CAPITAL ELITES

CAPITAL ELITES

High Society in Washington, D.C., after the Civil War

Kathryn Allamong Jacob

Smithsonian Institution Press

Washington and London

Edited by David Sewell.
Production editing by Rebecca Browning.
Designed by Kathleen Sims.

Library of Congress Cataloging-in-Publication Data is available.

Jacob, Kathryn Allamong.
    Capital elites : high society in Washington, D.C., after the Civil
War / Kathryn Allamong Jacob.
        p. cm.
    Includes bibliographical references (p.   ) and index.
    ISBN 1-56098-354-X
    1. Elite (Social sciences)—Washington (D.C.)—History—19th
century. 2. Washington (D.C.)—Social life and customs.   I. Title.
    F198.J33   1994
    305.5'2'09753—dc20   94-11050

British Library Cataloguing-in-Publication Data is available.

Manufactured in the United States of America.
03   02   01   00   99   98   97   96   95   94
10   9   8   7   6   5   4   3   2   1

    ∞ The paper used in this publication meets the minimum requirements of the
American National Standard for Permanence of Paper for Printed Library Materials
Z39.48–1984.

    Cover image: First Lady Ida McKinley and President William McKinley at a White
House dinner. (Library of Congress, Prints and Photographs Division)

For Rob,
Charlotte,
and
Annie

Sources will be found in the Bibliography and, for a particular item, in the Notes, identified by page number and a key phrase from the text.

Contents

Acknowledgments

When I was a little girl growing up in Harrisburg, Pennsylvania, my grandfather would take our family on car trips to a different historic site each month. Winter or summer, these trips always included a wonderful lunch that my grandmother would cook and pack in special boxes my grandfather designed and built. I liked the Gettysburg battlefields best, especially in the fall because that meant hot macaroni and cheese. The acres of markers topped with dying bronze soldiers and bearing vivid descriptions of suicidal charges were thrilling. I could really imagine the troops swarming over the hills in the shimmering heat of July one hundred years before. With history so exciting, and linked with family and food I loved, it seemed only natural that I should become a historian and choose a topic in which the Civil War figured prominently.

I am deeply grateful to my family for planting the kernel of interest in history, and to the many teachers, especially Jean Baker at Goucher College, who nurtured it over the years. If this interest had lacked such deep roots, it would not have supported me over the years this book was in the making. Equally sustaining was my perpetual delight in burrowing into manuscript sources, a pleasure enhanced by helpful staff everywhere, but especially at the Huntington Library, the Chicago Historical

Society, the Cincinnati Historical Society, the Society of the Cincinnati in Washington, D.C., and the New York Public Library. To a decade of staff at three particular institutions—the Historical Society of Washington, D.C., the Manuscript Division of the Library of Congress, and the Washingtoniana Division of the Martin Luther King Public Library—go my special thanks. More recently, staff of the National Archives Library, particularly Jeffery Hartley, the Prints and Photographs Division of the Library of Congress, and the Still Pictures Branch of the National Archives, have been unusually helpful.

As this project percolated, many, many people contributed their talents to keep it moving along. To all those who proofread and edited, led me to obscure sources, contributed their knowledge of nineteenth-century America, buoyed sinking spirits, and, above all, who read the manuscript with a critical eye and offered invaluable suggestions, go my thanks. Without implicating them in any of its shortcomings, I would especially like to acknowledge the many forms of support of my colleagues at the Senate Historical Office and at the National Archives, Michele Bogart, Diane Dimkoff, David Glassberg, Cynthia Harrison, Jill Jonnes, Philip Pauly, Jim Perry, Bruce Ragsdale, Ronald Walters, Anne Yeoman, and the members of my reading groups.

My greatest intellectual debt is owed to John Higham. When he took me on as a graduate student at Johns Hopkins, we both knew it would be a long haul. Though he may have privately despaired of my ever finishing, he never betrayed any doubt in me or in my work. He combined kindly understanding, intellectual grace, and always wise counsel with exacting standards to be my teacher in the truest sense of the word.

This book is about elites—men and women who are among the very best in their field, the crème de la crème, the top bananas. Specifically, it is about the social elite in Washington, D.C. My experience with high society is entirely vicarious, but I have been blessed with firsthand knowledge of many other elites. John Higham has been the best of mentors. Mark Hirsch, my editor at the Smithsonian Institution Press, has been the best of editors. My friends are the best of friends, standing by me through many ups and downs. My mother, Doris Allamong, is the best of mothers, making sacrifices unappreciated at the time but valued now that I am "grown up." My children are the best of children. Charlotte, born near the beginning of my research, doesn't remember the microfilm reader next to her crib, but I am grateful to her for sleeping so soundly as I squeakily cranked away. Annie, born in the middle of the process, assumes that all mothers write at nap time and into the night and has accepted that fact with her usual good humor. Finally, my husband, Robert Jacob, to whom I owe my greatest personal debt, is the best of husbands. He, more than anyone else, has provided the encouragement and the environment that have not only made this book possible, but made the long road that led to its completion so interesting to travel. His tangible aid—program design, education in SGML, chocolate—has been enormously helpful, but it is for his intangible contributions of love, optimism, and forbearance that I am most grateful.

1 Introduction

"Washington is a place quite out of the ordinary run," claimed *Century Magazine* in an 1884 article entitled "The New Washington." "It is unlike any other American city." Washington is indeed unlike any other American city, and it has been that way from its beginnings. In fact, it was planned that way.

The seeds of the city's uniqueness were sown when the deal that led to its establishment was struck during the First Congress in New York in the summer of 1790. Alone among American cities, Washington was planned as the home of the new federal government, the capital of the United States. This new city was designed to be the Constitution made tangible. Its parks and fountains, the very stones of its buildings and the broad sweep of its avenues, were intended to embody the dignity and the ideals underlying the new republic. While the site President Washington chose for the new capital included the ports of Georgetown, Maryland, and Alexandria, Virginia, neither town was intended to be the seat of government. A new city, capital of a new nation, would rise from the largely empty acres that lay in between.

Ten years in germinating, the new capital city had just begun to sprout in the spring of 1800 when sloops that had set sail from

Philadelphia bearing all of the young government's possessions docked at Tobias Lear's wharf on the Potomac. Promoters had promised that a decade would be plenty of time to make ready a suitable home for the federal government and time was up, but the first officials on the scene looked with dismay on the village's half-finished buildings and barely passable roads. Others outside of Washington saw this near-wilderness as the perfect home for a federal government with little real power and even less impact on its citizens' daily lives, but about which they felt mistrust and suspicion.

Seventy years later, Washington finally flowered into a handsome national city, a suitable home for the vastly larger, far more powerful federal government at the heart of the new "Union," the talisman wreathed with reverence that emerged in the years after the Civil War. Mark Twain and Charles Dudley Warner captured the exuberance of this "New Washington" in 1873 in *The Gilded Age: A Tale of Today,* one of the most hilarious and cynical Washington novels ever written, whose title became the eponym for the era it skewered.

The high society that flourished in this New Washington in the last half of the nineteenth century is the subject of this study. Like the capital city itself, Washington's high society came of age in the years after the Civil War. For decades a miserable backwater to which few would voluntarily go, beginning in the 1870s Washington took its place among the most fashionable cities in the country. Society reporters, a postwar phenomenon, arrived in Washington with the Grant administration and began to churn out column after column of saccharine prose for eager readers nationwide. By the 1890s, in gossip tabloids like *The Club Fellow,* which billed itself as the "National Journal of Society," Washington had a column all its own, which, in inches of lurid rumors, rivaled those of New York, Boston, Philadelphia, and summertime Newport.

Washington's social elite during the Gilded Age was also "quite out of the ordinary run." Man of the world Harry Brierly explains the capital's special qualities to beautiful country girl Laura Hawkins early on in *The Gilded Age:* "It doesn't need a crowbar to break your way into society there as it does in Philadelphia. It's democratic, Washington is. Money or beauty will open any door." High society in Washington was, and still is, unique in all America. And, just like the city, it was planned that way.

Several important factors set early Washington apart from its neighbors and shaped its high society. One factor was the city's extreme youth. While Boston (founded in 1630), New York (1653), Philadelphia (1682), and even nearby Baltimore (1729) were already paying homage to venerable families of homegrown gentlefolk, Washington in 1790 was still pastureland, a city in name only. If, as Oliver Wendell Holmes claimed, it took three generations to produce a gentleman, the nation's capital could not hope to harvest its first crop until at least the middle of the nineteenth century.

By virtue of its special purpose, Washington would be a one-company town, owned and operated by the federal government. Constraints of topography and policy rendered futile nearly all large-scale private efforts to attract business and diversify the city's economy. Unlike other cities with manufacturing or commercial bases, Washington became a city that expanded less in years of economic prosperity than in periods of war and national crisis. It would not prove attractive to the floods of European immigrants, nor would it witness the labor unrest that plagued industrial cities. As the *Nation* noted in 1874, "The 'seat of the Government' is not a commercial or manufacturing town. It is simply what it was designed to be—a dwelling-place for the National Government."

Thus Washington's self-conscious origin gave it many distinctions: it was a brand-new city, dropped in the midst of well-established metropolises; it sprang full-blown from the heads of the Founding Fathers, who found it harder than they had expected to translate plans into reality; and it alone was the federal capital. All of these distinctions, but especially the latter, determined the special qualities that marked high society in the capital city.

As the nation's capital, Washington would have a society with a unique and exotic feature not found in any of its older neighbors: high society in Washington included an ironclad official elite. Boston might have its Cabots and Lodges and Philadelphia its Cadwalladers and Biddles, long-established families recognized as society leaders by virtue of their antiquity and wealth. Washington alone would have an official society based on specific elected and appointed offices, regardless of the pedigree or affluence of their occupants. Whoever held the office, no matter how low-born or venal, could lay claim to that office's assigned place at table.

The rules that governed this official society were not a loose collection of informal maxims, subject to the whims of individual hostesses. Rather they were codified into a rigid, printed protocol. To break one of these rules was not merely a faux pas, but an Affair of State that could cause a cabinet to crumble or a foreign minister to be recalled.

President Washington himself felt strongly that official rules of protocol were important for the new government. In May of 1789, he wrote to Vice President John Adams, Chief Justice John Jay, and Secretary of the Treasury Alexander Hamilton, asking for their "undisguised opinions" about the matter. Should the president mingle with "all kinds of society" or live in "total seclusion from society"? Should he receive visitors one day a week? More? Less? Or would making himself available merely "prompt impertinent applications"? At the heart of his queries, as at the heart of all protocol, stood the dignity of the office. "The President," Washington reminded the three, "can have no object but to demean himself in his public character, in such a manner as to maintain the dignity of the office, without subjecting himself to the imputation of superciliousness or unnecessary reserve."

Only Adams's and Hamilton's replies survive. Of the two, Hamilton's, the more restrictive, prevailed. His suggestions, like Washington's solicitation, relied on the premise that "the public good requires as a primary object, that the dignity of the office should be supported." His plan, which he hoped steered "clear of extremes," offered minutely detailed prescriptions for every sort of occasion, such as these rules for a presidential levee:

> The President to have a levee day once a week for receiving visits; an hour to be fixed at which it shall be understood that he will appear, and consequently that the visitors are to be previously assembled. The President to remain half an hour, in which time he may converse cursorily on indifferent subjects, with such persons as shall invite his attention, and at the end of that half hour disappear. . . .

Official protocol and rules of precedence were outward, visible signs of the unique character Washington's status as the nation's capital conferred on its high society, but the impact of this special status appeared in other areas as well. The fact that Washington was the capital of a democracy guaranteed a high rate of turnover among its official population, which had important consequences for the stability of its social elite. Capitol Hill in particular was a community of birds of passage. During the first four decades of federal government, between one-third and two-thirds of the congressional community, the largest group within official society, left office every two years, never to return.

Margaret Bayard Smith, a leader of Washington's residential elite, poignantly noted one consequence for her own life of so temporary a population after Andrew Jackson's election victory in 1828:

> I . . . live as it were in a land of strangers. To say this in a land where I have dwelt for twenty years seems strange and yet is true. The peculiar nature of Washington society makes it so. Had the intimate acquaintances I formed when I first came been continued, twenty years would have ripened them into friendship. But one after another have been separated by death, the ocean, or mountains and water.

Mrs. Smith did not personally dislike or fear the new president. What she dreaded was the loss of old friends, rare commodities in a community of transients, that his victory promised. Women friends were particularly dear to Mrs. Smith because they were so scarce. Few politicians chose to subject their wives and families to the hardships of a primitive town where their tenures were uncertain. Most officials came to the capital alone and, like a flock of all-male migratory birds, merely wintered along the Potomac.

The existence of this official, mostly male elite, which cycled through the capital in shifts of two, four, and six years, gave Washington's high society an unusual flavor, but the social milieu of the capital was stirred up even more by the fact that official high society was not the only social game in town. Embedded in the Founding Fathers' plans for the capital were the makings for *two* social elites destined to become rivals. As the home of the federal government, Washington had plenty of transient officials with their own special rules of precedence, but it was also planned to have a permanent "civilian" population as well, made up of men and women like Mrs. Smith and her husband, Samuel Harrison Smith, who came to Washington in 1801 to publish the *National Intelligencer*. City boosters tried all sorts of schemes, all largely unsuccessful, to lure wealthy families to the new capital city. George Washington himself, who had a financial interest in the city's success, marched in a parade to try to drum up business.

By the 1820s, for reasons discussed in Chapter 2, the rapport between the early residents and the first officials began to fade. By the 1840s, residents were drawing a sharp line between those like themselves who regarded the capital as home, and those interested only in its federal functions.

Thus, in the years before the Civil War, there emerged in the District of Columbia an unusual city with an unusual social makeup. It was a brand-new city rising ex nihilo almost a full century after its neighbors got their start. It was the capital of a new nation and little else. It played host to a volatile group of male officials whose public social behavior was governed by strict rules of precedence. And it contained the nuclei of two rival social groups. A unique city with a unique high society, Washington does not fit into any of the sociological and historical molds to which other cities and their social elites conform.

The word "society" is used throughout these pages in its popular sense as "an aggregate of leisured, cultured or fashionable persons regarded as forming a distinct class or body," a modern usage that appeared at the beginning of the nineteenth century. Lord Byron used it in this sense in *Don Juan* in 1823: "Society is now one polished horde / Form'd of two mighty tribes, the *Bores* and *Bored*." Julia Ward Howe, of impeccable old New York stock, clearly understood "society" to mean a conspicuous, self-defined status group based on common, costly lifestyles, when she wrote "The Sociomaniac" in mid-century:

> Her Mother was a Shaw and her father was a Tompkins,
>> Her sister was a bore and her brother was a bumpkins.
>> Oh, Soci-, oh, Soci-, oh, Soci-i-i-i-ety!
>
> Her flounces were of gold and her slippers were of ermine,
>> And she looked a little bold when she went to lead the German.
>> Oh, Soci-, oh, Soci-, oh, Soci-i-i-i-ety!
>
> For my part I never saw where she kept her fascination,
>> But I thought she had an awful conceit and affectation.
>> Oh, Soci-, oh, Soci-, oh, Soci-i-i-i-ety!

Society, as Howe and her contemporaries had come to understand it, should not be confused with an upper class, of which it is only one facet. Upper classes dominate all, or almost all, of the primary community functions of religion, economics, politics, war, and culture. Fundamental upper-class features include predominant power, wealth, and social status. Upper-class sovereignty is legitimized by shared community traditions, and its membership consists of families who pass their rank on to their children.

Not every member of every group, including an upper class, is equal in power, wealth, esteem, or skills. Members with a disproportionate share of the advantages in any one area become an intraclass elite. There are elite scholars, elite athletes, even elite criminals. In sociological and political writing the term "elite" was first widely used in Europe in the late nineteenth century, and in England and America in the 1930s, largely popularized by the translation into English of the works of Italian sociologist Vilfredo Pareto, who helped define the term with examples like the following:

> Let us assume that in every branch of human activity each individual is given an index which stands as a sign of his capacity, very much the way grades are given in the various subjects in examinations in school. The highest type of lawyer, for instance, will be given 10. The man who does not get a client will be given a 1—reserving zero for the man who is an out-and-out idiot. To the man who has made his millions—honestly or dishonestly as the case may be—we will give 10. To the man who has earned his thousands we will give 6; to such as just manage to keep out of the poor-house 1, keeping zero for those who get in. . . . So let us make a class of the people who have the highest indices in their branch of activity and to that class give the name of *elite.*

Upper classes exercise generalized hegemony; elites do not. While certain extraordinary individuals may claim membership in several elites within a larger group—in both the political and social elites, for example, in Washington—most members of an elite enjoy celebrity in just one of many aggregates of specialized individuals within a class. While upper classes are groups of families who bequeath their rank and role, elites are composed of individuals who are personally successful and stand out in a particular field, whether it be waging war or giving parties.

High society in Washington or anywhere else is an elite—a social elite—a subgroup of the upper class. Historians and sociologists have given a great deal of thought to how social elites come into being, how they are sustained, how they deteriorate, and how they are reconfigured and renewed. Now-standard works by Frederic Jaher, E. Digby Baltzell, Edward Pessen, and others have created a yardstick by which urban American upper classes and social elites can be measured. Jaher's *The Rich, the Well Born, and the Powerful,* and *The Urban Establishment,* which examines New York, Boston, Charleston, Chicago, and Los Angeles; Baltzell's *Philadelphia Gentlemen* and *Puritan Boston and Quaker Philadelphia: Two Protestant Ethics and the Spirit of Class*

Authority and Leadership; and Pessen's *Riches, Class and Power Before the Civil War,* which examines New York, Brooklyn, Boston, and Philadelphia during the second quarter of the nineteenth century, offer useful models which scholars have applied in recent studies of cities like Pittsburgh, Cincinnati, Charleston, Atlanta, Cleveland, the boom towns of Colorado, and the river towns of the Midwest.

During most of the nineteenth century, the upper classes of these cities and their component social elites fit the model best articulated by Jaher, who identifies several characteristics shared by them all. Most important, they were made up of families whose origins stretched back to their city's misty beginnings, families who lived side by side in the same neighborhoods, whose children attended the same schools and dancing classes and later intermarried, who joined the same clubs, supported the same charities, voted the same way—often for a neighbor or fellow club member—and were buried in the same cemeteries. These social elites and the upper classes of which they were a part were marked by members with shared origins and common ancestors, and by cohesion, solidarity, continuity, and the hegemony they exercised over all of the major aspects of their city's life.

These are hardly the characteristics of Washington society. Its early residential elite, the closest the capital could come to an upper class, built fine homes close together, established the city's first churches, and founded its first charities. But these early residents mostly came from somewhere else. Their roots in the new capital city were shallow. They were considered "old families" by virtue of having lived in Washington for several years, not several generations. Unlike the Brahmins, the early Knickerbockers, and other urban upper classes, Washington's residential elite could not bring the crucial spheres of economic and political power under their domination: the chief business of the capital was government, and local government, such as it was, rested in the hands of a capricious Congress in which District residents had no representation.

Jaher notes that high rates of geographical diversity and population turnover are deleterious to upper class solidarity and continuity. Yet these were exactly the attributes that Washington's most visible population—government officials—possessed in abundance. These were men who came from all over the country and came alone, and who, with defeat or retirement, returned from whence they came. The criteria developed by Jaher, Baltzell, and others, with which the tenacity of upper classes and social elites in cities like Boston, Philadelphia, and New York can be

measured—rates of residential persistence, of intermarriage, and so on—
do not apply to Washingi. n. The cultural glue of shared childhoods,
common schools, churches, clubs, and intermarriage that bound the social elites of other cities together had no hold on these transients of dis-
parate backgrounds.

The concrete horrors of civil war and its wrenching aftermath also
set Washington apart from its neighbors. As Chapter 2 will illustrate, no
other city experienced the Civil War quite as Washington did. Prior to the
war, Washington's high society had been composed of two groups—the
residential and official social elites—both dominated by Southern
Democrats. Antebellum Washington was a thoroughly Southern town. It
even looked like one. While Northern officials, accustomed to bustling
cities like Philadelphia and Boston, balked at subjecting their loved ones
to the crudeness of the backwater capital, Southerners felt at home in its
rustic, small-town ambiance. Away from the tight cluster of federal buildings, Washington's quiet, shady streets and its fragrant gardens of crepe
myrtles and boxwood were far more akin to Richmond or Mobile than to
Hartford or Albany.

For these Southern political and social elites, the war spelled abrupt
disaster. Not since the departures of wealthy loyalists from Boston and
New York during the American Revolution had any American city experienced so sudden a loss of its social leaders. Suddenly Washington's old
Southern elite was gone—dispersed, defeated, disgraced, or impoverished, sometimes all four.

Into the vacuum created by the demise of the old Southern aristocracy rushed a host of newcomers eager to fill the vacancies they left behind. Other newcomers were tugged in the direction of Washington by
one or more of the new forces unleashed there in the years after the war.
There was a whole new political elite, dominated by Northerners and
Republicans. Scientists and scholars were pulled to the capital by the
magnet of government support from new and newly aggressive agencies
like the Smithsonian and the Geological Survey and by the desire to be
on hand at the creation of what promised to be a new America.

Interesting though these new political and intellectual elites are, this
book is not about them. This is the story of Washington's postwar social
elite. Chapters 4 through 8 will follow the course of these elegant, ostentatious newcomers and the unique high society they created in the nation's capital in the decades after the war. Only when politicians and scientists ventured into high society—and they often did—is this their story.

Another elite group also emerged in postwar Washington, but none of its members intermingled with high society. This was Washington's African-American elite. While it represented one of the most important concentrations of black wealth, intellect, culture, education, and leadership in postbellum America, this group was invisible in the newspapers and magazines that covered white high society so exhaustively. Aside from the handful of black men in official life who *had* to be invited to official functions, these two social elites, which thrived in the same city at the same time, were trains traveling on parallel tracks with no connectors. Constance Green's pathbreaking *Secret City* (1967) and, more recently, Willard B. Gatewood's *Aristocrats of Color: The Black Elite, 1880–1920* (1990) tell the story of Washington's African-American elite in detail.

The unique white high society that emerged in Washington after the Civil War caught the nation's imagination and holds it still. Society reporters relayed tales of its opulence and excesses to eager readers across the country. Writers of etiquette books began to churn out a steady stream of volumes detailing the special rules that governed Washington society, which newcomers would have to master if they wanted to "make a splash" in the national pond. The authors of these etiquette books stressed the unusual importance of proper behavior in Washington. Readers were reminded of George Washington's personal attention to official etiquette and of the Peggy Eaton affair, during which the snubbing of a cabinet member's wife enraged President Andrew Jackson and brought down his cabinet. In Washington, as one of these authors noted, "politeness is power," and the converse was also true: impoliteness could mean impotence.

In an incident less dramatic than the Peggy Eaton affair, but equally revealing of the special consequences social behavior could have in Washington, Henry Adams, one of the young intellectuals drawn to the capital after the war, felt the sting of his own social behavior in January 1881. Back in Washington after a research trip to Europe, Adams had settled into a lovely house on H Street, across from the White House, and he was once again deep in research in the State Department archives for his volumes on American history. He had been granted privileged access to browse at will through the early State papers during the Hayes administration by his friend Secretary of State William Evarts.

Adams's problems began when newly elected President James Garfield, in an effort to conciliate rival Republican factions, awarded the State Department portfolio to Senator James G. Blaine of Maine. Many reformers were dismayed by Garfield's choice, but for Adams the appointment spelled disaster. Henry Adams loathed Blaine and viewed him as the embodiment of all that was wrong with American politics. Only months before, Adams had published—anonymously—his popular political novel *Democracy,* featuring the despicable Senator Silas P. Ratcliffe, a very thinly disguised James G. Blaine. No one knew for certain who had written the novel, but many in Washington, including Blaine, believed it to be the work of either Henry Adams or his wife Marian.

Blaine couldn't prove that the Adamses had libeled him in *Democracy,* but he knew that they had cut him and his wife, Harriet, socially. Most of the shining lights of Washington's social, intellectual, and political elites received coveted invitations to the Adamses' select salon—but not the Blaines, whose absence was conspicuous. The Adamses refused to call on the Blaines. The clever but savage bons mots Marian Adams included about the couple in her letters to her father in Massachusetts were repeated in Boston and made their way back to the Blaines. Henry Adams had even gone so far as to turn his back on Blaine during an unexpected encounter at a Washington reception.

Since they were not part of official society, the Adamses smugly told their friends, they were not required to be polite to the Blaines. But in January 1881 it was clear that Henry Adams was going to pay for his high-minded contempt. The State Department archives were about to fall under the control of the man Adams referred to as his "pet enmity." Marian Adams wrote to her father of Blaine's appointment: "For us it will be most awkward; never having called on them before, it will simply be impossible to make up to them now. . . . Henry will hurry up his work there so as to finish by March 4th, not wishing to be a protégé of a man he does not recognize socially."

Henry Adams found it impossible to finish his work by March 4, but equally impossible to "make up" to the Blaines. He withdrew from the State Department archives.

Adams's exile proved brief. Within the year, President Garfield was assassinated, and President Chester Arthur replaced Blaine as secretary of state with Frederick Frelinghuysen, an old friend of the Adamses. In December 1881, Henry Adams gleefully wrote his friend E. L. Godkin of the *Nation:* "I go in for Arthur. No harm he can ever do will equal the good of ejecting Blaine. Today has been a day of bubbling joy to me, and I have returned to my work in the State Department." A few weeks later, Adams self-righteously described his "ordeal" of the past year to his

British friend Charles Gaskell: "I assure you that to stand alone in a small society like this, and to cut the Secretary of State for Foreign Affairs, without doing it offensively or with ill-breeding, requires not only some courage but some skill. . . . I trust Mr. Blaine is blown up forever."

James G. Blaine and Henry Adams, when he deigned to participate in society, clearly belonged to different factions within Washington's high society. Just as there were several different elites in the capital in the last half of the nineteenth century, there were also several different subelites within the social elite. Mark Twain, who was in Washington just after the war on the staff of Nevada Senator William Stewart (much to Stewart's eventual dismay), had a front-row seat from which to watch this new high society take shape. After close firsthand observation, Twain discovered what he branded "three distinct aristocracies" within the capital's social elite and lampooned them mercilessly in *The Gilded Age.*

Most numerous and most powerful were the officials. While Henry Adams modeled Senator Ratcliffe after James G. Blaine in *Democracy,* Twain's sanctimonious and thoroughly corrupt Senator Abner Dillworthy in *The Gilded Age* was unmistakably Senator Samuel C. Pomeroy of Kansas, who was repeatedly accused of buying his way into office but always managed to shake off the charges.

Twain also singled out the "Parvenus," the most ridiculous of the "three distinct aristocracies," personified by the Patrique Oreillés (formerly the Patrick O'Rileys), who dribbled mispronounced French phrases and allusions to dear friends in "Pary." Having earned their fortune elsewhere but finding that their millions could not buy them entry into the more select society of older cities, the Oreillés, just like many a real-life arriviste family in the years after the war, set out to "do" Washington.

The third of Twain's "three distinct aristocracies" was the group he labeled the "Antiques." Embodied by the formidable, faultless, fusty Fulke-Fulkersons, the Antiques were the remnants of Washington's old residential elite who prided themselves on their good breeding and their old family silver and wrapped themselves in the comforting mantle of their past glory days.

Had Mark Twain been a cultural anthropologist, his unflinching analysis of high society in Washington could not have been more accurate (and would probably have been less entertaining). The "three distinct aristocracies" in *The Gilded Age*—the officials, the Parvenus, and the Antiques—capture the three chief subelites that composed the unique, real-life, non-fictional high society in the postwar capital. The chapters that follow chart the shifting fortunes of these "three distinct aristocracies" through the last half of the nineteenth century.

Theirs is the story of first ladies overly fond of glamorous clothes, of beautiful wives of cabinet members who turn heads and excite gossip wherever they go, of congressmen who buy their way into office and sell their souls for a few thousand dollars, of ambassadors who complain about this country and embarrass their own, of nouveaux riches hostesses whose extravagant villas overstep the bounds of good taste, of blue-blooded matrons decrying the death of polite society, of insinuating lobbyists whose oiled tongues wheedle favorable legislation for their clients. Individuals such as these have become stock characters in the continuing saga of Washington society. That names from another postwar era—the post–World War II years—can so easily be substituted for those from the post–Civil War years partially accounts for the lively fascination Washington society still holds for the nation.

High society in Washington continues to excite the national imagination for other enduring reasons as well. The social elite in Washington is the closest parallel to the courts of Europe this democracy can offer to devotees of power, intrigue, romance, and scandal on a national scale. The fascination also emerges from the understanding that Washington society connects to the national life as society does in no other city in America. High society in the capital resonates to national themes—war, depression, the gold rush, the age of the tycoon, industrialization, bureaucratization, professionalization—that determine the cast of players on the national social stage. Finally, social life in Washington also connects with political life in a fascinating pas de deux of power. As the author of a popular Washington etiquette book warned her readers, "Society is the handmaiden of politics especially in a capital city." There were, and are, few purely social encounters in Washington.

2 High Society Gets Underway in the New Capital

1800–1860

"This Embryo Capital . . ."

High society in Washington, so glamorous by the end of the nineteenth century, got off to a modest start on New Year's Day, 1801. President John Adams, his wig freshly powdered and gathered in a queue, stood amid wet plaster in the oval library of the unfinished Executive Mansion that afternoon, bowing stiffly to the congressmen, foreign ministers, cabinet members, and residents of the District of Columbia who had come to pay their respects. Beside Adams stood his wife Abigail, dressed in brocade and velvet. Though Mrs. Adams made up in warmth and grace for her husband's austerity, she had been schooled in the formal English court where her husband had been American minister and in Martha Washington's stately "court" in Philadelphia, and she bowed as well.

With this, the first official White House reception, a conspicuously self-regarding social life got underway in the nation's capital. Though it was a subdued inauguration, the few local residents of the District of Columbia who enjoyed the marine band and the syllabub, trifle, and tarts that day were greatly relieved. Many had come to doubt that they would ever live long enough to see the city, much less a social life, take shape.

Lack of historical precedent for building a capital ex nihilo had not deterred the founders of the District of Columbia. In 1790, with great fanfare, they revealed their grand design for the new city and promised that a decade would be more than adequate to ready it. The government would reside in Philadelphia while Washington was created. Most government officials were unfamiliar with the area that was to be their new home. Had they visited it, they would have realized that the promised completion date of 1800 was extremely optimistic. In the spring of 1791, the future site of the nation's capital was a pastoral idyll of forests, ferns, and streams. Wild geese rose in clouds from the marshes. An apple orchard bloomed on what would become Lafayette Square.

The first auction of lots for the new city in 1791 was sobering. Only thirty-five of the ten thousand lots were sold. A second auction a year later brought little improvement. Although preceded by the town's first parade, featuring President Washington, two brass bands, a militia unit, and marching Masons, a third sale in 1793 fared even worse than the first two. Lack of buyers was only one symptom of public apathy toward the new capital. No one was moving there. The 1800 census counted 14,093 people in the Federal District, but more than half of these lived in Georgetown and Alexandria. (As a comparison, Philadelphia's population in 1800 was 69,403 and New York's 60,489.) Despite pressure from George Washington to reside in the city, even the District's own commissioners begged off, claiming that "no decent houses" were to be had. By 1800, the entire city contained only 109 habitable brick houses and 263 wooden ones.

The sight that greeted the first officials, who arrived in May 1800, was dismal indeed. The only public buildings were the half-finished President's House, the Capitol, and the Treasury. Pennsylvania Avenue was a dusty path choked with elderbushes and stumps. The new capital, grumbled Connecticut Representative Roger Griswold, was "both melancholy and ludicrous . . . a city in ruins." It gave "the appearance of a considerable town, which had been destroyed by some calamity." Treasury Secretary Oliver Wolcott, who arrived in July, was furious at the lack of progress and at the proprietors. He wrote his wife: "No stranger can be here a day and converse with the proprietors, without conceiving himself in the company of crazy people. . . . Their delusions with respect to their own prospects are without parallel."

Accustomed to the amenities they had enjoyed in Philadelphia for the past ten years, officials were extremely disappointed to find cows

The heart of the nation's new capital city was still sparsely populated when surveyor Nicholas King painted this watercolor in about 1803. Blodgett's Hotel, home of the city's first theatrical production in 1800 and later home to the Post Office Department and the Patent Office, at Eighth and E Streets, NW, is on the far right; the Treasury Building and the President's House are in the distance; the area of trees in between marks "the marsh," a favorite haunt of snipe hunters like the gentlemen depicted in the foreground. (Library of Congress, Prints and Photographs Division)

grazing in future plazas and bullfrogs chorusing on the Mall. Congress-men led the lamentations: the climate was intolerable and a menace to health, the flies and vermin were legion, the public buildings were hideous, the cuisine atrocious, accommodations terrible, and polite soci-ety a "golgotha of numbskulls." Wealthy Pennsylvania Senator Robert Morris complained to a friend, "All we lack here are good houses, wine cellars, decent food, learned men, attractive women and other such trifles to make our city perfect. . . . It is the best city in the world to live in—in the future."

After the pleasures of sophisticated Philadelphia, Washington was dull indeed. By day, "in the very heart of the city . . . not a sound is to be heard," and, by night, only the baying of dogs, squalling of cats, and do-mestic feuds from the shacks dotting the woods broke the silence. The "yelling of savages in the wilderness would be as much if not more en-tertaining," a Treasury auditor noted. There was a race track and a crude theater, but "one must love the drama very much," claimed one official, "to consent to pass three hours amidst tobacco smoke, whiskey breaths, and other stenches, mixed with the effluvia of stables, and miasmas of the canal, which the theatre is exactly placed and constructed to receive."

The officials who began to arrive in the winter of 1800–1801 found the tiny capital's few diversions scant compensation for the crowded living conditions they had to endure. Secretary Wolcott wrote his wife, "I do not perceive how the members of Congress can possibly secure lodgings, unless they will consent to live like scholars in a college or monks in a monastery, crowded ten or twenty in a house." House Speaker Theodore Sedgwick was the only member of the Sixth Congress to have a bedroom in a boardinghouse to himself.

Society at the Seat of Government

These disappointed, grumbling men—Wolcott, Morris, Griswold, Sedgwick and their colleagues—made up the earliest official society in the new capital. Death, defeat, or retirement would eventually send most of them back home, but the official society that began with President Adams's reception continued without them and continues still.

Its first decades in residence in Washington were official society's "shake down" years. The members of each new administration looked to the Executive Mansion to set the tone of official society. If the president and his wife chose, they could lead society. If they abdicated this role—and many did—vice presidents, cabinet members, and wealthy congressmen and their wives were usually more than eager to fill the void.

Presidents Washington and Adams had put great stock in form and formality. To President Thomas Jefferson, their protocol reeked of kings and England. He discontinued the old Federalist tradition of weekly levees and recognized no precedence at his table. To make his point, he installed a circular dining table so that no guest could be seated higher than another. Jefferson, however, knew as well as George Washington that the presidency must have a certain luster. While his detractors labeled his policies "the rule of *pele-mele*," Jefferson's official entertaining was actually far more stylish than was either of his predecessors'. It was just less ceremonial and more French. Jefferson's informal dinners for twelve or fourteen included the best cuisine in the capital. His French steward might spend fifty dollars in one day marketing in Georgetown. Jefferson's bill for wine alone totaled eleven thousand dollars for eight years (paid for out of his annual salary of twenty-five thousand).

When James and Dolley Madison moved into the Executive Mansion in 1809, the official social season lengthened. Where once the cycle of dinners and balls was completed in six weeks, when official social life resumed after the War of 1812, it extended for ten, beginning with the opening "drawingroom" at the White House on the first Wednesday evening in December and lasting until the middle of February. The social season was not only longer under the Madisons, but it sparkled with gaiety. To the delight of official wives and lonely congressmen, Mrs. Madison restored the Wednesday night "drawingrooms" that Jefferson had jettisoned. Beginning at sundown and lasting until nine o'clock, these evenings drew as many as two hundred people. Washington Irving described one such pleasant night:

> I emerged from dirt and darkness into the blazing splendor of Mrs. Madison's drawing-room. Here I was most graciously received; found crowded collection of great and little men, of ugly old women and beautiful young ones, and in ten minutes was hand in glove with half the people in the assemblage. Mrs. Madison is a fine, portly, buxom dame who has a smile and a pleasant word for every body.

Court dress for men on these occasions, wrote another guest, "appears to be a black or blue coat with vest, black breeches and black stockings. The ladies were not remarkable for anything so much as for the exposure of their swelling breasts and bare backs." This same guest, a Philadelphia merchant who had known Dolley Madison as a young woman, did, however, concede that "few of her sex at forty-five look so well" as his hostess.

There had never before been such easy access to the president and his wife as under the Madisons. Dolley Madison loved to entertain and did so often, bringing warmth and openness to the Executive Mansion. Her interest in and influence over official society endured for the next eight administrations.

Efforts by President and Mrs. James Monroe to change prevailing official protocol inaugurated a period Juliana Seaton, wife of William Seaton (publisher of the *National Intelligencer*) and a leader of Washington's residential elite, labeled one of "earthquake, upheaval, and cyclone." Citing

Dolley Madison wears white satin and a turban in this engraving after a portrait by Bass Otis, painted around 1817 near the end of her husband's presidency. As wife of Congressman and then Secretary of State James Madison, she had learned the rules of official society by heart before becoming first lady in 1809. (Library of Congress, Prints and Photographs Division)

the growing size of official society and the increasing demands on his time, President Monroe let it be known that thenceforth he would receive foreign ministers only by appointment. This, plus Mrs. Monroe's announcement that she would neither pay nor return calls, raised the ire of a community that had grown accustomed over the previous eight years to a cordial give-and-take with the president and his wife.

"The 'social revolution,'" noted Mrs. Seaton, "created no little heart-burning." The subject dominated diplomatic correspondence for weeks. There was a virtual boycott of the Monroes' weekly drawing-rooms. In December 1819, Mrs. Seaton reported: "The drawingroom of the President was opened last night to a beggarly row of empty chairs. Only five females attended, three of whom were foreigners." Acknowledging the importance of the situation, the president assigned Secretary of State John Quincy Adams the task of working out a new formula for presidential etiquette. Adams revised Hamilton's "Code" and produced a voluminous treatise on protocol, absolving President Monroe and future presidents of many of their old social duties.

Commenting on the new protocol, Mrs. Seaton speculated, "I suppose it will eventually go down, though this alteration in the old regime is bitter to the palates of all our citizens, especially so to foreign ministers and strangers."

A far more serious social crisis rocked official society during Andrew Jackson's presidency, revealing the close relationship between official life and private life, politics and society. Jackson arrived in Washington with the reputation of a social barbarian, and his chaotic inaugural celebration in 1829 did little to allay the fears of local society matrons. It was not, however, Jackson's manners or those of his supporters that began the "petticoat war." It was his championing of a lady. Jackson believed that malicious gossip had hounded his beloved wife Rachel into an early grave, and he was adamant that Mrs. John Eaton, the new wife of his longtime friend and campaign manager Senator John Eaton of Tennessee, be accorded every courtesy to which her rank in official society entitled

Margaret Bayard Smith, seen here in a pastel after an 1829 portrait by Charles Bird King, arrived in Washington in 1800. Mrs. Smith's diaries, letters, and novels written over the next forty-five years chronicle the growth of the capital and the vicissitudes of its high society. (Fine Arts Commission Collection, National Archives)

her. But Peggy O'Neal Timberlake Eaton, the beautiful daughter of a Washington tavern-keeper, was rumored to have had a checkered past. When most of the women in official society, including Mrs. John C. Calhoun, wife of the vice president, and Emily Donelson, Jackson's own niece and official hostess, refused to acknowledge her, the stage was set for battle.

Margaret Bayard Smith, a leader of Washington society since she had come to the capital in 1801 as a young bride, chronicled the escalation of the "Peggy Eaton Affair" in her lively letters. She first hinted of trouble on Senator Eaton's wedding day, January 1, 1829:

> Tonight Gen'l. Eaton, the bosom friend and almost adopted son of Gen'l. Jackson, is to be married to a lady whose reputation, her previous connection with him both before and after her husband's death, has totally destroyed. . . . She has never been admitted into good society, is very handsome and of not an inspiring character and violent temper.

Another observer who watched the events unfold in early 1829 saw the Eatons' problems a little differently. Senator William Barry of Tennessee was fond of both John Eaton and his new bride and cautioned his daughter not to believe all she heard:

> The truth is, there is an aristocracy here, . . . claiming preference for birth or wealth, and demanding obeisance from others. . . . Mrs. Eaton was the daughter of a tavern-keeper belonging to the democracy: she has by good fortune (if it may be so considered) moved into the fashionable world. This has touched the pride of the self-constituted great, awakened the jealousy of the malignant and envious, and led to the basest calumny.

When Jackson named Eaton his secretary of war, giving Mrs. Eaton the higher status of cabinet wife, the tension in society increased. Jackson became wholly absorbed in the issue. He called a cabinet meeting specifically to discuss it in September 1829 and presented the results of a private investigation he had ordered, complete with hotel registers checked to see if the Eatons had passed themselves off as husband and wife before their marriage. The meeting solved nothing. Instead, it became a catalyst for bringing into the open serious animosities and questionable loy-

THE CELESTE-AL CABINET.

An 1836 engraving by Henry R. Robinson, entitled *The Celeste-al Cabinet*, lampoons the "Peggy Eaton Affair," which broke apart President Jackson's cabinet. Thinly disguised as Madame Celeste, Peggy Eaton dances for a delighted Jackson and a more ambivalent cabinet. (Library of Congress, Prints and Photographs Division)

alties within the president's political family. Cabinet members resigned in protest.

A resolution to the crisis did not come until the spring of 1831, when Secretary of State Martin Van Buren, who had shrewdly championed Mrs. Eaton, urged Jackson to reorganize his cabinet. Life went on, but the deep rift opened in official society healed only with time and the Eatons' departure from Washington. Years later, Mrs. Eaton exclaimed, "God help the wom[e]n who must live in Washington! . . . They require the sympathy of the civilized world."

President Martin Van Buren and his four sons kept bachelors' hall until 1839, when matchmaker Dolley Madison brought together the oldest son, Abraham, and Angelica Singleton of South Carolina, who then served as the president's hostess. The White House under Van Buren sparkled with excellent food, fine wine, and witty conversation. He wrangled a sixty-thousand-dollar appropriation from Congress to refurbish the

Executive Mansion and spent it on gold plate, goblets, marble mantles, and Royal Wilton carpets.

As Van Buren soon learned, however, too great a love of luxury could be politically harmful. His enemies successfully used his elegant lifestyle against him in the 1840 presidential campaign. Supporters of General William Henry Harrison transformed their wealthy, well-born candidate into a rugged backwoodsman and contrasted this fiction with the effete Van Buren in satirical jingles:

> Old Tip he wears a home-spun coat
> He has no ruffled shirt-wirt-wirt;
> But Mat he has the golden plate,
> And he's a little squirt-wirt-wirt.

Another popular pro-Harrison poem read:

> No parties exclusive, no minuet balls
>   No Levees a la Royale shall flout in his halls
> The string of his door shall ne'er be drawn through
>   Always Welcome the world with Old Tippecanoe.
> No banquets he'll give a la mode de Paris
>   No wines of great price on his board you will see
> But Sirloin and Bacon and Hard Cider Too
>   Shall be the plain fare of Old Tippecanoe.

After the grandeur of the short-lived Van Buren administration, with few exceptions neither controversy nor charm stirred the the presidential social circle during the administrations of Presidents Harrison, Tyler, Polk, Taylor, Fillmore, and Pierce. From her house on Lafayette Square, the much beloved Dolley Madison offered a perpetual stream of advice on White House entertaining to its occupants. She befriended ailing Letitia Tyler when her husband suddenly became president. After Mrs. Tyler's death in 1842, Dolley Madison helped her daughters and daughters-in-law cope, and when President Tyler remarried two years later, she came across the park to offer young Julia Tyler advice, too. Mrs. Madison also befriended Mrs. Polk, who trusted her to be the last word on proper White House form.

Zachary Taylor's wife Margaret was ill and his newly married daughter Mary Elizabeth was an inexperienced hostess, so Taylor paid one of his first visits after he took office in 1849 to the shabby yellow mansion of eighty-one-year-old Dolley Madison. As she had many times before, she gave this new president her benediction. Four months later, on July 12, 1849, Dolley Madison died in her bed. Every church bell in the capital tolled the sad news and hundreds of mourners filed past her coffin in St. John's Church for a last glimpse at the last remaining link with the Founding Fathers.

During these years when it had little else to boast of, official society in Washington did embrace one very special group no other bigger or older city could claim—the staffs of the foreign legations. The presence of this colony of foreigners gave even the crude capital a cosmopolitan flair. The sophistication of the ministers' entertainments and the elegance of their wives provided grist for many a diary entry. Representative Thomas Hubbard of New York, who arrived in Washington in time for the 1817–18 social season, gratefully attended a score of parties at the French, British, and Spanish legations. His eager anticipation of these events probably reflected the feelings of many a miserable congressman far from home. Young Alfred Shelby, son of Governor Isaac Shelby of Kentucky, visited Washington in 1826–27 and spoke glowingly of the various ministers' hospitality. Dinner at one especially grand evening at the British legation was "splendid," with oyster pies, "turkey stuffed with everything that was nice after every bone had been taken from it . . . pickles of every hue." But while he heartily approved of the food, the dancing was another matter: "There was dancing—a complete band of music—the lascivious waltz has its devotees—they were however all either French or foreigners who engaged in it. May the time never come when American ladies will be open to the promiscuous embrace of every wanton at such an assemblage!"

While adding a touch of glamour to the city, the ministers and their underlings could also be a source of friction. Throughout the early nineteenth century, Washington was considered a diplomatic hardship post. Britain made an effort to assign only bachelors to the unprestigious North American capital. Widower Stratford Canning, British minister in 1822, bemoaned his fate in a letter to his sister:

> In the present imperfect state of this celebrated metropolis the life of a foreigner must ever be one of privation and restraint. . . . I try to make the best of my bargain; I swear occasionally—you women cannot con-

ceive the comfort of swearing—and I occasionally repeat to myself old saws and fag-ends of verse about patience. If I cannot get the last new novel I shut myself up and wait for better times.

The disappointment of several ministers with their surroundings was unconcealed. The informality of the Jefferson White House was particularly offensive. British Minister Anthony Merry, arriving at the Executive Mansion in full dress to present his credentials, was outraged when Jefferson received him wearing an old brown coat and slippers. Reporting the offense to his government, Merry huffed, "The excess of the democratic ferment in this people is conspicuously evinced by the dregs having got up to the top."

Arrogant ministers or international tensions occasionally elicited a nasty, nationalistic response from their American hosts. As England and America moved toward war in 1812, one congressman inspired a local drinking song entitled "The Extinction of the British Fire" by putting the British minister's fireplace to an unorthodox personal use during the Queen's birthday ball.

"A Congregation of Strangers"

From the beginning, a key factor shaping all of high society in Washington was the continual turnover of its official component. The perpetual motion of the revolving electoral door, sweeping familiar faces out and unfamiliar ones in with each revolution, made friendships between officials and local residents and between the officials themselves difficult to establish and impossible to maintain. The executive branch, while less volatile than the legislative, was no more immune from turnover. While Jeffersonians held sway, the personnel changes wrought by each new administration were largely limited to the topmost positions, below which there emerged a seemingly entrenched group of functionaries. To this latter group, Andrew Jackson's victory in 1828 spelled catastrophe. Both his enemies and friends predicted a clean sweep of all incumbents. There was, fretted Margaret Bayard Smith, "quaking and trembling" in all quarters.

Although the anticipated massive housecleaning never occurred (of the approximately three hundred men who had held posts under John Quincy Adams, about two hundred were still on the rolls in 1831), dismissals were nevertheless plentiful enough to alter greatly the composition of Washington's high society. Few ousted officials remained in the city, and the melancholy sight of belongings stacked up for auction prior to flight was repeated daily. Mrs. Smith lamented:

> Never before did the city seem to me so gloomy—so many changes in society—so many families broken up, and those of the first distinction who gave a tone to society. Those elegantly furnished houses, stripped of their splendid furniture—that furniture exposed to public sale. Those drawingrooms, brilliantly illuminated . . . distinguished by rank, fashion, beauty, talent—resounding with festive sounds—now empty, silent, dark.

The "elegantly furnished houses" being broken up were those of the few officials who had brought their wives with them to Washington. Most officials came alone. Only the wealthiest could afford to maintain two households—one in the capital and one back home among their constituents. Long weeks of confinement in cramped boardinghouses with only their male colleagues for company resulted in a flurry of love letters sent home by lonesome congressmen. In March 1802, after only a few weeks in Washington, Representative Samuel Mitchill of New York wrote his wife Catherine, "I anticipate great comfort from restoration after so long a separation from my wife and home. It seems to me that I shall prize you more than ever. One never knows so completely the want of a good thing as by being deprived of it."

When Senator George Mifflin Dallas of Pennsylvania left Philadelphia for Washington in 1831, it was the first time in fifteen years of marriage that he and his wife, Sophy, had been apart for any length of time. Dallas wrote to his family constantly, and urged his wife and children (his "little pig-tails") to write him daily. Anticipating a visit from Sophy, he coyly cautioned, "Bring no servant to worry or be expensive. Come alone and I will be your slave, lacer, hairdresser and packer." In his first letter home on December 4, 1835, freshman Maine Representative John Fairfield wrote his wife Anna, "I had no idea before being put to the trial how hard it would be for me to quit you and ours." Ten days after his arrival in the capital, Fairfield received word of the birth of his third son.

The absence of families gave early Washington high society a peculiarly masculine tone. English visitor Frances Trollope commented upon the fraternal lifestyle in the late 1820s:

> There is another circumstance which renders the evening parties in Washington extremely unlike those of other places in the Union: this is

the great majority of gentlemen. The expense, the trouble, or the necessity of a ruling eye at home, one or all of these reasons, prevents the members' ladies from accompanying them to Washington. . . . Female society is chiefly to be found among the families of the officers of state [the cabinet], and of the few members, the wealthiest and most aristocratic of the land, who bring their families with them.

Until the 1840s, most congressmen lived the bachelor's life in the numerous boardinghouses that sprang up around the Capitol to accommodate them. Members tended to congregate by region, with certain "messes," as the various boardinghouse cliques were known, being easily identified as Southern, Western, or Northern. When he arrived in 1817, Representative Thomas Hubbard of New York linked up with a colleague from Poughkeepsie and several other New Yorkers, "all gentlemen of the best habits and all extremely well-bred," to go looking for a "mess." Massachusetts Senators Nathaniel Silsbee and Daniel Webster could be found with other New Englanders at Mrs. Bayliss's boardinghouse opposite Center Market in the mid-1830s. John Fairfield of Maine took a small room on the fourth floor of Mrs. Hill's boarding house on Pennsylvania Avenue for eight dollars a week and lived there with several other congressmen from Maine, New York and Connecticut.

An official society made up mostly of men suddenly thrown together and often just as quickly pulled apart hardly constituted a social elite based, as they were in other cities, on long-standing family ties and deep roots in common ground. These men differed widely in age, wealth, occupation, politics, and region. New Englanders, Southerners, and Westerners were cultural aliens to each other. After scrutinizing his colleagues from New England, Representative John Randolph of Virginia concluded that there was "not one [who] possesses the slightest tie of common interest or of common feeling with us." New Englanders returned the ill will. Observing several Southerners on the House floor, Massachusetts Representative Josiah Quincy noted, "With men of such states of mind and temperament, men educated in . . . New England could have little pleasure in intercourse, less in controversy, and of course no sympathy." Commented English visitor Harriet Martineau, "No English person who has not traveled over half the world, can form an idea of such differences among men forming one assembly for the same purpose, and speaking the same language." Describing official society to his wife in 1841, North Carolina Senator William A. Graham wrote, "It is a congregation of strangers who never met before, and don't care (most of them) if they ever meet again."

Deprived of the comfort of their homes, lonesome for their families, and finding friendships difficult to cultivate, many officials came to despise Washington. For all their complaints, however, federal officials made no serious efforts to have the causes of their irritation corrected. During its first two decades in Washington, the government spent less on the improvement of its headquarters than it spent each year on the president's salary. Grumbling was easier and cheaper. Margaret Bayard Smith shared the opinions expressed in the local newspapers that the transient nature of so large a segment of the city's population contributed to the callousness with which federal officials viewed the urban problems surrounding them. In the midst of the terrible cholera epidemic of 1832, Mrs. Smith noted:

> The population of our city is made up of individuals from all parts of America . . . , dependent on the government and changing with the changing administrations, each family standing as it were by itself and caring only for itself, unconnected by any of those ties of common interest, which unite the permanent inhabitants of other cities, and without the bonds of kindred, long acquaintanceship or connections which form the cement of society, destitute of that pride of citizenship, that love of country, that home feeling, which stimulates the people of other cities, to make exertions and sacrifices for the common good.

To the mounting irritation of local residents, government officials proved unwilling to recognize that Washington's unique status as a city devoted solely to government—a status they had created—made the city especially deserving of their help. Residents' pleas for assistance with everything from physical improvements to poor relief were rebuffed. Officials failed to acknowledge that the indigent men and women who flocked to Washington in times of economic depression came because it was the seat of the government they hoped could help them. They failed to see that the money congressmen and visitors spent on consumer goods pumped little capital into the economy, or that the seasonal nature of federal building operations often forced upon local citizens the burden of caring for laborers' families during long winter layoffs. Government officials presumed that charity was a local affair, ignoring the fact that, unlike other cities, Washington had a population made up largely of men like themselves, transients, whose civic allegiance lay elsewhere.

The "We's" and the "They's": Residential and Official Society

Though ridiculously new when compared to their counterparts in Boston or Philadelphia, within the first decade of the capital's existence a core of local families emerged who styled themselves as leaders of the fledgling residential elite. This nucleus contained a few individuals who really were original Washingtonians. Among them was Marcia Burnes, heir of David Burnes, one of the original proprietors, and Daniel Carroll of Duddington, a commissioner and owner of the busiest brick kiln in the city. Several wealthy old families from the surrounding Maryland and Virginia countryside, such as the Tayloes, Keys, Calverts, Dorseys, Peters, Ogles, and Lewises, also established handsome town homes in Washington and made the new capital their winter social headquarters.

In addition to those with long-standing ties to the area, Washington's early residential elite included many individuals who were as new to the capital as the capital was to the region. Among the early arrivals who quickly became entrenched was British land speculator Thomas Law, whose marriage, though unhappy, to Martha Washington's granddaughter Eliza Parke Custis gained him instant entree into the new capital's best society. William Cranch, nephew of Abigail Adams, originally came to town as the business agent of Robert Morris of Philadelphia, but stayed to become a commissioner and judge. Robert Brent, owner of the quarry at Acquia Creek, Virginia, which furnished stone for the new federal buildings, established a town house in the city, as did Colonel Tobias Lear, former secretary to General Washington, who came in hopes of establishing an import-export business. Publishers Samuel Harrison Smith, Joseph Gales, and William Seaton and their families came to provide the town and the nation with news. Architects like James Hoban and William Thornton came to provide handsome buildings. By 1810, lawyers, physicians, pastors, and priests swelled the list of notable first residents.

These were Washington's "first families," the capital's equivalent of Boston's Brahmins and New York's Knickerbockers. Like the early leaders of these two older cities, it was they who built the capital's first churches—Christ Episcopal and St. John's Episcopal Church, and Methodist, Baptist, and Catholic churches and a Friends meetinghouse all by 1816. It was they who founded Washington's first dancing assemblies, private academies, and charities, like the Washington City Orphan Asylum. But while they might dominate the city's religious, cultural, and philanthropic spheres, they were not omnipotent.

In particular, these early Washington leaders could not control certain important areas of their city's development. Economic and political power were beyond their grasp. Large tracts of choice property within their borders were federal land, not theirs to tax, sell, or develop. The largest employer in their town was the federal government, not a privately owned ropewalk, textile mill, or foundry. A kaleidoscope of governmental experiments imposed on the District by the federal government meant that mayors and councils were sometimes appointed by capricious presidents, sometimes elected by the citizens, and sometimes abolished altogether, often with politics rather than the city's welfare in mind.

While some realms of power and control were beyond their grasp, high society fell within these first families' domain from the beginning. Throughout the capital's early years, Washington's residential society was sufficiently numerous, wealthy, and stable to constitute a matrix within which the unstable official society could find some continuity. Until the late 1840s, when more officials began to rent homes and bring accomplished hostesses, residential society's entertainments were the most genteel, its ladies the most abundant, and its tastes the most refined in the city. The finest private homes in the young capital belonged to three local residents—Mr. Brent, Mr. Carroll, and Col. John Tayloe III, whose Octagon House was the most spacious and elegant of all. The first lonely officials flocked to handsome drawingrooms such as these.

As long as the capital remained small, residents and officials mixed freely. In 1802, in one of the first grand weddings in Washington, local girl Marcia Burnes married New York Congressman John Van Ness. Their beautiful mansion became a social center for both residential and official society. An assortment of neighbors and officials, sometimes President Jefferson himself, also gathered at Mr. and Mrs. Samuel Harrison Smith's home nearly every night to talk, play chess or whist, and enjoy the newspaperman's excellent wines. Jefferson reciprocated. The Smiths were frequent guests at the president's table, as were most of the "respectable citizens" of the town.

The residential and official social elites could also be found together enjoying the hospitality of Col. Tayloe and his wife Ann at Octagon House. Despite Mrs. Tayloe's frequent pregnancies and the Colonel's poor health, they entertained often. In addition to friends and neighbors who, like themselves, had deep roots in Virginia, their guests included local residents like the Thorntons and the Decaturs, and officials like

Representative Harrison Gray Otis and, when she came to visit him in Washington, his wife Sally and British Minister Charles Bagot and his wife Mary.

Mrs. William Thornton recorded in her diary the pleasant unhurried social life of the early capital and the constant interaction between the residential and official elite. Her husband William had just won the design competition for the Capitol Building when they moved to Washington in 1794. Twenty years old when she arrived, Anna Maria Brodeau Thornton viewed society from both camps during a residence of over forty years as her husband held a variety of official positions and sometimes none at all. She described visits to and from the local Law, Peter, and Dorsey families, as well as most of the members of official society. Between bouts of

"A Party in Georgetown at Mrs. Peters Tudor Place, 1840 by Mr. Glass." Before the rift between residential and official society became unbridgeable in the 1850s, the two groups mixed amicably at the elegant homes of the city's local elite. Tudor Place in Georgetown was one of the most beautiful of these homes and is one of the few that remain. Designed by William Thornton, it was built at the turn of the century for Thomas Peter and his wife Martha Parke Custis Peter, a granddaughter of Martha Washington. (Tudor Place Foundation, Inc.)

baking (during which she seemed continually to run out of raisins) and attending funerals, Mrs. Thornton gave dinner parties or dined out, sometimes every night of the week. Guests and hosts included members of all three branches of the government, foreign ministers, the Smiths, the Tayloes, and the Ogles. In one week in 1803, the Thorntons were the guests of President Jefferson, Vice President Aaron Burr, and Secretary of the Treasury Albert Gallatin.

Perhaps because she was an architect's wife, one of Mrs. Thornton's favorite pastimes was watching new homes go up in the capital. On a springlike day in January 1800, she and Mrs. Peter stopped before the almost-finished home of a friend: finding it locked, she wrote, "we entered by the kitchen window and went all over it—It is a very pleasant roomy house but the oval dining room is spoiled by the lowness of the ceiling, and two niches which destroy the shape of the room."

Thomas Law described a similar give-and-take between official and residential society during these early years. Law and his wife, when they weren't publicly quarreling, dined with President John Adams and the Samuel Harrison Smiths and entertained neighbors and officials at their beautiful home near the riverbank. Law also frequently dined out without his wife. Apparently a sought-after guest, Law confined his cynical views of his hosts and hostesses to his journals and to poems like the following:

"Reflections After Seeing a Crowd At An Evening Party"

The expense of hackney coach and fancy dress
By every one is carried to excess
Though called republican for ranks we fret
and daily quarrel about etiquette
The ladies chiefly to great parties go
For few prefer domestic scenes to show.

Until churches could be built, officials and residents worshiped together in the chamber of the House of Representatives or in the corridor of the Treasury Building. Mrs. Smith described the less-than-reverent services in the House, where the marine band valiantly tried to accompany the hymns:

I have called these Sunday assemblies in the capital, a *congregation,* but the almost exclusive appropriation of that word to religious assemblies, prevents its being a descriptive term as applied in the present case, since the gay company who thronged the House of Representatives looked very little like a religious assembly. The occasion presented for display was not only a novel, but a favourable one for the youth, beauty and fashion of the city, Georgetown and environs. The members of Congress, gladly gave up their seats for such fair auditors, and either lounged in the lobbies, or round the fire places, or stood beside the ladies of their acquaintance. . . . Smiles, nods, whispers, nay sometimes tittering . . . beguiled the tedium of the services.

The House and Senate chambers served the entire community's secular needs as well. Their proceedings provided some of the best "theater" to be found in the infant capital, and their galleries became a "lounging place of both sexes, where acquaintance is as easily made as at public amusements." There the wives of both residents and officials spent their afternoons, chatting and evaluating the merits of the congressmen below.

In the 1820s, the rapport that residents and officials had enjoyed began to fade. Sheer growth was partly responsible for the decline of intimacy. The white population of Washington jumped from 2,464 in 1800 to 9,606 in 1820. In official society, the number of House members alone rose from 142 in 1800 to 213 in 1820. The rapid expansion of the residential population and the dramatic growth of official society made intimate social intercourse among the leading families of the city difficult to maintain. The collapse of the "era of good feelings" after the Madison administration and the Monroes' new official protocol also helped drive a wedge between residential and official society. The most potent factor, however, driving the two groups apart was the democratization of American politics, which began to churn up the social waters as well as the political seas in the 1820s. Successive waves of presidential fever began to sweep over official society. To the disgust of many residents, politics began to dominate social occasions as never before. Rival cabinet members, each of whom established a salon, tried to recruit residents and officials alike to their "evenings," and they expected those who joined up to remain loyal throughout the winter season. Secretary of State Henry Clay, afflicted with the presidential virus, sent out his autumn bids in the following form: "Mr. and Mrs. Clay, request the favour of Dr. C——'s company, on Wednesday evening, the 30th inst., and on every alternate Wednesday, till the 20th of March."

Increasingly, social life became just another arena for partisan politics. Who was and who was not invited to tea, who accepted and who declined, became fraught with political significance. John Quincy Adams routinely noted who was and was not calling upon whom in his diary. In such an atmosphere, noted Margaret Bayard Smith, one was "obliged to go to other peoples' parties, sick or well, for fear of giving offence."

The 1824 presidential contest vividly underscored the changed atmosphere. Three of the five contenders were members of the cabinet (Secretary of State John Quincy Adams, Secretary of War John C. Calhoun, and Secretary of the Treasury William Crawford), Henry Clay was a representative from Kentucky, and Andrew Jackson was a senator from Tennessee. All save Jackson were well known in Washington's social circles, and each formed his own cabal of partisans.

All sides recognized that society could be used toward partisan ends, but Louisa Catherine Adams was particularly aware of the power of entertaining to enhance political position. At the end of December 1823, her

A reluctant Louisa Catherine Adams agreed to give a ball honoring Andrew Jackson, her husband John Quincy Adams's rival for the presidency, on the anniversary of the Battle of New Orleans. Among the other prominent figures in official society depicted in this engraving of the grand evening are Jackson (center), the Adamses (far right), and John C. Calhoun with Daniel Webster at his side (far left). (Library of Congress, Prints and Photographs Division)

husband, John Quincy Adams, was begging her to give a ball in honor of his rival Andrew Jackson on the ninth anniversary of the Battle of New Orleans. A display of his republican and personal virtues by unselfishly commemorating one of his competitor's military victories, Adams reasoned, would enhance his position, especially if it attracted newspaper coverage and reached a wide constituency. But Mrs. Adams didn't want to do it. She was already weary of the tense social season. Earlier in the month, at her husband's request, she had given a dinner that had not been a success. "It was," she wrote, "what we call a snarling dinner composed of such opposite materials it was not possible to prevent sharp speeches. Mr. Clay as usual assumed a very high tone and forced our Secretary of War [Calhoun] completely in the background."

On December 20, barely within the proper time frame for sending out invitations, Louisa Catherine Adams gave in, "overpowered by John's arguments," and agreed to have a ball on January 8. Her husband drew up the guest list that included many residents and nearly all of official society and eventually totaled over five hundred people. Mrs. Adams confided to her diary, "The number of persons who come to be invited on this occasion exceeds belief." After two frenzied weeks of preparation, the ball went off smoothly. John Quincy Adams was delighted. Louisa Catherine Adams was exhausted. Both felt the evening had achieved its purpose, but they would have to wait until November to be sure.

In the intervening months before the election, as the presidential contest heated up, Mrs. Smith, an ardent Crawford supporter, noted that

> society is now divided into separate battalions as it were. Mrs. Adams collected a large party and went one night [to the theater], Mrs. Calhoun another, so it was thought by our friends that Mrs. Crawford should go too, to show our strength. Caroline and I got in the carriage after dinner, and in one hour collected a party of ten ladies and about twenty gentlemen. . . . With a strong Crawford escort we went and passed so agreeable an evening that this week they wanted to go again.

On the eve of the election, Mrs. Seaton, another Crawford partisan, reported: "Party spirit is now fiery hot, and will increase every day. We have never been so much aware of it, not even in war and embargo times, as it has severed the most intimate links of friendship and good will."

John Quincy Adams's victory proved a sobering reminder to many residents that to ally oneself with a loser could mean social calamity. The loser's political cronies in official life could, and usually did, return home to mend their fences, but residents of Washington, who had sunk their fortunes into the capital city, could not slink away. Washington *was* home. They had no choice but to remain and endure for at least four years the chilly social shadows cast by a victor who knew they had opposed him. Residents quickly learned either to choose a candidate with extreme care and not to denounce his opponents so viciously that they could never again face them in society, or to stay out of partisan politics altogether.

The increased partisanship of the 1820s also sharpened the line between residents and officials in another way. As already noted, the relative stability of the executive branch for nearly two and a half decades after the government moved to Washington had permitted an entrenched group of second-tier officeholders to emerge who often remained in the city for many years. In the mid-1820s, this pattern abruptly changed. The new principle of rotation in office tended to make temporary residents of all federal officials. And as it did, a sharper line dividing those who thought of the federal capital as home—the "we's"—and those officials to whom only its federal functions were important—the "they's"—was drawn by the settled families.

In various subtle ways, after the 1820s residential society started to set itself apart from transient official society. A note of superiority began to creep into the older residents' comments about their official neighbors. As the number of congressmen spiraled, old Washingtonians detected a corresponding decrease in "quality," especially among the Westerners, whose typical representative, they were eager to believe, was foul-mouthed Davy Crockett of Tennessee. Juliana Seaton belittled the wives of a new crop of government officials:

> I suppose there have never been in the city so many plain women, in every sense of the word, as are now here among the families of official personages. I have always heard it asserted without contradiction, that nothing was easier than to learn to be a lady; but I begin to think differently, being morally certain that many among the new-comers will never achieve that status.

While the older residents spoke condescendingly of the newer members of official society, beneath their snobbery lay the uneasy knowledge that they were beginning to be outspent by some of the newcomers. During the capital's first decades, residential society had laid undisputed claim to the finest homes and best coaches in town. And in fact residential society continued to hold the social edge throughout the antebellum years. The fortunes of a few newcomers in official society in the Jacksonian era, however, surpassed those of the residents, and these very visible new arrivals spent money freely on housing and entertainments. Likewise, although some of the country-born wives of new officials were still mastering the social graces, many of the families arriving with wealthier officials brought with them the latest in fashions and manners from Europe.

Mrs. Smith's correspondence reflected the regret and envy felt by some longtime residents over the new developments. At the height of the season in 1830, she informed her sister:

> The city is thronged with strangers, fashionable ladies from all quarters, a great many mothers with daughters to show off, a great many young ladies coming to see relatives and to be seen by the public and all coming in such high ton [i.e., Fr. *ton*, "tone"] and expensive fashions, that the poor citizens can not pretend to vie with them and absolutely shrink into insignificance.

In 1836, Mrs. Smith ended another letter describing the excesses of official society on a prophetic note: "The increasing luxury of dress and living in this place, will soon oblige the poor gentry to form a separate association." Though the rift between residential and official society was not yet so wide as to require the local gentry to form such a "separate association," each year of the 1840s saw it grow a bit larger.

Society in a House Divided

By the 1850s, the widening gulf between official and residential society paled in significance beside a far more serious fissure dividing the city along other stress points. Washington and the nation were splitting open along regional fault lines. Though its location midway between North and South had been considered an asset in 1790, by the 1850s the capital's strategic position and the unique composition of its population meant that it was a city torn in two by the escalating sectional tension. That decade and the war years that followed were especially painful for Washington because of the city's dual nature. Washington was a Southern

city, yet it sheltered a national government that was increasingly dominated by Northerners. The city's sole function was to be hospitable to a
government with which much of its residential population felt a diminishing kinship. Geographically teetering between North and South and
politically straining in both directions, Washington in the 1850s was a
house divided, neighbor against neighbor, resident against official.

From the beginning, Southerners and Southern ways had dominated
the capital. The builders of the capital's first fine homes were drawn from
neighboring planter families. In the 1820s, 1830s, and 1840s, when few
congressmen brought their families to Washington, the few who did were
almost invariably Southerners. Moreover, Maryland and Virginia, the two
states that had contributed not only the land for the federal district in
1790 but also many of the new capital's first residents, were slaveholding
states. There were 3,244 slaves in the District of Columbia when the government moved there from Philadelphia in 1800. Few Northern or
European visitors to the city failed to note that one could stand in the
doorway of the Capitol Building and watch coffles of slaves shuffle by on
their way to the pens to await sale to the deep South. The St. Charles
Hotel on Pennsylvania Avenue, a favorite with visiting Southerners,
boasted of six cells, equipped with iron doors and wall rings, in its basement to house slaves and ran the following advertisement in newspapers
throughout the South: "The Proprietor of this hotel has roomy under-
ground cells for confining slaves for safekeeping, and patrons are notified
that their slaves will be well cared for. In case of escape full value of the
negro will be paid by the Proprietor."

Except for some unpleasant exchanges over the Missouri Compromise and the Nullification Crisis, Northerners and Southerners had at first
mixed amicably in Washington's official and residential society. Cordial
relations, however, began to deteriorate in the late 1840s, especially so in
1849 when Illinois Congressman Abraham Lincoln proposed the abolition
of slavery in the District of Columbia. Residents, who had no representative in Congress, had to listen to others argue their case. The final compromise, providing not for the abolition of slavery in the District but only
for the outlawing of the odious slave trade, strained what sectional harmony had existed in Washington society.

The months leading up to the Compromise of 1850 were anxious
ones for everyone in Washington. Americans everywhere felt the strain as
the battle over the extension of slavery threatened to burst the bonds of
the Union, but in other parts of the country men could occasionally for-

get the danger. Not so in Washington, where the heated debates and sometimes the debaters themselves spilled out of the Capitol and onto the streets. The Kansas-Nebraska Act, the caning of Massachusetts Senator Charles Sumner by South Carolina Representative Preston Brooks, the Dred Scott decision, and John Brown's raid on Harpers Ferry, all helped widen the chasm between Northerners and Southerners until it became unbridgeable.

Despite the escalating tension, the intermingling of Southerners and Northerners, residents and officials, in high society continued throughout the 1850s. Southerners still dominated the increasingly polarized residential and political social circles. Among the leaders of residential society, local millionaire William Corcoran and the wealthy Riggs, Tayloe, and Parker families, all Southern Democrats, entertained most handsomely. Leading official society were Southerners like the families of Senators John Slidell of Louisiana, Robert Toombs of Georgia, and William Gwin of California; Representatives Roger Pryor of Virginia and Williamson Cobb of Alabama; Secretary of the Interior Jacob Thompson of Mississippi; and Secretary of War Jefferson Davis, whose sharp-tongued wife Varina had shown in society since the Taylor years.

Virginia Clay, wife of Alabama Senator Clement Claiborne Clay, was one of the gayest newcomers to official society during the decade. When the Clays arrived in 1853, they were welcomed into the prestigious Southern "mess" at Brown's Hotel. (Brown's and the National Hotel were known as Southern strongholds, while Yankees favored the Willard and Kirkwood.) Virginia Clay looked forward to entering society, but found it already a quagmire of sectionalist sentiment. While the niceties of formal etiquette were still being observed, beneath the surface she discovered an official society infused with tension:

> Feeling ran high in the Senate and the House. . . . To be sure, courtesies were exchanged between the wives of some of the Northern and Southern Senators, and formal calls were paid on Cabinet days, as etiquette demanded, upon the ladies of the Cabinet Circle; but, by a tacit understanding, even at the entertainments given at the foreign legations, and at the houses of famous Washington citizens, this opposition of parties was carefully considered in the sending out of invitations, in order that no unfortunate *rencontre* might occur between uncongenial guests.

As the Kansas debates unfolded, the strain on cordiality increased. "We are," wrote Mrs. Clay in 1856, "dancing over a powder magazine. . . .

Southern blood is at boiling temperature all over the city, and with good cause, too." A rabid Southern partisan, Mrs. Clay did little to help matters. At a fancy dress ball at the home of Senator and Mrs. Gwin on Eye Street, Mrs. Clay theatrically refused to shake the hand of abolitionist New York Senator William Henry Seward. Though her husband urged her to greet his colleague, she claimed she responded, "Not even to save the Nation could I be induced to eat his bread, to drink his wine, to enter his domicile, to *speak* to him!"

In 1857, with the arrival of bachelor President James Buchanan and his twenty-six-year-old niece and hostess Harriet Lane, the White House came alive with gaiety and warmth, once again the focus of official society. Striving for the near-impossible in such deeply troubled times, Miss Lane tried valiantly to mix men and women of opposing views at her en-

As official society split open along sectional lines in the 1850s, it became increasingly difficult to hold large receptions without guests coming to verbal and even physical blows. This engraving depicts President James Buchanan and his niece and official hostess Harriet Lane in the East Room of the White House at one of the last great receptions of his administration. Guests were on their best behavior, but the tension, reported one, was palpable. (*Harper's Weekly,* March 13, 1858; Library of Congress, Prints and Photographs Division)

tertainments. For a few years she succeeded, but in the end the task became impossible even for her formidable social skills. As sectional tensions increased, no hostess in the capital could honor the rules of precedence at the dinner table and still keep political enemies apart. In January 1860, Elizabeth Blair Lee, daughter of Andrew Jackson's loyal friend Frances Preston Blair and an ardent Unionist, wrote from her home across the street from the White House to her husband, naval officer Samuel Phillips Lee, about a terrible fight at a dinner party:

> Mr. Tombs and General Scott [Senator Robert Tombs of Georgia and General Winfield Scott, "Old Fuss and Feathers"] had a bout at No. 4 (John Rs) [the home of John R. Thomson, Senator from New Jersey]. The first called the Old Hero a liar—where upon the General rushed into him—but they were promptly parted—it was at a dinner party—Civil War seems inevitable—even at friendly dinner parties.

Little could distract Washingtonians from the escalating crisis. A much-publicized visit by the young Prince of Wales, a "peachy-cheeked beardless boy," provided a brief respite in 1860, but the grim reality of a nation dividing quickly returned. After John Brown's raid on Harpers Ferry in October, senators and representatives buckled on revolvers under their coats. When local Southerners' worst nightmare came true with news of Abraham Lincoln's electoral victory in November, they draped their houses in black.

A few days before Christmas in 1860, outgoing President James Buchanan attended a fashionable Washington wedding. As he sat in the parlor, breathing in the unseasonable fragrance of roses and lilies, he was startled by a commotion in the hallway and asked a nearby lady whether the house was on fire. It was, in fact, the Union that was in flames. The shouts came from those outside rejoicing over a telegram announcing the secession of South Carolina.

With news of South Carolina's secession, fear for the nation's economy swept the big Northern cities. For Washington, however, dissolution of the Union would spell far more than economic disaster; it would mean the town's virtual annihilation. On the one hand, if the nation peacefully split in two, Washington, perched on the Northern border of one new country and the Southern border of the other, could hardly expect to be the capital of either. Without the government business upon which it was dependent, Washington would quickly sink into insignificance. On the other hand, if the incoming Republican administration refused to "let erring sisters go in peace," civil war would surely follow, and the capital, straddling North and South, would become a beleaguered battleground. As it had been in 1814 for the British, Washington, the capital of the Union, would be a tantalizing, highly symbolic prize for any enemy.

Rumors began to fly that the South would try to secure Washington before Lincoln could be inaugurated. When on Christmas Day in 1860 the *Richmond Examiner* brazenly asked, "Can there not be found men bold and brave enough in Maryland to unite with Virginians in seizing the Capital in Washington?" it fanned the fears of all loyal citizens. If residents collaborated, Northerners knew that a coup might easily succeed. The 1860 census had shown that twenty-four percent of the capital's population had been born in Maryland and Virginia, and nearly fifty percent of those born in the District had ties to Southern families. The Capitol was checked for explosives each night.

Many residents clung to the hope that the unraveling strands of the Union might still be rewoven. That hope dimmed dramatically on January 21, 1861, when the senators from Florida, Alabama, and Mississippi delivered stirring valedictories and stalked out of the Senate chamber. One by one, the ties of unity were snapping. Amid the crush of Southern ladies weeping and waving handkerchiefs in the galleries sat a tearful Mrs. Clement Claiborne Clay, watching her husband take his leave of the Union. As one by one the Southern ex-congressmen left Washington, it was clear that the capital would never be the same again. Packing to return to Alabama, Mrs. Clay noted:

> From the hour of this exodus of Senators from the official body, all Washington seemed to change. Imagination can scarcely conjure up an atmosphere at once so ominous and so sad. . . . Farewells were to be spoken, and many, we knew would be final. Vehicles lumbered on their way to wharf or station filled with the baggage of departing Senators and Members.

3 Washington Society Transformed

The Civil War and Its Aftermath in the Capital

The Capital at War: "The City Now Is a Huge Crowd"

Despite threats of assassination, Abraham Lincoln took the oath of office on the afternoon of March 4, 1861—with fifty armed men concealed inside the platform beneath his feet. That night, the inaugural ball went off smoothly in a "white muslin palace of Aladdin," a temporary structure of wooden frames covered with cloth, behind City Hall. It was a Northern crowd that danced quadrilles to the music of the Marine Band. Most of the revelers were strangers to high society in the capital, and, by the looks of them, said their detractors, strangers to polite society anywhere else.

In the days that followed the inauguration, there was guarded optimism that the new president, who spoke of the "bonds of affection" uniting North and South, might yet mend the breach in the Union. Even this slim hope, however, quickly evaporated. On April 12, secessionists in Charleston, South Carolina, shelled Fort Sumter and President Lincoln called for seventy-five thousand volunteers. Five days later, the State of Virginia, directly across the Potomac from the capital, seceded. Little more than a month after the reassuring inauguration, civil war had begun.

Washington is unique among American cities in the transformation it underwent during the Civil War. No other city was subjected to the same constant threat of capture, the suspicions of disloyalty, the mushrooming of its population, and, most important from the standpoint of high society, the swift decimation of its old ruling elite, as Washington was during the war. Unlike other cities in the Union that experienced the struggle from a distance, Washington knew the war intimately, and that experience would exert a strong influence over the capital's high society forever after.

The first and most dramatic effect of the outbreak of war on Washington was the exodus of the Southern members of official society. What began as a trickle of departures with the fall of Fort Sumter quickly became a flood in the weeks that followed. Southern representatives and senators left as one after another of their states seceded. Justice John A. Campbell of Alabama stepped down from the Supreme Court and left town. Federal offices emptied as Southern-born clerks left to offer their services to the Confederacy. On April 18, 1861, Colonel Robert E. Lee rode into Washington from his home on the Arlington Heights in Virginia to reject an offer to command the Union army and hand in his resignation. Following his lead, Southern-born officers, many of whom had been among the most dashing members of official society, resigned from the military by the score. Between April and December 1861, 313 of the army's 727 officers resigned and departed.

The residential elite suffered similar losses. Southern-sympathizing, socially prominent, longtime Washingtonians, including former Mayor Walter Lenox, closed their homes and slipped away to Canada, Richmond, Mobile, and New Orleans. Elizabeth Blair Lee's letters in the spring of 1861 to her husband in the Union navy tell of neighbor after neighbor packing to leave. Auction notices filled the local newspapers. Financier William Corcoran rented his beautiful mansion on Lafayette Square to the French legation and spent the war years abroad with his daughter Louise and son-in-law George Eustis, who was secretary of the Confederate legation at Paris. Corcoran's neighbor on Lafayette Square, Mrs. Ogle Tayloe, who had strong family ties to Virginia and whose drawingroom was one of the most popular in the city, ordered summer dress for her rooms. When the world was righted and her friends returned, said Mrs. Tayloe, her red silk upholstery would be uncovered and she would receive once again.

One prominent Southern hostess who remained behind in Washington, Mrs. Philip Phillips, wrote to Mrs. Clement Claiborne Clay, back home in Alabama, of their friends' departures:

What can I tell you, but of despair, of broken hearts, of ruined fortunes, the sobs of women, and sighs of men! . . . For days I saw nothing but despairing women leaving suddenly. . . . You would not know this God-forsaken city, our beloved capital, with all its artistic wealth, desecrated, disgraced with Lincoln's low soldiery.

By May of 1861, as the city emptied out, advertisements of handsome homes for rent "for indefinite time" filled the *Evening Star*. The Reverend George W. Smith noted of the first two months of the war:

Property could be had 'for a song,' even badly sung. A small brick house opposite General Scott's headquarters which the owner had been about to sell for $7,000 to a customer who no longer wanted it was offered for $2,000, but there was no purchaser. No one wanted to buy a house in a city that might be on the eve of destruction.

Among the Southerners who stayed behind in the capital, many, like the large Francis Preston Blair and Phillips Lee families, remained loyal to the Union. Others, however, did not. When Mayor James Berret refused to take the loyalty oath, Union soldiers promptly hustled him off to Fort Lafayette in New York harbor where he remained imprisoned for a month. At one point in the war, three hundred District residents were in the Old Capitol prison for proven or suspected disloyalty. The arrest of prominent local hostesses like Mrs. Philip Phillips and Mrs. Rose Greenhow for spying for the Confederacy fueled Northern suspicions of the entire population's treachery. Even Joseph Henry, the august head of the Smithsonian Institution, became suspect: it was whispered that he was actually signalling the enemy from the Smithsonian's turrets and only pretending to conduct meteorological experiments. From within the White House, Lincoln's young secretary John Nicolay wrote his wife in that first spring of the war, "We are not only surrounded by the enemy, but in the midst of traitors."

The arrests of leading civilians on mere rumor of collaboration cast heavy shadows over every household in Washington. Elizabeth Blair Lee worried constantly about the loyalty of her neighbors in the Maryland countryside, many of whom would later be arrested. In the words of one longtime resident, "a social mildew fell upon neighbors and old friends who now looked upon each other askance with mutual distrust."

Though it shrunk at first with the exodus of Southerners, Washington's population mushroomed during the course of the war. In 1860, the population of the District of Columbia was 75,080. By the end of 1861, it had jumped to 100,000, and it exceeded 200,000 before the war's end. Contributing to the population explosion were soldiers—thousands and thousands of them. Over 200,000 young men in blue would pass through the city during four years of war on their way south to fight or on their way back home on litters to convalesce.

Washington quickly became a city of barracks and hospitals. The British actress Fanny Kemble marvelled at the military presence in the capital when she visited in the spring of 1862:

> The aspect of this place when first I came here a month ago was the strangest imaginable. Every eminence by which the city was

All through the early days of April 1861, Washingtonians loyal to the Union listened nervously to rumors of a Confederate blockade of the Potomac, cut communication lines, and terrorists slipping into town with bombs in their suitcases. The first Union troops who arrived to guard the city were greeted with outpourings of gratitude. This wood engraving shows crowds welcoming the New York 71st Regiment as it arrived at the B & O railroad depot in mid-April. (*Frank Leslie's Illustrated Newspaper,* May 18, 1861; Library of Congress, Prints and Photographs Division)

surrounded—and it lies in the midst of a sea of small hills—was covered with camps and shanties—the streets were incessantly filled with huge trains of army wagons—ambulances—great processions of hay and wood carts and covered wagons marked with regimental insignia bringing sick men into the hospitals— . . . the sound of drums and trumpets and artillery practising never ceased.

In addition to the soldiers crowding into the capital, thousands of desperate freedmen sought protection there. Their shanties sprang up in the malarial swamps along the canal known as "Murder Bay." Adding to the confusion, hundreds of new government clerks, needed to perform the myriad tasks generated by the war, packed themselves four and six to a bed in already bulging boardinghouses.

Whenever there was a lull in the fighting in Virginia, tourists flooded into the capital and signed up with cartmen for excursions to the battlefields. Souvenir sellers, hawking everything from the haversacks to the Bibles of fallen Confederates, followed and reaped a rich harvest. Reporter Noah Brooks, correspondent for the *Sacramento Union,* described another more poignant group of strangers who crowded into the city whenever the fighting ceased: "These people came in quest of friends who had been taken to the hospitals, or perhaps left dead on the field. It was easy to recognize them by their anxious and distressed faces, their strangeness in the city."

Confidence men, counterfeiters, and pickpockets slithered through the crowds. Dancers, actors, and prizefighters came to Washington to entertain the living. Embalmers and casket-sellers came to profit from the dead. Ambitious madams in New York, Philadelphia, and even Chicago and St. Louis closed their houses and brought their prostitutes to the capital. When General Joseph Hooker tried to concentrate the "daughters of Eve" in one section of town, the women promptly became known as "Joe Hooker's Division." In the wake of the prostitutes came "doctors" promising permanent cures for syphilis and gonorrhea in just three days.

Julia Ward Howe, visiting the capital in the fall of 1861, was struck by the diversity of the crowds: "Politicians of every grade, adventurers of either sex, inventors of all sorts of military appliances, and simple citizens, good and bad, flocked thither in great numbers." Louisa May Alcott was one of the many young women from New England who came to Washington to nurse the wounded. Arriving in 1862, she remarked on the feverish gaiety of the city: "Pennsylvania Avenue, with its bustle, lights, music, and military made me feel as if I'd crossed the water and landed somewhere in Carnival time." For the first time ever, Washington's hotels were crowded even in the months Congress was not in session. In November 1861, Mrs. John A. Kasson, wife of the First Assistant Postmaster General, noted in her column for the Des Moines *Register:*

> The city now is a huge crowd, and the strivings and pushing for houses and rooms, afford laughable contrast to the panic of last summer. . . . Demand for accommodations is so pressing, that one cannot help pitying the rueful faces of those who might have made small fortunes had they not been too readily scared by southern braggadocio, and anticipation of Jeff Davis' dread presence!

Amid the chaos, social life continued. A brand new cast of players, however, enlivened the wartime capital. For almost three generations—over half a century—Southerners had dominated Washington's high society, but no longer. When the steamers full of Southern families pulled away from the city's docks, a regime ended. Their sudden departure created a social vacuum. Into the void swarmed a horde of newcomers—a motley assortment of Northern Republicans, ambitious generals, and political adventurers of every stripe—who would transform Washington's official and residential high society.

The new president's wife, Mary Todd Lincoln, looked forward to leading the new official society of which she was the titular head. She was anxious to win for herself and the Republicans the kudos Harriet Lane had earned for the Democrats. Instead, unable to conceal her Southern sympathies or curb her unseemly extravagance, Mrs. Lincoln won only enmity. Elizabeth Blair Lee noted during the very first summer of the war that "the women kind are giving Mrs. Lincoln the cold shoulder."

Mrs. Lincoln gave her enemies ample cause to berate her. While Union soldiers shivered for want of blankets, she spent ten thousand dollars on a single carpet. Her lavish entertainments during the 1861–62 season drew harsh criticism, and none more than her enormous reception in February 1862. Mrs. Lincoln's new low-cut gown for the occasion was made of white silk flounced with ruffles of black lace and was said to have cost two thousand dollars. Not content with local caterers, Mrs. Lincoln hired Maillard's of New York, who produced a fountain held aloft by nougat water nymphs, sugar hives swarming with lifelike marzipan bees and filled with charlotte russe, and an immense Japanese punch

Mary Todd Lincoln, wearing a gown of white silk taffeta, posed for this carte de visite by Mathew Brady in November 1861, three months before her extravagant reception and the death of her son Willie. (Mathew Brady Collection, National Archives)

bowl that held ten gallons of champagne punch. Letters chastising Mrs. Lincoln for these extravagances poured into the White House, but by the time they arrived she was oblivious to their sting. On the night of the festivities, her two little boys lay upstairs sick with colds. Two weeks later, little Willie died of typhoid fever. Grief-stricken, Mrs. Lincoln never again entertained on such a scale. Her unseemly acquisitiveness, however, forever marked her as a spendthrift, callous to the agony of a nation at war.

Though mourning darkened the White House, there was no lack of elegant official drawingrooms in the wartime capital. The homes of Speaker of the House Schuyler "Smiler" Colfax and Representative Fernando Wood, the wealthy former mayor of New York, shone brightly. Outshining all the others, however, was the mansion of Secretary of the Treasury Salmon P. Chase. The widowed secretary's beautiful and savvy daughter Catherine, called Kate, ruled its parlors. Because of the illness of Secretary of State William Seward's wife, Kate Chase served as the chief hostess of the cabinet, but she was much more than that. While Mrs. Lincoln was the titular head of official society, Kate Chase was its sovereign in fact. The two women detested one another.

Kate Chase's wedding to Senator William Sprague of Rhode Island on November 12, 1863, stood out among the social events that took place in the capital during four years of civil war. Though it was rumored that she was marrying the uninspiring Sprague for his twenty-five million dollars to finance her father's presidential ambitions, the press carried only breathless accounts of the bride's beauty and the groom's good fortune. On the day of the wedding, spectators packed the street outside the Chase mansion hoping to catch a glimpse of the military heroes, congressmen, cabinet members, and diplomats alighting from the continuous line of carriages inching along E Street. President Lincoln arrived alone; Mrs. Lincoln pleaded mourning.

Each year of the war, the capital's official high society seemed to become more and more festive and frenetic. Perhaps with pain, death, and fear of attack and capture omnipresent in Washington, officials sought release in hectic gaiety. Though hundreds of men lay dying in makeshift hospitals and battles upriver sent bloated corpses floating down the Potomac to get tangled in its bridges, the social pace did not slacken. Most visitors to the capital were appalled by the frivolity. "Washington seems crazy," wrote one newcomer early in 1863: "Four or five parties in one evening seems the fashion." "One would hardly think we were at war," complained one army wife that same winter, "to see the crowds of well dressed men and women flitting about."

The 1863–64 season was even gayer. As it got underway, the London *Times* correspondent wrote home, "There is something saddening, indeed revolting, in the high glee, real or affected, with which the people here look upon what ought to be, at any rate, a grievous national calamity. . . . The jewelers' shops . . . have doubled and trebled their trade; the love of dresses and ornaments on the part of women amounts to madness." In February 1864, the Springfield, Illinois, *Republican* reported, "At present Washington is mad with gaiety, reeling in the whirl of dissipation, before it sits down to repent in the ashes of Lent. There are three or four grand parties a night; theaters, operas, fairs, everything to make its denizens forget that war and sorrow are in the land." Fourteen-year-old Violet Blair, granddaughter of Frances Preston Blair, Sr., recorded in her diary that she attended parties, balls, receptions, and tableaux nearly every night that winter. Secretary of State Seward's son Frederick noted, "Gaiety has become an epidemic in Washington this winter. . . . A year ago the Secretary of State was 'heartless' or 'unpatriotic' because he gave dinners; now the only complaint of him is, that he don't have dancing."

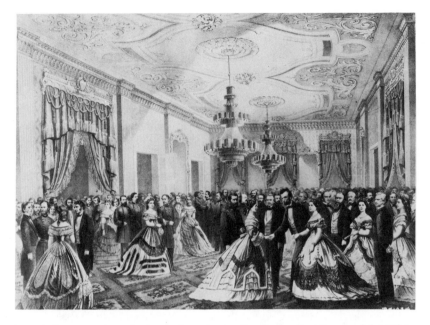

An artist's conception of a large, formal reception in the East Room of the White House late in the war. President and Mrs. Lincoln are surrounded by nearly everyone of official prominence in Washington. Vice President Andrew Johnson stands beside the president. General Ulysses S. Grant, in uniform, waits to shake the president's hand. Ben Butler is at Grant's left arm. Kate Chase Sprague, flanked by Edwin Stanton on her right and William Seward on her left, stands behind Mrs. Lincoln, whom she loathed. (National Archives)

    Noisy celebrations and serenading crowds marked President Lincoln's reelection in November 1864. In late December, howitzers boomed, bunting blossomed, and Harvey's Restaurant broke out Rappahannock oysters, the first served since the war began, to celebrate Sherman's victory in Georgia. The jubilation continued through February 1865 and the inauguration in March. On April 3 came news of the fall of Richmond. Convalescents panted out of hospitals, children streamed out of schools, and government clerks abandoned their offices to celebrate. Freedmen sang hymns in front of the White House. Major Benjamin Brown French, Commissioner of Public Buildings, decorated his own house and ordered the Capitol to be illuminated. Only the "secesh" houses remained conspicuously unadorned and shuttered. The next week brought General

Lee's surrender at Appomattox, and the city celebrated again with massive illuminations, fireworks, and parades.

The following week, Holy Week, President Lincoln was assassinated, and the capital plunged into deep mourning. Yards of black crepe smothered the gay bunting of the week before. Prudent "secesh" tacked up crepe as well. Those who failed to share in the public grieving paid a price: a Southern preacher who spoke ill of the slain president in his Easter sermon was dragged from his pulpit by the Union soldiers in the congregation. Come May, in the midst of the trial of the assassin's accomplices, the black crepe was taken down. The city bloomed once more with swags of red, white and blue. The capital revived for the last and greatest pageant of the war—the grand review of the armies of the Republic. Even after four years of teeming crowds, Washington staggered under the invasion of visitors intent on watching the spectacle. In New England, Marian Hooper, who later married Henry Adams, wanted desperately to see the triumphant parade and, against her father's wishes, found a chaperone to escort her and four other young ladies to the capital from Boston. Major General Rutherford B. Hayes insisted that his wife Lucy leave their children with family in Ohio and travel to Washington to see the review by his side.

Crowds began to line the parade route at dawn on May 23, the first day of the two-day review. Isaac Bassett, Assistant Doorkeeper of the Senate, who was watching from the Capitol, claimed that "from one extremity to the other, Pennsylvania Avenue was lined on both sides with a forest of faces." At nine o'clock, a signal gun heralded the beginning of the review. First to swing into sight was a solitary horseman, bespectacled General George Meade, at the head of the Army of the Potomac. The crowd took up the cheer of the Pennsylvanians in the stands— "Gettysburg, Gettysburg, Gettysburg!" For the next six hours the even lines of men, stretching from curb to curb, passed down Pennsylvania Avenue, their gleaming bayonets turning the street into a sparkling river. For Marian Hooper, the long trip from Boston had been worth it. That night she wrote a cousin:

> And so it came, this glorious old army of the Potomac, for six hours
> marching past, eighteen or twenty miles long, their colors telling their sad
> history. Some regiments with nothing but a bare pole, a little bit of rag
> only, hanging a few inches, to show where their flag had been. . . . It was
> a strange feeling to be so intensely happy and triumphant and yet to feel
> like crying.

Crowds gather early in the morning in front of the Treasury Building to await the Grand Review of the Armies of the Republic. While troops stretching from curb to curb marched down Pennsylvania Avenue from the Capitol for six solid hours on May 23 and 24, 1865, thousands watched, cheered, and wept as the last great pageant of the Civil War passed by. (National Archives)

The next day, "humanity of all ages, sexes and conditions" packed Pennsylvania Avenue once again and stood in the warm sun to cheer the Army of the Tennessee and the Army of Georgia. As the starting signal boomed, Generals William Tecumseh Sherman and Oliver O. Howard rode out onto the Avenue. In Sherman's honor, the bands played a jubilant new tune, "Marching through Georgia." Sherman was worried that his rough, gangling, ill-clothed Westerners might compare unfavorably with the polished Eastern troops that had passed by the day before. But as he topped the rise at the Treasury Building and turned in his saddle for a backward glance, his fears were put to rest. His men were magnificent. They were cheered and pelted with flowers as they marched down the Avenue. After they disbanded, the city was kept awake by their rowdy celebrating long into the night.

The grand review had ended. Noah Brooks cabled back to Sacramento:

> The pageant faded. The men-at-arms who had spent their years and lavished their energies in camps or on fields of battle went from the national capital to their own homes, to take up once more the arts of peace and the cares and joys of sweet domesticity. In a few weeks this army of two or three hundred thousand men melted back into the heart of the people from whence it came, and the great spectacle of the Grand Army of the Republic on review disappeared from sight.

"The Old Provincial Southern City Is No More"

Major Benjamin Brown French, who had lived in Washington for thirty years, regretted the decision to hold the grand review. The capital, he reasoned, had already had plenty of excitement, and he, for one, would be glad when the city subsided back into "its old jog trot way of life." But Washington would never again settle into the "old jog trot" Major French longed for. The war had swept away the old life. Although the outlines of the new order were still vague in 1865, as the city felt the rush of the receding tides of soldiers, Washington was clearly a changed city, the capital of a changing nation. Returning "secesh," soldiers, and others who had been away from Washington during the war were astounded by the physical transformation the capital had undergone during their absence. One young local boy who had fled in 1861 to fight for the Confederacy noted that "the returning parole bearer, who rubbed the smoke of a four-year battle from his eyes as he recrossed the Potomac, beheld with wonder and amazement the changes wrought by the Federal Aladdin."

One change was the crowds. Despite the mustering out of soldiers and the gradual departure of the prostitutes and con men, the city still seemed about to burst its seams. In 1867, when city leaders conducted a special census to prove to Congress that their requests for additional funds for city services were justified, the population had leveled off at 126,000, nearly double the 1860 census figures.

The war had also left the capital physically shabby. The rotting carcasses of mules were piled high behind splintering, makeshift stables on the Mall. Hardly a tree stood in the whole city—the cold troops camped in the town over four winters had used them all for firewood. The *New York Tribune*'s Horace Greeley described the postwar capital as a place where "the rents are high, the food is bad, the dust is disgusting, the mud is deep, and the morals are deplorable." Diagnosing the situation as hopeless, Greeley urged that the capital be moved west, preferably to St. Louis. By 1869, Cincinnati and Chicago each had supporters as well, and Congress appeared on the verge of considering relocation.

District businessmen, keenly aware that their livelihoods were irrevocably tied to Washington's official status, were prodded into action by this agitation to move the capital. Their strategy was to make the city so attractive, so accommodating, that talk of moving the government would cease. Their plans represented the final discarding of the last lingering dreams of exploiting the capital's commercial potential in favor of making the city a profitable service center for the steadily expanding federal government. As a first step, in 1870 a group of 150 influential citizens, including the unlikely pair of philanthropist William Corcoran, returned from Europe, and gasfitter's assistant turned real estate developer Alexander Shepherd successfully petitioned Congress to establish a territorial government for the District of Columbia, giving local leaders more autonomy.

The short life of the Territory of the District of Columbia was tumultuous at best, but everyone agreed that it did indeed change Washington. Its problems started immediately when President Grant began using his appointive powers to pay off political and personal debts. He appointed a newcomer to the capital, Henry Cooke, as Territorial Governor. Cooke, who had come to Washington in 1861 to lobby his old Ohio friend, Secretary of the Treasury Salmon Chase, on behalf of his brother, financier Jay Cooke, had become deeply involved in his own financial schemes in the District and become great friends with the Grants.

Grant named another crony, Shepherd, to the Board of Public Works. A tall, powerfully built man, Shepherd exuded confidence, and Governor Cooke and the other territorial officials quickly deferred to him as the "Boss." Shepherd ordered old buildings torn down, railroad tracks ripped up, streets paved, sidewalks lit, sewers buried, mosquito-infested canals filled in, aqueducts dug, parks laid out, and sixty thousand trees planted.

At first, few questioned what these improvements were costing them. Those who did, however, learned that by March 1872 Shepherd had spent over $2 million and sanctioned an indebtedness of $9,450,000, a debt larger than those of all but seven states of the Union. In addition, rumor had much of the money disappearing into the pockets of Shepherd and his friends. A congressional investigation followed, but the committee members proved to be less than aggressive watchdogs. Almost all friends of Shepherd and some in debt to Cooke, who was also president of the First Bank of Washington, they ascribed Shepherd's transgressions to excessive but well-intentioned zeal and warned Territorial officials to be more exacting in the future.

Shepherd ignored even this mild rebuke. By midsummer in 1873 the District of Columbia was bankrupt. In September, the banking house of Jay Cooke and Company failed, precipitating the Panic of 1873 and the beginning of a long nationwide depression. The First Bank of Washington closed its doors, and its humiliated president, Henry Cooke, resigned as governor of the District. President Grant named Shepherd to fill the governorship, but when he began levying new assessments, desperate taxpayers demanded a second congressional investigation into the affairs of the District of Columbia. After listening to witnesses tell extraordinary tales of jobbery, bribery, and other skullduggery, Congress

As chairman of the Board of Public Works and Governor of the Territory of the District of Columbia in the early 1870s, Alexander Shepherd transformed the postwar capital from an ugly village into a handsome city. A powerfully built man with a strong personality, "Boss" Shepherd created his "New Washington" in record time, though by means that proved to be corrupt. (Fine Arts Commission Collection, National Archives)

pronounced the experiment a costly failure and dissolved the territorial government.

Shepherd fled Washington for Chihuahua, Mexico, leaving behind a mixed legacy. Though he left the capital burdened with an enormous debt, he had turned a squalid town into a beautiful city of magnificent tree-lined boulevards. Whatever his faults, Shepherd had created an environment perfect for enticing to the nation's capital the growing numbers of rootless rich men and women who had formerly regarded the city as a social wasteland.

In 1873, Mary Clemmer Ames, a Washington correspondent for the New York *Independent,* offered an effusive, but fairly accurate, description of the changes Shepherd had wrought:

> The old provincial Southern city is no more. From its foundations has risen another city, neither Southern nor Northern, but national, cosmopolitan. Where the 'Slough of Despond' spread its waxen mud across the acres of the West End, where pedestrians were 'slumped,' and horses 'stalled,' and discomfort and disgust prevailed, we now see broad carriage drives, level as floors. . . . Where streets and avenues crossed and re-crossed their long vistas of shadeless dust, now plat on plat of restful grass 'park' the city from end to end. Double rows of young trees line these parks far as the sight can reach. . . . Old Washington was full of small Saharas. Where the great avenues intersected acres of white sand were caught up and carried through the air by counter winds. . . . Now where streets and avenues cross, emerald 'circles' with central fountains, pervading the air with cooling spray, with belts of flowers and troops of children, and restful seats for the old or the weary take the place of the old Saharas. . . . The green pools which used to distill malaria beneath your windows are now all sucked into the great sewers, planted at last in the foundations of the city. . . . Peace, prosperity and luxury have taken the place of war, of knightly days and of heroic men.

In 1876, crowds of visitors on their way to the Centennial Exhibition in Philadelphia stopped off in Washington to see the federal sights. Those who had never seen the capital were appreciative of its handsome, wide streets. But those who had known the crude town of only a decade before were amazed. It truly was, as Shepherd himself had dubbed it, a "New Washington," the ideal stage for the new high society drama unfolding in the nation's capital.

The Great Republic

The New Washington played host to a new government. Washington was still a one-crop town, with only government to export to the rest of the nation, but that single crop had changed dramatically. In the decade after the war, a strong new bureaucratic hybrid took root and flourished along the Potomac, providing high society in the postwar capital with a dazzling array of new members.

Shepherd's New Washington represented this new government in concrete form. In the decades before the war, the slovenly capital had been the physical embodiment of American distaste for centralized government. The town's small size indicated the slightness of the federal government's function. But the Civil War brought new vigor and a vastly expanded scale to the federal bureaucracy in Washington. Only a centralized government could provide the leadership that the war effort ultimately demanded. Ironically, the same war that strengthened the federal government initially left the city that housed it a mess of mud-filled streets and slapdash buildings. The immediate postwar capital was the ugly antithesis of the almost mystic image of the "Great Republic," the "Nation," the "Union" filling the print and oratory of the day. The new federal officials who wanted the scope of government enlarged also wanted a capital that would symbolize its grandeur. They were well aware that a capital city embodies a nation's self-image, and they were willing to cooperate with a "ring" of locals to create one. Under Shepherd, the capital was transformed into a beautiful city, the proper sort of grand home for the new, glorified state.

A Japanese visitor to Washington in 1871 observed, "It is . . . claimed by the best thinkers that the American Government was never more powerful and influential for good than it is at the present time." The federal government was indeed more powerful and more influential than ever before, and the nation's intellectuals, particularly the younger ones, initially embraced the new state as an agent for good and looked forward to playing an important role in the active new era. Harvard law professor Joel Parker predicted, "There is, or is to be a new epoch. . . . The opinions of men *under thirty* are to be the ruling opinions. They were educated by the war, and have lived a *deeper life* than falls to the lot of ordinary sluggish generations." Twenty-four-year-old E. L. Godkin wrote to Frederick Law Olmsted during the war, "I am duly thanking Heaven that I live here and in this age." In 1865, Godkin began editing the *Nation* with the hope of wielding its journalistic influence on behalf of the "new epoch."

Though the outlines of the new nation were still blurry to him in 1868, Henry Adams, thirty years old and just back from seven years in England, was optimistic that there would be a place in it for him. He wrote a friend in 1865, "We want a national set of young men like ourselves or better, to start new influences not only in politics, but in literature, in law, in society, and throughout the whole social organism of the country—a national school of our own generation."

The powerful new state to which the intellectuals initially gave their blessings extended its influence into every aspect of its citizens' lives. Whereas in the early part of the century Americans rarely felt the presence of the federal government except when their mail was delivered, by the 1870s they couldn't help but feel it nearly every day through pensions, railroads, resumption, patronage, patents, claims, schools, even free seeds. Each of several newly created departments—Agriculture in 1862 and Justice in 1870—and a variety of new agencies and offices— the National Academy of Sciences, the Commissioner of Immigration, the Bureau of Statistics and Bureau of Education, the United States Weather Bureau, and the Office of the Commissioner of Fish and Fisheries—extended the federal government's presence into vast new areas of national life.

The Congress was also newly powerful and aggressive. During the 1850s, it was little more than a cave of the winds, in which the venting of sectional passions supplanted the business of lawmaking. After the war, Congress set about flexing its legislative muscle. Its new vigor was apparent in the sheer scope of its lawmaking. Between 1855 and 1865, an average of 1,700 bills and resolutions was introduced in each Congress; about 430 became law. During the next ten years the average introduced grew to 4,800, and an average of 824 were passed.

Washingtonians could see that the government was expanding by the growing number of clerks necessary to keep it running. In 1802, there had been fewer than 300 government employees in Washington. In 1829, there were 625, including clerks, congressmen, the president, and the Supreme Court justices. By 1861, there were 2,199 civilian employees of the government in Washington; 6,222 in 1871; and 14,124 in 1881. Much of the increase from 1861 to 1871 reflected the demands of the war, but the rise from 1871 to 1881 reflected the growth of the federal bureaucracy.

Representatives of a host of special interest groups arrived in the capital to try to channel the new powers within the scope of the federal government toward their own ends. The Civil War had schooled a generation in the uses of federal power to effect social change. In its aftermath came calls upon the state to enter into good works appropriate to a purified Republic. Spokesmen for the poor and the sick, for criminals, for temperance and education, for civil rights for Negroes, for justice for American Indians, for votes for women, and for fair treatment of labor converged on Washington to plead their cases before the new agencies and departments.

Others were attracted to the New Washington not by the potential in the new government for good but by its potential to make men millionaires. "The truth is," wrote Ohio Senator John Sherman to his brother General William T. Sherman, "the close of the war with our resources unimpaired gives an elevation, a scope to the ideas of leading capitalists, far higher than anything ever undertaken in this country before. They talk of millions as confidently as formerly of thousands." Reporter George Townsend described the situation more bluntly: "The opportunities for gain at the public and general expense had been too vast during the war to be suddenly relinquished at the peace. . . . The harpies who had studied the government to take advantage of it . . . continued their work."

The lucrative new areas coming under the federal government's purview were the bait that lured this group to the capital and began the ruthless era that historians have branded "The Great Barbeque," "The Age of the Spoilsmen," "The Age of Excess," and "the saturnalia of plunder," and that Mark Twain and Charles Dudley Warner lampooned in *The Gilded Age*. The vast unsettled land in the West was the most sought-after of all the dishes at the Great Barbeque. Between 1862 and 1871, the government granted 128 million acres to new, federally chartered railroads. Business interests eyed tariff schedules and patent rights hungrily. Securing a single patent, such as Andrew Carnegie's for the Bessemer process for making steel, or Alexander Graham Bell's patent No. 174,465 for the telephone, could mean millions of dollars. Other coveted items were mining and timber rights, Indian trading posts, and military contracts for arms and supplies.

"Doings in the Social World": The Gilded Age Begins

Given the drastic physical and bureaucratic changes Washington had undergone during the war, it was hardly surprising to find that its high society had experienced a similar overhaul. Despite the acrimony engendered by Reconstruction politics, Washington society was especially gay during the winters immediately after the war. Returning to Washington in 1867 after two years as secretary to the American legation in Paris, John Hay found a city very different from the one he had known while secretary to President Lincoln. He wrote to John Nicolay, still in Paris as consul, "The town is gayer than you ever saw it. Balls nearly every night—receptions without number." Henry Adams said of the capital city he found in 1868, "The social side of Washington was to be taken for granted as three-fourths of existence. . . . Politics and reform became the detail, and waltzing the profession."

Much more, however, had changed about Washington society during the years these young men had been away than just its pace. The cast of characters waltzing across the postwar social scene bore little resemblance to those who had led the quadrilles when Henry Adams had last seen the capital in 1861. Noted one returning Southerner, "Great as is the superficial transformation of a provincial village into a cosmopolitan center, it dwindles when compared with the change in the social configuration of this literally central city."

In the years before the war, there had been two main groups within Washington's high society—residential and official society—both of which were dominated by Southerners. The "deep-dyed" Southern Democrats of official society had contended fairly good-naturedly with the old Southern residential families for the top social honors, with the residents generally acknowledged as holding the upper hand. After the war the old Southern residents would no longer call the social tune in the New Washington. Their numbers, fortunes, and reputations had been seriously eroded by the war. While William Corcoran was able to return from Europe and resume his active social life with little stigma, most other openly Southern sympathizers in the city were not so fortunate. Former mayor Walter Lenox returned to die in a federal prison. Richard Cox, the former mayor of Georgetown whose home had been seized and turned into a home for destitute former slaves, was unable to reclaim his confiscated property for years. A score of other leaders of the antebellum community faced similar problems. Few of the old houses that had sparkled before the war reopened after it. Mrs. A. A. Parker's mansion and Mrs. Ogle Tayloe's home, with its summer slipcovers still in place, were among the once-fashionable salons that remained shuttered and dark. Clouds of suspicion not quickly dissipated by peace enveloped families once honored as among the best in the city and the nation.

In Confederate strongholds like Charleston, the old antebellum elites had also suffered crushing losses during the war. Fires had gutted entire blocks of the downtown and the city had been bombarded for nearly six hundred days before its surrender. Members of the old elite had taken work on the railroads and taken in boarders and sewing to stay alive during the war. But in Charleston this old elite arose from the ashes to dominate the city once again. In fact, according to one study, eighty percent of the city's prewar leaders persisted and provided leadership to postwar Charleston. Ardent support for the Confederacy was worn as a badge of honor. Not in Washington. Families once prominent in the capital dropped from sight, never to rise again.

During the American Revolution, when the loyalists left Boston and New York for Britain, the Bahamas, and Canada, they left behind a social vacuum. In their absence, the ranks of the upper class became more accessible to newcomers. The Revolution created openings, opportunities at the top of the social ladder. The Civil War did much the same thing in Washington.

A host of newcomers rushed in to fill the vacancies at the top of the capital's social ladder. The "new" high society they created grew apace with the New Washington. In fact, the physical layout of the city mirrored this new postwar society. As one observer of the social scene noted:

> When Pierre Charles L'Enfant laid out the city on paper, with its streets straight and diagonal, with triangles and circles, it is clear he had in mind a prophetic vision of the social system that was to develop, with its rings and circles and angles, shortcuts to greatness if you know the way, and divergences that leave you on the rim of outer darkness if you miss the path.

High society in the New Washington was indeed very like "Boss" Shepherd's new traffic circles that would soon be named for such heroes of the recent war as John Logan, Philip Sheridan, Winfield Scott, and Samuel Dupont. The two main social circles, residential and official, were replaced by a complicated system of several circles, each with its own subcircles. The prophet Ezekiel's vision of wheels within wheels was no more intricate than Washington's postwar high society.

Shepherd's new traffic circles were linked by streets over which an increasing number of carriages passed back and forth. Likewise, there was also a great deal of traffic back and forth between the new social circles and subcircles. Henry Cooke, for example, first traveled between the circles of the press and the lobbyists, then added the circle of friends and sycophants orbiting around President Grant, and finally, before disappearing into social oblivion, Cooke himself became a member of the official social circle when he became governor of the Territory of the District of Columbia. English author Beatrice Webb's description of London's fluid society of the 1870s applied equally well to the American capital:

> Society appeared as a shifting mass of miscellaneous and uncertain membership. It was essentially a body that could be defined, not by its circumference, which could not be traced but by its centre or centres. . . . There was the Court, representing national tradition and customs; there was the Cabinet and ex-Cabinet, representing political power; there was a mysterious group of millionaire financiers representing money; there was the racing set. . . . These four inner circles crossed and recrossed each other owing to an element of common membership.

Official society, no longer predominantly Southern and Democratic, emerged as the most important of the many interconnecting social circles in Washington during the first decade after the war. Gone were the Pryors, the Davises, and the Gwinns. Mrs. Clement Claiborne Clay came back to Washington in 1865, but this time it was to plead for her husband's release from Fortress Monroe. The new official society was Northern or Midwestern and Republican. In the Thirty-fifth Congress, 1857–59, there had been 39 Democrats, 20 Republicans, and 5 "others" in the Senate, with 131 Democrats, 92 Republicans and 14 "others" in the House. In the Forty-first Congress, 1869–71, there were 11 Democrats and 61 Republicans in the Senate, 73 Democrats and 170 Republicans in the House.

War heroes popped up like mushrooms after a rain in postwar official society. Military service in the late war proved invaluable in seeking offices from foreign ministries to postmasterships. Three Republican Union generals from the Midwest marched into the White House one right after the other—Ulysses S. Grant, Rutherford B. Hayes, and James A. Garfield. In the Forty-third Congress, 1873–75, one-third of the 293 members of the House of Representatives had fought in the war (73 Union and 30 Confederate veterans, including 30 generals).

While official society was the biggest social story of the first postwar years, its leadership did not emanate from the White House during the Johnson administration. Illness forced Mrs. Johnson to live a life "as secluded as a nun's," and her husband's views on the reconstruction of the South and presidential prerogatives made him a pariah to many members of his own party. Johnson's enemies joked that the biggest boost he gave to Washington society was his own impeachment trial: demand for the yellow tickets for gallery seats drove senators and representatives to distraction.

Though the Johnson White House failed to shine, other prominent houses kept the social spotlight focused squarely on official society. Each of the rival political factions among Congress, the cabinet, and the military had its own social headquarters. After he astonished friends by marrying a rich, beautiful widow half his age in 1866, fifty-five year old Charles Sumner briefly became not only the Radicals' leader on the Senate floor but their social leader as well. Secretary of War Edwin Stanton and Commanding General of the Armies Ulysses S. Grant used social gatherings at their homes to enhance their political positions. When presidential fever struck Chief Justice Salmon Chase in the spring of 1867, Kate Chase Sprague cut short a shopping trip to Paris to return to Washington to reopen her salon and entertain on her father's behalf.

Late in 1868, after the impeachment trial had ended and General Grant had been elected president, the fuzzy outlines of the new social order in Washington grew clearer. Two things became apparent to sharp-eyed Washingtonians: official society would call the tune to which the rest of Washington would dance, and the new music to which all would whirl would be the sound of money.

In January 1869, Emily Edson Briggs, Washington social correspondent for the *Philadelphia Press,* reported on the new ostentation:

> A gradual change is coming over the face of events in Washington. The old monarchy's dying. Andrew Johnson is passing away. . . . In many respects it would seem as if time were taking us backward in its flight and that we were living over again the last luxurious days of Louis XV. If Madame Pompadour is not here in the flesh, she has bequeathed to this brilliant Republican court her unique taste in the shape of paint-pots, rouge, patches, pointed heels and frilled petticoats.

There were already, complained one old resident, "indications of a passion for notoriety to be won by prodigal display. . . . The doings in the social world became a distinct department in the newspapers, second in interest only to politics. As the masculine pen balked . . . at descriptions of fashionable gowns, the woman society reporter made her appearance." He was right: conspicuous consumption had never been so much in evidence in Washington as in the era that dawned with Grant's inauguration, and this glamorous society did indeed attract that new postwar phenomenon, the woman society reporter. Emily Edson Briggs was one of the first and her prose was among the most effusive of the genre. Her description of Mrs. Sprague in the Senate gallery at President Johnson's impeachment trial typified her style:

> Paris has Eugenie; Washington has Mrs. Sprague, the acknowledged queen of fashion and good taste. . . . Her costume is just as perfect as the lily or the rose. She is a lilac blossom to-day. . . . A single flower, of lilac tinge . . . rests upon her head, and is fastened to its place by lilac tulle so filmy that it must have been stolen from the purple mists of the morning. An exquisite walking dress of pale lilac silk has trimmings a shade darker, whilst lilac gloves conceal a hand that might belong to the queen of fairies.

Many of the new officials who would shine in Washington society over the next few years were on hand to celebrate President Grant's inauguration on March 4, 1869. Society reporters anticipated a bonanza of frothy prose, but the inaugural ball, held in the unfinished Treasury Building, was a fiasco. Stonecutting dust filled the air. Guests choked and coughed and became covered with grit. The cloakroom was staffed by illiterate treasury employees. When they could not read the numbers on the coat checks, they threw all the hats and cloaks onto a heap and fled. "The breaking up of the inaugural reception baffles description," Briggs wrote the next day. "The tearing up of the icebergs in the Arctic seas of a spring morning might seem more solemn!" Ladies in filmy dresses either went home in the cold without wraps or took the first they found. "Delicate women, too sensitive to take the property of others, crouched in corners and wept on window ledges; and there the daylight found them."

The new day dawning in Washington was the "Gilded Age." While off to an inauspicious start, the golden age of official society had begun.

4 The Blossoming of Official Society

1868–1872

Most of the men and women waltzing at President Grant's inaugural ball were unfamiliar to longtime Washingtonians. Military men, sharing in their old commander's glory, and Midwesterners, drawn from Ulysses and Julia Dent Grant's large families and larger circle of friends, crowded into the capital. The fact that new faces appeared on Washington's streets was hardly surprising: every new president trailed a host of newcomers in his wake. The advent of the Grant administration, however, brought more than the usual round of departures and arrivals. This transition was no mere transfer of power from one Republican administration to the next.

The Grant administration was borne into Washington on a tidal wave of optimism. Anxious to put the bloody past behind them, Grant's supporters anticipated much: an end to the awful bickering among Republican factions that had torn the Johnson administration apart; an end to disorder in the South; efficiency; reform. For each of these bright hopes, voters could assign good reasons: the Republican party stood strongly united behind the new president; Grant's military record bespoke a stern exponent of order and discipline; and he was new to politics, very popular in his own right, and beholden to no single special-interest group for his election. George Washington and Andrew Jackson were military heroes who had made strong civil executives. Surely, his supporters argued, Grant's sagacity and force of character, having sufficed to win the war, would make him a powerful president, too. On March 4, 1869, as the new administration picked up the reins of power, E. L. Godkin, the young editor of the *Nation,* predicted that Grant would cleanse the government of unprincipled men, remodel the national machine, "and make it really democratic."

Within eight years, these high hopes were cruelly dashed as wave upon wave of scandal washed over Washington, sullying members of the cabinet and Congress, the president's closest aides, even his wife. Each retreating wave carried off a bit of the good will with which the era had begun and a bit of official society's cachet. So thorough was the erosion that by the end of Grant's second term scarcely any moral high ground remained upon which official society could stand.

This chapter and the next chronicle the course of official society during the Grant years and subsequent administrations through the end of the century. At the beginning of the story, official society dominates the Washington social scene. By the end, it has declined into second place behind the rich, unofficial newcomers who began to trickle into the handsome New Washington in the 1870s. As the rise and fall of official society is charted, the emphasis will be on how it changed in size, composition, wealth, personnel, leadership, and prestige. Many of Washington's colorful "characters"—some noble, some outrageous—personified the ups and downs of official society during the postwar years, and their brief biographies will be used to illustrate these changes.

A New Official Society Takes Root and Flourishes along the Potomac

The eventual eclipse of official society could scarcely be imagined during the heady months when the new Grant administration was unfolding. At least four and very possibly eight years of unparalleled political power stretched before the Republicans. The expanding federal government held out the promise of dozens of new, well-paying jobs to the ambitious young men flocking to Washington. With the hero of Appomattox in the White House, hundreds of Civil War veterans traveled to Washington to lay claim to his friendship. The debonair lobbyist Sam Ward watched the new administration settle in with detached amusement and likened the period of grasping for appointments to the rutting season among stags, with the decencies and amenities of civilization entirely forgotten. Within a few months the clamor for places died down. Hundreds of veterans accepted minor positions, while the unlucky left town, complaining about "the General's" ingratitude. Most of those who remained in Washington as additions to the federal payroll sank into obscurity—at least social obscurity. Only a very few, the richest cream of the new crop, rose to the top of official society to constitute the most powerful and plentiful of Mark Twain's "three distinct aristocracies."

This new postwar official society shared the social limelight with no one, least of all the old Southern families of Washington with whom the old official society had shared the social stage in antebellum years. This shift from prewar days, when official society had been part of an elite duet, to the early postwar years, when it became a solo performer, was only one of the changes affecting Washington high society in the years after the war. Other changes occurred in its size and composition.

In sheer numbers alone, official society dominated the postwar capital as never before. Its congressional component, always the biggest, had grown dramatically. In 1859, 32 states sent 237 representatives and 64 senators to Washington. By 1871, there were 37 states sending 297 representatives and 74 senators. These new states joining the Union did more than swell the size of official society. Three of the five new states, Minnesota, Nebraska, and Nevada, were in the West, and many of their first emissaries to Washington were rich, flamboyant "Bonanza Kings," who brought the spice of the untamed frontier and the dash of rough mining camps to the national melting pot of Congress.

Another large component of the new official society consisted of military men in splendid uniforms, full of thrilling tales of the battlefields. In 1859–60, the War Department had just 33 leading officers and the Navy Department 16, for a total of 49. By 1869, the chief officers of the Navy Department alone numbered 49, while at the War Department the number had nearly tripled to 89. Among these new officers were some of the most dashing heroes of the war: Brevet Major O. O. Howard, Brevet Major General Montgomery Meigs, Rear Admiral John A. Dahlgren, and the Commanding General of the Army himself, General William Tecumseh Sherman. Washington was also becoming a favorite place for venerable veterans like Admiral David Farragut to retire.

The diplomatic community was growing as well. In 1860, there had been 22 foreign legations in Washington, and the total number of ministers, secretaries of legation and attachés staffing them was just 43. By 1870, the number of legations had risen to 28, and the number of ministers, secretaries, and attachés had increased to 62. Diplomatic eccentrics added enormously to official society's cachet. The Peruvian minister's wife rode about the city in a white carriage lined with white satin with a white lap robe over her knees and snowy ostrich plumes bobbing from her head. News of soirees at the various ministries and the comings and goings of visiting royalty filled newspaper society columns across the nation.

More important to official society's general character than the growing number of men on the government rosters was the rapid growth of another group of individuals who held neither elected nor appointed office: women. The postwar years saw a dramatic increase in the number of officials bringing their wives, daughters, nieces, and other female kin to Washington. This influx not only nearly doubled the size of official society, but added to it precisely those individuals with the leisure, the inclination, and the training to pursue and perpetuate its intricate rituals and protocol.

The *Congressional Directories* chart both the increasing number of women in official society and changes in housing patterns. Although first published around 1810, it was not until 1845 that the *Directories* began to include information on whether or not congressmen were accompanied by family members. Reflecting the growth of Washington's official society beyond the point where everyone could know everyone else and know who was in town and who was not, the 1845 *Directory* included a helpful new feature: "Those gentlemen to whose names an asterisk (*) is affixed have their families, or part of them, in the city," read the legend accompanying the list of members of Congress.

In 1845, asterisks preceded the names of 74 of the nearly 300 members of Congress. There was no indiction of the number, age, or gender of the members of a congressman's party, but inadequate accommodations, a paucity of good schools, and the brevity of congressional sessions all worked against the uprooting of families with young children. Most of the congressional families in town for the 1845–46 social season were Southerners. The majority of members, Southern and Northern, with and without their families, lived in the boardinghouses or "messes" clustered around Capitol Hill. The section of the *Directory* entitled "Members in Messes" helpfully provided their addresses. Few congressmen lived in the city's meager offering of hotels and fewer still in private homes.

As congressional sessions lengthened, keeping husbands away from home for longer periods of time, as rail transportation made the capital more accessible, and as Washington acquired the rudiments of urban amenities, more and more officials began to bring their wives along with them to the capital. By 1861, a mere asterisk designating the presence of an unspecified number of kin no longer sufficed as a guide to the growing congressional component of official society. A more specific breakdown of the congressmen's households was included in the *Directory* for 1860–61: "The asterisk (*) designates those whose wives accompany them; the section (§), those who have a single lady with them; two sections (§§), more than one lady; an asterisk and section (*§), wife and single lady."

Whereas fifteen years earlier only a quarter of the congressmen had brought any family members along to the capital, during the 1860–61 season more than a third of the 311 congressmen came accompanied by wives or single women, at least 179 in all: 85 *, 19 *§, 16 *§§, 1 *§§§ and 2 §§. Couples unencumbered by daughters, sisters, nieces or any other "§" predominated. While many of the congressional bachelors continued to live in the city's boardinghouses, many of the men accompanied by * and § had begun to eschew the "messes" in favor of the city's growing number of decent hotels. As in 1845, however, only a very few of the wealthiest members could afford to rent private homes in Washington while maintaining residences in their home states.

The *Congressional Directory* for the winter of 1871–72 revealed the changes that had taken place in official society since the war. Once again, the number of symbols used to designate the women in a congressman's party had multiplied to define more precisely this growing and ever more complicated branch of official society. To the * and § was now added the ‖: "The * designates those whose wives accompany them; the § designates those whose daughters accompany them; the ‖ designates those having other ladies with them." While in 1845 a quarter of the members of Congress brought some part of their family with them to Washington, and in 1861 a third did so, by 1871–72, more than half of the 367 members of Congress came to Washington accompanied by more than 250 women. They came in a dizzying variety of combinations: 95 *, 32 *§, 14 *‖, 8 *§§, 3 *‖ ‖, 2 *§§§, 2 *§§‖, 2 *§‖, 1 ‖ ‖, 1 §§‖, and 1 *§‖ ‖!

By 1871–72, so few members patronized the boardinghouses on Capitol Hill that the "Members in Messes" listing was eliminated. In their stead appeared the names of the city's new, fashionable hotels to which both the "bachelor" congressmen and those who brought their families

ALPHABETICAL LIST

OF

SENATORS, REPRESENTATIVES, AND DELEGATES,

WITH THEIR HOME POST-OFFICES, AND RESIDENCES IN WASHINGTON.

[The * designates those whose wives accompany them ; the § designates those whose daughters accompany them ; the ‖ designates those having other ladies with them.]

[The streets and avenues of Washington are now numbered on the "Philadelphia plan," starting north, south, east, and west from the base-lines, which run north and south, east and west, intersecting at the Capitol. Thus, in the northwest section of the city, the houses on any street designated by a letter, or on any avenue running east and west, which are between First and Second streets, are numbered between one and two hundred ; those between Second and Third streets are numbered between two and three hundred, and so forth. On the streets designated by numbers, or on any avenue running north and south, the houses between A and B streets are numbered between one and two hundred ; those between B and C streets are numbered between two and three hundred, and so forth. This system of numbering enables any one, with the aid of a map of the city, to determine the exact location of any house the number and street of which are given.]

THE VICE-PRESIDENT.

*‖§ SCHUYLER COLFAX...... South Bend, Indiana......7 Lafayette Square, west side.

SENATORS.

Name.	Post-office.	Residence in Washington.
Alcorn, James S..............	Mississippi....................	Metropolitan Hotel.
*Ames, Adelbert............	Natchez, Mississippi.........	1423 I street, N. W.
Anthony, Henry B..........	Providence, Rhode Island....	1518 H street, N. W.
Bayard, Thomas F..........	Wilmington, Delaware.......	1413 Massachusetts avenue.
Blair, Francis P., jr........	St. Louis, Missouri	1653 Penn. avenue, N. W.
Boreman, Arthur I.........	Parkersburgh, West Virginia..	Washington House.
Brownlow, William G......	Knoxville, Tennessee........	4 A street, N. E.
§Buckingham, William A...	Norwich, Connecticut........	819 Fifteenth street, N. W.
*Caldwell, Alexander......	Leavenworth, Kansas........	1417 G street, N. W.
*Cameron, Simon	Harrisburg, Pennsylvania ...	The Arlington.
*Carpenter, Matthew H....	Milwaukee, Wisconsin.......	1215 K street, N. W.
*Casserly, Eugene.........	San Francisco, California.....	12 Lafayette Square, west side.
*§Chandler, Zachariah....	Detroit, Michigan...........	1408 H street, N. W.
Clayton, Powell	Little Rock, Arkansas......	1214 F street, N. W.
*§Cole, Cornelius.........	San Francisco, California....	The Arlington.
*§Conkling, Roscoe.......	Utica, New York...........	736 Fifteenth street, N. W.
Cooper, Henry.............	Nashville, Tennessee........	825 Vermont avenue.
*Corbett, Henry W........	Portland, Oregon...........	514 Thirteenth street, N.W.
*Cragin, Aaron H.........	Lebanon, New Hampshire...	430 First street, east.
Davis, Garrett.............	Paris, Kentucky	310 Indiana avenue.
Davis, Henry G.........	Piedmont, West Virginia	825 Vermont avenue.
*§Edmunds, George F.....	Burlington, Vermont	1411 Mass.av.,[Highland Ter.]
*§Fenton, Reuben E......	Jamestown, New York	23 Lafayette Square, east side.
*§Ferry, Orris S..........	Norwalk, Connecticut......	1410 G street, N. W.
Ferry, Thomas W.........	Grand Haven, Michigan....	National Hotel.
Flanagan, J. W...........	Walling's Ferry, Texas......	Casparis House.
*§§§ Frelinghuysen, F. T..	Newark, New Jersey.......	1731 I street, N. W.
Gilbert, Abijah.............	St. Augustine, Florida......	National Hotel.
Goldthwaite, George.......	Montgomery, Alabama......	402 Sixth street.
Hamilton, Morgan C......	Austin, Texas	122 East Capitol street,
Hamilton, William T......	Hagerstown, Maryland......	218 Third street.
*Hamlin, Hannibal........	Bangor, Maine..	Metropolitan Hotel.
*§Harlan, James..........	Mount Pleasant, Iowa.......	1623 H street, N.W.
*§§Hill, Joshua...........	Madison, Georgia..........	1325 F street.
*Hitchcock, Phineas W....	Omaha, Nebraska...........	221 I street, N. W.
*§‖Howe, Timothy O....	Green Bay, Wisconsin.......	1708 I street, N. W.
Johnston, John W.........	Abingdon, Virginia.........	508 Twelfth street, N. W.
*Kellogg, William P.......	New Orleans, Louisiana.....	Metropolitan Hotel.

By the 42d Congress, 1871–73, it took three different symbols—* for wives, § for daughters, and ‖ for "other ladies"—to differentiate among the growing number of women who accompanied members of Congress to Washington. Lists such as this indicate that congressmen and their families, no longer content with boardinghouse life, were renting rooms in fashionable, expensive hotels such as the Arlington. (*Congressional Directory,* 42d Congress, 2d session, 1872) were gravitating. The Arlington Hotel, which boasted of elevators, five private dining rooms, and 325 suites of up to ten rooms with private baths, had opened its doors in 1865. Known as "the extension of the Capitol," the Arlington became home for dozens of senators and representatives and their families, as well as for cabinet officers, diplomats, and visiting royalty. All paid dearly to enjoy its amenities. In 1871–72, when a congressman's salary was five thousand dollars a year, Senator Ruben Fenton of New York paid a thousand dollars a month for a parlor, an office, and two bedrooms in the Arlington for himself, his wife, and his daughter.

By 1871, several members of Congress lived in large private homes in the city's most exclusive neighborhood, the area of elegant Federal-period homes surrounding Lafayette Square. While decent houses for rent had been extremely scarce in the antebellum capital, after the war many members of the city's Southern aristocracy supported themselves by renting out their fine old family homes to rich Yankees.

The postwar *Congressional Directories* confirmed that at least one aspect of antebellum official society still endured: its constant turnover. The perpetual changing of personnel constantly transformed official society, and the decade between 1860 and 1870 witnessed even greater change than usual. The roster of officials for 1870 was nearly wiped clean of all names that had appeared there only ten years earlier. Only a score of the 311 members of the Thirty-sixth Congress of 1860–61 were still serving in either the House or the Senate during the Forty-first Congress. Hardly a diplomat could be found who remembered the antebellum capital. Even on the Supreme Court, only three of the nine justices from 1860 remained on the bench in 1870.

What were the lessons to be learned from such clear-cut evidence of constant turnover by all who aspired to social prominence, especially by the women arriving in Washington in unprecedented numbers? Certainly the chief lesson was that one could not hesitate if one hoped to leave a mark on the capital's quicksilver society. No time could be devoted to a long apprenticeship while one learned the social ropes under the tutelage of a mentor with long experience in the capital's society. Not only were such mentors precious few, but time was of the essence—congressional elections, which always threatened defeat, came relentlessly every two years. If the social heights could be scaled at all, the trek must begin even before the bags were unpacked.

In many cases, the assault on the peaks of social prominence began with the purchase of one of the many books that appeared after the war to teach etiquette, a subject enjoying its biggest boom since its origin in medieval Europe. The Washington etiquette book became a burgeoning subset of the new genre. The most popular were by women with impeccable social credentials, whose reputations as prominent hostesses in the capital lent their works an air of authority. Among the first of such women was Madeleine Vinton Dahlgren. Mrs. Dahlgren, a rich widow, had served as her father's hostess during his twenty years in Congress, and she and her late husband, Rear Admiral John A. Dahlgren, had been popular and proper entertainers. Her manual of manners, *Etiquette of Social Life in Washington* (1873), was taken to heart by many newcomers, pushing it into edition after edition of larger and larger printings. Following in Mrs. Dahlgren's footsteps were Rose Cleveland, sister of President Grover Cleveland, Mary Logan, widow of Illinois Senator John A. Logan, and Mary Elizabeth Wilson Sherwood, daughter and official hostess of New Hampshire Congressman James Wilson, all of whom wrote popular etiquette manuals.

As the spate of Washington etiquette books, primarily written by and aimed at women, suggests, women were not only becoming more numerous in the increasingly complex official social circles, they were also becoming more important. While upperclass gentlemen in Boston and Philadelphia maintained a keen interest in and leadership of their respective cities' elite society until the turn of the century, women emerged as the arbiters of taste in postbellum Washington.

There are several reasons for this feminine hegemony. As the scope of the federal government expanded, so did the duties and prerogatives of the men who embodied it. Sessions of Congress lengthened, committee assignments multiplied, the Supreme Court docket grew, new cabinet departments appeared, and the oversight powers of both old and new agencies expanded. Men in official life seemed busier than ever before. Yet they realized that the social proprieties could not be ignored. Social and political success were linked just as closely in Washington as in other capitals like London or Vienna.

"The courtesies," the author of one etiquette book explained, "which are an indispensable part of civilized life are of peculiar importance in a national capital." "Society is the handmaiden of politics especially in a capital city," she warned, and "all these [people] know personal influence is a mighty power to conjure with." "Politeness is power," another author succinctly noted. The men in official life did realize the importance of "the courtesies," and they were anxious to do the right thing; they just didn't want to do it themselves. A wife or, if not a wife, a sister or a daughter, any woman who could serve as his official hostess, became increasingly important to the busy man who recognized the link between a successful social and political career.

The new women in Washington paying and receiving calls on behalf of their male kin took official society's stern rules of precedence and protocol very seriously. That they should set such stock by these artificial distinctions is not surprising. Their husbands, brothers, and fathers had an identity outside the drawing room that these ladies lacked. Men in official life could define themselves in terms of treaties negotiated, battles won, or legislation passed, while their womenfolk had few landmarks by which to measure self-worth save whether their place at table was above or below the salt. Wives of officials were always referred to in terms of their husbands' position—"Mrs. Representative Blaine," "Mrs. General Sherman," "Mrs. Secretary Seward"—and their place on the ladder of precedence was determined by their husbands' ranks. Small wonder then that women clung so jealously to their protector's prerogatives, and thereby their own, and were ever vigilant against the slightest encroachments upon their place in the social pecking order.

All of the changes in postwar Washington society—its increasing size, the increasing number of women, the shift from boardinghouses to hotels and private homes—fueled heated debates in 1873 over a pay increase for congressmen. The debates also highlighted still another change: official society was not just bigger, it was more expensive.

From 1789 to 1855, congressmen received a modest per diem compensation (six dollars from 1789 to 1817, eight from 1817 until 1855) that amounted to an average yearly compensation of about a thousand dollars. In 1856, congressmen voted themselves an annual salary of three thousand dollars per year, raised to five thousand in 1865 because of wartime inflation. The press had always ridiculed suggestions for additional increases, but it was with special disgust that the newspapers reported in 1873 that the congressmen not only proposed to raise their salaries to seventy-five hundred, but to make the increase retroactive for two years, dropping into each member's lap a windfall of five thousand dollars. The repellent scheme was quickly dubbed the "salary grab" and the "back pay steal," but despite a barrage of criticism, the congressmen pressed ahead. Why? Quite simply, they argued, they desperately needed the money. Cries of poverty went up from both the House and Senate, from both Democrats and Republicans.

Senator Simon Cameron, the millionaire Pennsylvania political boss, described how costs had escalated during his three decades in government service:

> I came here first at eight dollars a day [in 1845 as a senator] and that pay covered all my expenses then. . . . I boarded at Gadsby's, and we had canvas-back ducks on the table every day in the season, and everything else in proportion, and I only paid ten dollars a week board. . . . After a while I got $3,000 a year, and it took all of that to pay [my expenses]; and now I get $5,000 a year, and although I have no family here except my wife and myself it costs me twenty-five dollars a week more than I receive from the Government for my board.

Cameron cited examples of the increase in the housing costs: "A member of the Cabinet [Secretary of State Hamilton Fish] now lives in the house I occupied when I filled a place in the Cabinet [Secretary of War from 1861 to 1862]. . . . I had the furniture and the house for $100 a month. Now he pays $6,000 a year rent for the same house without furniture."

Senator Oliver H. P. T. Morton of Indiana backed up Cameron's claims with his own examples and alluded to the political consequences of the insufficiently elegant life in Washington. "I do not believe there are twenty members of this body," Morton claimed,

> who can save fifty dollars a month from their salary during the session of Congress, while many of them spend the whole of it, and some two or three times the amount. Most members of Congress who board at hotels in this city are paying from three to six hundred dollars a month for the board of themselves and families. . . . If you are to go to a place where you can be readily found and where you can receive your friends, those who have business with you, and your constituents who come from their homes either for business or pleasure, it will cost you from three to six hundred dollars a month, if you have your family with you, and we all know it.

Some wealthy members, like Senator John Scott of Pennsylvania and Senator Justin Morrill of Vermont, took the moral high ground, arguing that men should not aspire to a seat in Congress with an eye to a high salary but out of selfless desire to serve the public. Seeing that his lofty argument was getting nowhere, Senator Morrill eventually adopted the more practical argument of unseemliness. "I believe," said the Vermont senator, who had just moved into a handsome mansion on Thomas Circle, "we ought to set an example of frugality at the capital of our country."

Morrill's sanctimonious speeches only irritated his colleagues. Senator Matthew Carpenter, a wealthy lawyer from Wisconsin and one of the unabashed champions of the pay raise, managed to take a few well-aimed swipes at his high-minded colleagues while presenting an unvarnished assessment of the importance of wealth and socializing to a political career:

> The people of Wisconsin if they send a man here to represent them in the Senate wish him to live how? In the garret of a five-story building on crackers and cheese, to dress in goat skins and sleep in the wilderness? No. When they come here and ride by the mansions of my honorable friends from Vermont [Senators Morrill and George F. Edmunds] up on the Circle, see their elegant houses, brilliantly lighted, surrounded by acres of pavement, parks, fountains, &c., . . . and then come to the homes of the "poor white trash" of this Senate and find their own Senators among them, they will not like that. (laughter) They have manly pride; and expect to find their Senators living like other Senators. . . .
>
> The Senator from Pennsylvania [Scott] admits . . . that we poor fellows, we "white trash," must live on a scale entirely below the nabobs of the Senate. Well, Mr. President, it does not require any genius to see and know that if you make these discriminations in social life, of necessity you force just such discriminations upon the influence of men in this body. There is great sublimity undoubtedly in the idea of rising above all the accidents of human nature, looking at things in the abstract, and regarding a man dressed in goat skins precisely as one dressed like a gentleman; but unfortunately the sentiment is not respected in practical life.

Senator Carpenter and the other congressmen who claimed that their constituents supported increased salaries were sadly mistaken. Quite to the contrary, the storm of abuse that broke over Congress when the odious bill passed in March 1873 reflected their constituents' lack of sympathy with their plight. The deepening economic depression evoked a furious outcry, and members rushed to return their back pay to the Treasury or donate it to charity. In January 1874, congressmen worried about reelection that fall (among them Senator Carpenter) voted to repeal the salary increase, but the damage had already been done. That November, in bitter campaigns focusing on the "salary grab," the voters voted out member after member who had supported the "back-pay steal." Senator Carpenter's head was one of those that rolled. The folks back home might read with relish about the glamorous lives their representatives led in the nation's capital, but they did not want to underwrite them.

Circles within Circles: The Complexity of Official Society

The "salary grab" debates, the *Congressional Directories,* and the lengthening newspaper society columns all made it clear that the official society that flourished in the postwar capital bore little resemblance to the small group of grumbling bachelors who had constituted official society only a generation earlier. Within the larger, more costly, and more glamorous official social circle, however, there were still many smaller subcircles. Just as before the war, there were partisan, regional, and occupational cliques within official society. These subcircles within official society often intersected. Membership was nonexclusive, and most men in official life belonged to several. Crossover between the official and the unofficial social circles frequently occurred. The borders of all but the "Antiques" were highly permeable. When Senator Carpenter was turned out of office, for example, he remained in Washington, established a lucrative law practice, and became a distinguished member of the city's legal coterie, only to be returned to the ranks of official society in 1879 when Wisconsin voters sent him back to the Senate again.

A closer look at three gentlemen prominent in official society during the first Grant administration reveals how the smaller social subsets orbited and intersected within the larger official social sphere. The three— Senator Justin Morrill of Vermont, Senator William Stewart of Nevada, and Representative Benjamin Butler of Massachusetts—were all members of Congress, and thus all members of the same occupational subset of official society. All three were Republicans (although Butler changed his party affiliation many times) and thus all members of the same partisan subset. All three men were self-made millionaires. All three brought their wives to Washington.

Another distinction marked Morrill, Stewart, and Butler and reflected the postwar changes in Washington residential patterns. While more and more officials rented large homes in the capital in the late 1860s, few bought or built houses in a city where their tenure rested in the hands of capricious constituents. Indeed, ever since the 1840s, when the first members of Congress to build themselves Washington houses were defeated in the next election, it had been only half-jokingly said that to build a house in Washington was to seal one's political doom. Morrill, Stewart, and Butler tempted fate. In the early 1870s, each man built a handsome mansion in Washington.

Despite their similarities, these three self-made Republican congressmen had very little else in common. They were not friends; at times they were enemies. Each differed in personality and philosophy from the other two, and their social lives and houses reflected their differences. While they and their wives were among the leaders of official society, the social group each couple led was small. They were not among the leaders of official society in toto, nor even of the subset of Republican congressional society. Their domains were subsets of that subset—Morrill's that of fiscally and politically conservative New Englanders, Stewart's that of the Bonanza Kings from the West, and Butler's that of the Radicals and the slick, new "bosses" so distasteful to men like Morrill. Their little planets orbited on separate paths within the social galaxy and seldom intersected.

Justin Morrill was the only one of the three who remembered Washington before the Civil War. Born in 1810 into an old New England family of middling means, Morrill launched his career as a merchant with $150 saved from his earnings as a clerk in a village store and retired a millionaire at the age of thirty-eight. Elected as a Whig to the House of Representatives in 1854, he served throughout the war. In 1866, Morrill was elected to the Senate where he served for nearly thirty-two years, until 1898 when he died in office at the age of eighty-nine.

Respected for his eloquence and sound reasoning, Morrill was known as "The Nestor of the Senate" and "The Gladstone of America." Among his most notable achievements Morrill counted the Morrill Tariff and the Morrill Act establishing land grant colleges. Tall and angular, with closely trimmed side-whiskers, Morrill cultivated artistic and literary tastes. He also took a great interest in Washington. Unlike many of his Senate colleagues whose interest in the capital was pecuniary, Morrill's was altruistic. He played a large part in the beautification of the grounds around the Capitol, in the completion of the Washington Monument, and in the building of the Library of Congress.

Justin Smith Morrill served Vermont as a representative and then senator from 1855 to 1898. After seventeen years in Congress, he and his wife grew sick of boarding-houses and built a home of their own in the capital. The Morrill Tariff and the Morrill Act, establishing land grant colleges, bear his name. (U.S. Senate Historical Office)

In 1871, after seventeen years in Congress, Morrill correctly judged that his constituents might be willing to keep him in Washington for several more terms. The prospect of spending them in the boardinghouses and hotel suites he and his wife had lived in for a decade and a half had little appeal, so Morrill decided to build himself a home in the capital. He hired Edward Clark, the architect of the Capitol, to oversee the project. The Morrills' large, austere mansion arose at the corner of Vermont Avenue and M Street, directly on Thomas Circle, a well-established, solidly genteel neighborhood. Morrill took no risks in choosing his site; he was no speculator.

For nearly thirty years, the Morrills entertained sedately but elegantly at their Thomas Circle home and introduced a series of young relatives to Washington's society in their drawingrooms. Morrill preferred the company of conservative, old-fashioned Republicans like himself. He had little in common with the new politicians crowding into Washington along with General Grant, whom he had not known. All members of official society, however, were welcomed into his home for his annual birthday parties, grand affairs always held on April 14.

While Morrill's mansion was rising on Thomas Circle, a far flashier home was being built in the wilderness northwest of town by one of his more flamboyant Senate colleagues, William Morris Stewart of Nevada. Both Morrill and Stewart came from old New England families, but there the similarity ended. Morrill had made his life and fortune in New England and left Vermont only to serve its citizens in Washington. Stewart, born in upstate New York in 1825, caught the gold rush fever in 1850, abandoned Yale in the midst of his studies to head for California, and never looked back. Morrill was fiscally conservative with his own and the nation's money; Stewart was reckless with everyone's money, including his own. With his tidy side-whiskers and impeccably tailored suits, Morrill was the picture of New England probity. Over six feet tall, with a bushy, flowing beard that gradually turned from red to silver, and always sporting a wide-brimmed white hat, Stewart was the very picture of a rugged Westerner. In contrast to Morrill's understated gentility, Stewart shared the tastes of the other dazzling Bonanza Kings who burst upon Washington after the war.

Gold and silver made Stewart a millionaire before he was thirty years old. In 1855, he married Annie Elizabeth Foote, one of the reigning belles of San Francisco and the daughter of hot-tempered former Mississippi Senator Henry S. Foote. The young couple followed the gold rush to Nevada Territory. When the territory became a state in 1864, Stewart garnered one of its first two Senate seats. His arrival in Washington launched a flurry of newspaper articles that proclaimed him the richest man in the Senate. Like Morrill, Stewart took a moderate stand on Reconstruction. He helped draft the Fifteenth Amendment and laws for the regulation of mining and the opening of the mint in Carson City. For his vociferous championship of the free coinage of silver, his Senate colleagues and the press dubbed Stewart "The Silver Senator."

Like many of the other new arrivals in Congress, Stewart brought his family with him. They settled into an expensive suite at the Willard Hotel amid speculation that Annie Foote Stewart would attempt to occupy the same prominent place in official society that her mother, Elizabeth Foote, had once enjoyed. However, as soon as the war ended, Mrs. Stewart took her two daughters off to Europe and stayed there for six years. It was rumored that Senator Stewart anticipated unpleasant scenes with his Southern-born wife over the upcoming Reconstruction battles and had eagerly assented to finance her lengthy itinerary.

With his family gone, Stewart abandoned the fashionable Willard for the boardinghouse of Miss Virginia Wells, where his stormy relationship with Mark Twain began and ended. According to Stewart, Twain showed up in Washington one day looking for a place to stay while he completed a book about the Holy Land (*Innocents Abroad*.) Stewart claimed he took pity on Twain, hired him as his Senate clerk, shared with him his cramped living quarters, and invited him to "help yourself to the whiskey and cigars, and wade in." For his part, Twain maintained that Stewart had offered him the job months before, and that from the bargain Stewart expected to use Twain's popularity in the West to advance his political career. Whatever the case, their arrangements lasted barely two months. According to Stewart, Twain "waded in" to the whiskey, not his writing. Twain was, claimed Stewart, a disreputable, seedy, sinister character who sported a frazzled cigar and tormented the landlady by lurching drunkenly through the halls and smoking in bed. Miss Wells decreed that both

Known as the "Silver Senator," William Morris Stewart was one of Nevada's first two senators and served for thirty years. Though he was from New England and had attended Yale, Stewart styled himself a Westerner; this is a rare picture of him without his wide-brimmed white "cowboy" hat. Stewart and his wife Annie Foote Stewart were among the leaders of the rich, flamboyant "Bonanza Kings." (U.S. Senate Historical Office)

men would have to leave unless Stewart ordered Twain out, which he did. Twain resigned his Senate position without regret, and, to Stewart's acute embarrassment, poked fun at the whole episode and his former patron in print.

Like Morrill, Stewart took a great interest in the capital city, but his was not altruistic. He and a syndicate of wealthy Westerners invested six hundred thousand dollars in land at ten cents a foot in the wilderness near the city's northwest limits. Old-time Washingtonians dubbed the isolated outpost "The Honest Miners Camp," and labeled the mansion Stewart proposed to build there "Stewart's Folly." The "Honest Miners," however, had the last laugh. The grand plans of Stewart's friend "Boss" Alexander Shepherd, to which Stewart and a few others were privy, called for the city to grow in just that direction. To longtime citizens' surprise, water mains, sewers, and sidewalks sprouted in the "Camp" and property values in the "West End" skyrocketed. By 1875, land in the area was selling for three to five dollars a foot. When Stewart's mansion arose on Pacific Circle, later called Dupont Circle, it was known as "Stewart's Castle."

The huge, five-story, Second-Empire mansion, with its soaring entrance tower, was designed by Washington architect Adolph Cluss, who also designed Shepherd's home the same year. "Stewart's Castle," one reporter claimed, surpassed in "magnificence anything to be seen in this city. . . . Visitors neglected the White House itself in their desire to see and exclaim over the sharp windows, steeple and columned porticos." Gilded chairs upholstered with Aubusson tapestry, purchased in Europe by Mrs. Stewart, lined the walls of the seventy-foot-long ballroom. Massive Chinese teak furniture filled the main hall. Annie Foote Stewart reveled in her "castle" and in the pomp of official society. As a little girl, she had watched her parents entertain. Now her own dinners were famous. With two teenaged daughters in residence, Stewart's Castle became one of the most festive of official homes. Bessie Stewart's wedding at the Castle in May 1874 was so brilliant an affair that it threatened to eclipse Nellie Grant's White House wedding later that same month.

The Stewarts sought and won the company of President and Mrs. Grant and of the richest and most glamorous members of the cabinet and Congress. The subset of official society that the Stewarts elected to join was that of new men, willing to take risks, proud of their wealth, and eager to show it off. The sedate circle of conservative New England Republicans in which Justin Morrill traveled held little appeal for men like Stewart.

When Senator William Stewart let it be known that he intended to build a mansion in the undeveloped northwest part of town, old-time residents ridiculed him and called his unbuilt home "Stewart's Folly." By the time his house was built on the north side of Dupont Circle in 1873, however, land for which Stewart had paid ten cents a foot was selling for five dollars a foot. The mansion was demolished in 1901. (Historical Society of Washington, D.C.)

In 1874, Stewart announced that he would not seek reelection. His family's years in Europe, the Castle, and lavish entertaining had depleted his fortune. Another richer Bonanza King, William Sharon, coveted Stewart's Senate seat, and he was willing to outspend him to win it. Perhaps Stewart recalled the old warning about public officials building houses in Washington as he closed up the Castle in which he had lived for only two years and headed West. For over a decade, the Castle stood empty while Washington grew up around it. In 1886, Stewart rented it to the Chinese for their legation. The next year Stewart, who managed to earn a second fortune, was again elected to the Senate. When they ousted the Chinese, the Stewarts found the house in need of extensive repair:

opium smoking had burned holes in the furniture, and the house reeked of the fish that had been cooked over coal braziers on the bathroom floors.

Once reensconced in their mansion, the Stewarts tried to resume their grand social life. They quickly found, however, that the capital had changed greatly during their fifteen-year absence. William and Annie Stewart no longer seemed so exotic. Their red-brick Castle was dwarfed by the huge, white marble, neoclassical palaces of richer men that now surrounded it. Stewart's fortune was modest when compared to the millions possessed by some of his new colleagues in the Senate. The Stewarts could not keep pace with the more opulent official society of the late 1880s. The Castle went up for sale and was purchased by another Bonanza King, Montana Senator William A. Clark, who demolished it. After his wife's death in 1902, Senator Stewart dropped out of official social life altogether and, in 1905, he left the Senate where he had served for thirty years.

The year after the Stewarts built their Castle, Massachusetts Representative Benjamin Franklin Butler built a four-story, granite, Italianate mansion on Capitol Hill. Morrill had placed his sober mansion in one of Washington's staid, long-respectable neighborhoods. Stewart, the speculator, had placed his spectacular house on undeveloped acres that he was betting would earn him a second fortune. Butler's house and its location bespoke his personality as clearly as did Morrill's and Stewart's. The huge Butler mansion overwhelmed its site just as the overbearing Butler overwhelmed his colleagues in the House. It towered over the southeast corner of Independence and New Jersey Avenues, as close as a private residence could get to the Capitol Building. In choosing his site, Butler served notice that his plans for the future included domination of the Congress.

Like Morrill and Stewart, Butler belonged to several subgroups within official society, including one for which these two colleagues were not eligible. Unlike Morrill and Stewart, Butler was a proud veteran of the Civil War. Though known by a host of epithets, he was above all *General* Butler, one of the many military men who traded on their wartime prominence to win public office. Conservative values might unite a group like Morrill's, and great wealth a group like Stewart's, but the ties that bound together the Civil War veterans were forged in blood and common experience under fire. More important, the same ties that bound them together bound them to the president, who regarded his old comrades-in-arms, whether worthy or not, with special favor.

Like Morrill and Stewart, Butler came from old New England stock. When he spoke to crowds of Massachusetts mill workers, he made much of his humble childhood, but in fact his family was moderately prosperous. Butler had gone to college and become a lawyer. He also became a millionaire before his fortieth birthday. His military career had been one of the most controversial of the war. While commander of occupied New Orleans, he issued his famous Order #28, which stated that Union soldiers were to treat as prostitutes women who showed them discourtesy. Southerners labeled him "Beast Butler." Jefferson Davis ordered him hanged if captured. Many Northerners found Butler's grandstanding

Benjamin Franklin Butler represented the laborers of Lowell, Massachusetts, in the House of Representatives for just ten years, but his career in Congress was as stormy and controversial as his earlier service in the Union Army during the Civil War. Infamous throughout the South as "Beast Butler," he had ordered Union soldiers in New Orleans to treat as prostitutes any women who showed them disrespect, and was rumored to have looted gold and silver from the homes of that city's elite. (National Archives)

equally disgusting, but, among the laborers whose support he cultivated, it only enhanced his reputation, which remained untarnished in their eyes despite military failures and charges of corruption. When the war ended, Butler, a former Democrat, transformed himself into a militant Radical Republican. In 1866, he made the issue of President Johnson's impeachment the springboard that catapulted him into the first of five terms in the House.

Even as a freshman congressman, Butler was easily recognized on the streets of Washington. Not a handsome man, his acutely crossed eyes and droopy eyelids lent a perpetual leer to his countenance. "The bag-eyed bullion-bagger," one enemy called him, with reference to the gold Butler allegedly stole from residents of New Orleans. Butler's shiny, bald head was abnormally large, his figure was short and stocky, and, as he got older, he got fatter until he waddled like "a bass walking on its tail." His oratory was equally memorable: "Not eloquent, but he was savage— as savage as a meat ax," declared one Republican colleague.

The early Grant years benefited Butler politically, financially, and socially. To the disgust of many of Grant's admirers, the two generals, who had once feuded, became more and more intimate. The growing friendship brought Butler handsome rewards: federal jobs and consulships for his family and constituents, and large munitions contracts and flag orders for the cartridge and bunting companies he controlled. While Southerners still decorated their chamber pots with his pudgy visage and conservative Massachusetts Republicans plotted to unseat him, Butler's loyal labor constituents voted for him in overwhelming numbers again and again.

The parties that Butler and his wife Sarah gave at their Capitol Hill mansion were always well attended. The press marveled at the number of Butler's avowed enemies who dined at his table, but even his bitterest adversaries conceded that Butler could be exceedingly charming. When he avoided politics, his easy gaiety, quick wit, and sparkling conversation made him a delightful host. Invitations to Butler's various homes or to sail on his yacht *America* were usually accepted eagerly.

When Butler began his fourth term in the House in 1873, the wave of popularity he had been riding was about to break. While too clever himself to become entrapped in the Crédit Mobilier scandal, his vigorous defense of its chief culprit, Representative Oakes Ames, was repugnant to more men than he realized. Next, Butler led his House colleagues in pushing for the "salary grab," heedless of the disaffection growing among his working-class constituents. Finally, evidence implicated Butler in the

Sanborn contracts scandal, a slimy scheme whereby the government paid informers for intelligence on persons delinquent in paying taxes.

Butler's enemies in Massachusetts overthrew him in the November elections in 1874. When the Forty-fifth Congress opened in 1875, Butler found himself in the embarrassing position of living in a huge new house right across the street from the House chamber where he was no longer welcome. Butler had good reason to recall the old saw about congressmen who build houses in the capital. He stayed on in Washington, however, and, after beginning a law practice, he continued to entertain handsomely as a member of unofficial society. In 1876 he won one more term in the House, but found himself hopelessly out of step with the new president, Rutherford B. Hayes. He retired from politics and, after his wife's death, from society for good. Ben Butler died in his Capitol Hill mansion on January 10, 1893.

A Bouquet of Hostesses

The Morrills, Stewarts, and Butlers dominated small sub-subsets of the congressional subset of official society. During the first Grant administration, several women emerged who dominated, or attempted to dominate, all of official society. A look at three of them—Julia Grant, Kate Chase Sprague, and Kate Williams—and their ascent and descent of the social ladder helps make more concrete the complexity of official society, the intricacies of its rituals, and the ramifications of dismissing their importance.

In theory, President and Mrs. Grant were the leaders of all official society. In fact, while Julia Dent Grant was handicapped by neither the eccentricities of Mrs. Lincoln nor the ill health and unpopular husband of Mrs. Johnson, she fell short of possessing the poise and elan required to make the White House the focus of official society. But if not *the* leader of official society, Mrs. Grant was certainly *one* of its leaders. Society reporter Emily Edson Briggs watched her receive her first White House callers in 1869 and described her as "fair, fat and forty." Like Ben Butler, Mrs. Grant suffered from strabismus, an uncontrollable twitching eye, of which she was self-conscious. Still, while no beauty, she was good-hearted, well-meaning, and friendly. Briggs noted approvingly, "She appears in grace and manner just as any other sensible woman would who

had been lifted from the ranks of the people to such an exalted position."
"She squints like an isosceles triangle," reported Henry Adams, "but is not
more vulgar than some Duchesses."

The nation delighted in reading of Mrs. Grant's plans to convert the
basement of the Executive Mansion into a playroom for her boys. Fred,
the oldest, attended West Point, but Buck and Jesse romped through their
grand new home with glee. Nellie, a lovely girl of just thirteen when her
doting father became president, was to have a room of her own on the
second floor. Two weeks after the inauguration, with renovation only
begun, the Grants moved in. The president's aides, Horace Porter and
Orville Babcock, moved in, too. So did the president's irascible father-in-
law, the old unreconstructed rebel Col. Frederick Dent, who insulted
phalanxes of guests until his death in 1873.

With the nation eagerly looking on, Julia Grant held her first reception. "I felt a little shy," she recalled in her memoirs, but the visitors "all
looked happy and greeted me very kindly. I soon felt at home." She continued, "I am very fond of society and enjoyed to the fullest extent the
opportunity afforded me at the White House." The "fullest extent" was
very full indeed. The White House social calendar sprouted dozens of
levees, balls, dinners, and special parties. More than any previous residents of the White House, the Grants dined out, made social calls, and attended evening parties.

Mrs. Grant's "Tuesday afternoons" were extremely popular. Guests,
once counted by the score, swarmed into the White House by the hundreds. Reflecting the dramatic growth of Washington society, the explosion of visitors overwhelmed not only Mrs. Grant's receptions but the "at
homes" of all official wives. Taking matters into her own swollen hands,
Mrs. Grant bravely tackled existing protocol and invited other ladies in
official society to receive by her side. "For instance," she explained,
"Mrs. Fish, wife of the Secretary of State, would stand near me while the
members of the diplomatic corps were passing; and when the officers of
the army and navy were passing, the ladies whose husbands were heads
of these departments would . . . come to my side . . . thus making it easy
and pleasant for me and also for the company." Mrs. Grant's seemingly
small innovation drew instant comment, almost all of it favorable, and
her lead was gratefully followed by other beleaguered hostesses. By her
second season in the White House, Mrs. Grant's reform had become the
custom.

At first, when the Grants dined at the White House, they dined simply. The president liked well-done beef, over-boiled vegetables, bread, and rice pudding. He installed as White House steward the Army quartermaster who had served him all of the things he liked best during the war. The president was content, but Mrs. Grant was not. Anxious to do the right thing, she noticed the raised eyebrows at state dinners when slabs of beef and slices of pie were set before the guests. Out went the quartermaster, replaced by suave Italian restaurateur Valentino Melah.

In no time, thanks to Melah, Mrs. Grant was winning high praise and comparisons to Thomas Jefferson for the exquisite taste shown in the selection of the wines and food served at the White House table. For state dinners, Melah planned banquets of some thirty dishes, most of which the president left untouched, with different wines served between every

Thanks to the guidance of her Italian steward Valentino Melah, Julia Grant's elegant dinners rivaled Thomas Jefferson's. Though President Grant detested them, Mrs. Grant revelled in vast banquets of as many as thirty dishes, served amid the statues and vases of the "Monroe Plateau." This engraving shows a state dinner in 1871, featuring the Monroe Plateau with arches added by Mrs. Grant. (*Frank Leslie's Illustrated Newspaper,* April 1, 1871; Library of Congress, Prints and Photographs Division)

third course. He had less control over seating. Seated according to rank, guests were arrayed in the State dining room around a large table with a huge flower-decked mirror running down the center, which, rumor had it, the president ordered arranged to hide from his view the guests whom he was least anxious to see. Melah's tastes were impeccable but costly. Briggs claimed that each one of his dinners "cost from three to fifteen hundred dollars, with the average cost about seven hundred," not including the wine. Almost every penny of the president's salary of twenty-five thousand dollars and much of his small personal savings were consumed by official entertaining during his first term in the White House.

Mrs. Grant, the president, and their family—what they ate, what she wore—interested the press intensely. Reporters like Briggs scrutinized the White House as never before. The press enjoyed greater rapport with the Grants than with any previous occupants of the White House. Mrs. Grant gave occasional interviews, the first president's wife to do so, and Melah, when approached by Briggs, became the first White House majordomo to disclose the secrets of the household. Many criticized the new reporters and their new style of reporting but Briggs held her ground, drawing a distinction between private parties and White House parties. Of the White House, she wrote, "It is public. It belongs to the people. When we go to the Executive Mansion we go to our own house. . . . Whoever goes to a levee at the mansion becomes public property, and has no more right to complain because he has been caught in the net of a newspaper correspondent than the fish who has swallowed the hook of an honest fisherman."

"My life at the White House was like a bright and beautiful dream and we were immeasurably happy," Julia Grant wrote of her eight years there, the longest period she and Ulysses lived together anywhere in their married life. Yet while "life at the White House was a garden spot of orchids, a constant feast of cleverness and wit," these years were not, Julia Grant admitted, without "some dark clouds in the bright sky." Most of those clouds appeared during her husband's second administration, but the darkest for her personally intruded before she had lived in the White House a full year. "There was," she lamented, "that dreadful Black Friday"—September 24, 1869, when the gold market collapsed, ruining scores of Wall Street investors. To Grant's great embarrassment, the investigation that followed revealed that Julia Grant was probably involved with the speculators.

Both the Grant and the Dent families had proved vulnerable to the

One of the first of many women reporters to cover Washington's postwar high society extensively, Emily Edson Briggs reported for the *Philadelphia Press*. Under the pen name "Olivia," between 1866 and 1882 she wrote hundreds of vivid columns, chronicling the personalities and antics of Washington's social elite. (Emily Edson Briggs, *The Olivia Letters* [New York, 1906])

attentions of unscrupulous schemers. Shortly after his inauguration, Grant's thirty-seven-year-old sister Jennie was swept off her feet by sixty-one-year-old New York financier Abel Rathbone Corbin, who, in league with Jay Gould and James Fisk, had plans for making a fortune in the gold market predicated on the government's not selling off any of its reserves and driving down the price. To reassure nervous investors, they floated a rumor on Wall Street that Corbin, in addition to carrying an account in gold of two million dollars for himself and his wife, the president's sister, was speculating with a half million each for Julia Grant and the president's aide Horace Porter.

When Grant learned of the plot, he ordered Mrs. Grant to write to his sister, informing her that he would make his decision to sell gold without reference to possible harm to his wife, his sister and her husband, or his new New York friends. When runaway speculation pushed the price of gold unreasonably high, he ordered four million dollars of the government's gold dumped on the market. In the hysterical trading that followed, dozens of men, including Corbin, were ruined. Congress voted to investigate the circumstances surrounding the panic. Democrats were anxious to question Mrs. Corbin and Mrs. Grant, doubly embarrassing the president, but the Republican majority won the women a reprieve.

Black Friday was the Grants' first brush with corruption. This time their involvement in the affair was soon forgotten by the press, still in a forgiving mood, but the honeymoon would not last much longer.

At the beginning of the Grant administration, the woman who seemed most likely to eclipse dowdy Julia Grant and dominate official society was Kate Chase Sprague. Young, beautiful, shrewd, witty, and rich—all things Julia Grant was not—Mrs. Sprague also had the benefit of

The marriage of Kate Chase, the beautiful daughter and official hostess of Secretary of the Treasury Salmon Chase, to millionaire Rhode Island senator William Sprague in 1863 was one of the major social events of the war years in Washington. The Spragues were considered the most fashionable couple in the capital, but their marriage quickly deteriorated and both were eventually engulfed by scandal. (Signal Corps Collection, National Archives)

intimate knowledge of statesmen, statecraft, and official protocol gained as hostess for her father, now chief justice, and her senator husband. But instead of dominating official society, Kate Chase Sprague became an example of how precarious prominence within it could be.

There was little cordiality between President Grant and either Chief Justice Chase or Senator Sprague. Grant was suspicious of the former, and he ignored the latter. Still, Mrs. Sprague expected Mrs. Grant to seek her out, as the Johnson women had done, for whatever social advice she might condescend to give. Julia Grant, however, had no intention of turning to an arrogant young woman who, she learned, cruelly ridiculed her behind her back. To Kate Chase Sprague's surprise, Mrs. Grant turned to other, older women for guidance through the social wilderness, leaving her cut off from the social cachet an "in" at the White House conferred no matter who its occupants. Mrs. Grant had also undoubtedly heard the rumors that the Spragues were seeking a divorce and the gossip about Senator Sprague's drunkenness and visits to brothels. Although her husband still financed her elaborate parties, in the opening months of the Grant administration Mrs. Sprague's high social standing was in jeopardy.

When in the spring of 1869 Senator Sprague astonished all of Washington by spewing out a series of sensational speeches on the Senate floor, he didn't help matters. Ostensibly tied to pending fiscal legislation, Sprague's sulphurous harangues were far-reaching. He assailed the president, his father-in-law, the framers of the Constitution, the Senate, and his fellow officers during the Civil War. He claimed that America and American women were losing their virtue. His audience sat in embarrassed silence as Sprague thundered, "Where is there a husband who closes his doors with satisfaction?"

Mrs. Sprague herself appeared in the Senate gallery to hear her husband's next diatribe. Looking straight at her, Sprague attacked the fashionable folk who went to Europe and came back laden with extravagant purchases and the lax morals of corrupt civilizations. It was well known that his wife had just made two trips abroad. The insult, said one observer, "was like a hot cannon ball hissing through the chamber." It hit its mark. Mrs. Sprague turned scarlet and sailed rapidly out of the gallery and out of Washington to Narragansett.

When she returned to the capital for the 1869–70 season, Kate Chase Sprague found that a new official social hierarchy had arisen around the Grants. Speaker of the House James G. Blaine and his wife Harriet now drew to their salon the most prominent men and women in society. Mrs.

Sprague also faced stiff competition from several other lovely, young new official wives, among them Mrs. John Creswell, wife of the postmaster general, and Mrs. William Belknap, the new bride of the secretary of war, who were receiving the adulation of reporters that had once been reserved for her.

Mrs. Sprague was much subdued that season. Mrs. Lincoln, spending the winter in Europe, noticed the absence of her old rival's name from the reports of Washington society. With some satisfaction, in February 1870, she wrote a friend in Philadelphia: "I do not see Mrs. Sprague's name among the gay notices of the winter. Is she in Washington—or South?" Later that month, Austine Snead, the gossip of the New York *World,* whose byline was "Mrs. Grundy," noted, "Two or three years ago no sketch of Washington society would have been complete without giving Mrs. Sprague a conspicuous place in the foreground. . . . Of late she has passed very little of her time in Washington, and when here entertained but seldom, having given herself up in great measure to her maternal duties." (Mrs. Sprague had returned from Rhode Island with a baby girl named Ethel, her second child.) Briggs announced with disappointment that "the elegant wife of Senator Sprague" had "retired before the noon of life to the substantial comforts and enduring peace to be found only in the smooth waters of domestic life." In fact, as both reporters surely knew, the waters of Kate Chase Sprague's domestic life were hardly tranquil.

Briggs was not the only spectator who noticed handsome New York Senator Roscoe Conkling glance frequently toward the Senate gallery when Mrs. Sprague appeared each day. The flowers sent regularly to Conkling's desk were rumored to come from her conservatory. One day, Briggs noted, Mrs. Sprague even wore to the gallery a Worth gown of royal purple velvet that exactly matched the blossoms below on the chamber floor. When, in the midst of the 1871–72 season, Mrs. Sprague gave birth to a third daughter, Portia, there were rumors that the child was not her husband's.

In April 1872, Kate Chase Sprague gave the last and most elaborate reception she ever attempted for her father, whom she believed might yet be president despite his rapidly deteriorating health. It was a balmy spring night and refreshments were served outdoors. Lights sparkled, a fountain splashed, and music wafted from the house. Mrs. Sprague wore a headdress of flowers and feathers and her favorite diamond and turquoise jewelry. She posed her ailing father in a shadowy corner, where he weakly greeted his colleagues, old friends, and influential editors. Despite her best efforts, no one was fooled, either about the motives behind the party or the real condition of the chief justice. Mrs. Sprague's friend Senator Carl Schurz watched the grim spectacle with genuine sadness: "Gossip had it that the reception was given for the very purpose of convincing the political society of Washington that [Chase] was physically as fit to be President as ever," but in fact, "[Chase's] futile efforts to appear youthfully vigorous and agile were pathetically evident."

Mrs. Sprague bitterly accepted Schurz's verdict and backed her father's friend Horace Greeley against Grant that fall. Grant's reelection came as a blow. It meant four more years during which neither her father nor her friends would control the White House, and she would not control official society.

In 1869, Kate Chase Sprague's most often mentioned rival for the leadership of official society was Kate Williams, wife of Senator George Williams of Oregon. Every few years a woman would take it upon herself to try to alter the protocol that ruled official social life in Washington, and Mrs. Williams was the gadfly of the early Grant years. She learned the hard way that one did so at one's peril.

Prior to his remarriage, widower George Williams had seldom been seen in Washington society. His early career and his congressional record were unimpressive. Little distinguished him until, while on a trip back to Oregon in 1867, he married Mrs. Kate George, a beautiful widow, and his days of social invisibility were over. The Williamses abandoned the senator's old bachelor quarters in favor of an expensive suite at the National Hotel. Not waiting for the wives of her husband's colleagues to call on her, Mrs. Williams inaugurated a series of elaborate receptions to introduce herself to official society. One reporter covering her debut described the newcomer as "a tall, shapely, handsome, brilliant brunette, with fresh complexion and graceful carriage, vivaciously trying her repartee on her companions."

The *Oregon State Journal* was soon claiming that "Mrs. Williams has no superior among the leading ladies of the nation" and prophesied that her "agreeable and ingratiating manner and keen intelligence promised her the scepter" of Washington society. And indeed Mrs. Williams did seem to be one of the most likely candidates to whom the social scepter might pass. But she began to press too hard for the honor. She injected herself into politics as well as society. Worse yet, she bragged of her successes. After the entire Oregon congressional delegation had appealed to President Grant without success to pardon an Oregon official convicted of embezzlement, "Mrs. Senator Williams," announced an Oregon reporter, "visited the White House . . . and the fair diplomatist . . . had more influence with the stubborn President and a cold and calculating Attorney General than could have been exercised by a score of members of Congress." When the official was pardoned, Mrs. Williams claimed the credit.

When the Democrats swept Oregon in 1870, Williams lost his Senate seat. President Grant offered his old friend the attorney generalship, and, to the publicly expressed dismay of many prominent jurists, Williams accepted the post in December 1871. The Williamses moved to a large home on Eye Street, and, shortly after that, to an even larger one on Rhode Island Avenue. Mrs. Williams was soon seen out driving in the most expensive landau in the city, pulled by a pair of horses rumored to cost $750 and attended by two liveried servants. Had she only spent money ostentatiously, she would have provoked comment but not censure, but she went further than extravagance in her efforts to scale the social heights: she embarked upon a campaign to change long-standing official protocol and give herself a quick boost up the social ladder.

Mrs. Attorney General Williams announced that thenceforth she expected Senate wives to make the first call upon her. After four years as a Senate wife herself, Mrs. Williams should have known better. No group guarded their prerogatives more jealously than the Senate wives, and they cherished their superiority over cabinet wives in the intricate hierarchy of calling above all else. Mrs. Senator John A. Logan of Illinois found Mrs. Williams's peremptory antics outrageous:

> George Williams, of Oregon, was appointed Attorney-General, greatly to the delight of his beautiful and ambitious wife, whose elevation from obscurity on the frontier to the wife of a United States senator had inspired her with an ambition which was destined to be her undoing. . . . Mrs. Williams became so elated over her sway that she undertook to change the time-honored rules of etiquette at the national capital. She induced Mrs. Grant to call the ladies of the cabinet together in the White House to consider the changes she deemed necessary. . . . Mrs. Grant insisted that it was foolish and could not be done, but gratified Mrs. Williams's whim by calling the ladies together for a confidential talk about social affairs. The majority, in fact all but Mrs. Williams, agreed with Mrs. Grant that they had no power to change Jefferson's code of official eti-

quette. Mrs. Williams said she, for one, would not make the first call on the families of senators. She very unwisely so informed many of the senators' wives and insisted they must call first on her, as the wife of the Attorney-General. This provoked the indignation of the senatorial ladies and many of their husbands, among them Senator Matthew H. Carpenter of Wisconsin.

No other cabinet wife followed Mrs. Williams's lead, and the "provoked" ladies of the Senate refused to make the first call upon the attorney general's wife.

Soon nasty gossip began blowing through Washington about the Williamses. The attorney general was not a wealthy man and his eight-thousand-dollar salary seemed hardly sufficient to cover his elegant new lifestyle. Rumors floated that the funds used to underwrite his entertaining were the public's. It was also whispered that both he and Mrs. Williams took "presents" from individuals with business before the Justice Department. Mrs. Williams's past, which could bear little scrutiny, suddenly became of great interest to the ladies of official society. Journalist Abigail Dodge often included in her private letters to her family the Washington gossip she could not print in her columns. In March 1872, it concerned Mrs. Williams. The attorney general's wife was, Dodge wrote,

> the daughter of a steamboat man, [who] ran away at fifteen with a miserable fellow, had one child, and finally found the man so bad that she got divorced from him by Judge Williams of Oregon. . . . Subsequently she married again and went to California, kept a tavern in Austin—a regular miner's inn—did the work herself, sometimes made forty beds in a morning for those rough pioneers. Then her husband's partner failed, and the firm not having been legally dissolved, he became responsible and they lost the whole they had made. . . . Then her first streak of luck came in the death of her husband. She went to Boston, I think, first, then to Portland. . . . and Judge W., having in the meantime lost his wife, married her and she is now Mrs. Att. Gen. Williams of Grant's cabinet.

Although Dodge's information was essentially correct, she omitted the more salacious suggestions that Mrs. Williams' first marriage was so hasty because she was about to bear the man's child, that she left that child with the husband when they divorced, and that the Georges' frontier "tavern" had really been a brothel with Kate George one of its attractions.

As the first Grant administration ended, Mrs. Williams sat in splendid isolation in her Rhode Island Avenue mansion. Invitations dwindled to only those for official entertainments to which protocol required that all cabinet members be invited.

Rather than to Kate Chase Sprague, Kate Williams, or any of their other young counterparts, Julia Grant turned to Julia Kean Fish for social guidance. The wife of Secretary of State Hamilton Fish, Mrs. Fish literally stood by Mrs. Grant for eight years, guiding her across official society's minefields with a deft, subtle hand.

Mrs. Grant admired Mrs. Fish enormously and in her memoirs called her "my ideal of an empress." The two women first met in the spring of 1865. While General and Mrs. Grant were visiting West Point, from across the Hudson came Mrs. Fish, Mrs. William Morris Hunt, and Mrs. George Templeton Strong to pay a call. Julia Grant, whom they found "simple-mannered, plain and quiet," was overawed by this triumvirate representing New York's most patrician old Knickerbocker families. She would never forget their graceful gesture.

Mrs. Fish could have easily intimidated Julia Grant with her stately grace and flawless manners. Like Kate Chase Sprague, she could have ridiculed Mrs. Grant behind her back. But Julia Fish did neither. She was, instead, kind. She and her husband were unstintingly respectful of the president and his lady, and the Grants were deeply appreciative.

Mrs. Fish was neither young nor beautiful. Fifty-two years old when her husband became secretary of state, Julia Fish was called "queenly," generous, and pious by the press (adjectives never used to describe Kate Chase Sprague). Mrs. Fish was also well acquainted with the capital's quirky protocol, having mastered it when her husband had been a senator from New York in the 1850s, and she happily shared her knowledge with newcomers. Reporter Abigail Dodge found Mrs. Fish "a lady *par excellence,* intelligent, elegant, *au fait."* Emily Briggs saved her highest praise for the secretary of state's wife: "Mrs. Fish—ah! where shall words be found to describe the woman that wakens that exalted sentiment, and makes one long to call her mother or some other endearing name? She has an intellectual countenance, noble enough to belong to a nun."

During the Grant years, when official Washington was uncertain how to meet a social crisis, it waited until Mrs. Fish took the first step, then followed. Mrs. Fish perceived what a forbidding place Washington could be for young, unschooled congressional wives. She was often the first official wife to climb the four or five flights of boardinghouse stairs to the cramped quarters of the newest, poorest congressmen to invite their wives to tea. Mrs. John A. Logan recounted how Mrs. Fish insisted that she accompany her to pay a call upon the pretty young government clerk who had recently married Senator Isaac Christiancy of Michigan, many, many years her senior. The girl was embarrassed by her distinguished visitors, but Mrs. Fish's warmth and graciousness soon put her at ease and placed upon her the stamp of social approval. Kate Chase Sprague was incapable of such gracious gestures.

With their charm and personal fortunes, the Hamilton Fishes were admirably suited to entertain foreign ministers and the heads of state beginning to visit Washington. Once settled into a handsome house at 15th and Eye Streets, just a five-minute walk from the White House, they set about shouldering the formidable social burden that falls on any secretary of state. It was said that the Fishes spent seventy-five thousand dollars a year on official entertaining. Each week during the social season, they held two formal dinners for an average of twenty guests, several smaller dinners, and a reception, during which as many as twenty-five hundred people passed through. Every Wednesday afternoon, Mrs. Fish was "at home" to an endless stream of callers.

Portent of a Killing Frost to Come

The Fishes and most of the other leaders, or aspiring leaders, of official society during his first administration were on hand for Ulysses S. Grant's second inauguration in March 1873. As a group, these Republicans from the North and Midwest had enjoyed unusual hegemony over all of Washington society for the past four years, and they looked forward to extending their reign for four more.

The second inauguration was a disaster even worse than the first. The day dawned "piteously cold" and blustery. A gale blew from the southwest, and a glittering blanket of ice and sleet had covered the city during the night. Flags along Pennsylvania Avenue froze stiff or tore from their moorings. The parade in the morning failed dismally. The breath of the musicians condensed and froze in the valves of their instruments, silencing the music. A constant stream of ambulances transported frostbitten cadets from the line of march to local hospitals.

Since no building deemed big enough or elegant enough for the evening's inaugural ball could be found, an enormous temporary ballroom, made of "light boards, lined with lighter muslin," had been erected in Judiciary Square. Several hundred canaries, dangling from the ceiling in cages, were to provide entertainment. It was all quite lovely, but the room was a frosty horror as the guests arrived, bundled to their eyes in furs.

President and Mrs. Grant arrived at half past eleven o'clock, trailed by the cabinet, the diplomatic corps, the Congress, and a host of other dignitaries and their wives. Mrs. Fish, "as stately, lovely, and serene as ever," huddled in ermine. The "handsome" Mrs. Williams and "dream-like" Mrs. Creswell ventured out of their cloaks only briefly. "Tall Lady Thornton [the British minister's wife] bent like a reed in the blast." Henry Cooke, still Governor of the Territory of the District of Columbia, and his wife, flashy in emerald green satin, shivered on the officials' platform. All of the diamonds and beautiful dresses especially saved for this grand night were "eclipsed by layers on layers of wrappings, till, at a little distance, the whole platform seemed to be filled with a crowd of animated mummies."

Guests swore that the champagne froze solid. Mrs. Logan claimed the coffee turned to frappé. Hot roasts congealed into greasy white lumps. The canaries did not sing. Those that hadn't perished were shivering balls of yellow fluff, "as paralyzed with cold as the bipeds below." Had the president been a superstitious man, he might have viewed his second inauguration as an omen of bad times to come.

5 Official Society Sullied by Scandal, Cleansed By Time

1873–1900

The frigid gusts that froze the canaries at Ulysses S. Grant's second inaugural ball foretold the cooling of the warm winds of optimism that had first blown him into office four years before. Early missteps like Black Friday had been chalked up to the new president's trusting nature, which his supporters assumed would be tempered with experience. But it was not: all his life Grant proved as loyal in sticking by his friends as he was indiscreet in choosing them. Even as the shivering dancers waltzed in their overcoats, rumors of corruption circulated among them. Few leaders of official society remained unsullied by the taint of wrongdoing. During the first Grant administration, official society was like a dense forest, thickly wooded with many aspiring social leaders, all competing for a place in the sun. As official after official was toppled by the blight of corruption during the next four years, they fell with a crash that reverberated around the nation, and with them plummeted the nation's respect for officialdom and for official society. By the end of the second Grant administration, only a few sturdy trunks like the Hamilton Fishes remained in the clearing unblemished.

The political consequences of the revelations of corruption were great. As scandal engulfed the members of the administration, disaffection grew within the Republican ranks. Each official's downfall provided one more rock upon which eager Democrats hoped to drag themselves back up to power. The social ramifications of the scandals were equally great. When the muddied waters finally began to recede with the election of Rutherford B. Hayes in 1876, the social beaches in Washington were nearly wiped clean. The revelations of corruption left a stigma attached to official society, sapping it of the enormous prestige its members had enjoyed in the years just after the war.

For almost two decades, official society labored under the shadow cast by the scandals of these four years. It was unseemly in years of nationwide depression for public officials to entertain extravagantly and, even as prosperous times returned, to do so remained suspect. Official society drifted from administration to administration without direction or leadership. In time it revived. By the turn of the century, a glamorous rejuvenated official social life was very much in evidence in the capital. It did not, however, dominate all of Washington society as it had in the heady days of the first Grant administration. Once again, as in antebellum days, official society was part of an elite duet. In 1900, official society's rival for the top social honors was not the old residential elite of the capital, but the group of rich newcomers without portfolios first attracted to "Boss" Shepherd's New Washington in the early 1870s, just the moment when scandal made official society vulnerable to their challenge.

The Tallest Social Timbers Fall

No sooner had the second Grant administration begun than it was faced with the Crédit Mobilier and "salary grab" debacles. As early as 1868, rumors about the Crédit Mobilier, a corporate front set up to strip the Union Pacific Railroad of its assets, had circulated through the capital. In the summer of 1872, the full story began to come out, and when it did Vice President Schuyler "Smiler" Colfax was among the first casualties. Colfax had accepted a bribe of Crédit Mobilier stock from Massachusetts Representative Oakes Ames. Republicans hastily dropped the handsome vice president from the ticket in favor of Senator Henry Wilson of Massachusetts, whose own involvement with the Crédit Mobilier wasn't revealed until after the election.

When a congressional investigation into Crédit Mobilier began, the list of casualties rose quickly. Ames produced a memorandum book which implicated many of his colleagues. In January 1873, the *Nation* offered a preliminary assessment of the damages: "Total loss, one Senator; badly damaged and not serviceable for future political use, two Vice Presidents and eight Congressmen. The condition of Ames' reputation language is inadequate to describe." The senator was James Patterson, a Republican from New Hampshire; the vice presidents were Colfax and Wilson; and the damaged representatives included Henry L. Dawes of Massachusetts and James Garfield of Ohio, though the *Nation* was wrong about the latter's future serviceability.

Speaker of the House James G. Blaine of Maine, Representatives William Boyd Allison of Iowa, George Boutwell of Massachusetts, John Bingham of Ohio, William "Pig Iron" Kelly of Pennsylvania, James Harlan of Iowa, all Republicans, and James Brooks of New York, a Democrat, were all implicated in the mess. In February, Secretary of State Hamilton Fish lamented the plunging into disgrace of reputation after reputation: "Tis sad and sickening to see reputations which one loved to believe well-earned and pure knocked to pieces, and leave no chance for friends to say a word. For most purposes the present Congress is practically demoralized, so many are struck at, and they too leaders."

In the same weeks that the Crédit Mobilier investigations unfolded, congressmen were embroiled in the "salary grab" debates discussed in Chapter 4. The connection between the two issues was emphasized in the press along these lines: it required a great deal of money to live, to entertain, and to dress decently in Washington; if congressmen could not cover their expenses with their meager salaries, they would turn to men like Oakes Ames, who offered alternative means of procuring the required funds. Better to raise their salaries, argued the pay raise's proponents.

After the debris of the reputations shattered by the Crédit Mobilier investigations had been cleared away, the next leader of official society to fall was Territorial Governor Henry Cooke. After the smash-up of the House of Cooke in September 1873, Cooke hastily resigned as governor and sank into social and political oblivion, only to be followed within months by Alexander Shepherd. When the president appointed him governor after Cooke's resignation, Shepherd increased the number of entertainments at his mansion on K Street to include more and more members of Congress in hopes of staving off an embarrassing investigation into the District's finances. He could not; the president's close ties to both Cooke and Shepherd were revealed; Congress dissolved the territorial government; and Shepherd fled to Chihuahua, Mexico.

In February 1876, the *New York Daily Graphic* printed this engraving of a grand reception given by ex-Governor and Mrs. Alexander Shepherd. The Shepherds' friend Ulysses S. Grant, seen here being received by Mrs. Shepherd, was joined by a host of luminaries from official society. President Grant's attendance, at a time when Shepherd was suspected of gross corruption, angered the *New York Sun,* which fumed, "The President not only gave this fellow the countenance of his official presence, but he took his whole family with him, and sat down on a level with the thieving contractors, fraudulent measurers, notorious jobbers, and colluding clerks." (*New York Daily Graphic,* February 5, 1876; Library of Congress, Prints and Photographs Division)

The next tall trees in the social forest to topple were Attorney General and Mrs. George Williams, whose new round of problems began in the spring of 1873 with the death of Chief Justice Salmon Chase. At first, President Grant considered appointing New York Senator Roscoe Conkling to the high court, but Conkling turned the offer down, as did several other candidates. The year dragged on with no appointment, until, finally, in early December, the president nominated Attorney General Williams, who had so badly mismanaged the government's case against the Crédit Mobilier Company that he lost it.

The press, bar associations, and law reviews all publicly protested Williams's nomination, emphasizing his mediocrity and rumors of malfeasance in office. The private objections raised against Williams's nomination in Washington drawingrooms were more personal and lethal. The attorney general and his wife had antagonized not only a great many congressmen but their wives as well, whose egos were still bruised by Mrs. Williams's aggressive campaign to usurp their time-honored prerogatives. Writing of Williams's nomination, C. H. Hill of the Justice Department referred to the "animus" of the Senate wives and noted that "the fair sex are to a man (or to a woman) opposed to the appointment and of course under such circumstances exert great pressure." The animus of official wives, added to Mrs. Williams's checkered past, her extravagant entertaining, and her flaunted landau, all became one festering sore of bitterness that burst when her husband's name was sent to Capitol Hill.

When Williams's nomination came before the Senate committee, rumors of wrongdoing were replaced by serious, specific accusations. Allegations surfaced claiming that Williams had blocked investigations that could have embarrassed him, that he accepted bribes, and that he used Justice Department funds to pay for his wife's extravagances. Groaned a Justice Department official, "that unfortunate carriage and horses (2,350$) has of course attracted attention." Congressman James Nesmith of Oregon, Williams's longtime enemy, caused much hilarity in the House with his attacks on the attorney general, dubbed "Landaulet Williams" by the press:

> This constituent of mine is the only one who indulges in this gorgeous oriental splendor of riding in a sixteen hundred dollar landaulet. Why, sirs, lawyers in my State of his caliber ride upon the outside of a fifty-dollar mule, and think they are doing well at that. . . . There is a Spanish proverb, I believe, "Put a beggar on horseback and he will ride to the devil." . . . I have no objection to the termination of this journey in that direction, but I do not want the people to pay for the transportation.

Mrs. Williams came in for her own share of abuse. Senator Matthew Carpenter, whose wife despised Mrs. Williams, was still a member of the Judiciary Committee. According to Mrs. John A. Logan, at his wife's prodding Senator Carpenter arose in Committee and made "a violent speech against the confirmation of General Williams' name, making many charges against Mrs. Williams, accusing her of numberless peccadilloes." Mrs. Williams sought to help her husband's case by spreading spiteful gossip about the members of the Judiciary Committee. She made her unfounded charges to Mrs. Fish, who told Mr. Fish, who told the president, who was furious. It was unclear whether Grant also heard the rumors, apparently groundless, linking his own name with that of Mrs. Williams. The gossip about Mrs. Williams's virtue, which had first surfaced when her husband was named attorney general, grew uglier. "Mrs. W. is not a favorite with her own sex, however much she is with ours," hinted one Justice Department official. Less subtle were the observations of *New York Sun* reporter Jerome Stillson to his editor Charles A. Dana:

> Williams' appointment to the chief justiceship is more horrible perhaps than even you know it to be. He, Williams, has said within two days that *his wife* knew of Grant's purpose to nominate him on Saturday night— that he did not learn it till Monday morning—Who is his wife? She was a handsome adventuress in San Francisco known as Kate George publicly kept as a mistress by one George, a prosperous stage proprietor. She has a son in the Maryland Penitentiary, a convict for the crime of robbery, his second offense. The old Senators and Representatives who "know things" in Washington believe that Kate "screwed" her husband into the Attorney Generalship—one of the shrewdest of the old Senators said yesterday in conversation about this appointment—"Mrs. W. has the most profitable c——t that has been brought to Washington in my day. . . . By Jupiter it is horrible."

Williams's position was hopeless, and he withdrew his name from consideration in January 1874. Grant permitted him to remain as attorney general for another eighteen months, until new evidence surfaced indicating that both husband and wife had demanded money from businesses to drop suits before the Justice Department. Threatened with impeachment, Williams finally resigned in the spring of 1875. The Williamses remained in Washington for several years, but once no longer part of official society they could be snubbed, and were. Their retreat to Oregon in 1881 went largely unnoticed.

The Williamses' humiliation revealed the dangers of excessive social ambition. Mrs. Logan claimed, "General Williams's confirmation was defeated, the real trouble originating in Mrs. Williams's arrogance toward the wives of senators who joined Carpenter in his determination to humiliate Mrs. Williams." Mrs. Logan's assessment was widely shared. When news of Williams's withdrawal reached Oregon, a local judge wrote to Representative Nesmith: "Among many there is much rejoicing, and the irreverent say that 'Aunt Kate' has withdrawn George." Observed another

Oregonian, "Society in Washington has something to do with promotion there."

Before his second administration was one year old, the president's friends Henry Cooke, Alexander Shepherd, and George Williams had been exposed as inept, if not as thieves. Before the second year ended, another scandal was uncovered whose trail led to a desk right outside the president's office. Secretary of the Treasury Benjamin Bristow had launched an investigation into irregularities in the whiskey business that were robbing the government of millions of dollars in taxes. He cast a wide net and caught dozens of corrupt small fry in a ring centered in St. Louis. But Bristow suspected that the big fish swam in Washington in the White House pond. Rumors implicated the president's brother Orvil, his brother-in-law Lewis Dent, his oldest son Fred, and the president himself, but solid evidence pointed toward the president's secretary Orville Babcock, a man whom Grant regarded as fondly as a son.

Babcock had moved into the White House with the Grants in 1869 and lived with them until he married, exploiting his ties to the president for all they were worth. During his courtship of Annie Campbell, he shamelessly intimated how his closeness to the Grants would bring him success and riches, which she would share. The young Babcocks were not among the wealthiest couples in official society—it was one of the mysteries of the Whiskey Ring that after five years' participation in the frauds, Babcock had not made more money—but they were ubiquitous fixtures at Washington parties. Men who could not afford to offend this Cerberus who guarded Grant's door invited the Babcocks to all their entertainments. After Julia Grant began inviting ladies of the official family to receive with her, Annie Babcock was almost always at her side.

Babcock counted on his friendship with the Grants and the favors owed him by men both in and out of official society to save him from a jail cell. In fact, the president did believe Babcock innocent, and when his trial opened in St. Louis in February 1876, Grant astounded his cabinet by proposing to take the stand in his friend's defense. While talked out of this rash scheme, Grant insisted on giving a five-hour-long deposition at the White House in which he emphatically testified to Babcock's good character. There was little doubt that the president's testimony achieved Babcock's acquittal. Convinced of his guilt, however, the majority of the press blamed the president for protecting a scoundrel. The Whiskey Ring revelations were another serious blow to official society's prestige. Orville Babcock had worked hard to have his name linked in the public's mind with the president's, and it was, in both honor and disgrace.

Throughout Grant's second administration, one scandal was hardly put to rest before another was unearthed. On New Year's Day 1876, while Babcock awaited trial, the last year of Grant's presidency began with the traditional White House reception. Before the year was two months old, yet another scandal would erupt, dragging down one of the most glamorous couples in attendance at the open house that day. Reporting on the festivities, columnist Rebecca Felton of Georgia wrote admiringly of the "charming grace and manner" of Amanda Belknap, the new wife of Secretary of War William Belknap. Just a few weeks later, Felton had less happy news to report about the secretary's wife, as rumors about the Belknaps "ran through the city like a prairie on fire."

In February 1876 there began a congressional investigation into suspected corruption within the War Department. On the morning of March 2, as he was leaving the White House to sit for his portrait, President Grant practically ran into his secretary of war, "nearly suffocated with excitement," in the front hall. In tears, Belknap confessed to what the investigating committee had discovered but Grant did not yet know: he had accepted large payments for an Indian post tradership. Belknap begged Grant to accept his one-sentence letter of resignation, which the astonished president did. His resignation, however, did not prevent the outraged House of Representatives from proceeding with a motion for his impeachment that same afternoon. Within days, the sordid details of the Belknap case were splashed across the pages of the nation's newspapers. "Washington has written a dime novel," crowed the New York *Herald*. The press camped out on the Belknaps' front steps as one of Washington's most popular couples went into hiding behind the doors of their elegant mansion on Lafayette Square.

Seclusion did not suit Mrs. Belknap. Since her marriage in 1873 to her late sister Carrie's handsome widower, Amanda Tomlinson Brown Belknap had become one of the most prominent young hostesses in the capital. Her marvelous figure was set off by beautiful Worth gowns and splendid diamonds and pearls. Until the congressional investigation, few had stopped to wonder how General Belknap, not a man of means, had managed to maintain two expensive wives in a row on a cabinet member's salary of eight thousand dollars a year.

As the press managed to piece the story together, the bargain that paid for Amanda Belknap's fine clothes had been struck by her sister. After her husband became secretary of war, Carrie Belknap arranged for a New York contractor, Caleb Marsh, to obtain the lucrative trading post concession at Fort Sill, in Oklahoma Territory. In return, Marsh was to pay her six thousand dollars a year. A hitch temporarily arose when the holder of the tradership, John Evans, refused to give it up quietly, but he and Marsh made a contract whereby Evans would keep the tradership but pay Marsh twelve thousand dollars a year. Marsh promised to pass on to Mrs. Belknap half of his proceeds.

Carrie Belknap lived to enjoy only one payment. She died in December 1870, leaving behind a baby boy. When Marsh called on her sister Amanda to pay condolences, he assured her that the infant would continue to be the beneficiary of the arrangement, to which she was privy. When the baby died in June 1871 and Amanda left for Europe, the payments went directly to the secretary of war. After Belknap married his sister-in-law, the payments continued to arrive regularly. The couple had received at least twenty thousand dollars before the scheme was uncovered.

The Belknaps' fall from grace struck official society full force. That the secretary of war should stand accused of selling offices was bad enough, but having the good names of two of the city's most charming hostesses, one of whom had died a new mother, dragged into the mire was worse. Few rejoiced in the Belknaps' downfall as they had at the toppling of the Williamses. Julia Grant, who grew to despise the Williamses, genuinely liked the Belknaps. "I do feel *so* sorry for them," she had sobbed as she unsuccessfully tried to convince cabinet members to urge their wives to call on Mrs. Belknap. No rumors of misconduct preceded this golden couple's fall as they had the Williamses'. Two weeks after Belknap's hasty resignation, *Harper's* noted:

> The disclosure in regard to Secretary Belknap was . . . astounding because there had been no suspicion. He had long been a member of the cabinet, and although not the most eminent among his colleagues, he bore from his service in the army, and as an officer of the internal revenue, an unsullied reputation. . . . There were no whispers or insinuations against him.

Though shocking, understandable stresses drove men in public life to enter into such sordid transactions, claimed *Harper's,* which summed up the temptations to which Belknap, Williams, and others had succumbed:

> The peril of official life at the capital is immensely increased by the "great pace" of society. The profusion and splendor and reckless expense are

captivating and fatally alluring. The imagination and ambition and rivalry of women are inflamed to passion. The temptation falls upon his [the official's] family with enormous power and he has ten thousand dollars a year salary.

Belknap's trial in the summer of 1876, as the nation celebrated its centennial, proved a gaudy spectacle. Like the debates over the "salary grab," it highlighted once again the high costs of maintaining a genteel lifestyle in Washington. After two months of damning testimony, the senators voted to acquit Belknap not because they believed him innocent, but because they believed the Senate had no jurisdiction over an individual who was no longer in office. The Belknaps followed the Cookes, the Shepherds, the Williamses, and the Babcocks into disgrace.

At the beginning of the second Grant administration, three women had been the chief grist for the society reporters' mills—Kate Williams, Amanda Belknap, and Kate Chase Sprague. During these four years, the erosion of Mrs. Sprague's social position accelerated. No headlines heralded her demise, as they had the others. News of her sinking fortunes was passed around the capital in whispers and sly winks.

After her father's death, Kate Chase Sprague moved out of her husband's mansion on E Street and reopened her salon at the late chief justice's country estate of Edgewood. She abandoned the large parties she had once enjoyed in favor of small dinners for select groups of prominent politicians. Senator Roscoe Conkling was a frequent guest, and the gossip about the two, which had begun three years earlier, escalated. At first glance, the two seemed mismatched. Roscoe Conkling had not admired her father, whom she adored. He did admire Grant, whom she belittled. The New York senator and Mrs. Sprague did, however, share certain qualities, among them ambition and arrogance. Conkling was as handsome as Kate Chase Sprague was beautiful. Over six feet tall, red-haired, athletic, and fond of striking poses, Conkling was the darling of the Senate ladies' gallery, the "Apollo of the Senate." Horace Greeley acidly labeled him "the Pet of the Petticoats," and other enemies tagged him "the curled darling of Utica."

Conkling's wife, Julia, preferred Utica to the capital. She cared little for Washington society and less for her husband. Thus unencumbered, Senator Conkling and Mrs. Sprague, whose husband was often absent from the capital, went out together more and more frequently after Chief

Justice Chase's death. "They were so much seen together that it was generally supposed that she was his mistress," claimed Violet Blair Janin, a formidable leader of residential society, explaining to a friend why she refused to receive Mrs. Sprague, adding, "He is not by any means the first man she has been suspected to have sinned with." Not coincidentally, Kate Chase Sprague's name began to appear in society columns less and less often. She still received invitations to the official affairs to which all congressmen and their wives had to be invited, but the fact that the senator who often was her escort was not her husband accounted in part for her decreasing visibility.

With her husband's last Senate term ending in March 1875, the 1874–75 social season was Kate Chase Sprague's final one as a member of the official society she had dominated since her arrival in Washington as an ingenue a decade and a half earlier. As soon as she was no longer a member of the official social circle, reporters boldly linked her name with Conkling's in print. Still only thirty-five, her beauty at its height, Kate Chase Sprague's official position, with its guarantee of a special place in the capital's society, was gone, as was her reputation.

The Social Whirl Spins On

Despite the scandals that swept some of its most prominent members out of office and tainted those left behind, official society remained at the forefront of the Washington social scene in the mid-1870s. As it had always been, official society was still made up of smaller subcircles, each of which had its own stellar hosts and hostesses. Congress, the largest of the subsets, had the greatest number of shining stars. Within the cabinet circle, decimated by resignations, only the Fishes endured.

As the leaders of the other official subcircles were disgraced, society reporters increasingly focused their attention upon the diplomatic circle, led by British Minister Sir Edward Thornton and his wife. Japanese Minister Jushie Yoshida and his young bride were great favorites during these years. Mrs. Logan was among those they thoroughly charmed, and she related a story from an evening at the Japanese ministry:

> General Logan and I were dining at their home one night, when Associate Justice Field sat on Madame Yoshida's right and I sat next to Justice Field. The Justice was a very agreeable conversationalist and Madame Yoshida

had learned to speak English quite well. Justice Field said: "Madame Yoshida, how many children have you?" She replied: "I have two American and one Japanese children," at which Justice Field smiled. Quickly realizing the fact that she had made a mistake, she said: "Two born in America, and one in Japan. One is named Ulysses Grant, and one other Roscoe Conkling."

The press and all of official society were also smitten by the handsome new Danish Minister Johan de Hegermann-Lindencrone and Madame de Hegermann-Lindencrone, formerly Lillie Greenough of Cambridge, Massachusetts, who arrived in 1875. With her trunks still only partially unpacked, Madame de Hegermann-Lindencrone wrote her mother: "There seems to be no end of card-leaving and card-receiving, and a list of rules on etiquette (Ten Commandments of a Diplomat) as long as your arm. I never knew of anything so confusing. . . . I am knee-deep in engagements, actually wading in them."

Lillie de Hegermann-Lindencrone's letters to her family provide a glimpse of official society free of the saccharine gloss of society reporters. She wrote of harpies who stole the legation silver and impossibly boring dinner partners. After the Mexican minister's first ball, she reported:

> The assemblage was promiscuous, to say the least. . . . And as for the supper, it was in a room out of all proportion to the gathering! There was no question of getting into it. . . . The chairs intended for the guests were utilized as tables on which to put unfinished plates of food and half-empty glasses. Everything that was not spilled on the floor was spilled on the table. Gentlemen(?) broke the champagne-bottles by knocking them on the table, sending the contents flying cross the room. The lady guests drew out the silver skewers which ornamented the *plats montes* and stuck them in their hair as mementos of this memorable evening.

The social calendars of the de Hegermann-Lindencrones and the other men and women of official society were filled with events like the Mexican minister's soiree. No diplomatic dinner or congressional ball could compare, however, with the premier social event of the second Grant administration—the wedding of the president's daughter Nellie to Algernon Sartoris in 1874. There had been no young girls in a presidential family since the Tylers a quarter century earlier, and the press had doted on Nellie ever since her father's election.

On the way home from a European tour in 1872, seventeen-year-old

Nellie had fallen in love with Algernon Sartoris, a charming young Englishman of the minor gentry. The president was disconsolate, but with her mother's help Nellie prevailed. All of official society received invitations requesting their presence at the White House on May 21, 1874. Among the guests crowding into the East Room reporters sighted the Spragues, making an unusual appearance together, Senator and Mrs. Conkling, the latter making one of her rare visits to the capital, the Belknaps, and the Fishes. Despite the trials and tribulations with which it was beset, official society rallied to witness Nellie Grant and her "Algy" stand beneath a bell of white camellias and exchange their vows.

After Nellie Grant's wedding, the ladies of official society threw themselves into preparations for the nation's upcoming centennial. By means of countless teas, bazaars, and benefits, they raised money for the Centennial Exposition in Philadelphia. For days before the grand opening in May 1876, train after train pulled out of Washington as much of official society migrated to the former capital to watch President Grant open the Exhibition on one of the hottest spring days in a decade. Beneath the cascades of patriotic rhetoric that poured forth that day and throughout the centennial summer ran an undercurrent of dismay. Even as orators extolled the integrity and sagacity of the Founding Fathers, fresh scandals were making it all too clear that those virtues were sorely lacking in many of the nation's then-current leaders.

Disenchantment with politics and politicians in Washington encompassed all of official society. During the first Grant administration, with few exceptions the press had reported with uncritical relish on the lavish parties and handsome mansions of the members of official society. The New Washington, reporters had enthused, rivaled the most glamorous courts of Europe. As scandal followed scandal and a serious financial depression settled over the nation, however, notes of caution and disapproval began to creep into descriptions of official society. Even effusive chroniclers like Emily Edson Briggs began to temper their reports with admonishments against unseemly extravagance.

After the corruption in the District of Columbia's government was exposed, the *Washington Evening Star* retreated from its enthusiastic coverage of official society. "Let us have cheaper pleasures," the *Star* chided in January 1874, "and it cannot be doubted that we shall soon hear less of 'rings' and deficits from the public treasury." After the Belknap scandal in the spring of 1876, Republican journals began to play down the brilliance of social life in Washington as the fall elections loomed. James

The German-American humor magazine *Puck* carried this bitter cartoon by Joseph Keppler, featuring "Columbia" as the tattooed lady, in its election issue of November 1876. Columbia's shameful tattoos depict the many scandals that had sullied the Grant administration, including Crédit Mobilier, Black Friday, and the Whiskey Ring. (*Puck,* November 1876; Library of Congress, Prints and Photographs Division)

G. Blaine, one of the Republican presidential hopefuls, found his reputation as one of the capital's leading hosts a liability. Reporter Mary Abigail Dodge, Blaine's wife's cousin, had previously regaled her readers with accounts of Washington high life, but in June 1876 she published a long article in *The Galaxy* protesting that "The rich men in Washington are the exception and not the rule":

> The President and the Cabinet are seldom wealthy men. . . . The Judges of the Supreme and other courts are always of small salaries. . . . The Senate has perhaps a baker's dozen of rich men and householders but the large majority make no pretensions of wealth and live quietly in the most modest of boardinghouses. . . . It is idle to imagine such a society as this dominated by wealth or corrupted by extravagance.

It was true that the majority of officials did live modestly in Washington. But these, as Dodge well knew, were not the men who gave official society its *ton*. It was the "baker's dozen of rich men" who built "castles" in the capital and spent thousands of dollars on a single party that brought official society national visibility and set the expensive standards their less-wealthy colleagues sought to emulate. It was not "idle" to imagine that Washington society was "dominated by wealth"; it was a fact.

In 1876, the nation was in no mood to hear about liveried footmen. What had once seemed vicariously exciting had become unseemly. To pay hundreds of dollars for violets in January was obscene when thousands of men were out of work. The thirst for social news from the capital had been slaked. Mary Clemmer Ames turned from reporting on society to writing book reviews and advertising copy. Emily Edson Briggs's columns tapered off with the Grants' departure. The euphoria with which the Grant years had begun had evaporated, and official society had lost its cachet.

Undistinguished Years: The 1880s

While the number of officials rose steadily throughout the late 1870s, 80s, and 90s, these were undistinguished years for official society. At first, depression still gripped the nation and the memories of the Grant-era scandals were fresh. Yet as the depression eased and the memories faded, official society remained relatively lackluster. Leadership more than money was wanting: there were plenty of millionaires, but few stellar entertainers. With few exceptions, the White House provided as little social leadership as it did political initiative. Nor did the Congress, even during this era of unprecedented power in the legislative branch, or any of the other subcircles of official society provide enough fascinating hosts and hostesses to galvanize official society and make it outshine its competition again. This is not to say there were none at all. During this period official society provided sufficiently intriguing characters—crass Bonanza Kings, sullied diplomats, amazingly rich robber barons—to keep it in the national news and to lure newcomers to the capital who wished to enjoy their company.

Mrs. Hayes set the subdued social tone that would characterize the Hayes administration at its very beginning. On the eve of her first diplomatic dinner in 1877, she decreed that no wine or spirits would be served in the White House during her tenure there. The new first lady also introduced morning worship and Sunday evening hymn-singing to the

White House. Young Ohio Representative William McKinley was usually among those booming out "Blest Be the Tie That Binds," the hymn that regularly closed the gatherings. The Hayeses' social style mirrored the mood of the country, as they intended it should. They had the means for far greater splendor. Unlike the Grants, Rutherford and Lucy Webb Hayes had never been poor. They were, in fact, among the richest occupants of the White House in the nineteenth century. The Hayeses wanted to set an example of sober, wholesome pleasures and the press noted the change with approval. Reporters like "Mrs. Grundy," who complained of Mrs. Hayes's "economical dressing" and her "Columbus-cut dresses" were in the minority.

The Hayeses had the financial means to entertain lavishly, but they consciously set an example of sober, wholesome pleasures. At the Sunday evening White House hymn-singing depicted in this engraving, Secretary of the Interior Carl Schurz plays the piano, Vice President William S. Wheeler stands by the president, Secretary of the Treasury John Sherman sits on the couch next to Fanny Hayes, and little Scott Hayes stands by his mother. (*Frank Leslie's Illustrated Newspaper,* April 3, 1880; Library of Congress, Prints and Photographs Division)

When the lively Garfield family moved into the White House in March 1881, Mrs. Garfield reinstated wine, dancing, and cards. But if she was laying additional plans to overhaul the White House social calendar, Lucretia Garfield never got to carry them out. In July, while she was convalescing from malaria and nervous exhaustion at a seaside resort in New Jersey, her husband was shot by a disappointed office-seeker in Washington. All official entertainments ceased as the president's life hung in the balance for two-and-a-half agonizing months, until his death on September 19.

One of Garfield's cabinet appointments, James G. Blaine as secretary of state, looked very promising for official society. James and Harriet Blaine had been among the leaders of official society for over a decade. Both looked forward to the elevation in their social status that came with the State Department portfolio, which they expected to be their stepping-stone into the White House. On January 16, 1881, Mrs. Blaine gleefully wrote to her son Walker, "All the world is paying court to the coming or expected Secretary of State. Socially you know it is about the best position."

To her daughter Alice, Mrs. Blaine wrote in mock despair, "Truth to tell, the new position gives me a mighty wrench. . . . All the afternoon I shall be paying visits, and the letters, notes, accounts I have to notice before then make my heart sink into my shoes." Mrs. Blaine was more than up to the task. Her letters expressed her delight over her new place at table and her overcrowded reception days. They were also filled with news of the new house, "so huge and so expensive," the Blaines were about to build on a prime lot in the West End near Stewart's Castle. On June 22, 1881, she wrote her daughter, "The new house is starting. He [Blaine] likes to watch every spade-full of earth which he can snatch the time to see thrown out."

But eleven days later President Garfield was shot, and in December 1881 his successor, Chester A. Arthur, replaced Blaine as secretary of state with Frederick Frelinghuysen. Blaine accepted the removal for the expedient political move that it was, but a devastated Mrs. Blaine would never forgive Chester Arthur. For the first time in twenty-three years, the Blaines found themselves outside of official society. "I cannot help feeling a little blue over the loss of place," Mrs. Blaine wrote her son with considerable understatement. There was talk of Blaine as a presidential candidate for 1884, but for the moment the Blaines had no real reason to stay in Washington. What they did have, however, was a half-finished mansion, eating up the money of a man with no salary and an uncertain future. By the time it was completed in 1882, the house cost nearly a hundred thousand dollars, and when the Blaines finally moved in, they found they couldn't afford to maintain it. After only a year, the Blaines moved out and put the house up for rent.

The White House under Chester Arthur was glamorous, reflecting both the return of prosperity and the new president's tastes. Arthur was a widower, and his daughter Nellie was too young to be his hostess, so the president asked his sister, Mary Arthur McElroy, to preside. Mrs. McElroy and her brother both enjoyed entertaining. Thomas Donaldson, a Philadelphian also familiar with the Hayes and Garfield White Houses, found in the winter of 1881–82 that "parties, receptions, etc. were more extravagant than ever before known in Washington," and that "Grant was mentioned, Hayes cursed, Garfield forgotten, and Arthur hailed as the rising sun."

During the Arthur years, two incidents—the arrival of a new British minister in 1881 and the outlandish antics of Colorado Senator Horace Tabor in 1883—enlivened the official social scene and raised new questions of protocol and propriety. Official society's reaction to each reflected a still-viable social group still grappling with the question of boundaries of tolerable behavior and precedence.

In 1881, Sir Lionel Sackville-West, a handsome bachelor, replaced retiring British minister Sir Edward Thornton. Sackville-West was well known in England to have enjoyed a long liaison with a Spanish dancer, who had borne him several children before her death. The British minister to America was expected to entertain often and well, and it was clear that Sackville-West would need an official hostess in Washington. Though scandalized by their brother's bastard brood, Sackville-West's sisters, the duchess of Bedford and the countess of Derby, used their influence to convince Foreign Secretary Lord Granville and Queen Victoria that his charming, convent-educated, eighteen-year-old illegitimate daughter Victoria should be permitted to accompany her father and act as his hostess.

The Queen agreed, provided official Washington society would accept the highly irregular arrangement. The delicate question was put to then-Secretary of State Blaine, who referred it to the most competent judge of official society he knew—his wife. Mrs. Blaine convened an informal "ladies' committee," composed of the first lady, the wife of Under Secretary of State Bancroft Davis, and Elizabeth Sherman Cameron, the accomplished young wife of Pennsylvania Senator Don Cameron, and

Eighteen-year-old, convent-educated, illegitimate Victoria Sackville-West became the official hostess of the British legation in Washington in December 1881, with the blessing of Queen Victoria and the leading women of Washington's official society. When she and her father Sir Lionel Sackville-West arrived in December 1881, they called first on former Secretary of State James G. Blaine and Mrs. Blaine to thank them for smoothing Victoria's way. (Library of Congress, Prints and Photographs Division)

asked them to consider whether they would accept as hostess of the most important legation in Washington the new minister's illegitimate daughter. Mrs. Blaine knew that if these prominent women would acknowledge Victoria Sackville-West, the rest of official society would follow. Their answer was favorable, the cable was sent, and the Sackville-Wests set sail for America.

When they arrived in December 1881, the Sackville-Wests first called upon the Blaines, now private citizens, to thank them for smoothing their way. Next, Sackville-West took Victoria to meet Mr. and Mrs. Henry Adams, to whom he had letters of introduction. Both Adamses, who knew of Victoria's background from both English friends and from their friend Elizabeth Cameron, were charmed. Henry found Victoria

a sweet girl, just out of a French convent, talking very broken English in a delightful accent. She is the ideal ingénue of a French comedy. . . . The poor child is illegitimate, we are told. . . . I've no doubt she will be happy here if none of her relatives come over. It is a kind society and covers all the sins it can.

At first it appeared as if Henry Adams had overestimated the kindness of Washington society. The newspapers got wind of the irregular circumstances of the British minister's household and protested. Mrs. Adams informed her father:

> The Sunday papers opened fire at first but were instantly throttled—probably by Blaine as he holds them all even today, and Mrs. Blaine, so one of her intimate friends told me, was consulted by West, so she has to stand by him. Luckily for him the girl is sweet and refined in manner and attracts everyone; she will help him rather than hinder him—still, it's a horrid position; there are *three* other children in England. [Actually there were four, two girls and two boys.] You had better not show this . . . gossip travels fast enough.

Whether due to the Blaines' influence, Victoria's charm, or the special attention for which President Arthur singled her out, criticism soon stilled. Official society watched closely as Victoria presided over her first official entertainments at the British legation, and the verdict was overwhelmingly in her favor.

A potentially great embarrassment in the Sackville-West affair had been averted. In the case of Senator Horace Tabor such a potential was fully realized. During a whirlwind thirty days in office, Tabor's tasteless behavior recalled the improprieties of the Grant years, memories Republicans were trying hard to erase.

Tabor had been a Vermont quarryman when he caught gold fever in 1859. For nearly twenty years, he dug for elusive veins of gold across Colorado, while his wife Augusta supported the family with a bakery, a general store, and a boardinghouse. Then, suddenly, Tabor struck it rich in silver and lead. By 1879 his mines were bringing in over a hundred thousand dollars a month. At the age of fifty-two, he began to sow wild oats, developing tastes for gambling, liquor, rowdy Republican politics, and a dazzling twenty-year-old divorcée named Elizabeth McCourt Doe, better known as "Baby" Doe.

When Colorado Senator Henry Teller was named secretary of interior in 1882, the state legislature had to elect someone to fill the remaining thirty days of his Senate term, as well as someone to fill the six-year term to follow. Horace Tabor desperately wanted the six-year term. The wives of the state legislators, however, sympathized with Augusta Tabor, whom he had discarded in a messy divorce, and urged their husbands not to award either term to him. The *Rocky Mountain News* called the eager candidate a "shambling, illiterate bore." Teller refused to support him. "You are mistaken in supposing that I could elect you if I wished," Teller wrote Tabor. "I could not do so if I wished, I would not if I could." But Tabor had not paid the drinking tab of the Republican members of the legislature for nothing. He reportedly spread an extra two hundred thousand dollars around the capital, but he received only the thirty-day term.

Though he would have to work fast, Tabor's dream of a big Washington wedding for "Baby" Doe was still possible. He set out for the capital immediately, rented a ten-room suite at the Willard Hotel, and un-

"Bonanza King" Horace Tabor of Colorado allegedly spent more than $200,000 to buy himself a thirty-day term in the Senate in 1883. Even in that short time Tabor managed to embarrass senators and most of official society with his unseemly bragging and his wedding to "Baby" Doe, who was less than half his age. (U.S. Senate Historical Office)

In order to marry Elizabeth McCourt Doe, the young divorcée everyone called "Baby," Horace Tabor divorced his wife of nearly thirty years. Though they were dogged by scandal and fell on hard times, theirs was a happy marriage. After Tabor's death in 1899, "Baby" Doe clung to his Matchless Mine and froze to death guarding it. (Library of Congress, Prints and Photographs Division)

packed his nine bags and thirteen trunks. Included in their contents was a silk-and-lace nightshirt with gold buttons for his wedding night that he obligingly showed to reporters while revealing that it had cost a thousand dollars.

When Tabor took the oath of office on the Senate floor, he was ablaze with diamond rings, cuff buttons, and studs. Kansas Senator John Ingalls wrote his wife, "The Colorado millionaire, Tabor, took his seat last week. A fouler beast was never depicted. . . . Such a vulgar, ruffianly boor you never beheld; uncouth, awkward, shambling, dirty hands and big feet turned inward; a huge solitaire diamond on a sooty, bony blacksmith hand." Once sworn in, Tabor began to give expensive dinners, one of which was for President Arthur. The ladies of the Colorado delegation refused to attend any of Tabor's entertainments, but their husbands felt obliged to go.

"Baby" Doe and her wedding dress, which cost seventy-five hundred dollars and had a daring décolletage, arrived in Washington only days before the wedding. Tabor had put the nuptials off until the next-

to-last day of his Senate term because he was worried about a techni-
cality: "Baby" Doe was Catholic and insisted on being married by a
priest. Since knowledge of her divorce and Tabor's would have made
that impossible, they had simply decided not to tell the priest who had
agreed to officiate. The wedding took place in the candlelit parlor of the
Willard Hotel on the evening of March 1, 1883. Tabor had boasted that
his great friend President Arthur would attend, and the president
obliged. The male members of the Colorado delegation also attended
but, noted one reporter, "the ladies of the delegation refused to see Miss
McCourt married to Mr. Tabor at all." The wife of Colorado Senator
Nathaniel Hill returned their invitation torn in half. After the nuptial
mass, President Arthur and the other guests devoured the buffet of "elaborate viands."

The Tabors beat a hasty retreat to Colorado, but within days of their
departure the secrets surrounding their marriage began to leak into the
Washington newspapers. The priest, upon learning that he had been de-
ceived, returned the wedding fee and declared the marriage illicit. Next,

Horace Tabor and "Baby"
Doe were married in the
candlelit parlor of the fashionable Willard Hotel. The
newspapers described the
decorations seen here as "a
massive wedding bell of
white roses, surmounted by
a Cupid's bow, with arrow
on a string, tipped with a
heart of violets, the rest
being composed of various
hued roses." (Courtesy,
Colorado Historical Society)

the press discovered that Tabor and "Baby" Doe had been secretly married in St. Louis in September 1882, three months prior to Tabor's legal divorce. President Arthur was said to be mortified that he had attended the wedding. The whole incident, declared Mrs. Henry Adams, made the "Senate blush." Most of official society echoed the thoughts of Secretary Teller, who wrote a friend shortly after the Tabors' departure:

> Tabor has gone home, I thank God he was not elected for six years; thirty days nearly killed us, I humiliated myself to attend his wedding because he was a senator from Colorado (but Mrs. Teller would not). I felt as if I could not afford to say that the state had sent a man to represent her in the Senate, that I would not recognize socially, but I could not have kept it up.

Official Society Revives

In 1884, after the Tabor scandal had died down, the press considered the social consequences of the upcoming presidential election. Should the Republican nominee, James G. Blaine, be victorious, the prospects looked bright: Harriet Blaine was entirely capable of making the White House sparkle again as the focal point of official society. The social prospects of a Cleveland victory, however, looked dismal even for Democrats, anxious to end a quarter century of Republican dominion. The forty-eight-year-old bachelor governor had no hostess in Albany and gave few receptions. "If he goes to the White House," one of his confidants told a reporter, "I imagine he will be a very uninteresting social figure. He might have his sister, Rose Elizabeth, with him, but she is a rather sharp-tongued young lady with a predisposition to Woman's Rights."

Cleveland, of course, did win; he did ask his sister to act as his hostess; and, as predicted, the receptions she organized were "uninteresting." The one spark of social interest generated by the new president was the persistent rumor that he might marry, which he did in the spring of 1886. On June 2, Miss Frances Folsom, the twenty-two-year-old daughter of the president's late law partner, wed Grover Cleveland, twenty-seven years her senior, in the Blue Room, becoming the first bride of a president ever to be married in the White House and the youngest first lady ever. To the members of the new Democratic official society aching for a major social event to call attention to themselves, the wedding was dismayingly small. The president himself wrote out the simple invitations to a handful of guests only a few days before the ceremony.

There was much speculation over whether or not a young woman fresh from college was capable of shouldering the heavy White House social burden. But, claimed a reporter, "she ran the gauntlet of the Washington society critics," and emerged with flying colors. She particularly endeared herself to workers nationwide by instituting Saturday open houses for working women.

The White House under Frances Folsom Cleveland's direction was festive and open, but was still overshadowed in glamour and style by a dozen dazzling homes of lesser members of official society. The premier entertainers of official society could be found in the Congress, which was attracting men of greater and greater wealth. Among the leaders of the congressional social circle were the Camerons, Ohio Senator "Gentleman George" Pendleton and his wife, and New York Representative Levi Morton and his wife, millionaires both.

The two richest men in Congress were the two California senators, Leland Stanford and George Hearst, whose combined worth topped a hundred million dollars, or so reporters claimed. Stanford had made his millions from the Central Pacific Railroad and investments; Hearst had been a miner. Stanford was quiet and dressed in cheap suits; Hearst was flamboyantly gross. Neither man enjoyed society, but both married women who enjoyed it enormously. Mrs. Stanford and Mrs. Hearst happily cooperated with society reporters, supplying tidbits of trivia and tours of their homes. Mrs. Stanford, readers learned, served lunch on china plates costing one hundred dollars apiece, poured tea from a solid gold teapot, and owned three sets of diamonds, one of which was said to have belonged to Queen Isabella of Spain.

George Hearst was not troubled by charges that he had bought his way into the Senate. He had, and he wasn't ashamed of it. He wanted the Senate seat partly because he thought his wife, Phoebe Apperson Hearst, a former schoolteacher who had stuck by him through the ups and downs of his stormy career, would like Washington society. Hearst bought a huge, nearly new mansion in the West End and spent thousands of dollars overhauling the facade from the Colonial Revival to the Romanesque style Mrs. Hearst preferred. Once her dream house was finished, Mrs. Hearst began to entertain prodigiously, throwing parties for two to three hundred guests each week. For these occasions, Mrs. Hearst liked to array her rooms with vegetation:

> The mantels [at one reception] were decorated with poinsettia blossoms and Annunciation lilies. In a doorway between the parlor and the ballroom there was an umbrella covered with California moss, sprayed over with carnations, with a pendant fringe of gilded cypress cones. In the back parlor, the mantels were draped with Nile green silk, held up with bunches of silver and gold pine cones, with pampas grass suspended in the center. The hall and the library were filled with palms and calla lilies, and the tower room off the main parlor was fragrant with roses on tables and stands.

The magnificent entertainments of congressional couples like the Stanfords and the Hearsts easily eclipsed the more sedate White House receptions under the Benjamin Harrisons. First Lady Caroline Scott Harrison was more interested in the National Society of the Daughters of the American Revolution, the new Johns Hopkins Medical School, china painting, and her family than in society. Harrison's cabinet, however, initially showed great social promise. James G. Blaine was secretary of state again, and Mrs. Blaine looked forward to resuming the social duties she had so enjoyed eight years before. But the Blaines' happy prospects quickly soured. As the 1889–90 social season began, their son Walker died. Scarcely three weeks later, their daughter Alice (Mrs. Colonel John Coppinger) also died. Two years later, their son Emmons died as well. The Blaines were devastated by their losses. After promising to be one of the gayest official salons in Washington, the Blaines' drawingroom was one of the saddest.

When the Clevelands moved back into the White House in 1893, baby Ruth, who had been born in New York, came too. The public took keen interest in Ruth and in the births of her sisters Esther in 1893 and Marion in 1895, the first children of a president to be born in the White House. But with three little girls to care for, Mrs. Cleveland had considerably less time to devote to society than she had had during her first experience as first lady.

In addition to the maternal constraints upon the first lady, by the early 1890s other important factors worked against too grand a White House social display and briefly restrained the most exuberant hosts and hostesses in the other subcircles within official society. The stock market crashed and a serious financial depression settled over the nation in the summer of 1893. By the end of the first year of the "Panic of 1893," sixteen thousand businesses had gone bankrupt, six hundred banks had closed their doors, and as many as four million citizens were out of work. As Coxey's Army of the unemployed marched on the capital, society columns carried fewer stories about solid gold teapots and more about official society's concern for the poor.

Official Society at Fin de Siècle

In the spring of 1897, as the depression eased, William McKinley was inaugurated president of the United States. His would be the last administration of the nineteenth century. McKinley would also be the last Civil War veteran in the White House. Within three years, a new group of military heroes, men who little dreamed of social prominence on inauguration day, would shine as heroes of another war, one that established America's reputation as a world and a colonial power.

After Frances Folsom Cleveland and her three lively little daughters, the McKinley White House seemed gloomy and dull. First Lady Ida McKinley suffered, said the press, from "delicate" health. In fact, Mrs. McKinley was a petulant invalid. She suffered from migraine headaches, phlebitis, and epilepsy, and her seizures were frequent and ghastly. At official dinners the president always sat by her side. At the first sign of the rigidity which heralded an oncoming seizure, he sprang into action, throwing his napkin over her convulsed face and whisking it off when she later revived. State dinners became tense affairs as guests wondered whether the first lady would suffer one of her "spells" that night. Marguerite Cassini, the daughter of the Russian minister, described one of her first White House dinners:

Mrs. McKinley, looking fragile and drawn in a gown of pale jade satin with lovely Valenciennes lace, with high neck and long sleeves, has been eating little and saying less, only now and then casting loving looks at her husband, beside whom she sits, contrary to usage. Suddenly, making no sound, she stiffens in her chair, and begins to quiver violently. Calmly the president throws his pocket handkerchief over her face, rises, lifts her gently in his arms and carries her from the room without a word. . . . My dinner partner explains quietly that Mrs. McKinley is subject to these seizures. In a moment the President is back and resumes his place as if nothing has happened.

Mrs. McKinley professed to love little children and demanded that they be brought to visit her. Many, however, came away remembering only a frightening face suddenly covered with a twitching cloth. Mrs. Senator Henry Keyes recalled being taken to visit the first lady in 1898, when she was twelve:

> I completely forgot I had been told to curtsy to Mrs. McKinley instead of shaking hands with her. . . . I seized one of the blue-veined transparent hands lying relaxed in the white lap . . . Then I was stricken with terror. Suppose she had a paroxysm then and there, in the middle of the party!. . . My agitation was so evident that my mother refrained from scolding me. But it was a long time before she took me to the White House again.

Because First Lady Ida McKinley was subject to seizures, President William McKinley insisted on sitting at her side at White House dinners, in defiance of traditional protocol. (Library of Congress, Prints and Photographs Division)

With the exception of Vice President and Mrs. Garret Hobart, the entire executive branch was as lusterless as the chief executive. Secretary of War Russell Alger, an affable millionaire, entered official society amid a flurry of elegant entertainments, but he became extremely unpopular during the Spanish-American War as a result of the "tainted beef" scandal and resigned. Secretary of State John Sherman was seventy-three and growing feeble. In 1898 he was replaced by William Day, who was in turn replaced by the urbane John Hay, who, along with his wife Clara, brought some belated savoir-faire to a dull cabinet.

Despite the lackluster executive branch, fin de siècle official society was gayer and more glamorous than it had been for nearly thirty years. Marguerite Cassini called these the "butterfly years," referring to the richly colorful creatures like herself who flitted across the Washington scene. The brightest social butterflies were still found in the Congress, followed by the military, enjoying a renaissance of prestige, and the diplomatic corps.

The Senate of the 1890s was called the "Rich Man's Club" and the "Millionaires Club" with good reason. Many senators were indeed millionaires but, more important for official society, with the abating of the financial depression, many members of Congress were once again spending freely on huge houses and extravagant parties without incurring censure from the press or their constituents.

At the turn of the century, when a congressman's annual salary was only six thousand dollars, a reporter claimed without exaggeration, "It is hardly possible for a member of Congress to make any figure in the social life of the capital on less than $20,000 a year, and he may easily spend $100,000 per annum without immoderate display." To rent a handsome house in the capital could easily cost ten thousand dollars a year; servants, horses, and carriage, fifteen hundred; one large evening reception a minimum of five hundred; and the eight or ten smaller dinner parties incumbent upon anyone who hoped to be mentioned in the city's society columns at least a hundred dollars each. The funds of even a moderately well-off congressman could quickly be depleted by his wife's obligatory Thursday afternoon receptions alone:

> It is expected that she will serve a cup of tea, a sandwich, a salad or a croquette, ice cream and cake, salted almonds and other confectionery and she must provide for at least 200 people. This will cost from $50 to $100, and it must be repeated five or six times during the season.

Congressional high society was clearly a rich man's game, but there were plenty able to play it. The number of millionaires in Congress had been rising steadily ever since the Civil War. An article in the *Saturday Evening Post* in 1901 entitled "How Our Congressmen Live in Washington" described the phenomenon: "The millionaire Senator is a postbellum product. . . . Great fortunes built up during and soon after the War brought a good many men into the Senate, but it was not until after 1870 that millionaires began to be common in that body." Commonplace by 1901, these millionaire congressmen "have adorned Washington with some of its most magnificent residences, and to-day they contribute much to the social brilliancy of the capital city, giving frequent and costly entertainments." Some of these millionaires, claimed the *Saturday Evening Post,* sought a seat in Congress for the glory and some for the power, but more and more "regard as of most importance the social and other non-political advantages offered to the statesman resident in Washington." Such men "like to play at politics under such agreeable circumstances as are afforded to a rich man occupying such a position at the capital of the nation." For these men, the article continued, the Senate, not the House, was their goal: "The Senate is, of course, a place of highest dignity."

The *Saturday Evening Post's* description fits the Bonanza Kings perfectly. After they had made their fortunes in the West in gold, silver, copper, and lead, many came East to spend them. Some sought membership in the elite Eastern clubs like New York's Union Club, but many sought out the most prestigious club of all, the Millionaires Club in Washington.

Ten Bonanza Kings managed to obtain the status symbol of a Senate seat. Except for Nevada Senators John Jones, a Comstock King, and William Stewart, however, most served a single term without distinction. For most of them, service in the Senate was a costly diversion, often a chance to please wives and daughters, rather than an opportunity to serve the public. While undistinguished as senators, the Bonanza Kings cut a wide swath in official society. They built, bought, or rented the showiest mansions in town, filled them with the most expensive furnishings, and then invited their colleagues and friends to the most lavish dinners the city had yet witnessed.

In addition to Senators Stewart, Hearst, and Tabor, the Bonanza Kings in the Senate in the 1880s and 90s included Nevada Senator John Jones, Senator Thomas Kearns of Utah, better known for his fine clothes than any legislation, Senator William Sharon of Nevada, who set a new record for absenteeism, and Senator James Fair, another Comstock King who was rumored to have spent $350,000 to defeat Sharon. Colorado Senator Jerome Chafee felt his efforts to secure a Senate seat were well worth it when his daughter Fannie married U. S. Grant, Jr. Colorado Senator Nathaniel Hill and his wife, Alice, set new records for costly entertaining. William Clark of Montana, the copper king who bought Stewart's Castle and then tore it down, was elected to the Senate but forced to withdraw over charges of election fraud, was then appointed to a Senate vacancy for which he did not qualify, and was finally elected and seated only to decline to run for reelection. It was said that Clark relished the title but not the work. His fondness for huge, ornate houses, excessive even among the Bonanza Kings, made him and his enormous New York mansion the butt of a caustic poem by Wallace Irwin:

Senator Copper of Tonopah Ditch
Made a clean billion in minin' and sich.
'Hiked for New York, where his money he blew,
Buildin' a palace on Fift' Avenoo.
"How," says the Senator, "kin I look proudest?
Build me a house that'll holler the loudest.
None of your slab-sided, plain mossyleums!
Gimme the treasures of art an' museums!
Build it new-fangled,
Scalloped and angled,
Fine, like a weddin' cake, garnished with pills.
Gents, do your duty.
Trot out your beauty.
Gimme my money's worth—I'll pay the bills."

Not all of the members of the Millionaires Club of the 1890s were Bonanza Kings, and not all of the rich men in Congress were interested in society. Quite a few, however, were very interested in it. Writing about the Senate at the turn of the century, Mrs. Senator Joseph "Fire Alarm" Foraker of Ohio, one of the most formidable of that circle's social leaders, enumerated some of the other front-runners:

The hospitable crowd included the [Chauncey] Depews . . . , the [Stephen] Elkins, [George] Wetmores, [Eugene] Hales, [Elihu] Roots, [Charles] Fairbanks, [Julius] Burroughs [i.e., Burrows], [John] Keans and

[Philander] Knoxes. Both Mrs. Eugene Hale and Mrs. Elkins enjoyed the distinction of being daughter, wife and mother of a Senator. You may imagine that they knew their way about!

Among the nine couples on Mrs. Foraker's list, the Elkinses were the most dazzling. The rise to prominence of Stephen Elkins typified the experience of several members of Congress in the late 1890s. Elkins had been a schoolteacher in Missouri when the Civil War erupted. He joined the Union Army, then migrated to the New Mexico Territory at the war's end. By the early 1870s, Elkins had acquired more than a million and a half acres of land, making him one of the richest men in the West.

Shortly after Elkins arrived in Washington in 1873 to represent the Territory of New Mexico in the House of Representatives, he courted and married Hollie Davis, daughter of wealthy West Virginia Senator Henry Gassaway Davis. The fact that Elkins was a Republican and Davis a Democrat didn't prevent the newlyweds from moving in with the Davises at their mansion on K Street. In 1878, Elkins moved from New Mexico to West Virginia, made another fortune in railroads, mining, and timber, and eventually became a senator from his adopted state. In 1891, after Elkins was named secretary of war by President Benjamin Harrison, he and his wife finally built a home of their own. It was one of the grandest homes in a city filling up with elegant houses. Their four-story Georgian Revival house included a ballroom hung with gray satin that could accommodate two hundred guests and a secret vault beneath the stairs for Elkins's treasure of wine and scotch. Their Thursday evening dinner parties, always planned for twenty-four because of the size of their silver-gilt dinner service, became Washington institutions.

On May 2, 1898, another socially prominent congressional couple, Representative and Mrs. James Slayden, reported, "Last night at 12:30 we were awakened by loud shouts of 'Extra Post' from boys running madly through our usually quiet streets." The "extra" heralded Admiral George Dewey's victory over the Spanish fleet in Manila Bay in the Philippines. The end of the Spanish-American War a few months later, like the end of the Civil War thirty-three years earlier, sent a cascade of famous military men pouring into Washington. Their presence fortified the turn-of-the-century military social circle, which had begun to flag as the old Union generals died off.

General Nelson Miles, the beau ideal of a soldier, with gleaming silver mustaches and a broad chest sparkling with medals, and his wife, the niece of General John Sherman, settled into the beautiful mansion the grateful citizens of Massachusetts bought for them on N Street and began to entertain splendidly. General Henry Corbin, a handsome widower, found himself beseiged with dinner invitations from Washington hostesses. Most famous of all the new military men was Admiral Dewey. In the months after his victory at Manila Bay, the nation was afire with Dewey mania. Babies, yachts, racehorses, hotels, cocktails, cigars, and a new brand of chewing gum (Dewey Chewies) were all named for him.

On a cool October night in 1899, spectators jammed the pavements and searchlights poured a river of light down Pennsylvania Avenue as the nation's capital welcomed the Admiral. The city had not known such a night of military splendor since the Grand Review in the spring of 1865. For almost two months thereafter, official and unofficial society feted Dewey with dinners, receptions, and balls. A national subscription drive raised fifty thousand dollars to buy him a mansion on Rhode Island Avenue, and the dapper Admiral prepared to settle down in the capital.

In November the Dewey euphoria suddenly died when the Admiral, a sixty-two-year-old widower, married Mildred McLean Hazen of Washington. Mrs. Hazen, a rich forty-nine-year-old widow, was the sister of the ruthless Ohio Democratic boss John R. McLean, who, by spending millions of dollars and marrying into the respected Beale family, had pushed his way to the top of Washington's unofficial society. Mrs. Hazen was, claimed reporters, cold, arrogant, ambitious, and Catholic. News of the Admiral's marriage stunned his legions of admirers. The press reacted as if it had been jilted by its sweetheart. Talk of the Democratic presidential nomination stilled, much to the new Mrs. Dewey's annoyance. The subscription drive to build a Dewey Arch in New York faltered and died. Officially, however, there was nothing to suggest the change in Admiral Dewey's status. Nothing could change the rules of official protocol that prescribed the social honors to which the Admiral and his wife were entitled. Whether or not they approved of the match, the members of official society were obliged to seat the Deweys according to the Admiral's rank and pay them the deference due gold braid and four stars.

The diplomatic corps, like the congressional and military official social circles, helped make up for the glamour that the McKinley White House lacked. Beginning in 1893, several European nations acknowledged the growing importance of the United States in world affairs by elevating their legations in Washington to embassies, and their ministers to ambassadors. As it had since the city's beginning, this growing community of foreigners added not only glamorous titled aristocrats but tension to the Washington social mix. In the spring of 1897, it was again the British who were causing social "heartburnings." The question was an old one of precedence. Should British Ambassador Lord Julian Pauncefote, dean of the diplomatic corps, and his wife pay the first call upon Vice President Garret Hobart and Mrs. Hobart or should the Hobarts first call on the Pauncefotes?

The matter was not considered a trivial one. To pay the first call acknowledged superior rank and Pauncefote, his position only recently elevated from minister to ambassador, claimed he represented the "body of Queen Victoria" and was second to none but the President of the United States. The Hobarts, supported by President McKinley, felt just as keenly the dignity of the Office of the Vice President. Though the French, German, and Italian ambassadors called on the Hobarts, Pauncefote would not and a stalemate ensued. Hostesses stopped inviting the two couples to the same party, noted Jennie Hobart, "lest the storm might break in one of their dining rooms."

The question hung fire as the Pauncefotes left Washington to summer in England. While in London, Pauncefote's superiors ordered him to give in and make the first call, which he did as soon as he returned in the fall. Mrs. Hobart claimed that they were congratulated by "everyone." From London, American Ambassador John Hay wrote Vice President Hobart, "I congratulate you on the peaceful outcome of your battle for precedence. I have always heartily approved the position you assumed and think it was imposed by a proper sense of dignity of the great office you hold." Assistant Secretary of the Navy Theodore Roosevelt wrote, "I must just write a line to tell you the great admiration and respect I felt for the way you have met this trying crisis. We are all under a debt to you."

No sooner was this question of precedence settled than another arose, this one precipitated by sixteen-year-old Marguerite Cassini, the daughter of Russian Ambassador Count Arthur de Cassini. Her arrival in Washington revealed once again the tenacity with which the members of official society clung to their prerogatives.

Count Cassini, a gambler and libertine in his youth, was twice divorced when he secretly married the Dutch singer who bore him Marguerite. In 1898, when Cassini was reassigned from China to America, his wife went along as "governess" to the young woman he claimed was his "niece" and ward. Upon their arrival in Washington, the ambassador was written off by the press as a pomaded, pompous bore; his "niece," with her dark curls and pretty, inscrutable face, was labeled a minx. The *Star* predicted that with her "good looks, youth, distinguished ancestry and many accomplishments," Marguerite Cassini was "likely to shine conspicuously amid the many brilliant women of diplomatic society at the Capital." Marguerite certainly hoped the reporters were right. After eight years in China, she was more than ready to enjoy high society in a Western capital. She made her Washington debut at the first big ball of the 1898–99 social season, with Del Hay, Secretary of State John Hay's handsome son, as her escort.

Life for Marguerite Cassini and the other young women of official society was not all parties. Her memoirs offer the daily detail of the lives of these young turn-of-the-century social butterflies. Her hectic days matched those of her friends, one of whom was Vice President Theodore Roosevelt's oldest daughter, Alice. Miss Cassini arose early and rode her horse in Rock Creek Park with a groom. Home again, she changed for breakfast, the first of about five costume changes each day. After breakfast, she sent and answered invitations,

> writing carefully worded acceptances or regrets—so much could be read between the lines; organizing my own calendar of engagements, making out my list of calls and cards to be dropped for the afternoon, . . . drawing up the list of official dinners . . . , deciding on the seating, and conferring with Leon [the chef], and with Dada [her mother] about the arrangements.

When her duties to her father were over, the morning was hers. She and her friends preferred shopping to any other form of recreation:

> We usually ended up in Woodward and Lothrop's where we bought wrist-length, elbow-length and shoulder-length kid glacé gloves by the dozen and tulle by the mile. The wet greeny stems of the bouquets we carried at dances were ruinous to gloves and by four o'clock in the morning when the ball ended we would be knee deep in tulle. For such things, gloves, veils, pins, and so forth, girls were made an allowance called "pin money." Mine—$500 a month—was never enough. Every month when the bills came I had always a difficult session with my Father.

After shopping, there were calls to be made:

> Each afternoon I sallied forth in the carriage with my list and my cards, carefully cornered, praying some at least of my hostesses would not be at

home. Once I cheated and left my card without asking. Once only! The Cabinet member's wife was peering through her curtains and returned my card—torn in half—to my father with a stiff note. I was called on the carpet—it was very unpleasant, ending as always with, "Remember who you are!"

Marguerite Cassini's social calendar for the 1899–1900 season began with a typically crowded schedule:

January 1, President McKinley's New Year's reception

January 4, lunch at the British Embassy for actor Sir Henry Irving

January 5, luncheon at the Embassy for her own friends

January 8, dinner in honor of the Cramps of Philadelphia (wealthy shipbuilders)

January 9, dinner for twenty-four for the Spanish Minister and his wife

January 11, the Pauncefotes' dinner for Admiral Dewey

January 13, dinner dance at Senator Depew's

January 17, the diplomatic dinner at the White House

January 19, musicale at the McLean's for Admiral and Mrs. Dewey

January 22, dinner at the Austrian Legation for Lillian Pauncefote and her fiance

January 24, dinner at the Russian Embassy for Prince DeCroy of Belgium

January 30, reception at Assistant Secretary of State David Hill's for the McKinley nieces

January 31, the second bachelor's ball.

And these, she claimed, were only the "high spots"; interspersed were afternoon teas, small dinners, and her own reception days.

From the moment of the announcement that an ambassador's sixteen-year-old "niece" would be the official hostess of a major embassy, the hostesses of official society had been on the defensive. Trouble, however, had actually been brewing ever since the McKinleys had introduced peculiarities into the traditional seating at state dinners. Status at the White House table was measured by proximity to the president and first

Sixteen-year-old Marguerite Cassini, daughter and official hostess of Russian Ambassador Count Arthur de Cassini, took Washington by storm when she arrived in 1898. Here she is dressed for a tableaux: "Wearing a costume made from a pair of lace curtains, some Chinese brocade, the jade earrings the Buriat chieftain's daughter had given me for a pot of cold cream, and a Japanese sword . . . I appeared as a dramatic and sultry Judith." (Marguerite Cassini, *Never a Dull Moment* [New York, 1956], p. 204; Frances Benjamin Johnston Collection, Library of Congress, Prints and Photographs Division)

lady, who had always been seated across from each other at the center of the table, with the ranking guests arrayed beside them. The McKinleys upset this scheme by insisting on sitting side by side in case the first lady should become indisposed, thus canceling two places of honor in one swoop. Under the McKinleys' new seating scheme, the secretary of state sat across from the president, and the first three ranking ladies present were seated in order to the president's left and to the right and left of the secretary of state. The unorthodox arrangement was highly unsatisfactory to the European diplomats, who took a condescending view of the secretary of state as an appointed official. It was into this messy state of affairs that Marguerite Cassini waltzed.

Young, unmarried official hostesses like Miss Cassini were not new to Washington society. In the McKinley administration, Flora Wilson presided over the household of her father, Secretary of Agriculture James Wilson, and Helen Long, daughter of Secretary of the Navy John D. Long, substituted for her stepmother. However, career diplomat and stickler for protocol that he himself was, Count Cassini must have known that the diplomatic wives would reject the claim of rank for an unmarried girl within their circle. Victoria Sackville-West had at least been eighteen and the minister's recognized daughter, albeit his illegitimate one. Marguerite Cassini was not only young, but a mere "niece." Nevertheless, Cassini persisted, and his demands were met in seating the diplomatic dinner of 1899.

As the wife of the dean of the diplomatic corps, Lady Pauncefote was entitled to the highest available place on the president's left. But Miss Cassini was given second best, Secretary of State Hay's right, taking precedence over all other ladies present. The next day a steady stream of notes and visitors to the State Department made the displeasure of the diplomatic corps clear. Baroness von Hengelmüller, wife of the Austrian minister, was outraged. Lady Pauncefote was vexed. German Ambassador Dr. von Holleben claimed to have been doubly injured—both by Miss Cassini's place at table and his own next to her.

The resolution of the dinner table crisis was considered important enought to be assigned to Secretary Hay himself, who personally supervised the seating arrangements for the diplomatic dinner of 1900. He demoted all unmarried girls and squeezed all the ambassadors and their wives (and wives only) together on the McKinleys' side of the table, while on his side he grouped the ministers of lesser kingdoms and the South American republics. To everyone's relief, Miss Cassini did not appear—she had conveniently fallen ill.

Hay's handling of the crisis was pronounced a success. The next year, however, Count Cassini made an unexpected move. Realizing the weakness of a "niece's" claim to precedence, while on a visit to St. Petersburg he made a full confession of his marital irregularities to the Czar, who received the news indulgently. Marguerite not only returned to Washington as Cassini's acknowledged daughter, but as a countess by imperial ukase. There were rumors that Cassini was planning a fresh assault on the White House dinner table, but Countess Cassini was not allowed to repeat her triumph of two years earlier. At the diplomatic dinner in 1901, the countess found her place on the inferior side of the board, Hay's side, between the Portuguese and Chinese ministers.

While Secretary Hay wrestled to shore up fragile official egos, the century turned. In the fall of 1900, voters reelected William McKinley to lead them into the twentieth century. He was the first president to succeed himself since Grant. As President McKinley took the oath of office for the second time on March 4, 1901, the capital city and its official society offered a remarkable contrast to the physical and social wasteland of mud and brambles in which Thomas Jefferson had sworn the same oath a century before. One hundred years after it had begun with the Adamses' first White House New Year's reception, official society in Washington was alive and well, the gayest it had been in years. True, official society no longer ruled all of Washington society as it had in the heady days after the Civil War. It had suffered drastic setbacks in prestige during the scandals of the Grant years, from which it had struggled for over two decades to recover. But Washington's official society was a delightful pond in which to make a splash nonetheless.

As the century turned, Julia Grant, a widow for fifteen years, joined by her daughter Nellie Grant Sartoris, a divorcée for ten, watched from her home on Massachusetts Avenue as a glamorous official society shone in the social limelight in Washington again, attracting the attentions of society reporters and again inviting comparisons with European capitals.

6 The First Rich Newcomers Trickle into Washington

1865–1880

While the members of official society were enjoying their unparalleled domination of Washington's high society in the late 1860s, a phenomenon was unfolding in the capital that would lead to their eclipse. The scandals that would soon engulf many of them and sully official society's reputation coincided with the arrival of the vanguard of a glamorous new group of unofficial social dazzlers. Together these two factors insured that official society would eventually have to share the social limelight of the capital once again.

These new arrivals will be called the "Newcomers." The term is a broad umbrella that shelters a diverse group of characters, with little in common save money and their desire to shine in the high society of the New Washington. Who these rich newcomers were, where they came from, and why they came to Washington when they did will be the topics of this chapter and the next. Sketches of several archetypical newcomers will illustrate how widely their origins, motives, and chances for success varied, and how their presence further transformed high society in the nation's capital in the last decades of the nineteenth century.

Who Were These Strangers in Washington?

Who were the rich newcomers arriving in the postwar capital on every in-bound train? For Mark Twain, this ostentatious new crowd was made up of the outrageously gauche "Parvenus," second in numbers of Washington's "three distinct aristocracies" only to the officials.

In *The Gilded Age,* Laura Hawkins first encounters the Parvenus when a shiny coach, festooned with complicated monograms, showy coats of arms, Latin mottoes, and footmen in elaborate livery, deposits "the Hon. Mrs. Patrique Oreillé (pronounced O-re *lay)* and Miss Bridget (pronounced Breezhay) Oreillé" upon her doorstep to pay a call:

> When the visitors swept into the drawing-room they filled the place with a suffocating sweetness procured at the perfumer's. Their costumes, as to architecture, were the latest fashion intensified; they were rainbow-hued; they were hung with jewels—chiefly diamonds. It would have been plain to any eye that it had cost something to upholster these women.

The Hon. Patrique Oreillé, a "wealthy Frenchman from Cork," and his family had clambered out of steerage at Castle Garden as the Patrick O'Rileys. Mr. O'Riley, a hod carrier, caught the eye of William Weed, a thinly disguised Boss Tweed, and quickly rose through New York's Democratic ranks. "By and by the newspapers came out with exposures and called Weed and O'Riley 'thieves,'—whereupon the people rose as one man (voting repeatedly) and elected the two gentlemen to their proper theatre of action, the New York legislature," whence O'Riley's "Hon." To celebrate their success, the O'Rileys decided to "do" Europe. There they "learned to speak English with a foreign accent" and returned to America miraculously transformed into the ultra-fashionable Patrique Oreillés. Buoyed by this triumph, the Oreillés, their conversation full of mispronounced French phrases, set out to "do" Washington.

Twain's fictional Oreillés reflect the nationwide rise of the nouveaux riches in the second half of the nineteenth century. Fortunes were being made overnight all across America. The swing of a pickax might reveal a vein of silver ore so rich that it could catapult a man from miner to mil-lionaire in the time it took him to reach the assay office. Two decades be-fore the Civil War there had not been one hundred men in America worth a million dollars. By the turn of the century, when two New York news-papers engaged in a heated contest to count the number of American millionaires, the *World* counted 3,045 and the *Tribune* 4,047. Regardless of the exact number, it was clear that millionaires were becoming common-place. They made their millions, however, in ways barely dreamed of be-fore the war—in steel, steam engines, air brakes, oil, telephones, min-ing—and in places barely heard of in antebellum America—Denver, Dayton, Abilene, Altoona.

Few of these new millionaires remained content for long in the iso-lated mining outposts and small towns where they got their start. Older cities like Boston and New York, as well as newer cities like Washington and Chicago, were awash with real live parvenus like the Oreillés, anx-ious to show off their new wealth, in the years after the Civil War. Successful Forty-Niners came in from the goldfields and built fanciful mansions on San Francisco's Nob Hill. Newly rich coal barons from Scranton, Wilkes-Barre, and Hazelton converged upon Philadelphia. Yet, while the appearance of so many nouveaux riches was a nationwide phe-nomenon, each of these cities experienced it in a distinctive way. Differ-ent individuals gravitated to different cities for different reasons. Wash-ington's arrivistes were its own, drawn to the Potomac's shores, not to Boston, not to Philadelphia, for reasons unique to the capital.

Laura saw only outlandish parvenus like the Oreillés when she in-spected the rich newcomers in the postwar capital. She might be forgiven her inability to distinguish among all the rich men and women arriving in Washington in the late 1860s because the nouveaux riches were indeed by far the most dazzling. In fact, however, there were several other sub-groups of newcomers. Not all of the rich newcomers were newly rich, nor did all parvenus resemble the Oreillés. Crowded beneath the rich newcomer umbrella, in addition to the parvenus, were at least three other groups, which, while represented in the antebellum capital by a few in-dividuals, grew dramatically after the war. They included the old rich from elsewhere, a handful of newly-rich native sons, and a small group of lobbyists.

The old rich from other cities brought with them fortunes that had already taken on the patina of age. While new to Washington, they were not new to money or to society. The homegrown arrivistes were just the opposite: while new to money and new to society, they were not new to Washington. Other cities in America experienced influxes of wealthy men and women whose fortunes had been made elsewhere long before, as well as the rise of a few local parvenus, but the wealthy lobbyists who swarmed to Washington after the Civil War represented a phenomenon unique to the nation's capital. No other city, not even state capitals like

Albany, New York, or Harrisburg, Pennsylvania, proved so strong a candle to so many of these wily moths.

In the early 1800s, before the Capitol's lobbies were even finished, the representatives of special interest groups had begun lining up to press their cases. Only after the Civil War, however, when the coals were hot and ready for the "Great Barbecue," did lobbyists begin to descend upon Washington in great numbers. Among these new postwar lobbyists were a few who were not only very highly paid but socially well connected as well. Notable among these new-style lobbyists was Sam Ward, who will be discussed below, and former Mississippi Senator and Secretary of the Treasury Robert Walker. Also, for the first time, the enormous profits to be made by exploiting the powers of the expanding federal government began to attract the captains of industry themselves. In 1869, reporter Emily Edson Briggs vividly described one of the latter, Collis Huntington, head of the Central Pacific Railroad, and his style of lobbying:

> Floating in Congressional waters . . . at all hours of the legislative day may be seen the burly form of [Collis] Huntington, the great, huge devil-fish of the railroad combination. . . . He ploughs the Congressional main, a shark in voracity for plunder, a devil-fish in tenacity of grip. . . . At the beginning of every session this representative of the great Central Pacific comes to Washington as certain as a member of either branch of Congress; secures his parlors at Willard's, which soon swarm with his recruits, both male and female. . . . Every weakness of a Congressman is noted, whilst the wily Huntington decides whether the attack shall be made with weapon of the male or female kind.

Joining Huntington at the sordid end of the scale of rich men who personally "worked" Congress were Samuel Colt, the munitions manufacturer, Cyrus McCormick, the reaper baron, Erastus Corning, the New York railroad magnate, and Sidney Dillon, president of the Union Pacific Railroad.

The likes of Huntington, Colt, and Corning did not seek admission into Washington's high society or the front parlors of the officials they hoped to influence. They were too impatient to wait for the warm glow of friendship nurtured at genteel dinner parties to develop and shine in their favor. The slow, careful cultivation of contacts was not their style. More patient rich men followed in their wake, however, and, by the 1880s there had emerged in Washington what was known in the press as the "social lobby." Its members didn't pass out cash and stock certificates; their methods were more subtle, more social. Men like George Pullman,

George Westinghouse, Andrew Carnegie, and Alexander Graham Bell began coming to Washington for the social season. They bought beautiful mansions and entertained official society on a gracious, grand scale, only casually mentioning matters in which they had an interest.

Another new feature of the postwar lobby to which Briggs alluded was the "lobbyess." In the late 1860s, a woman known as "Comanche" lobbied for the ironclad ship builders, another worked for Samuel Colt, and another for Jay Gould. Briggs described one such "dazzler," against whom, it was said, no senator could hold out, as

> a luscious, mellow banana; a juicy, melting peach; a golden pippin, ripened to the very core. From India's coral strand comes the two thousand dollar cashmere wrap that snuggles close to her fair shoulders. Diamonds, brilliant as the stars in Orion's jewelled belt, adorn her dainty ears, whilst silk, satin, velvet, feathers, and laces prove what a railroad can do when its funds are applied in the proper direction.

Well known "lobbyesses" like Briggs's "mellow banana" were part of the city's demimonde, but reporters hinted that "lobbyesses" could also be found undercover on the highest rungs of Washington's social ladder. High society "lobbyesses" like Twain's Laura Hawkins began to appear in fiction, where they always kept their true identity a secret and, when exposed, literally died of embarrassment. In fact, however, while society women like Mrs. Attorney General George Williams might use their own or their husbands' influence for personal gain, if paid high society "lobbyesses" existed outside of fiction, they have successfully hidden their true identity.

Whether nouveaux riches from the hinterlands, old rich from old cities, or members of the "social lobby," most of the rich newcomers who arrived in Washington after the Civil War had in common certain characteristics that they shared with the members of official society as well. These common traits—principally lack of both roots in and ties to Washington—explain why both groups are unlike more traditional social elites in more traditional cities.

Save for a handful of homegrown parvenus, the rich newcomers in the postwar capital were by and large men and women who had grown up somewhere else, married and raised their families somewhere else, and made their fortunes somewhere else outside of Washington. Most were native-born Americans, and most were born in the Northeast, but few had stayed in their hometowns. Some had moved a dozen times before arriving in Washington, and few but the Bonanza Kings, who at least shared the common experience of mercurial mining camp life, knew more than a handful of their new dinner partners in the capital.

With few exceptions, the rich newcomers came in couples, and they came after both husband and wife had reached middle age. A few were in their thirties, a few more in their early forties, but most were in their late forties or fifties. These were not families with little children, interested in finding proper schools and playmates for their youngsters. Many came precisely because their children were already young adults on the verge of entering society, and Washington seemed to offer them their best chances for success.

Thorstein Veblen's concept of "conspicuous consumption" applied to all of America's arrivistes, including Washington's. To build a strikingly opulent mansion was an impulse that seized almost all of them. The massive homes rising along Massachusetts, Connecticut, and New Hampshire Avenues in Washington's West End stood as testament to the power of that impulse. Such houses not only symbolized their owner's wealth and loudly proclaimed it to all, but they provided a site for sumptuous banquets, an extensive, expensive library, and exhibit space for a costly (even if mediocre) art collection. Whether they built, bought, or rented a huge Washington mansion, these rich newcomers rarely lived in it for more than six months of the year. They came for the winter social season only, and during their stay they took little interest in any aspect of the city that did not touch upon their pleasures. The capital's schools, churches, and charities meant little to them. Among local institutions, only the city's prestigious social clubs caught their attention.

Some of the newcomers returned to Washington every winter and departed each summer year after year, like the swallows of San Juan Capistrano. No matter how many seasons they might spend in the capital, Washington would never be "home." Home was somewhere else—perhaps a ranch in California or a mansion on Denver's Capitol Hill—but not this new discovery of midlife, where they had arrived full blown.

Where Did the Newcomers Come From?

The rich newcomers arriving in the postwar capital came from every corner of the nation but the South, where parvenus and intact old fortunes were generally too rare to be exported. Some came from the Northeast. The older cities with deeply entrenched social elites, like Boston and Philadelphia, rarely lost members of their oldest families to the capital. More often it was the heirs to relatively new fortunes, to whom the doors of the older city's aristocracy were closed, who migrated to Washington. Most of the rich newcomers from the Northeast came from newer, smaller, industrial cities like Albany, Utica, Springfield, New Haven, Rochester, and Scranton, with fortunes made in railroads, glass, lumber, iron, coal, and steel.

The steadiest stream of rich newcomers flowed into Washington from the Midwest. Beginning in the 1870s and showing no signs of abating at century's end, parvenus poured into the capital from Dayton, Toledo, Cincinnati, Cleveland, and especially Chicago. The richest, most flamboyant newcomers came from the West, with fortunes made in mining, real estate, and livestock. The procession began with California Forty-Niners, then fanned out to include the Comstock Lode millionaires and the Bonanza Kings of Colorado, Montana, and Nevada. And finally, there was the small group of newcomers who were actually native sons. Many of these homegrown nouveaux riches had taken advantage of the opportunities afforded by the New Washington, quickly amassed sizable fortunes, and burst upon society in the early 1870s. While the same soil had nurtured them both, however, the local arrivistes were as alien to the old Washington families as if they had come from Carson City.

Why Did the Newcomers Come?

The rich newcomers came in many varieties from many places, but why did they come to Washington and why in such numbers only after the Civil War? Many of the rich claimed they chose to spend their winters in Washington because of its mild climate. It was, of course, true that Washington's winters were milder than those of Boston or New York, but they were no milder in the 1880s than they had been in the 1850s, when few New Englanders voluntarily ventured South to the capital. Nor were Washington's winters any more temperate than the winters in Charleston or New Orleans. More than a few degrees' change in temperature was luring rich men and women to Washington who had not come before.

Clearly the postwar capital possessed something antebellum Washington lacked. In fact, it possessed many new attractions. One of the most striking changes in postwar Washington was in the physical city itself. Warm winters meant nothing to rich newcomers contemplating spending a season in the capital without decent avenues along which to promenade and beautiful homes with large ballrooms in which to dance. Boss Shepherd provided these and other luxuries in abundance in the New Washington. Despite the scandals that accompanied the transformation, Shepherd created a lovely city, filled with all the right amenities to appeal, as he intended they should, to the restless rich of the era. Thanks to Governor Henry Cooke's press connections and Shepherd's influence with Republican journals, glowing articles in the nation's major newspapers and periodicals spread the news of the new, beautiful capital city, the perfect place to winter, far and wide.

The press touted the New Washington as a city of leisure. Reporters commented favorably on the city's lack of "bustle." "The pleasant thing here is the absence of business," Henry James noted during his first visit to Washington in 1882. "Compared to New York or Chicago," wrote a visiting English clergyman, "Washington . . . is a city at rest and peace. The inhabitants do not rush onward as though they are late for the train or the post, as though the dinner hour being past they were anxious to appease an irritable wife." Another Englishman spoke of the capital's "air of comfort, of leisure, of space to spare, of stateliness you hardly expected in America. It looks the sort of place where nobody has to work for his living, or, at any rate, not hard." Still another commentator observed, "The rich men, who are coming to Washington more and more, find the variety of the social panorama amusing and attractive, while the absence of the tremendous pressure and competition of modern business gives to all more leisure."

When comparing the capital to New York in 1882, one reporter hit upon perhaps the most important carrot that Washington dangled before the nation's nouveaux riches:

In New York the chief talk is of money; in Washington gossip and great men are the leading subjects. In New York a fall in stocks sets all tongues buzzing; in Washington, if a bureau chief loses his job, the same result is accomplished. . . . New York is a city of things, as well as of money. Washington is a city of persons. . . . With all its great men, there is more opportunity for a nobody to become a somebody than in the whirl-pool of New York.

The ease with which "a nobody" could become "a somebody" was one of Washington's chief attractions, especially to the Western and Midwestern parvenus. When in *The Gilded Age* Henry Brierly assures Laura Hawkins that "money or beauty will open any door" in Washington, he is not entirely correct: beauty alone was a weak reed on which to lean. Money, however, did open the doors to high society in the capital in the Gilded Age. While the city's old residential aristocracy remained impenetrable to even the wealthiest arriviste, this aging, fading elite no longer led high society. In Washington's new postwar society, which Twain observed close up, origins counted for little, immediate assets for all.

High society in other East coast cities was more insular. Philadelphia admitted few outsiders. Neither had many auslanders scaled Boston's social heights. By comparison, high society in New York was more open to new wealth and diverse geographical origins. But even in New York antecedents counted for more than they did in "democratic" Washington. Parvenus sought out Washington because of its growing reputation as a city where money, rather than pedigree, counted. Many found it difficult to break into society in the cities where their fortunes had been made, but where their humble origins were also well remembered. In *A Child of the Century,* a Washington novel by reporter John Wheelwright, lovely Genevive O'Hara, who arrives in Washington after several unsuccessful seasons in her home-town of Cincinnati, explains why she wasn't accepted in society there: "You see, there were two dreadful blots on my escutcheon, in the eyes of the fashionable people. Papa was an Irishman, in the first place; and he kept a 'one-price clothing store,' in the second." Her Washington confidant accurately predicts greater success in the nation's capital:

> The "one-price emporium," instead of being a detriment to the young
> girl's success, as it had been in Cincinnati, was, on the contrary, a great
> help to her in Washington, for a "one-price emporium" was known by all
> to be a gold-mine; and was not this charming young woman the sole
> heiress of the nuggets which had been dug from it?

Why should Washington in the 1870s have more fluid criteria for admittance to its high society than Boston, or Philadelphia, or New York? The answer lay, in part, in the fact that the capital had been stripped of its old Southern aristocratic families, its longtime arbiters of taste and gentility, by the Civil War. Unlike Boston, Philadelphia, and New York, postwar

Washington had no sizable, viable upper class dominating all aspects of the city's life, including its high society. Such an upper class would be made up of men and women who had lived all their lives in Washington, men and women socialized together since birth in schools, clubs, churches, and neighborhoods to share common values.

The Civil War veterans who dominated the postwar capital's political and social elites shared only the common experience of battle. Most of the other leaders of official society after the war shared even less. Drawn from far-flung cities and towns, with widely dissimilar backgrounds, most had never met before being introduced in Washington receiving lines. Without a Cerberus, like New York's Ward McAllister, to guard them, the portals to the capital's high society stood open to the wide variety of rich newcomers who sought admittance.

The unguarded entryway into postwar Washington's high society was actually a revolving door, with men and women of unknown backgrounds whirling in and out with each social season and each election. "Washington always gives one the impression of a great hotel," claimed one observer, where "everything is transient and the last thing one expects is permanency. . . . People stream through the great houses of Washington as they do through the corridors of a hotel, and everyone feels that tomorrow or the next day there will be new faces at the table." One sharp-eyed reporter spelled out the effect of Washington's unique state of constant flux on the city's high society:

> Washington society is so constituted that it is impossible to guard it with
> anything like the restrictions of McAllister's Four Hundred in New York or
> those of the bon ton society of any other American town. Here every
> season the people change. Every Congress a new batch of maidens and a
> new set of hangers-on appear on the capital stage. Every four years a
> new administration turns the social world topsy-turvy, and the old order
> gives place to the new. Under such conditions anyone can make his way
> into society. . . . Washington seldom bothers itself about the skeletons in
> its inhabitants' closets. Lucifer himself will be welcomed if he will dress
> well, keep his hoofs hidden in patent leathers, and his tail out of sight.

The rich newcomers didn't stop to ponder explanations for their easy access to Washington's high society. They just took advantage of its vulnerability. The possibility of exploiting its porousness to slip easily into high society drew to Washington people who knew they could not successfully storm more vigilantly guarded gates elsewhere.

In addition to its reputed porousness, Washington was also rapidly earning a reputation among parvenus as the premier marriage mart of America. After the much-publicized marriage in 1874 of Brooklyn-born Jennie Jerome to Lord Randolph Churchill, younger son of the duke of Marlborough, more American mothers than ever before were anxious for their daughters to marry titled Europeans, and Washington was the best place in America to find European nobility in significant quantities. Rich, eager mothers began arriving in the capital at the start of each season with their aspiring young countesses in tow. While the press condemned the "incurable mania for aristocratic distinctions" as "unrepublican," each news story reporting the engagement of another Midwestern belle to a baron or a count who was an undersecretary at a foreign legation identi-fied Washington as the best place for the "mania" to be cured and sent more hopeful mothers and daughters on their way.

To warm winters, urban amenities, and a highly permeable society, must be added still another important factor that increased the postwar capital's allure for some rich newcomers. Even after its transformation into the New Washington, other cities had greater beauty and a richer cultural life than the capital. Cincinnati had superior museums, art schools and music, and yet it was from cities like Cincinnati that the greatest num-bers of rich newcomers came to Washington. A powerful magnet pulling many newcomers eastward was the power and prestige of the new post-war federal government discussed in chapter three.

The city's new beauty, its social fluidity and increasing prestige, and the growing federal power concentrated there, combined to insure that postwar Washington would be a national—eventually an international—pond in which to make a social splash. The kings, queens, and princes who visited America after the war almost always stopped in the nation's capital, though they might bypass New York and Boston. The visits of these foreigners, covered by the nation's newspapers in vivid stories made even more intimate by the introduction of photographs, added an extra shine to Washington's high society that no other American city could duplicate.

The Avant-Garde Arrives: 1865–1875

Whatever the carrot that tempted them on to Washington, the avant-garde of rich newcomers arrived in the capital in the years just after the Civil War. "Marie Columbia," who grumbled about the nouveaux riches in the pages of the *Delineator,* recalled the sudden arrival in the late 1860s of "the millionaire ex-tradesmen," before whom "the old sets in holy horror grumblingly retreated and finally disintegrated into the limbo of 'has beens.' The new day, the new Washington, dawned—the day of palaces, champagne, and orchids."

Among the first of the "new set" to arrive were three colorful individuals who represented some of the subgroups gathered under the broad newcomer umbrella: Sam Ward, the "King of the Lobby," Ned Beale, a local boy who made his fortune in California, and Amzi Barber, an outsider who became a millionaire by exploiting the opportunities of the New Washington. As official society's cachet was fading in the early 1870s, rich newcomers like these were coming to the fore.

While Sam Ward was already established in the capital in the early 1860s, he rose to prominence by exploiting the new powers of the federal government in the postwar years. One of the few paid lobbyists who was also a member of polite society, for a decade after the Civil War he reigned in Washington as the acknowledged King of the Lobby. His lineage and family connections were as impressive as his title. He was born in 1814 into an old and prosperous New York family that claimed as ancestors a colonial governor of Rhode Island, Francis Marion, the "Swamp Fox" of the American Revolution, and a signer of the Constitution, and his father was head of the highly respected New York banking firm of Prime, Ward and King. His favorite sister, Julia, married Samuel Gridley Howe, the abolitionist. His cousin, Ward McAllister, coined the phrase "the Four Hundred" to describe the glamorous New York society that he helped define and guard. Sam Ward's first wife, Emily Astor, who died in childbirth, was the granddaughter of John Jacob Astor.

The path that led Sam Ward to Washington was circuitous. When his father died in 1839, he left more than a million dollars to Sam, who promptly squandered it. When he took his father's place at Prime, Ward and King, the other partners, anticipating disaster, dissolved the firm. Indignant, he set up his own banking house and went bankrupt within the year. Next, he joined the Forty-Niners, made a fortune in mining and California real estate, and lost that, too. He then traveled throughout Mexico and South America, intimating that he was acting as semiofficial diplomat and secret agent, sometimes for old friends at the State Department and sometimes for private companies. Someone—it was not clear exactly who—found Sam Ward's assessment of the turbulent political and business situation in Latin America astute and paid him handsomely for his information. He was rich again, but his family was distressed by his wanderings and shady dealings. "Come back to the old Puritan morals," his sister Julia pleaded, "shake yourself loose from this nightmare. Wake up, and find yourself all that you ever were—the honest son of an honest man."

Sam Ward did come back to the United States, but to a profession Julia Ward Howe did not find entirely honorable. Armed with a contract sealed with a thousand pounds sterling to lobby on the government of Paraguay's behalf, and hoping to turn his many government connections to profit, he headed for Washington in 1860. He took a house at 258 F Street and began to give the dinners that would make him famous. He wrote teasingly to Julia, "I have my own crockery and a set of silver marked S. W., which I earned by the sweat of my brow and the oil of my tongue."

During the Civil War, Ward accepted annual fees "plus dinner expenses" from his old friend Comptroller of the Currency and later Secretary of the Treasury Hugh McCulloch, "to court, woo and charm Congressmen, especially Democrats prone to oppose the war" into passing McCulloch's fiscal policy. He used his extensive network of friends and relatives in the South to get information for another friend, Secretary of State William Henry Seward. He also became the Washington agent of Samuel L. M. Barlow, a wealthy New York lawyer, whose chief business interests lay in railroads, shipping lines, and international finance.

Ward's reputation as a successful lobbyist and as a member of the "social lobby" grew throughout the 1860s. More thoroughly than any of his competitors, he had divined the powers of the new federal bureaucracy and mastered the names and peccadillos of its new officials. For substantial fees, he maneuvered certain bills through Congress and sidetracked others. His domestic clients included insurance firms, telegraph companies, and railroads. He represented foreign interests in such matters as tariffs, shipping rights, and claims. He boasted to Julia that he was a sort of Figaro:

> Everybody wants me, everybody calls me!
> *Tutti mi chiedono, tutti mi vogliano, son il factotum della citta.*

What "everybody wanted" was the charming blend of gentility, intellect, and guilelessness that made Sam Ward so irresistible—and they wanted

Dapper and spry at sixty-eight, Sam Ward, the retired "King of the Lobby," posed at a New York photographer's studio about 1882. Though he had already squandered several fortunes, Ward was rich again and enjoying the good life. (Maud Howe Elliott, *Uncle Sam Ward and His Circle* [New York, 1975])

an invitation to one of his dinners, too. "Uncle Sam's" motto was that the shortest distance between a pending bill and a congressman's "aye" lay through his stomach. To this end, he entertained on a scale befitting his potentate title. No delicacy was too costly or rare for his table. He shopped for his own terrapin and canvasback ducks, imported his own teas, and personally blended his own coffee. The results were, gushed one guest, *"noctes ambrosianae!"* Sam Ward's dinners, enthused another, were "the climax of civilization."

Ward's company was as delightful as his dinners. He was, said *Vanity Fair,* "the one man who knows everybody worth knowing, who has been everywhere worth going to, and has seen everything worth stepping aside to see." Sam Ward "knew more of life," wrote Henry Adams, "than all the departments of the Government together, including the Senate and the Smithsonian." He captivated Lillie de Hegermann-Lindencrone, the wife of the Danish minister. Mr. Sam Ward was, she wrote her mother, the "diner-out par excellence . . . the King of the Lobby par preference . . . and the most delightful talker, full of anecdotes." His guests knew that absolute discretion was his rule, and it promoted expansiveness. Sam Ward never leaked a confidence and never brought up at his dinner table a measure in which he was interested. Instead, a reporter explained, "He treated his friends so well that they were always anxious to do something for him, and usually asked how they could help." On the morning when a measure which he was shepherding along came up for a vote, a friend might receive a gay little note on delicately tinted blue paper reading, "This is my little lamb. Be Good. Sam Ward."

Ward was frank about his occupation, and his openness disarmed critics. He offered an eloquent and humorous explanation of how the lobby, in particular the social lobby, worked before the House Ways and Means Committee in 1875, when it investigated the large sums of money spent by the Pacific Mail Steamship Company to obtain a subsidy to carry the United States mail to the Orient. Ward was called to testify when his name appeared on a list of those who allegedly shared in the booty, and he readily admitted receiving four thousand dollars. After answering the Committee's questions, he launched into a defense of his profession. He described for the Committee the frustrations besetting the lobbyist in Washington:

> To introduce a bill properly, to have it referred to the proper committee, to see that some member in that committee understands its merits, to attend to it, to watch it, to have a counsel to go and advocate it before the committee, to see that members of the committee do not oversleep themselves on the mornings of important meetings, to watch the coming in of the bill to Congress day after day, week after week, to have your men on hand a dozen times, and to have them as often disappointed; to have one of those storms which spring up in the Adriatic of Congress, until your men are worried and worn and tired, and until they say to themselves that they will not go up to the Capitol to-day, and then to have the bird suddenly flushed, and all your preparations brought to naught—these are some of the experiences of the lobby.

Warming to the topic, Ward went on:

> Another point—the question of entertainments—is spoken of. There is
> nothing in the world so excellent as entertainments of a refined order.
> Talleyrand says that diplomacy is assisted by good dinners, but at good
> dinners people do not 'talk shop,' but they give people who have a taste
> in that way the right, perhaps, to ask a gentleman a civil question, and to
> get a civil answer; to get information which his clients want, and that can
> be properly given. Sometimes a railroad man wants information; some-
> times a patentee wants his patent renewed; that is a pretty hard fight.
> Then a broker wants to know what the Treasury is going to do about a
> certain measure. Sometimes the banker is anxious about the financial
> movements in Congress, or a merchant about the tariff. . . . We keep up a
> certain circle of friends, and once in a while an opportunity comes of
> getting something that is of real service, and for which compensation is
> due and proper. But the entertainments are proportioned to the business
> of the session. When the business is good, so are the entertainments, and
> when the business is not good, the entertainments are meager.

One skeptical member asked, "Is there not a great deal of money wasted
on good dinners?" Ward indignantly replied, "I do not think money is
ever wasted on a good dinner. If a man dines badly he forgets to say his
prayers going to bed, but if he dines well he feels like a saint."

Sam Ward's widely reported testimony spread his reputation across
the nation. Though famous, however, he was not rich. He entertained
the best of Washington society, but with other men's money. At sixty, he
was still scratching for a living. Large sums came to him, but just as
quickly slipped away. The long depression that followed the panic of
1873 tightened the corporate purse strings that had been wide open to
him. Then Sam Ward's luck changed once again. In 1877, California millionaire James Keen, whose life Ward had saved many years earlier,
came East to visit his old friend. He bestowed upon Sam the profits of a
block of railroad stock he had earmarked for him years before—nearly a
million dollars.

After this dramatic alteration in his circumstances, Washington and
the halls of Congress saw little more of Sam Ward. The King of the Lobby
had no successors. He was a unique character who thrived in the flamboyant milieu peculiar to the Gilded Age in Washington. Sam Ward's
memory lived on for decades in the capital, kept bright by the appearance on the menus of the city's finest restaurants of delicious dishes *à la*

In 1875 Sam Ward's spirited, witty testimony before the House Ways and Means Committee on the hazards and rewards of lobbying in Washington made him famous across the nation. In this cartoon Ward is cooking up another of his lobbying dinners. (*New York Daily Graphic,* December 20, 1876)

Sam Ward, and by the bar patrons who ordered a "Sam Ward," a drink he had concocted of cracked ice, a thin peel of lemon, and yellow Chartreuse.

Sam Ward was one of the first members of the social lobby in postwar Washington. Others in the vanguard of newcomers to the capital were old friends of the Grants from the Midwest, former comrades-in-arms of the new president, and rich Republicans who had contributed to their party's victory in 1868. Even if Washington's streets were still canals of mud in the late 1860s, high society in the nation's capital was more glamorous than what most of them had known back home: one met very few diplomats in Salinas. These early newcomers expected to be included in the festivities planned by the genial Grants and other grateful officials, and they were not disappointed.

One of the first of this group of new arrivals was General Edward Fitzgerald Beale, an old friend of Ulysses S. Grant, a fellow army officer, and a very rich Republican. These three factors, plus their early entry onto the field, guaranteed the Beales a special role in the capital's postwar society.

Sam Ward delighted in his title of "King of the Lobby." On the front of this "King" calling card, Ward drew himself girded with barrels. On the back he wrote out the menu for one of his lobbying dinners; it began with oysters, moved through several courses to veal sweetbreads in tomato sauce, and ended, several courses later, with macaroons, ice cream, and fruit. (Lately Thomas, *Sam Ward: King of the Lobby* [Boston, 1965])

Washington high society watched with interest in 1872 as the beautiful old Decatur House on Lafayette Square was reopened with a spectacular party. Salads were served on dishes made of ice, and Roman punches drunk from carved ice goblets. This lavish debut was Ned Beale's way of letting all Washington know that he, his wife, his son, and two marriageable daughters had arrived from California. His arrival was actually a homecoming of sorts. He had been born in the capital in 1822 into a wealthy family. His father, George Beale, was a naval hero in the War of 1812, and his maternal grandfather, Commodore Thomas Truxtun, was a privateer during the Revolution. After George Beale's early death, the family's means were greatly reduced. Young Edward entered the navy and saw little of Washington for nearly three decades until he returned in a burst of glory.

Young Beale became a hero in the Mexican War. Within the space of two years, he made six perilous journeys from ocean to ocean carry-

General Edward Fitzgerald Beale was one of the first of the rich Republicans to settle in Washington in the early 1870s. With his old friend Ulysses S. Grant in the White House and his wife anxious to introduce their son and daughters into East Coast society, the General felt the time was right to leave their 200,000-acre ranch in California to spend the winter social seasons in Washington. (Library of Congress, Prints and Photographs Division)

ing crucial dispatches. In the summer of 1848, he carried to Washington the first authentic news of the gold discoveries in California and a small bag of precious nuggets. In 1849, he married his childhood sweetheart, Mary Edwards, daughter of Representative Samuel Edwards of Pennsylvania. In 1851, Beale resigned his commission and settled in California. At the requests of Presidents Fillmore, Buchanan, and Lincoln, he served as superintendant of Indian affairs and surveyor general for California and Nevada, and he was appointed brigadier general in the California militia. After the Civil War, Beale retired to his ranch, Tejon Rancho, an immense tract of over two hundred thousand acres near what is now Bakersfield.

With Ulysses Grant's election in 1868, the Beales decided to come back East. General Beale's and General Grant's friendship stretched back to dark days in the early 1850s in California, when Grant's army career seemed about to end and Beale had wrestled with resigning from the military to support a growing family. Beale was also a generous contributor to Republican coffers. With his party in control and his old friend in the White House, it seemed the ideal time to return to his home town for the winter social seasons and to satisfy his wife, who was urging him to introduce their children into society.

Beale purchased historic Decatur House, designed by Benjamin Latrobe in 1818, for his family's social debut. According to tradition, he had coveted the house since he was a boy and had hunted snipe with his dog in the adjacent fields. It must have been the house's historical associations rather than its design that appealed to Beale, because he immediately ordered the exterior of the old house redesigned in the prevailing Grant-era style, and heavy sandstone trim spread over the simple Georgian facade. Beale's most dramatic addition to the house was the

Gen. Beale had admired Decatur House on Lafayette Square since he had shot snipe nearby as a boy. After he bought the historic house he ordered the facade changed to feature heavy Victorian sandstone trim around the ground floor windows and doors. Here workman are on the roof and the new mortar around the recently added trim is visible. (Historical Society of Washington, D.C.)

new second-floor drawingroom with a parquetry floor of rare woods emblazoned with a huge twenty-two-thousand-piece mosaic of the seal of California. Everywhere in the Beales' renovated home, said a reporter, there was "evidence of four things—leisure, wealth, taste and travel."

While the dramatic party that the Beales threw to open their new home provoked some negative comments from the city's old families, on the whole they stood ready to welcome this wandering son to their bosoms. Though Beale had been gone a long time, his family was still fondly remembered, and his wife was the daughter of a respected former congressman. The Beales appreciated the invitations from old family friends, and they often included William Corcoran and other members of the local aristocracy in their entertainments, but they had not come all the way from California simply to renew old acquaintances. Their closest friends and most frequent guests were members of the new administration and other rich men and women new to the capital. While they gracefully straddled the two groups, the Beales' social weight came to rest on the "nouveau" side of the society fence.

During the six months of the year they spent in Washington, the Beales made Decatur House the unofficial center of official society. President Grant spent many evenings there, reminiscing about old times. (Often General Beale would retire, assigning his son, Truxtun, to sit up and listen to Grant's stories.) Beale's reputation as a member of Grant's inner circle, and the likelihood of meeting the president at any of their numerous entertainments, guaranteed the Californians' invitations ready acceptance by newcomers and officials alike.

Beale's entertainments, political connections, and contributions to Republican war chests paid off handsomely. First he was named president of the National Republican League. Then in 1876, to the delight of Beale's wife and daughters, President Grant named his friend to the prestigious post of Envoy Extraordinary and Minister Plenipotentiary to Austria-Hungary's glamorous court. The post was a generous but ill-chosen reward. Beale had openly sympathized with the Juárez administration in Mexico, which had murdered the Emperor Maximilian, the younger and best-loved brother of the Austrian emperor. Beale resigned after a year, citing eagerness to oversee his American property, but other factors prompting his early return included his chilly reception in Vienna and the end of Grant's presidency.

When the Beales returned to Washington, they resumed their place at the center of the city's most glamorous social circle. Presidents Hayes,

Garfield, and Arthur were frequent guests. Former President Grant and many of Beale's influential friends strongly urged Arthur to name him secretary of the navy, a post he dearly coveted, but Arthur had other political obligations to meet and did not grant the favor. Beale suffered his disappointment in silence and continued to entertain on a grand scale at Decatur House until his death in 1893. His widow kept the house ablaze with parties until she died in 1902.

The Beales had come East partially for the sake of their three children. They had chosen Washington because old family and political ties to the city augured well for a successful debut into society there. Thanks to money, excellent connections, and their own and their parents' charm, the Beale children thrived in the capital. At the time of their father's death, the oldest daughter Mary (known as Mamie) was married to Russian diplomat George Bakhmeteff, who had courted her in Vienna. Truxtun was in Greece, where, through his father's influence, he was serving as American minister, and he was engaged to marry Harriet Blaine, the daughter of the late Secretary of State James G. Blaine. Beale's youngest daughter Emily was still living in Washington and playing a prominent part in unofficial society herself as the wife of John R. McLean, whose family was among the richest in the wave of newcomers who washed into the capital in the 1880s.

Sam Ward, the Beales, and the other early arrivals among the rich newcomers who were drawn to Washington in the late 1860s and early 1870s came despite the city's rawness. Local entrepreneurs suspected that a far larger group of potential newcomers still out in the hinterlands was more concerned with appearances. To entice these rich nomads to the capital to spend their money, businessmen and civic leaders set about transforming the dirty postwar capital into the dazzling New Washington. Several of these city boosters managed to transform themselves into millionaires in the process.

None profited more spectacularly than Alexander Shepherd. Shepherd could lay claim to membership in each of Twain's three "social aristocracies": although the "Antiques" refused to recognize him, he was still a local boy, the son of an old, but not rich, Washington family; when his friend President Grant appointed him governor of the Territory of the District of Columbia in 1873, he became a member of official society; and Shepherd was also one of the "Parvenus," having risen from gasfitter's assistant to near-millionaire in less than a decade. He took inordinate pride in the most visible sign of his affluence, his large bluestone mansion on K Street, with its imposing tower and drawingroom hung with mirrors, blue satin, and Brussels lace, where the president could often be found among the guests. Shepherd's days of glory, however, were brief. By 1876 he had declared bankruptcy and moved to Mexico. His was a shooting star, twinkling in postwar Washington's high society for barely half a decade before plunging into darkness.

Many other men became rich thanks to Shepherd's New Washington, and their wealth and fame outlasted his. Among them, the tale of Amzi Barber closely rivals Shepherd's own for drama. Born in Vermont in 1843 and raised in Ohio, Amzi Lorenzo Barber was the son of a struggling Congregational minister. Barber graduated from Oberlin College in 1867 and entered the Theological Seminary at Oberlin, but he interrupted his ministerial studies in 1868 to answer the call of General O. O. Howard to

Amzi Lorenzo Barber came to Washington in 1867 as an idealistic teacher to take a job at the new Howard University for Negroes. Lured from academe by the money to be made in creating the "New Washington," Barber abandoned teaching for real estate and then for road-building. By the 1890s, he was known as the "Asphalt King" of the world. (Library of Congress, Prints and Photographs Division)

When Amzi Barber developed the residential neighborhood of Columbia Heights in 1881, he saved the highest, most beautiful spot for himself. "Belmont," his massive gray stone mansion, completed in 1886, sat within a ten-acre private park. Its tall, pointed tower could be seem from miles away, until the house was demolished in 1915. (Frances Benjamin Johnston Collection, Library of Congress, Prints and Photographs Division)

come to Washington and take charge of the Normal Department of the recently opened Howard University for Negroes. After four years at Howard, however, Barber gave up all thoughts of pedagogy and abandoned academe for real estate. The fortunes being made in the New Washington were overwhelmingly attractive to a young man who had known only financial hardship.

Barber's first business venture was immensely profitable. In partnership with Ohio Senator John Sherman, one of the officials with whom Shepherd shared inside information about the plans for the city's development, Andrew Langdon, a local land speculator, and others, Barber developed LeDroit Park, one of Washington's first residential suburbs, in 1873. In 1881 he developed the fashionable residential neighborhood of

Columbia Heights, reserving the finest elevation for his own estate of "Belmont." The massive granite mansion, with its soaring tower, standing in the midst of Barber's personal ten-acre park, was one of the most imposing country residences ever built in Washington.

Barber closely watched the streets Shepherd's crews were paving through his new neighborhoods. Washington had always been a testing ground for all sorts of paving materials, and the durable asphalt laid down on city streets in the mid-1870s looked especially promising. Barber formed the Barber Asphalt Paving Company and began paving miles of streets in the capital himself. The former theological student proved to be a shrewd businessman. From Washington, Barber expanded his asphalt business to Baltimore, Philadelphia, and the Northeast, and then moved west and south. By the early 1890s, half of all asphalt pavement laid in the United States was Barber's. By 1896, through his tightly monitored asphalt trust, Barber was "asphalt king" of the world. To remain "king," Barber knew he needed close ties to the political establishment in Washington. He and his lobbyists kept one eye on potentially damaging tariff and importation legislation in Congress and another on State Department dispatches from far-flung pitch-producing countries like Trinidad.

Real estate and asphalt made Barber rich and enabled him to enjoy any luxury he chose. After beautiful houses in Washington and New York, Barber chose yachts. He spent his summers sailing with family, influential friends in official society, and other newly rich men and women like himself up and down the East Coast and to the Mediterranean on his famous three-hundred-foot yacht *Lorena*.

New "Stars of the First Magnitude" in the Social Sky

The glories of the emerging New Washington were broadcast across the nation by obliging reporters covering Grant's second inauguration, which Alexander Shepherd also orchestrated. Accepting the invitation to visit, grandly extended by Shepherd in every interview, more and more rich men and women with no official position began to arrive in the capital in the months that followed to see for themselves its new amenities and enjoy its gracious ambiance. Even as the House of Cooke closed its doors and a second investigation into the Territory's tangled financial affairs commenced in 1874, the trickle of rich newcomers that had begun to

seep into Washington at the close of the war widened into a steady
stream that even a nationwide depression did little to stem.

Their arrival did not go unnoticed. The transformation of Washington's high society, begun by the new cast of postwar officials, to which
this rising tide of newcomers contributed was as dramatic as the physical
transformation of the city and just as widely noted. In 1874, the *Nation*
commented that the improvements to the capital had begun to "attract a
respectable class of winter residents who formerly held it in great contempt." Privately, E. L. Godkin, the *Nation's* editor, wrote to Charles Eliott
Norton at Harvard, "Washington seems to be becoming more and more
of a resort for people who want to amuse themselves in the winter in a
mild climate, and is greatly changed in all respects. . . . A great many new
houses have gone up, and a general air of smartness and enterprise has
come over the place." Helen Nicolay, returning to Washington with her
father, John, in the 1870s after a nearly five-year absence, noted that the
city had begun "to take on its new character as a place of winter residence for people of wealth, unconnected with the government."

Reporter Emily Edson Briggs informed her readers in 1876 that "a
new set of people are pressing forward to blaze in the social sky as stars
of the first magnitude." Reporter Mary Clemmer Ames also took note of
the "new set" in town and, assuming her most superior tone, described
some of the recent arrivals promenading along the newly laid sidewalks:

> This lady, flashing by in many hues, represents what one sees continually
> in Washington—a new woman. Not new to the city merely, but new to
> position and honor. . . . All she has is new. She, herself, is new. Her
> bearing and her honors do not blend. There is no soft and fine shading of
> thought, of manner, of accent, of attire. The sun of prosperity may strike
> down to a rarer vein, and draw it outward, to tone down this boastful
> commonplace; but we must bear the glare, the smell of varnish, and the
> crackle of veneering, during the process.

Shepherd was delighted with the response to his invitation to the rich
men and women of America to come sample the New Washington's pleasures. Not surprisingly, the capital's old families, already smarting from
their eclipse by official society, were not. That so many of the Antiques
began grumbling about the rich newcomers in the mid-1870s marks the
perceived beginning of the deluge. The beleaguered old families found
most of the newcomers, with a few exceptions like the Beales, distaste-

ful, and the lavish lifestyle invading their home town shocking. To one member of the old elite, the New Washington was a horrid place, full of "veneer furniture and plated spoons," a place where "vulgar people who amass fortunes by successful gambling in stocks, pork, or grain can attain a great deal of cheap newspaper notoriety for their social expenditures." Postwar Washington society, complained another, was infected "by a demoralizing haste to be rich, a vulgar, consuming passion for display." Mourned still another in 1878:

> Ill-gotten and well-gotten wealth have usurped the leadership of society.
> It is a custom, we are informed, for a society woman to dazzle, not by
> her beauty or conversation, but by the quality of her dress and the value
> of her jewels, and that a costume is not remarked upon as being in good
> taste and becoming, but as having cost so many hundred dollars.

Neither the ill will of the old families, the depression that followed the Panic of 1873, the end of Grant's eight years in the White House, nor the sober administration of Rutherford B. Hayes stemmed the stream of rich newcomers flowing into the New Washington. Throughout the 1870s, the number of large, private receptions—described by one wag as "the easiest way to give the greatest possible number of people the least possible pleasure"—grew dramatically. While unemployment spread across the nation, the pace of the unofficial social whirl in Washington accelerated each year.

7 A Rising Tide of Rich Newcomers Floods the Capital

1881–1900

The rich newcomers captured the leadership of Washington high society in the 1880s, and their flag waved atop the social pinnacle for the rest of the century. Their only rivals were the members of official society, who had dominated high society after the war but ruled with diminishing credibility and vigor during the 1870s. As official society's prestige declined, the number of rich newcomers increased, until all that was wanting was the return of a milieu conducive to elaborate entertaining to make their victory apparent. The decade of the 1880s provided the perfect environment in which the rich newcomers could shine. The depression was easing and, as prosperity returned, so did the public's fascination with high society in the nation's capital. This renewed interest enveloped official and unofficial hosts and hostesses alike, but with official society's prestige at its nadir the newcomers were better situated to take advantage of it. In 1905, "Marie Columbia," who reported on Washington with a wry eye, noted that once "the millionaires arrived" the "wedge was driven. . . . As has been the case from time immemorial, the battle was to the strong, and the newcomers remained in entire possession of the field, nor have they lost ground with the passing of time."

"Pearls by the Bushel, Diamonds by the Peck": The 1880s

The decade of the 1880s saw the end of the era when three or four official wives ruled high society in Washington. During these years, a constantly changing baker's dozen of both official and unofficial hostesses jockeyed for supremacy, creating an atmosphere of constant flux. As the 1880–81 social season got underway, the ever-vigilant reporter Emily Edson Briggs took note of the new state of affairs:

> Since the retirement of the superb Katharine Chase Sprague "society," in a blundering way, manages to get along without an acknowledged "head." If the beautiful and accomplished woman is found, the immense wealth is lacking, for no woman can be a successful "leader" unless she has beauty, brains, and money. To a great extent beauty can be spared, because its loss can be made up by the artistic skill which the brain power will utilize. . . . The coming of the bonanza wives is watched with the most intense anxiety. The question is asked: "Has she the qualities to command or will inefficiency and cowardice consign her to the ranks?"

Briggs and her readers did not have to wait long before several women with brains, money, and even beauty stepped forward to try to fill the vacuum. During the 1880s, Washington was awash with newcomers of all categories—native sons and gilded Westerners, old rich from Eastern cities and nouveaux riches from all over, but especially from Ohio and Illinois.

This second, larger wave of rich newcomers was drawn to Washington by the same enticements that had tugged at the first. In 1884, *Century Magazine* spelled out the capital's various charms and the groups to which each one appealed:

> Its mild climate, its quiet streets, free from the hurried bustle and noise of a commercial center, and the character of its society, prove more and more attractive to certain classes. The merchant who has acquired a fortune in the fierce struggles of trade goes there to build himself a house and quietly enjoy with his family the results of his labors in a place where there is no business talk. The retired army or navy officer finds nowhere else so many friends or so much consideration—in fact nowhere else can he live on his pay with any comfort. . . . During the winter all the world and his wife goes there for a visit—some for sight-seeing, to see what Congress and public men look like; some because it is the fashion to go

to Washington in winter as to Newport in summer. . . . The society is thus
ever changing and kaleidoscopic . . . every winter brings its fresh supply
of mere temporary residents.

While the *Century Magazine* article listed many of postwar Washington's
attractions, it missed, or perhaps tactfully omitted, an important one that
"Marie Columbia" pointed out. Once word got out of how easy it was to
"make it" in Washington society, how easy "for the new-rich to come
to Washington and hob-nob with diplomats and officials," going to
Washington "became an epidemic that was as infectious as mumps or
measles. Trade from Chicago built a white palace. Patent medicine set up
a mansion. . . . These new mansions sprang up like beautiful white and
brown mushrooms upon all the fashionable thoroughfares."

The presence of these rich newcomers in their beautiful white
palaces, combined with the wealthy members of official society, made
the 1880s the most dazzling decade yet in the capital's history. It was during these years that high society in Washington came of age and took its
place alongside its counterparts in the nation's other fashionable watering
holes of the rich and famous like New York and Newport. By 1883,
claimed one reporter, it had become "as fashionable to have a winter
house in Washington as it is to have a summer one at Newport or at
Saratoga. . . . Washington in the winter is the gayest of the gay."

More reporters were assigned to cover the capital's social season in
the 1880s than ever before. Most of these reporters were women, but the
very best of them was Frank Carpenter, an engaging young man with un-
manageable red hair who covered the capital for the *Cleveland Leader*
using the byline "Carp." Within months of his arrival in 1882, Carp's lively
columns were being picked up by more newspapers than those of any
other Washington correspondent. Americans all across the nation sat
back in their antimacassared chairs and read his gossip from the capital.
Washington's horsecars and hotels, its salons and saloons, the rumors
about Grover Cleveland's marriage to his ward, the widespread disapproval of the nude statues in William Corcoran's art gallery, all came alive
for the readers of his colorful word pictures. In the fall of 1882, describing the opening of the social season, Carp captured the evanescence and
effervescence of the capital city:

Washington is like no other city in the world. It is a living curiosity, made
up of the strangest and most incongruous elements. There is a fairy-tale

sense of instability about it. As with the palace of Aladdin which flew away in the night, one feels that this city could easily vanish and that he could wake up some morning to find himself stranded on the empty Potomac Flats. The city looks as if it had sprung up in a morning, or rather as if a whirlwind had picked up some great town, mixed the big houses up with the little ones, then cast the whole together in one miscellaneous mass, keeping intact only the city streets.

Carp's dispatches told of beautiful women, handsome men, and breathtaking opulence. At the height of the season in 1885, he reported:

> There is enough silk worn here every winter to carpet a whole state; there are pearls by the bushel, and diamonds by the peck. . . . At the White House the other night there were at least five hundred women wearing diamonds of various sizes. I counted fifty pairs of solitaire earrings whose stones were as big as the end of my thumb, and thirty diamond stars and pendants any one of which would buy a large farm. One brunette beauty, dressed in a flowing red gown, had by actual count eighty-five diamonds on her person. Some of these, set in bracelets and rings, were not unusually large, but the solitaires in her ears were as big as hazelnuts. She shook at least five thousand dollars this way and that every time she moved her head.

The son of a wealthy Ohio banker, Carp enjoyed poking fun at the nouveaux riches flooding into his journalistic territory. He described a capital full of contrasts:

> The Washington nabobs are a strange conglomeration. Some have the bluest of blue blood in their veins, education acquired in the best of schools, and manners polished by long sojourns in Europe. Such persons have, as a rule, many friends among the great public figures of the day, and have little trouble about getting into the swim.
>
> There is, however, another class who have nothing but their money to recommend them. Their vulgar ostentation marks them as *nouveau riche,* and when you meet them at large receptions you have no difficulty in recognizing them. Many use bad grammar; the men cannot avoid mentioning their wealth; and the women, whether their figures make it advisable or not, dress in the most extravagant extremes of fashion. Stories of the crudities of such people are legion.

Henry James, briefly returning to America after six years in England, visited Washington in the winter of 1882, at the same time Frank Carpenter arrived on the scene. A keen observer of European high society, James, like Carp, missed few of the subtleties of society in his homeland's capital. He found much to dislike in "this democratic substitute for a court city." Nevertheless, he was fascinated by Washington: "It is very queer and yet extremely pleasant: informal, familiar, heterogeneous, good-natured, essentially social and conversational, enormously big and yet extremely provincial, indefinably ridiculous and yet eminently agreeable." For all its flaws and contradictions, James concluded, Washington was "genial and amusing": "The sky is blue, the sun is warm, the women are charming."

The Washington of the early 1880s described by Carp and James, with its appealing blend of naivete and sophistication, beauty and crassness, genuine and imitation, was a magnet for the nation's rootless rich, drawing them to the Potomac's shores in greater and greater numbers.

Many of the rich newcomers in Washington society in the early 1880s shone like holiday sparklers, spectacularly but briefly. Others, however, endured, taking part in society season after season. Among those who arrived in the early 1880s and whose stars remained undimmed a decade later were the Andersons, the McLeans, the Leiters, and the Pattens. Their stories illustrate not only the various wellsprings from which newcomers flowed to the capital, but also the attraction, the glamour, and the fluidity of Washington society in the 1880s.

Newcomers from Ohio

The Anderson family of Cincinnati arrived with the first newcomers from Ohio. Nicholas Longworth Anderson was the very proud descendant of Richard Clough Anderson of Virginia, an aide-de-camp to Lafayette during the Revolutionary War. After the Revolution, Anderson had moved first to Kentucky and then to Ohio, where his son Larz married Catherine Longworth, the daughter of Nicholas Longworth, known as the first millionaire of the West. Nicholas Longworth Anderson, born in 1838, was the second child, the first of ten sons, of Larz and Catherine Longworth Anderson. Like his father, Nicholas went to Harvard. He had just begun to study law when the Civil War began, and he and three of his brothers enlisted. Commended for gallant action, he became a major general at the age of twenty-six, one of the youngest officers of that rank in the Union Army.

In 1865, Nicholas Anderson married Elizabeth Kilgour, a member of another prominent old Cincinnati family. They honeymooned in Paris, and for the next decade and a half they and their two children, Larz, born in 1866, and Elizabeth (Elsie), born in 1874, spent most of each year in Europe. As the time for Larz to enter college approached, the Andersons returned to the United States and enrolled him in Phillips Exeter Academy. They decided to remain in America while Larz was in school, but the question was where. Cincinnati held few charms. Anderson's brothers had managed the family estates in his absence and become prominent figures in local politics, leaving little room for him. Cincinnati society, too, seemed quite provincial after Paris and Vienna. The Andersons had money and leisure, and they sought the glamour of the European cities they missed. In early 1881, they decided to settle in Washington.

The capital drew newcomers onward with a combination of postwar attractions. For the Andersons, Washington's leisurely pace and aura of sophistication weighed most heavily in the balance. The capital, with its legations staffed by people the Andersons had met while abroad, had a more cosmopolitan flair than Cincinnati or even New York. In addition, Washington in the 1880s was filled with friendly faces in high places. Anderson had known Ulysses S. Grant and fellow Ohioans Rutherford B. Hayes and James Garfield during the war, and he had contributed to their political campaigns. Like Ned Beale a decade earlier, Anderson's generosity to the Republican party, his friendship with President Garfield, the bond of common service to the Union shared with many veterans holding high positions, plus the Andersons' considerable wealth, sophistication, and eagerness to entertain, assured them a place on the highest rungs of the Washington social ladder.

On March 20, 1881, Marian Adams wrote her father that Henry's Harvard classmate had stopped by: "Friday Nick Anderson of Cincinnati turned up at five o'clock and stayed to dine; came for four days and to his own amazement bought a charming house." The "charming house" that the Andersons moved into was at 8 Lafayette Square, making them neighbors of both the Adamses, their old friends, and the Beales, who quickly became their new friends. Within a few months, the Andersons commissioned another of Nicholas's old Harvard friends, famed architect Henry Hobson Richardson, to design for them a mansion on the southeast corner of K and 16th Streets. Their letters to Larz provide an intimate glimpse of the problems engendered when wealthy newcomers and a strong-willed architect came together to build one of the "beautiful white and brown mushrooms" popping up all over Washington. In November 1882, Mrs. Anderson brought Larz up to date on the house's progress:

We have had Mr. Richardson here, and he has filled our time and thoughts. . . . His pleasure in the house was worth seeing and he proposed so many more nice (and expensive) additions that it made my head swim, and drove your father into a melancholy from which he has not recovered yet. I should be quite satisfied to have it simply finished and move in directly, but the interior is tempting for decoration, and Mr. R. will not let us off so easily. Mr. [Henry] Adams made some funny comments on the exterior, but was speechless on entering, declaring its arrangements were perfect.

Three months later, Richardson was back to inspect the final stages of construction, and the General wrote to Larz in exasperation:

Mr. Richardson is with us, but as his valet broke his arm and did not accompany him, our Edward has had to act as nurse and we find the said R. a great deal of trouble. He bullies and nags everybody; makes great demands upon our time and service; must ride, even if he has to go but a square; gets up at noon; and has to have his meals sent to his room. He is a mournful object for size, but he never ought to stay in a private house because he requires so much attention.

The Andersons' massive Romanesque house was completed in the fall of 1883, just in time for the social season. The interior was as elaborate as the exterior was severe. The walls of the drawing room were wood-paneled, painted many coats of white and then hand-rubbed with pumice powder until they resembled polished ivory. Decorative tiles ran like shiny necklaces throughout all the principal rooms. National magazines like *Harper's* and *Century* devoted several pages to the house, its architect, and the Andersons.

The Andersons' almost daily letters to Larz at Phillips Exeter, and later at Harvard, revealed how quickly the liveliest of the capital's social circles embraced them and how rapidly they came to identify themselves as Washingtonians. Just a few weeks after moving to the capital, the Andersons were entertaining and being entertained by the most prominent members of Washington's official and unofficial high society. By the spring of 1883, the Andersons were already taking pride in their adopted city and taking steps to insure that the Washington society they had

Nicholas Longworth Anderson of Cincinnati chose his Harvard classmate Henry Hobson Richardson to design his Washington house, which stood at the corner of K and 16th Streets, NW. One of only four houses Richardson designed for Washington clients, Anderson House was razed in 1925. (*Artistic Houses: Being a Series of Interior Views of a Number of the Most Beautiful and Celebrated Homes in the United States, 1883–1884* [rev. ed., New York, 1987])

elected to join would become even more lively. In May, the General wrote Larz:

> Washington is growing so that all the "corners" have been purchased and are being held at fancy prices. The Casino (a stock concern) including theatre, club, ball room, tennis courts, glass-covered gardens, etc. is almost an accomplished fact, and will be built on Connecticut Avenue just off Farragut Square. . . . I have subscribed, so as to have the privilege of securing seats in the theatre.

After three years in the capital, the Andersons felt quite at home. They never regretted their decision to settle in Washington rather than return to Ohio. Cincinnati compared very unfavorably in their eyes with the capital, and both Mr. and Mrs. Anderson were loathe to return even for visits. In December 1884, the death of an uncle forced the General to make the trip back to Cincinnati, where he complained to Larz: "I hate to come back. Cincinnati makes such a bad impression on me with its smoke, its dinginess, but I must go abroad and have my hand shaken." Vanity prodded him to add, "I was pleased, of course, to see all my relatives, who treated me with distinguished consideration."

Soon the General was grumbling just like a native Washingtonian about the "swarms of strangers" who infested the capital each season, about how the city was growing "in wealth and snobbery," and about its "vanity fair" quality. By 1891, such venerable old Washington institutions as the Bachelor's German, a social society that held a series of very select

The dining room of Anderson House was paneled in dark mahogany and featured two stained-glass windows by John La Farge and an inlaid portrait of Nicholas Anderson's father, Larz Anderson, attributed to Gilbert Stuart. The room was large—22 feet square—and uncluttered. From the built-in seat under the six windows along a concave wall, the Andersons could look to the left and see the White House a few blocks away. (*Artistic Houses*)

dances each winter, were seeking out the General as a patron. He was already a member of the city's prestigious Metropolitan and Alibi Clubs. In a city where many fashionables did not return from one season to the next, tenure of less than a decade entitled the Andersons to a place in the pantheon of "longtime" residents. In November 1891, the General wrote to Larz, "Eight years ago we moved into this house. How time passes! It does not seem so long, and now we are reckoned among the older residents of Washington, so shifting is its population."

The Andersons' letters to Larz also reveal just how hectic and varied social life at the pinnacle of Washington's high society was during the brilliant decade of the 1880s. The Andersons happily made the rounds of countless luncheons, dinners, parties, receptions, weddings, and balls, giving and attending a host of functions each week of the season.

Early in May 1883, Caroline Appleton Bonaparte, wife of Col. Jerome Bonaparte and granddaughter of Daniel Webster, took one hundred friends, including the Andersons, to a visiting circus. Afterwards, General Anderson described the fun to Larz and outlined the coming week's schedule: "Picnics are all the rage now. On Saturday we are invited to one given by the Secretaries of the British Legation on Rock Creek Road. Monday we go down the river by moonlight in aid of your mother's favorite charity, the Children's Hospital. Later Colonel Bliss [Alexander Bliss, son of Mrs. George Bancroft] gives his Great Falls excursion." These three outings were followed by a "gentlemen's dinner":

> Thirty of us gave a grand send-off dinner to Aristarchi [the popular Turkish Minister]. . . . I electrified the gang by making a speech in Greek, but Aristarchi and [Henry] Adams were the only two who knew I was reciting a poem of Anacreon's and they were so amused at the joke that they didn't expose me.

All this during the Andersons' very first spring in Washington, and in May, long after the busiest part of the season had passed. That fall, as another season began to unfold, General Anderson informed Larz that a few nights earlier he had been "invited to dine with the Secretary of War [Robert Todd Lincoln], but having the Secretary of State [Frederick Frelinghuysen] and the Attorney General [Benjamin Brewster] to dine with me, was forced to decline." Lest the impressive list of names sound boastful, the General hastened to add: "This sounds very grand and important, but it is in fact a very commonplace matter. Familiarity with men or things brings them down to a very ordinary level, and you will find as you advance in life that merit alone makes the man."

In the summer of 1884, the Andersons and other rich Republicans began to worry about the fall elections. "If a Democrat should be President," wrote the General, "our social cup of sorrow will be full." On November 5, when it looked as though Democrat Grover Cleveland had indeed beaten his friend James G. Blaine, General Anderson wrote to Larz, "I am not one of those who believe the country to be endangered by a change of administration, for in some respects it may be an advantage. . . . But our social life in Washington will not be changed for the better." In January 1885, returning from President Arthur's last diplomatic reception, the General lamented, "I rather imagine that the next four years will find us infrequent visitors in the Presidential residence."

In March, as the Democrats, who had been out of office for three decades, swarmed into Washington, General Anderson was in a conciliatory mood. He wrote to Larz a few days after Cleveland's inauguration:

> We in Washington have open-eyed amazement for the beginning of the new Administration, and wonder if the political millennium is come. Not only does Mr. Cleveland have as his motto *festina lente,* but he promises to observe the Civil Service Reform in its strictest sense. . . . This is simply marvelous!. . . . Can it last?

No, the General decided a few months later, it could not. Cleveland was not the great believer in civil service reform he claimed to be, and as more and more Republican heads rolled and other new Democratic policies chaffed the General, his assessment of the new administration grew more harsh. Grover Cleveland became "the obese head of government" and "the Buffalo sheriff." Though the Andersons entertained and were entertained by some of the new members of official society, they considered many affected. That fall the General wrote Larz:

> Your Mother begins to-day her winter season by lunching with Mrs. Adjutant General [Andrew] Drum to meet Mrs. Secretary of War [William] Endicott, where I presume she will also greet Mrs. Chief Justice [Melville Fuller], Mrs. Postmaster General [William Vilas] and other feminine adjuncts of the so-called Democratic Administration, but who, in defiance of their names and principles, air their titles and affect an aristocratic fondness for show, which is foreign to our institutions and at variance with

the preceding rules of political society. Put a beggar on horseback, and
everyone knows where he will ride.

Not surprisingly, as the Andersons' opinions became known, they began
to see less and less of the members of the new administration.

The Andersons' letters demonstrate that the tempo of Washington
high society was accelerating in the 1880s. Finding that all their balls, receptions, dinners, and card parties could barely be squeezed into the
long-established season, late December through April with a halt during
Lent, several hostesses began to nudge at the frontiers, scheduling more
and more events for early winter and paying no attention to the Easter
season. While the younger crowd responded enthusiastically, many of
the older members of society disapproved. In mid-March 1887, the
General grumbled, "A big *mi-carême* ball by the Bachelors to-morrow
evening awakes in me a little of the Puritan. I cannot justify a mid-Lent
spree as orthodox Christianity." A few days later, he noted with satisfaction, "Our mid-Lent ball was scarcely a success. In fact it was a dead failure, and people began to awake to the fact that gaiety is an epidemic,
like measles, and only when the fever is on, does it become delirious. All
attempts, before and after a 'season,' to rush things are likely to fail."

Apparently neither Mrs. Anderson nor Elsie shared the General's orthodox views. Though they did pause for Lent, over his objections they
planned dozens of dinners and accepted a score of invitations right up
until mid-June, when the city's intolerable heat forced the mass migration
of everyone who could afford to escape. In late spring 1887, the General
complained: "We are still dining out fast and furiously. . . . Two more dinners this week will, I hope, end the festivities in that line. . . . Elsie has
not lunched at home for the last twenty Saturdays and is invited out more
than any other girl in town."

The fall of 1888 brought the election of Benjamin Harrison, a
Midwesterner and a Civil War veteran like the General, and the reap-
pearance of many prominent Republicans in the capital. With his party
back at the helm, a friend in the White House, another friend, James G.
Blaine, in the cabinet as secretary of state, and still another, Robert Todd
Lincoln, in London as minister to the Court of St. James, the General had
but to let it be known that his son was looking for a "place" for Larz to
be offered the position of second secretary of the American legation in
London.

In October 1891 the Andersons began to plan an extended vacation

abroad. No sooner did word of their trip leak out than they were be-
sieged by families eager to rent their beautiful home. Housing, especially
elegant housing, was always scarce in Washington and so stunning a
house as theirs brought many offers—all turned down. The General
wrote Larz:

> The new Secretary of War, [Stephen] Elkins, has offered me anything (?)
> for my house for eighteen months. I accepted; your Mother declined. The
> reasons she assigned were the amount of damage which would be done
> the house by the public receptions which a Cabinet officer must give, and
> by the four small boys who form his family. So when we go to Europe,
> we shall close the house.

The Andersons sailed for Europe in the spring of 1892. Their first stop
was London, where Elsie was presented at court to Queen Victoria. From
England, they traveled on to Switzerland, where the General consulted
doctors about a worrisome illness. On September 18, 1892, he died in
Lucerne. There was never any question that Mrs. Anderson and Elsie
would return to Washington. The nation's capital had become their
home. The General, though a resident for little more than a decade, was
described in obituaries as a "long time Washingtonian."

The Washington McLean family, like the Andersons, arrived in
Washington in the early 1880s, but they represented a very different type
of newcomer. Like the Andersons, the McLeans were from Cincinnati, but
there the similarity ended. Back in Cincinnati, the Andersons had been
long-established members of the city's old, aristocratic elite. They did not
"know" the parvenu McLeans, who, while wealthier, represented unvarnished new money. The McLean and Anderson social circles seldom intersected in Ohio, and there would be little change in Washington. The
McLeans were attracted to the capital by a different siren's song than had
drawn the Andersons. Washington's chief attraction to this arriviste family was twofold: the political power concentrated there appealed to
Washington McLean's manipulative nature, while its high society's reputation for easy accessibility appealed to his wife, who had had little luck
buying her way into Cincinnati's elite circles.

Washington McLean was born in Cincinnati in 1816. He rose from
boilermaker's apprentice to owner of a boilermaking shop, made a fortune manufacturing Ohio River steamboats, and became involved in

Democratic politics. In the 1850s, he purchased the *Cincinnati Enquirer* and made it the leading Democratic mouthpiece of the Midwest. By 1880, McLean found his interest in Ohio politics waning as his interest in national politics grew. He and his ambitious wife decided to move to Washington, where their daughter, Mildred McLean Hazen, wife of Brigadier General and Chief Signal Officer William Hazen, was already a prominent hostess in official society. Dividing their time in the capital between a city mansion on fashionable K Street and a beautiful country estate named "Beauvoir," Mr. and Mrs. Washington McLean quickly became fixtures among the new "smart set" of parvenus in the capital.

After being asked to leave Harvard University, John R. McLean had gone to work for his father's *Enquirer*. He eventually took over the newspaper, as well as Ohio's Democratic party. After several visits to his parents' new home, however, he found, as his father had, that Washington held a greater fascination and the promise of greater power than did Cincinnati. On one of his early visits to K Street, John met his parents' new neighbors, the Beales, and fell in love with their youngest daughter, Emily. Old Washington society reacted with dismay and official society with surprise at the announcement of their engagement. General Beale, whose money was new but whose lineage was distinguished and old, had been welcomed back to Washington by the city's old aristocracy like a long lost son, and he was uncompromisingly Republican. The McLeans were pushy parvenus. Though he had not been in the city long, already John McLean had not made a good impression. Rumors circulated that he used blackmail and bribery in both journalism and politics, and he was a militant Democrat. Henry Adams, who was very fond of Emily Beale, was baffled by the match. McLean, Adams grumbled, represented "the cheaper, fatter, commoner measure of the Cincinnati regime."

Emily Beale and John R. McLean were married at the old Decatur mansion on Lafayette Square in 1884. Their union represented the merger of two of Washington's most socially and financially formidable newcomer families. Upon the deaths of their fathers (Washington McLean died in 1890, General Beale in 1893), both John and Emily Beale McLean inherited substantial fortunes. While their mothers and siblings remained active in Washington society, all were eclipsed by this ambitious young couple.

John McLean viewed social contacts as useful tools for extending the financial and political power he was beginning to wield in Washington, and he encouraged his wife to cultivate the capital's high society. She needed little urging. Emily Beale McLean was intelligent and witty and a skillful hostess. For the social campaign they planned to wage, the young McLeans wanted an "important" house, one that would surpass in magnificence the mansions of all the other rich newcomers in town. They hired New York architect John Russell Pope to design for them a Florentine Renaissance–style villa that took up an entire side of McPherson Square. The first floor, designed solely for entertaining, was decorated by the leading New York designer of the day, Elsie de Wolfe, in shades of mulberry. As McLean hoped it would, the house conveyed the sense of wealth and power that had belonged to the Renaissance princes.

John R. McLean and his wife Emily Beale McLean commissioned this enormous Florentine Renaissance-style mansion that covered one-third of a city block on the south side of McPherson Square. The entire thirty-foot-high first floor was designed solely for entertaining and included three huge reception rooms, a tapestry gallery, balconies, and fountains. The McLeans' huge house was demolished in 1939. (*The American Architect and Building News,* June 10, 1908; James Goode Collection, Library of Congress, Prints and Photographs Division)

From this palace, Emily Beale McLean set out to reign over Washington society as its queen. Her husband's newspapers readily bestowed the title upon her, but Washington society itself never did. Enthroned upon her high-backed Italian chairs in her enormous tapestry gallery, Mrs. McLean was until her death in 1912 the most regal of Washington's hostesses, but neither she nor any other woman was society's undisputed ruler.

Newcomers from "Pork Town"

Rich Chicagoans began arriving in Washington in the 1880s, and "Pork Town" eventually surpassed Ohio as a major source of newcomers flowing into the capital. In the vanguard were the Leiters, even wealthier than the McLeans and of just as recent vintage.

Levi Leiter was born in Maryland in 1834. At age nineteen, he headed west to seek his fortune, arriving in Chicago in 1854 when the city was booming. Leiter and two other store clerks, Marshall Field and Potter Palmer, pooled their resources and opened what became Chicago's preeminent department store. All three became millionaires within just a few years. Gradually, Leiter withdrew from the retail business, concentrating increasingly on his vast real estate holdings in Chicago and the West and on his mining investments. By 1881, when he was just forty-seven years old, Levi Leiter was worth more than six million dollars.

In 1866, Leiter had married Chicago schoolteacher Mary Teresa Carver. On their tenth wedding anniversary, when she realized that her husband was already worth several million dollars, Mrs. Leiter, whose social ambitions had been growing apace with her husband's fortune, decided that they should enter Chicago society. She worked indefatigably for various causes popular with the city's social elite, and Levi contributed generously to the city's cultural and charitable organizations. He supported the Art Institute and the Chicago Historical Society, and joined all the right clubs. Their efforts, however, met with only limited success. Said one newspaper gossip columnist, "The beef and pork element turned up its nose [at the Leiters]."

Rebuffed by Chicago's high society, the Leiters decided in 1883 to try their luck in Washington. Mrs. Leiter hoped to make matches for her three beautiful daughters that would put the "butchers" to shame. For their springboard into the capital's society, Levi Leiter paid an astounding $11,500 a year to rent the James G. Blaine house on Dupont Circle.

The Leiters' reasons for moving to Washington were uncomplicated. Mrs. Leiter was quite matter-of-fact about the situation: she wanted a glamorous social stage on which to perform and, if her husband's millions couldn't buy her entree in Chicago, she would try Washington, where other parvenus had already had great success. To their delight, the unaffected Leiters were indeed a hit in Washington. Their entertainments were spectacular but usually tasteful, and they had no political axes to grind. They wanted nothing more than the company of their famous guests, which included ambassadors, cabinet members, and William Corcoran. Mrs. Leiter threw herself into committee work to preserve Mt. Vernon, a project that brought her into contact with the "best ladies" in Washington. The elderly, extremely respectable historian George Bancroft and Levi Leiter shared a love of history and books and spent many evenings together. Mrs. Leiter was the recipient of vast bouquets of Bancroft's famed roses. Even the discriminating Henry Adams and Mr. and Mrs. John Hay soon became the Leiters' friends.

In 1891, the Leiters decided to build a home of their own in the capital. Mrs. Leiter, said Countess Cassini, "was naively pleased with her wealth" and "anxious that everyone else should be suitably impressed, too." They chose as their site a prime lot on Dupont Circle, the most fashionable part of town. Their enormous fifty-five-room white brick mansion dwarfed its little red neighbor, Stewart's Castle, and dominated Dupont Circle for half a century. The lot alone cost $83,000, the building $125,000, and the furnishings $300,000. Once ensconced in her palatial home, Mrs. Leiter soon became known as the "Duchess of Dupont Circle." Behind her back, she was also known as Washington's "Mrs. Malaprop." Mrs. Leiter once allegedly shocked guests by claiming that a dry-goods merchant constantly committed adultery—she meant that he adulterated his goods, a serious, but very different, offense. A hapless young attaché was once scornfully referred to by Mrs. Leiter as "no one important—only an *étagäre* of one of the embassies." After a stormy Atlantic crossing, Mrs. Leiter announced, "At last I am back on terra cotta."

Mrs. Leiter collected sculpture, silver and urns, but she always said her most beautiful possessions were her three daughters, Mary, Nancy, and Daisy. Mary Victoria was very beautiful, very smart, and, like her mother, very ambitious. She "came out" in Washington in 1888 and was the belle of the season. Her mother was delighted when Mary Victoria was befriended by Victoria Sackville-West, a mark of great distinction

In 1891 Chicago millionaire Levi Leiter built this enormous white brick house on the north side of Dupont Circle at New Hampshire Avenue and 19th Street. The mansion, with its fifty-five rooms and dramatic Ionic-columned porte cochere, dominated Dupont Circle until it was razed in 1947. (Frances Benjamin Johnston Collection, Library of Congress, Prints and Photographs Division)

conferred on few by the British minister's popular daughter. Mary Victoria Leiter also became close friends with First Lady Frances Folsom Cleveland and was a frequent guest at the White House.

Many thought Mary Leiter arrogant, but others, like Henry Adams and John Hay, found her enchanting. Cecil Spring-Rice, secretary of the British legation, was smitten by her, but her aims were higher than a lowly diplomat. "She never swerved," said Margaret Winthrop Chandler of her contemporary, "from her intention of making a great marriage, and she did." In 1890, on a visit to England, Mary met and fell in love with the Honorable George Curzon, the eldest son of Lord Scarsdale and a member of Parliament. Upon their engagement, her father gave her a dowry of three million dollars.

The marriage of Mary Leiter and George Curzon on April 22, 1895, at St. John's Episcopal Church on Lafayette Square, was the social event of the season. Washington's newspapers, as well as Chicago's, which belatedly sought to claim her, were filled with stories of the impending nuptials, of the groom's arrival with the family diamonds for his bride to wear on her wedding day, and of the Curzon estate of Kedleston. Mary Leiter's picture on a postcard was sold on street corners in both Washington and Chicago. Henry Adams, the Hays, the young Theodore Roosevelts, Mrs. Marshall Field, Mr. and Mrs. John R. McLean, Mr. and Mrs. Truxtun Beale, British Ambassador and Mrs. Pauncefote, almost the entire cabinet, First Lady Frances Folsom Cleveland, and a wide array of members representing all of the circles and subcircles of Washington's high society attended the wedding.

The Curzons honeymooned at Beauvoir, the McLeans' country estate, and then left for England. While sad to see her lovely daughter sail away, Mrs. Leiter was delighted with the match and felt avenged upon the Chicago "butchers" who had once snubbed her. Her joy was unbounded when, in 1898, her son-in-law was named Baron Curzon of Kedleston, Viceroy of India, by Queen Victoria. Photographs of Lady Curzon riding elephants and viewing the Taj Mahal, surrounded by hordes of servants, filled the American newspapers. News of Lord and Lady Curzon's exploits in exotic India filled the daydreams of countless young Washington girls who aspired to follow in the American-born vicereine's footsteps.

Newcomers from the West, the East, and the Capital's Own Backyard

While Bonanza Kings like William Stewart began to claim seats in Congress in the late 1860s and 70s, the first of the unofficial rich newcomers from the far West arrived in Washington in the 1880s. In the forefront was the Patten family from California.

Like most of the Western millionaires, the Pattens were looking for an Eastern city in which to gain a foothold in society, and Washington's social heights held out the promise of easy accessibility. And like many of the nouveaux riches, the Pattens quickly cast out lines and moored themselves alongside official society by entertaining and marrying into it. (For the latter undertaking, it helped to have eligible daughters, which the Pattens had in abundance.) The Pattens were unique, however, among newcomers in that the family was headed by a woman who ventured into the Washington social waters on her own, and they were very proudly Irish and devoutly Catholic.

Edmund Patten, born in Ireland, struck it rich in the American West. He mined a fortune in gold in California before he died suddenly in 1872. His strong-willed Irish-born widow Anastasia took her inheritance and her five young daughters, Katherine Augusta, Edythe Agnes, Josephine, Mary, and Nellie, to Europe for almost a decade, where the oldest girls were educated at a convent in Paris. In 1884, when Mrs. Patten brought her daughters back to the United States, she headed for Washington. Apparently she considered no other city when settling on the appropriate site for her daughters' introduction into American society. She established the younger girls at the highly respected Convent of the Visitation in Georgetown and built a massive, multicolored brick home just off Dupont Circle, where each successive daughter made her debut.

Unlike the obnoxious Oreillés (nee O'Rileys) in *The Gilded Age*, the Pattens had not been transformed into pseudo-Frenchwomen by their years in Paris. They were as militantly Irish and as staunchly Catholic when they returned to America as when they left. Though the Patten girls had been polished until they gleamed, their only accent was a softer version of their mother's pronounced Irish brogue. Their house on Massachusetts Avenue, which included its own chapel, became goodnaturedly known as "The Irish Legation."

The Pattens drew no national or sectarian lines in their hospitality. Nor did their Irishness or their Catholicism seem to hinder their rapid progress up the Washington social ladder. They were soon entertaining everybody and going everywhere in the capital. An 1887 newspaper account claimed the family was "at once received in the best circles of Society" in Washington. And indeed, within a very short time, invitations to Anastasia Patten's Sunday afternoon teas, where a visitor was likely to find the parlor filled with bishops, politicians, diplomats, and five pretty girls, were highly coveted.

Katherine Augusta Patten met and fell in love with John Milton Glover, a Democratic congressman from Missouri, at one of her mother's Sunday afternoons. Their lavish wedding in February 1887 was one of the many unions between official and newcomer society that year. Several hundred guests, including California Senator and Mrs. Leland Stanford (whose gifts to the newlyweds were a pendant of pearls and diamonds and solid gold opera glasses) and Senator-Elect and Mrs. George Hearst, friends from the California gold fields, watched as Katherine Augusta, preceded down the aisle by her four sisters, married Congressman Glover.

After Anastasia Patten's death in 1888, her four unmarried daughters continued to live together at the Patten mansion through the turn of the century, molding their "Sundays" into a Washington institution to which prominent visitors sought access. The Patten sisters were known as the chief stokers of the Washington gossip mill. For those who wanted to speed the spread of news, one wit prescribed, "Don't telegraph. Don't telephone. Tell-a-Patten."

During the 1880s, a rivulet of rich Easterners, both patrician and parvenu, joined the streams of Midwesterners and Westerners swelling the ranks of newcomer society in Washington. In 1887, the young Winthrop Chandlers, both from prominent old New York families, took a home in Washington for the season. Winthrop Chandler and Margaret Terry, a niece of Julia Ward Howe and Sam Ward, had been married in 1886, and spent that spring in New York amid a constant whirl of postnuptial celebrations. Warned that New York winters would be bad for Mrs. Chandler's delicate health, the newlyweds decided to spend the next season in Washington, where they had many friends, including the Henry Cabot Lodges and the Theodore Roosevelts, leaders of an ambitious new generation within official society.

Mrs. Chandler soon grew unhappy and restless in Washington. "There is no music," she complained, "No theatres to speak of, no operas, no university . . . few interests outside of politics and society." She was right, of course. But it was precisely for its politics and its society, not for its music or its universities, that so many other rich Americans prized the capital. The Chandlers tried living in New York; they traveled in Europe; but when their friends the Theodore Roosevelts settled into the White House, they became prominent fixtures in Washington high society and leaders of the "charming idlers," as Mrs. Chandler called her "set."

The Tuckerman family of New York found that the blend of society and politics in Washington, which so offended Mrs. Chandler, suited them perfectly. A wealthy New York iron manufacturer, Lucius Tuckerman was a founder of the Metropolitan Museum of Art. Despite his close ties to New York City, in 1881 failing health prompted Tuckerman to move to Washington, where the winters were milder but the society still delightful. He erected an unusual Romanesque-style home and filled it with his famous collection of paintings. Warmer winters notwithstanding, Lucius Tuckerman died in 1890, but his widow and children continued to play a prominent role in Washington society for two more decades.

While none were as rich as the wealthiest auslanders (no local fortunes could rival Levi Leiter's millions), during the 1880s several of Washington's newly rich native and near-native sons joined newcomer society. Among them was Brainerd Warner. Warner was recognized on the streets of Washington in the 1880s as the city's entrepreneur par excellence, but he had been an unknown country boy when he migrated to the city from a small town in Pennsylvania at the age of fifteen in 1863. He read law with Thaddeus Stevens, graduated from the Columbian Law School in 1869, and hitched his star to Alexander Shepherd's New Washington. Warner quickly became head of the city's largest real estate firm, founder and president of the Washington Loan and Trust Company, and president of the powerful Board of Trade. He built himself a huge red brick mansion on Millionaires Row (Massachusetts Avenue) above Dupont Circle and entertained with style.

Thomas Franklin Schneider, son of a German printer, was born in Washington in 1859. After an apprenticeship with the prestigious local architectural firm of Cluss and Schultz, which had designed Shepherd's Row, Stewart's Castle, and other prominent homes, Schneider set up his own firm in 1883. Within just five years, he accumulated a fortune by building entire blocks of handsome granite-faced townhouses. It was on his own fifty-room mansion near Dupont Circle, however, that Schneider lavished his greatest attention. Its stunning red and ivory ballroom, with its twenty-foot ceiling and stained-glass dome, awed even the most jaded waltzers. Unfortunately, the Schneiders, like several other overly ambitious couples, found maintaining their enormous house a financial burden. They moved into the Cairo, Schneider's acclaimed luxury apartment house, and rented their mansion first to the Chinese legation and later to wealthy New Jersey Senator John Fairfield Dryden, the founder of the Prudential Insurance Company.

The Tide of Newcomers Continues to Rise: The 1890s

During the 1890s, more rich Westerners, Midwesterners, and Easterners than ever before made Washington their social headquarters for the winter months. What one reporter dubbed "the nomadic community" grew each year: "Attracted by the social advantages of the capital, [they] reside at the hotels and boardinghouses, or take furnished residences or apartments for the season, spend their money freely, contribute to the gaiety of the winter, and flit off to Europe or to the watering places when the roses begin to bloom in the parks." This newest flock of rich newcomers were unpredictable birds of passage. Many of the earlier arrivals, like the Andersons and the Leiters, had pulled up stakes, moved their families to the capital, and settled in for an indefinite stay, summering in various fashionable spots, but returning to Washington every winter, season after season. These new newcomers were of a different migratory breed. They were members of an emerging, itinerant, national elite, who each year chose from a long menu of cities the spot where they would alight for the winter.

As the decade began, Washington was in the midst of a real estate boom. Scores of official and unofficial newcomers rushed to build or buy homes in the capital. Those who owned a pied-à-terre in Washington had little to lose. They knew that they could buy a residence in the capital, use it for entertaining a few months of the year, and, when they tired of the Washington scene, easily dispose of it and count on making a tidy profit.

The decade had barely begun to gather steam when ill financial winds blew over the city and the nation. Up until then, the capital had been relatively insulated. It had little heavy industry or commerce, few immigrants or labor unions. But even in this "city of leisure," by 1893 building enterprise had declined and wages had dropped. The full seriousness of the nationwide depression, however, didn't strike most Washingtonians until the spring of 1894, when "General" Jacob Coxey's ragtag "Army of the Unemployed" marched on the capital. This army of desperate men was a vivid manifestation of the hard times of which most residents had yet only heard rumors.

The depression ate away at both old and new fortunes. Late in July 1893, Henry Adams was called back to America from Switzerland by his brother Brooks to help determine the extent of the family's losses. A month later, from his home in Washington, Adams claimed that the depression had thrown the capital into turmoil. "For a thorough chaos," he wrote John Hay, visiting in London, "I have seen nothing since the war to compare with it. The world surely cannot long remain as mad as it is, without breaking into acute mania. Everyone looks on his neighbor as a dangerous lunatic." Several elegant Washington houses would not open for the coming season, Adams told Hay. Calvin Stewart Brice, the mil-

"At the Japanese Legation"

"Belles of Washington"

During the early 1890s, more and more magazines and journals ran flattering articles about Washington's glamorous high society, sending new waves of socially ambitious rich newcomers from the hinterlands to wash up on the city's beaches. In the spring of 1893, *Harper's* ran a long two-part article entitled "Washington Society," illustrated with a dozen lovely drawings of scenes from Washington's official and unofficial high society. (*Harper's,* March and April, 1893)

"The Jam at the Senator's"

lionaire Democratic senator from Ohio, who lived next door to Hay and Adams and also had a mansion on Fifth Avenue in New York, was, Adams reported, "busted, or, in his own words, is trying to find out whether he is busted for good or not. His family is supposed to be going abroad and the house is expected to be let."

Despite the darkened houses and Adams's dire predictions, the Panic of 1893 inflicted only a glancing blow upon Washington's newcomer society. By the mid-1890s, after only a brief ebb, the flow of rich newcomers resumed. "Pork Towners" continued to lead the way. Levi Leiter's former business partners, Marshall Field and Potter Palmer, and their wives, along with the extremely ambitious women of the Patterson and Medill-McCormick families, who had tried and failed to break into Newport society, were among the rich Chicagoans making winter forays to the capital. Prominent Chicagoans among the "younger set" wintering in Washington in the 1890s were the glamorous Mr. and Mrs. Reginald

DeKoven. Reginald DeKoven was well known as a composer of light opera and of the wedding standard "Oh Promise Me." Mrs. DeKoven was the daughter of millionaire and former Illinois Senator Charles Farwell, and she had spent her first seasons "in society" in Washington.

Chicago railroad car tycoon George Pullman and his wife, who had spent several seasons in Washington during the Grant years, brought their two daughters along for the winter season in the capital in the 1890s. A heavy contributor to the Republican party, Pullman came to the capital not only to enjoy the hospitality of the recipients of his largesse, but to press upon them his views on what was good for the nation and consequently for George Pullman. He was particularly interested in high tariffs, hard money, enforcement of patent rights, and discouraging regulation of sleeping-car rates. At his lavish entertainments he regularly exchanged advice on the stock market for information on legislation pertinent to his company.

The rest of the Midwest also continued to contribute rich newcomers to the capital. From Indiana came plow manufacturer Henry F. Blount and his wife, who turned the lovely old Dumbarton Oaks estate in Georgetown into one of the social and intellectual centers of the capital. The George Westinghouses were among Pittsburgh's first contributions to Washington society. For several winters the Westinghouses rented large homes in the city, but in 1899 they bought the James G. Blaine mansion on Dupont Circle. Their parties there became legendary—at one banquet, Mrs. Westinghouse enclosed a crisp one-hundred-dollar bill in every napkin.

The Hendersons of Missouri had been prominent members of official society in the 1860s. John Brooks Henderson had been a senator; his wife, Mary Foote Henderson, was the niece of Vermont Senator Solomon Foote. When the Hendersons returned to the capital as private citizens, built an enormous mansion atop Meridian Hill, and began to entertain on a grand scale in the early 1890s, they came as very rich newcomers. The long drive up 16th Street to the Hendersons' massive red sandstone home, designed by Thomas Franklin Schneider and known as "Hendersons' Castle," was impressive, and the guests who made the trip represented the best of both official and unofficial Washington society.

The Hendersons were connoisieurs of fine wine and food, and Mrs. Henderson had written several popular cookbooks. Her famous dinners became infamous when she suddenly became a vegetarian and denounced liquor, wine, coffee, and tea as poisons. Few turned down her invitations, but it was the conversation, not the food, they enjoyed. Mrs. Garret Hobart, wife of the vice president, was fond of Mrs. Henderson but had mixed feelings about the lumpy "something" her cook colored and molded into the shape of turkeys and fillets of beef.

Rich newcomers from older East Coast cities continued to flow into Washington as well. Two wealthy Philadelphia widows enlivened social seasons of the late 1890s: Mrs. George W. Childs, whose late husband had owned the *Philadelphia Ledger,* built a town house on K Street, and each year Mrs. Bloomfield Moore gave a pearl necklace to the young lady she deemed the most popular girl in Washington. New Yorkers also continued to find the capital attractive. These were the years, claimed Julia Foraker, when "the rich spectacular New York-crowd-with-the-names came over, took big houses, gave extravagant parties and exotically quickened the pace." Among the New Yorkers "with-the-names" in the capital in the 1890s were the John Trevors and the James Roosevelts. The Cornelius Vanderbilts occupied a huge house at Vermont and K Streets for several seasons. Their daughter Gladys, one of several Vanderbilt women to marry into European nobility, married the dashing Hungarian diplomat Count Szechenyi in a highly publicized wedding that brought New York's Four Hundred to Washington by the trainload.

Washington also continued to be the social mecca of the East for the Bonanza Kings. Among those who arrived in the 1890s was Tom Walsh of Colorado, perhaps the richest of them all. Born in Ireland in 1850, Walsh was building railroad bridges in Massachusetts when he caught gold fever and headed West. The summer of 1876 found him, along with Calamity Jane, Swill Barrel Jimmy, and Antelope Frank, penniless in Deadwood, South Dakota. Walsh married Carrie Bell, a schoolteacher in Leadville, Colorado, and together, year after year, they unsuccessfully chased rumors of rich strikes across the West. Finally, in the summer of 1896, their twenty-year-long streak of bad luck changed. Tom Walsh struck gold, and within months his Camp Bird Mine made him a millionaire.

The Walshes decided to move East. It would be a bitter tragedy, Mrs. Walsh argued, after laboring all those years isolated from the world, to be robbed of the well-earned good life. In 1897, Walsh announced that they were moving to Washington. His doctors had told him to seek a lower altitude, but almost any Eastern city had a lower altitude than the Rocky Mountains. Most likely he and his wife chose Washington after hearing reports from old mining friends like Horace Tabor and George Hearst of the glamour and ready acceptance that would await them in the nation's capital. In addition, it was becoming well known among the parvenus that a senator or president who had been assisted into office could be counted on to help the socially ambitious on their way up the Washington social ladder. Tom Walsh, known as the "Colorado Croesus," was a Republican and a generous one. (He could well afford to be: his Camp Bird Mine was producing five thousand dollars in gold each day.) He had supported William McKinley for president in 1896 and anticipated his rewards.

The Walshes took a large suite of rooms at a fashionable hotel, enrolled their children, Evalyn and Vinson, in the best private schools, and prepared to enter Washington society. Mrs. Walsh had never worn an evening gown and was embarrassed by her naked shoulders, but she overcame her modesty. The Walshes were quickly "taken up" by several Western senators and their wives, and Mrs. John R. McLean included Evalyn in the children's dancing class she sponsored. In no time at all, Evalyn rightly claimed, "we were in." One day, shortly after they had arrived in Washington, Evalyn recalled, "Vin and I were permitted, after washing our hands, to hold and examine something the postman delivered, a rectangle of cardboard, stiff, gold-edged, and bearing a gold shield. It was from the Executive Mansion—an invitation to Mr. and Mrs. Thomas Walsh to attend a reception at the White House."

Next the grateful president made Walsh a commissioner to the Paris Exposition. The Walshes occupied nearly a whole floor of the Elysée Palace Hotel. By day they visited the Exposition and by night, Tom Walsh gave sumptuous banquets that made him the talk of Paris. The highlight of the trip for him was entertaining King Leopold of Belgium, who promised to visit him in Washington.

As he sailed home, Walsh laid plans to build a Washington mansion commensurate with his escalating social status. When finished in 1903 at a cost of nine hundred thousand dollars, the mansion, known as "2020" after its Massachusetts Avenue street address, contained sixty rooms, including a rooftop garden and a gilded apartment on the third floor for King Leopold, and required a staff of twenty-three servants.

Success for the Second Generation

By 1900, the children of the first generation of rich newcomers to Washington were assuming positions of social prominence in their own

At the turn of the century, "Colorado Croesus" Tom Walsh spent $835,000 to build this sixty-room mansion at 2020 Massachusetts Avenue, NW, and almost as much again to furnish it. Gold and gilding were found throughout, from the gold brocade wall coverings to the dining-room table set with a service of gold made of nuggets from Walsh's Camp Bird Mine. Today "2020" is the Indonesian embassy. (Historical Society of Washington, D.C.)

right. Several highly publicized weddings confirmed in the parents' eyes the wisdom of their decision to move their families to the capital. To potential newcomers still back in Pittsburgh and St. Louis who were considering taking the plunge, these unions of wealth, power, and status affirmed that their dreams of social success in the nation's capital were not illusory.

Mary Leiter's much-publicized wedding to the Honorable George Curzon was only one of the unions so gratifying to the rich newcomers. Her sisters' marriages into the British aristocracy and Augusta Patten's happy marriage into official society were others. In 1901, after a thirteen-year hiatus, there was a second Patten wedding, again into official society. Edythe Patten, the next-to-youngest sister, married the charming widower General Henry C. Corbin, Adjutant General of the Army, one of President McKinley's most trusted aides, and the best "catch" in the capital.

The children of Nicholas and Elizabeth Anderson also married well and happily. Elsie Anderson married Philip Hamilton McMillan, the son of millionaire Michigan Senator James McMillan, and moved to Detroit, where she became one of that city's leading hostesses. After his father's death, Larz Anderson continued to move up the diplomatic ladder onto which his father's influence had given him a boost. While secretary of legation in Rome, he met eighteen-year-old Isabel Perkins of Boston. They became engaged after a two-year courtship by mail, and Larz resigned from the diplomatic corps in 1897 to return to the United States for their wedding. All of the nation's major newspapers carried stories about the impending Perkins-Anderson nuptials. Reporters disputed just how much Miss Perkins, the granddaughter and sole heir of New England millionaire William Wild, would inherit when she turned twenty-one, but all

Emily Beale McLean, whom her husband's newspapers called the "queen of Washington society," sits in the long gallery of McLean House beside her future daughter-in-law Evalyn Walsh about 1909. (Library of Congress, Prints and Photographs Division)

agreed that she was "one of the richest girls in the world." The *Chicago Tribune* put her likely inheritance at "upwards of $20,000,000."

Isabel Perkins was a member of an increasingly national high society. Newspapers reported on her high standing in Boston society as well as her membership in the "New York-Newport crowd." On the eve of her wedding, another newspaper noted that "all the 'four hundreds' from one end of the country to the other are on the *qui vive* of preparation, for both families are well known in all the principal cities of the North."

When the newlyweds returned to Washington from their year-long, around-the-world honeymoon, they built a mansion on Massachusetts Avenue that rivaled even Tom Walsh's home across the street. Built of seventeen types of marble and hung with costly French tapestries, Anderson House became the center of the young set's gayest entertainments.

The various marriages of two generations of McLean family members perhaps best illustrate the fluidity, and thus the continuing attraction, of Washington society. The children and grandchildren of Washington McLean married into official society, into the city's old families, and into a flamboyant family of arrivistes even richer than they. John R. McLean married into both the capital's old aristocracy and newcomer high society when he married Emily Beale. His sister Mildred, already the widow of one prominent military man, married into the heights of official society when she wed Admiral Dewey. In 1908, when John and Emily McLean's son Ned married Evalyn Walsh, daughter of Tom Walsh, two of the richest families of parvenus ever to come to the capital merged.

8 "Dying Snails"

The Old Elite Withdraws into Its Shell

What of the old Washington families, the descendants of the antebellum residential elite who had dominated the capital's high society from its beginning in 1800 until the Civil War? Surely all of them had not cast their lot with the Confederacy and fled to the South.

Many of the old Washington families did still reside in their ancestral homes in the capital in the years after the war. Their place in Washington high society, however, had changed dramatically. Once the city's undisputed social leaders, they found themselves outnumbered, outspent, and ignored by the members of the glamorous new official society inaugurated by the Grants and by the even more exuberant rich newcomers.

Under these adverse conditions, the members of the old residential elite struggled to carve out a niche for themselves in the New Washington. Their various strategies for survival met with limited success. By the end of the century, they had evolved into a well-defined group known as the Cave Dwellers. Though troglodytes, they were not on the brink of extinction. While they would never regain the glory of the antebellum years, they faced a new century as the widely recognized keepers of the flame of proper behavior and correct etiquette, and as the capital's living memory of its past.

The *"Antiques"*

Among the first outside observers to take note of the old families' diminished status after the war was Mark Twain. These were the families he
dubbed the "Antiques." Reporter Emily Edson Briggs, so fond of the ostentation of the new officials in town in the early 1870s, also took note of
the old families and commented on their bitterness and their eroding
clout. Describing their pained reaction to the capital's flashy new leaders,
Briggs derisively dismissed the "old aristocracy's" hauteur: "The few dying
snails of the old aristocracy drew coldly within their shells like the
monarchists under the Bonaparte reign." Other reporters branded the
members of the residential elite the "has beens." In 1884, *Century
Magazine* took note of the old families' place in the New Washington:
"The 'old resident' element which, in the days of Southern supremacy
before the war, ruled Washington society, is becoming every year more
and more in a minority, buried out of sight in the avalanche of Northern
wealth and numbers."

Though too preoccupied with their own declining status to see beyond Washington's borders, the Antiques were neither the first beleaguered elite to decry the decline of polite society nor the only one in late
nineteenth-century America. Nor was their reaction to their displacement,
specifically their disdain for the usurpers of their old prerogatives, unusual or new. It was the quite typical reaction of any elite that was becoming passé. As early as 1651, the leaders of the Massachusetts Bay
Colony expressed their "utter detestation" for the "men and women of
meane condition, education, and calling" who were taking "upon them
the garb of gentlemen." The Puritan fathers proved to be no more successful at protecting their prerogatives than the Antiques more than two
centuries later. The men of "meane condition" persisted in wearing "buttons or poynts at their knees" and the women "tiffany hoods or scarfs,"
just like their "betters."

Every fading elite sees in its own decline the disappearance of cherished virtues. Regret, anger, and sentimentality color their vision. At whatever point they sense their displacement, when they first feel the swirl of
the bath water and the tug of the drain at their feet, the members of the
elite being cast aside pronounce polite society dead. In the United States
in the years after the Civil War, the grumblings of Washington's "dying
snails" were just one voice in a chorus of lamentation rising up from the
nation's old Eastern cities. Polite society, in the eyes of each city's old

elite, was dying all over America; the epidemic, they were certain, was being spread by the nouveaux riches sweeping over the barricades of privilege and propriety and trampling out the old genteel culture.

Whether they were Washington Antiques, New York Knicker-bockers, Boston Brahmins, Huguenots in Charleston or the leading Quakers in Philadelphia, the old elites in America's cities shared much the same status and temperament in the late nineteenth century: their prestige was declining, and they were bitter. E. L. Godkin, who had been so optimistic as a young man at the war's end, lashed out angrily in mid-dle age at the "gaudy stream of bespangled, belaced, and beruffled bar-barians. . . . Who knows how to be rich in America? Plenty of people know how to get money; but . . . to be rich properly is, indeed, a fine art. It requires culture, imagination, and character." The old elites also shared a common popular image. To be called a Knickerbocker or a Brahmin implied much the same thing as did the Antique label: illustrious heritage, unassailable gentility, and unyielding propriety. Beneath a shared reputa-tion for haughtiness, however, each of the old elites was unique, shaped by the peculiarities of its own city's past. Each group of dying snails man-ifested their own particular anxieties and carved out their own special niche in the new social worlds that confronted them.

In Washington, the once-dominant residential elite evolved into Antiques amid a variety of circumstances unique to the nation's capital. Among them was the relative youth of Washington's oldest families. Boston, Philadelphia, and even New York could boast of families well into their fourth generations by 1790 when first-generation Washing-tonians were just settling in. The roots of Washington's oldest families were shallow. They had not sunk as deeply into the city's thin soil, nor entwined themselves as tightly within the city's unusual power system as had their counterparts in other cities. The Antiques were only ancient rel-ative to the hordes of transients who passed through the capital in two, four, and six-year cycles.

The presence of large numbers of transients was another important factor adversely affecting the capital's residential elite. Every elite—social, political, or professional—needs new recruits to continue. At the same time, it is essential that an elite group exercise tight control over the ad-mission of new members to its ranks if it is going to maintain its high sta-tus. Open the doors too wide, make admission too easy, and chaos re-sults. Status plummets. The coveted aura of exclusivity evaporates. Potential recruits lose interest. While all of the nation's old urban elites eventually faced the problem of assimilating large numbers of new members, Washington's Antiques confronted it earlier than most.

During the antebellum years, the old families of Boston, New York, and Philadelphia had been able to absorb new members gradually, after careful scrutiny. This leisurely assessment of likely candidates and their eventual acceptance only after years of apprenticeship was denied Washington's residential elite. From the capital's very beginnings, wealthy men—strangers from faraway places, of unknown pedigree, with dubiously acquired fortunes—descended upon the city after each election. And because of their official position, over which the old families could exercise no control, these newcomers instantly became members of official society. Before residents could evaluate their credentials and decide whether or not to admit them into their own more select elite, they were gone.

The very fact that such a concretely defined rival elite as official society existed at all was perhaps the most distinctive feature of the capital that shaped Washington's Antiques. There was no uncertainty about membership in official society, no heart-burnings over whether one would pass muster with older members. If one held a certain office, one's membership was guaranteed. Neither divorce, nor drunkenness, nor any other sort of misbehavior that stopped short of incurring expulsion from office could get a member thrown out of official society. Not only was its membership ironclad but official society also operated according to a rigid, well-defined protocol, which left no room for discretionary behavior. The notion that good breeding, elegant manners, and *quality* did not enter into the equation of acceptability for this official elite was anathema to the old families, who took such pride in the select nature of their group.

The fact that Washington was the capital of a nation being transformed by industrialization and bureaucratization also guaranteed that its eminent old families were destined to play a progressively smaller and smaller part in the capital's society. The ever-lengthening list of high-ranking officials constantly diminished the importance of the local aristocracy. With no elected officials of their own in Congress and thus no claim to patronage, and few job alternatives in the small local private sector, the old families from the Civil War onward watched their sons leave Washington to pursue careers elsewhere. Their daughters stayed behind a little longer and married, but with fewer and fewer native sons on hand many of them married government officials and, at the end of an administration, left with their husbands on the ebb tide. This steady trickling out of the city's human resources eventually eroded the core of influential old families conditioned by generations of devoted service and interest in local affairs.

Washington's youth, transitory population, and separate sets of official and residential social leaders, one growing and one not, all abetted the transformation of the old families from the capital's premier antebellum social elite into superfluous postwar Antiques. In addition, during the war, Washington's old families suffered a special, devastating blow more concrete and dramatic than any other city's old elite would endure. The core of the antebellum capital's old residential elite had been Southern and Democratic, with fortunes based on slaves and land in Maryland and Virginia. Their ranks were decimated by the war just as surely as the ranks of soldiers in blue and gray had been mowed down on the battlefields.

The social vacuum created in Washington by the Civil War was not total. A few Southern sympathizers, like William Corcoran, regained their old privileged positions. And there also remained a handful of prominent old families who had tried to remain neutral or sided with the North, like the Riggs, Carroll, and Mercer families, and the large Blair clan. But all of these together, added to the little band of old military families that had long chosen Washington as home base, formed too small a foundation upon which to rebuild a formidable residential social elite capable of dominating a capital now bulging with ambitious new Republican officials from the North.

A Policy of Gradual Disengagement

Almost immediately after the war, one group of disgruntled old residents took steps to distance themselves from the official and unofficial newcomers whom they regarded as "the mushroom aristocracy." In 1865, thirty-one of the capital's longest residents established the Association of Oldest Inhabitants of the District of Columbia—the Antiques' first and most self-conscious attempt to draw a boundary between themselves and the "intruders." William Corcoran was among the first members, as was Peter Force, mayor of the District in the 1830s, John Carroll Brent, descendant of two of Maryland's oldest families, and Colonel Benjamin Ogle Tayloe, who claimed to be *the* very oldest inhabitant, having arrived in the city in 1801 in time for Thomas Jefferson's inauguration.

The Oldest Inhabitants unanimously adopted a constitution committing members to

> cement and strengthen the interest and associations arising out of a common residence for a long period in the same locality; to keep alive the reminiscences of the past and the society and paternal communion of the present and the future. Assuming that, as the oldest residents of the District, we cherish the greatest solicitude for its welfare, it will be for the association to lend its aid in every way to its prosperity and improvement in good order, right government, and social intercourse, in hospitality, and in courtesy and respect to all public functionaries and authorities, without regard to section or political distinction.

While the founders readily agreed upon the Association's purposes, the question of whom to admit besides themselves fostered much debate.

Members of Washington's Association of Oldest Inhabitants, established in 1865, pose for the camera around 1870. (Historical Society of Washington, D.C.)

Finally the requirements for admission were set: any white male over the age of fifty who had been a resident of the District of Columbia for forty-five years could join and attend the Association's meetings, held the first Wednesday of each month. Left unstated in these specific requirements was still another attribute, perhaps the most important one, required for membership—good personal character.

The Oldest Inhabitants Association consistently attracted men of sterling character. Its membership list was a roll call of Antiquedom. However, while "cherishing the greatest solicitude" for the city's welfare, the Association proved powerless to rout any evils or make any changes. Its members were without clout. When proffered, their collective wisdom, the accumulation of decades of familiarity with the capital, was ignored by the new men capriciously awarded positions of power that old residents like Peter Force had once so conscientiously held. The Association was quickly reduced to a purely social organization, able to live up to only the first part of its constitution, the part which required it to keep alive the city's history, by the reading of historical papers to assemblages of members and their many women guests.

By establishing the Association of Oldest Inhabitants in 1865, the Antiques reacted to their declining status in much the same way as did the Brahmins, the Knickerbockers, and the other old urban elites who would soon found similar organizations: in New York City, the St. Nicholas Club (1875) and the Holland Society (1885); in Charleston, the Huguenot Society (1885); and even in Los Angeles, the Society of the Pioneers of Los Angeles County (1897). The establishment of these local genealogical and historical societies coincided with the founding of a host of similar national patriotic societies that looked to the past: the Colonial Order of the Acorn, the Order of Colonial Lords of Manors in America, the Colonial Dames of America, the Order of Colonial Dames, and the Sons, the Daughters, and the Children of the American Revolution.

The impetus behind these organizations almost always came from the same groups, the fading urban patriciates, and for the same reasons: to perpetuate the memory of their illustrious families, commemorate their long and intimate connections with the nation or city with which they so strongly identified, and provide a congenial setting where lineage outweighed wealth and the past meant more than the present. Through genealogical and historical research, members could keep alive old reassuring traditions and envelop themselves in the glory of their forefathers. Such organizations provided, as one Knickerbocker noted of New York's

Holland Society, a refuge "when a race is being outnumbered and over-run in its own land."

At first, it seems surprising and more than a little ironic that the "old-est inhabitants" of one of the East Coast's newest cities should be among the first to band together to keep alive memories of their relatively short past. In the chaos of the Civil War and its aftermath, however, Washington's old families were among the first to see into the future, and to see that it would no longer be theirs to shape. By 1865, it was evident in Washington that the days of prominence for all old elites based on kin-ship and tradition were numbered. The oldest inhabitants of the young capital city saw clearly the handwriting on their wall that was just be-coming legible to others like them in much older cities.

While the Association of Oldest Inhabitants was an early example of the Antiques' efforts to distance themselves from the official and unoffi-cial newcomers, the policy of disengagement developed gradually. Save for a few unreconstructed Southerners, most members of the first gener-ation of postwar Antiques were actually cordial to well-bred newcomers, even Northerners, like the ancient and eminent historian George Bancroft, and Republicans, like the gracious Hamilton Fishes. The divid-ing line between admission to or exclusion from their select group at first fell not between government officials and private citizens, Northerners and Southerners, Republicans and Democrats, temporary and permanent residents, or even between the affluent and the moderately well off. High standards of personal behavior and gentility were the principal criteria for admission into Antique drawingrooms.

Above all else, the Antiques were formidably correct. They were united by a shared dislike of bad manners and ill breeding. Twain cap-tured the unyielding formality of two august female members of Washington's "ancient nobility" in the fictional Mrs. Major-General Fulke-Fulkerson and her daughter, the antithesis of the Oreillés, who exuded the same contempt for all things new and gaudy as their real-life coun-terparts. The Fulke-Fulkersons paid a call to scrutinize newcomer Laura Hawkins shortly after her arrival in the capital:

> They drove up at one in the afternoon in a rather antiquated vehicle with a faded coat of arms on the panels, an aged white-wooled negro coach-man on the box and a younger darkey beside him—the footman. Both of these servants were dressed in dull brown livery that had seen consider-able service.

The ladies entered the drawing-room in full character; that is to say, with Elizabethan stateliness on the part of the dowager, and an easy grace and dignity on the part of the young lady that had a nameless something about it that suggested conscious superiority. The dresses of both ladies were exceedingly rich as to material, but as notably modest as to color and ornament. All parties having seated themselves, the dowager delivered herself of a remark that was not unusual in its form, and yet it came from her lips with the impressiveness of Scripture: "The weather has been unpropitious of late, Miss Hawkins."

By the early 1870s, as revelations of corruption began to ooze out of every branch of the Grant administration and official society reveled in increasingly showy receptions, the Antiques' initial cordiality toward the newcomers began to chill. So many new men and women of every stripe—official, unofficial, Northern, Western, Republican—were pouring into the capital at such a rapid rate that careful assessment of their credentials of gentility was impossible. There was no time for the Antiques to separate the social wheat from the chaff, not enough calling days in the season for them to drive up to each newcomer's door to scrutinize the behavior and plumage of these new birds of passage. As their ability to access the superficial trappings of the newcomers' gentility decreased, the Antiques' emphasis on more easily measured, and less easily bought, evidence of distinction, such as family lineage and length of residence in Washington, increased. Just as these became the qualities they looked for in others, these were the qualities that the Antiques began to boast of themselves.

Increasingly the Antiques gathered into their stately homes centered around Lafayette Square and wrapped themselves in the comforting mantle of genealogy. Journalist Mary Abigail Dodge noted in 1876 that "the old citizens are more likely to be proud of their poverty, and are far more inclined to take on airs over aristocratic seediness than over any parvenu wealth." A long line of illustrious ancestors, preferably based in the capital, became essential for membership in the Antiques' elite circle. One old Washington grande dame proudly let it be known that she kept her grandmother's visiting list and only the descendants of that lady's contemporaries appeared on her own lists for calling.

When eyeing new recruits, the early Antiques were prepared to waive long residence in Washington in favor of illustrious ancestors. Thus, New York Knickerbockers Hamilton and Julia Fish were welcomed into their genteel company, but Territorial Governor Alexander Shepherd, a local-boy-made-good, was not. Shepherd's family, though established in Washington for over half a century, was middling poor, his fortune was freshly and possibly illegally made, and his lifestyle was unacceptably exuberant.

The newly married Henry and Marian Adams were welcomed by the Antiques on both counts when they moved to Washington in 1877. Not only were they from illustrious New England families, but Henry's great-grandfather and grandfather had been presidents of the United States who had mingled with and respected the local population. Both Presidents John and John Quincy Adams were still favorably remembered in the capital as sticklers for proper etiquette.

Even Henry Adams's seemingly impeccable pedigree, however, did not satisfy the haughtiest of the Antiques. The old Blair family had a reputation for both hotheadedness and arrogance and the latter had been inherited in abundance by Violet Blair Janin, the granddaughter of Frances Preston Blair. Much to her annoyance, Mrs. Janin shared Lafayette Square with the Adamses, whom she regarded as upstarts. On January 10, 1883, displeased by some witty remark of Adams's making the rounds, she angrily noted in her diary:

> The Adams [sic] . . . run altogether on the fact of having two dead presidents in the family. Of course it may be nicer to have had your great-grandfather and grandfather presidents than to be one yourself, still as those who went before the great grandfather were very plain people, we of older blood do not think him [Henry Adams] such a great aristocrat.

Determining just who among the newcomers were "of older blood" and thus worthy of admittance to their circle became a major preoccupation for the Antiques. As for the already anointed members, they, as one of their daughters noted, began to view themselves "as a race apart." In John Marquand's *The Late George Apley,* a novel about the withering influence of Boston's Brahmins, Apley's Aunt Amelia tells him she comforts herself with thoughts of her good breeding: "Whenever I am depressed I remember I am an Apley." To the south of Boston, real-life Antiques like Mrs. Janin echoed Aunt Amelia's sentiments and found balm for their wounded status in their pedigrees.

By the mid-1870s, the Antiques' emphasis on pedigree was growing apace with their mounting antipathy toward the members of official society and the rich newcomers with no official position. Yet although nearly all of official and newcomer society was viewed with contempt by the old Washington blue bloods, the members of these two groups seemed scarcely aware of any lack of welcome. On the contrary, the officials and the rich newcomers justifiably felt themselves to be in command and attributed to envy alone the aloofness of the arrogant old residents who regarded them as social carpetbaggers.

It was more than envy, however, that fueled the Antiques' smoldering resentment. Not envy, or eclipsed wealth, or disgust with the ostentation of the parvenus alone explained the fissure widening between official and newcomer society and the Antiques. Most broadly put, the Antiques and their counterparts in other cities despised the newly rich and powerful because they believed they were corrupting American life and vulgarizing its culture.

Old aristocrats everywhere disliked everything that the new achievers represented, whether they were Washington politicos, Boston mill owners, or New York financiers. These brash, disrespectful interlopers were free from ties to the past and to any community. They could move anywhere and adjust to anything in search of opportunity. Free of ties to the past, these unfettered men could, as Frederic Jaher sums up, "more easily meet the needs of a rationalized, bureaucratically structured, dynamic social system. Against the modern demands for efficiency, mobility, adaptability, innovation, objectivity, achievement, and coordination, the genteel objectors raised only the feeble claims of loyalty, sentiment, inheritance, tradition, community, and authority." More than envious, the old aristocrats were bitter at a world that no longer required or valued their cherished attributes.

The old elites' general bitterness and mistrust took on a special dimension in Washington, where complete unknowns continually popped up to demand all of the deference due their official position. As the second Grant administration and its scandals unfolded, the Antiques emphasized more and more strongly the distinctions they drew between authentic quality (the type they possessed) and artificial quality (the type the officials possessed). Outspoken Antiques bemoaned the passing of the gentleman politicians still fresh in their memories of the antebellum capital. All of the gentlemen of the "statesmen series" who had ruled the nation in her youth were gone, lamented one old Southern Democrat, replaced by "politicians," the most derogatory term in her lexicon.

The Antiques Take Care of Their Own

Hand in hand with the Antiques' disdain for both official and unofficial newcomers and their preoccupation with the past was the increasing importance they placed on civic responsibility. While there was much the Antiques disliked about the newcomers, they especially resented their disregard for the day-to-day concerns of the capital city. It was an old irritant, which had chaffed ever since the two groups had first been thrown together in the early 1800s. The first officials to arrive in the capital in the 1790s held it in contempt and many of their successors did the same. Most officials and rich newcomers in the postbellum capital regarded Washington as a city that existed to give them pleasure while they were in residence a few months of the year. With few exceptions, they were blind to the capital's squalid alley dwellings filled with the families of freedmen and the rows upon rows of modest little houses filled with middle-class government employees.

At the turn of the century, Washington Episcopal Bishop Henry Y. Satterlee expressed the pent-up resentment of the capital's old families, who made up a large portion of his congregation, when he denounced from the pulpit those temporary residents of the capital who

> while they bring wealth, magnificence and luxury to the capital of the country, are, as a rule, actuated by no sense of civic, moral or religious obligation regarding the welfare of the community, and it is a very serious question whether the material advantages that they bring are any compensation for the atmosphere of careless irresponsibility which they create.

The absence of any sense of "civil, moral or religious obligations" among the newcomers enabled the Antiques to continue to control at least one aspect of life in Washington. Though pushed from the social pinnacle, the Antiques cornered the market on civic responsibility by default. Though praised by none save their peers, they would clothe Washington's poor, feed its hungry, house its orphans and lunatics, and educate its children.

The Washington City Orphan Asylum, the Guardian Society, the children's branch of the Washington Humane Society, and the House of Correction for Boys, which local citizens had opened in 1866 on a farm above Georgetown, were among the favorite charities of well-meaning

Antiques. Of these, the Washington City Orphan Asylum was the oldest and most cherished. Founded in 1815 by Marcia Burnes Van Ness, whose father's farm had once flourished where the White House stood, and Mrs. Obadiah Brown, wife of the pastor of the First Baptist Church, it had long enjoyed the strong support of the city's most august families. Women like Elizabeth Blair Lee, who joined the board of the Asylum in 1849 and served as directress from 1862 until 1906, devoted countless hours to its operations. In the face of insufficient federal funds for health care, the old families also generously supported Garfield, Providence, Freedmen's, and Children's hospitals, the Home for Incurables, and the Columbia Lying-In Asylum, which Congress chartered and then abandoned. In the severe winters of 1878–79 and 1893–94, it was a citizens' committee of longtime residents that raised money to buy food, fuel, and clothing for the poor.

Among these charitable institutions, one founded by the wealthiest and most prominent Antique, financier William Corcoran, was also the most symbolic. Antiques, as Corcoran's example shows, looked after their own if they had the means. After his return to Washington from Europe at the close of the Civil War, Corcoran channeled his considerable philanthropy toward rebuilding the South and caring for those cut adrift by the fighting. He financed the rebuilding of schools and churches destroyed by the conflict, paid for the creation and upkeep of cemeteries for the Confederate dead, and set up pensions for impoverished widows and orphans throughout the South. In 1869, Corcoran focused his benevolence on his home town and his less fortunate fellow Antiques. He announced the establishment of the Louise Home in Washington as a memorial to his beloved wife and daughter, for whom it would be named. As Corcoran envisioned it, the Louise Home was intended "for the comfortable maintenance and support . . . of destitute but refined gentlewomen," with priority given to those who were loyal daughters of the South and the descendants of Washington's oldest families. The Louise Home, which Corcoran endowed with $250,000, opened in a beautiful Second Empire-style building, built at a cost of $200,000, on Massachusetts Avenue in the spring of 1871.

Corcoran was ever mindful of the pride of the gentlewomen who would inhabit the Louise Home. They were, after all, as one reporter noted, "educated and accomplished, having basked in the bright sunshine of comfortable means until the dark day came, and the cloud of misfortune burst ruthlessly upon them." Corcoran sought to give them the same elegance of surroundings they had once enjoyed. Paintings and

A native son, financier
William Corcoran amassed a
fortune by selling millions of
dollars of government bonds
in England to underwrite the
Mexican War. During the
Civil War, Corcoran's loyal-
ties lay with the South, and
he left Washington to wait
out the war in Europe. He
was one of the few Southern
sympathizers to return to
Washington whose reputa-
tion and place in society
were undiminished. (Library
of Congress, Prints and
Photographs Division)

statuary from his extensive personal collection added opulence to the
marble halls, black walnut-paneled library, and high-ceilinged drawingrooms. In these surroundings would dwell the kin of Confederate officers
and old Washingtonians, such as Mrs. Letitia Tyler Semple, daughter of
President John Tyler of Virginia. When he learned of a case of economic
hardship from friends, as in the case of Miss Letty Lewis from her brother-
in-law Smithsonian archeologist William Henry Holmes, Corcoran would
graciously write to "invite" the lady to be his "guest" at the Louise Home.
Miss Lewis just as graciously accepted, telling Corcoran his Louise Home
was "the most noble, the most tender and touching tribute that ever the
knighthood of a man's heart has offered to womanhood, to age, or to
misfortune."

Each year the "guests" at the Home expressed their gratitude by
throwing Corcoran a birthday party. Marian and Henry Adams attended
the festivities for their friend and landlord in December 1881, and Marian

William Corcoran established the Louise Home, opened in 1871, as a "last refuge" for "destitute but refined and educated gentlewomen." The building was designed in the Second Empire style that Corcoran had admired in Paris. The Louise Home's elegant interior rooms, decorated with art from Corcoran's own extensive collection, were to remind his "guests" of better days. The Louise Home was razed in 1949. (Historical Society of Washington, D.C.)

described the event for her father: "Tuesday, a birthday party, in honour of Mr. Corcoran's eighty-third year, at the Louise Home, his almshouse for some forty decayed gentlewomen. It was from eight to ten and really very pleasant; the Solid South of course, but others beside."

As he grew older, Corcoran grew increasingly concerned about the fate of the Louise Home after his death. In 1879, he once again spelled out his criteria for admission and emphasized

> the absolute necessity of selecting for future appointment ladies cultured and refined, whose dignified bearing will render them a desirable acquisition to the home. Let them also be chosen from that class of individuals who have known brighter days and fairer prospects, yet who through

reverses that human foresight could not obviate have been compelled to contend with adverse circumstances, while the sensibilities of their nature interposed an insuperable obstacle to their personal solicitation for aid.

Corcoran's wishes were strictly adhered to for many years after his death in 1888. Isabel McKenna Duffield, daughter of Supreme Court Justice Joseph McKenna, described the Home in the 1890s as the

> last port of comfort and ease for those gentle-bred women bereft of the support of their mankind, for there was then a slight odium attached to the idea of self-support for those born to the purple. Within those kindly red brick walls on Massachusetts Avenue many a former great hostess, a daughter of a President, an unfortunate widow of the South, or a spinster of renown, donned her best silk on reception days, and served tea and cherry bounce—"made in Georgia, my dear, by a relative of the Lee family"—behind the lustre of her own tea set.

The institutions that the old families founded and to which they proudly pledged allegiance were not all charitable. Even the Antiques occasionally enjoyed an evening of entertainment, provided all was done decorously. The dances given each winter by the Bachelor's German Club, their premier social organization, were the highlights of the Antiques' social season. "The Bachelor's" had been established in 1868 by many of the same men who had founded the Association of Oldest Inhabitants three years earlier and for many of the same reasons. They were revolted by the rising tide of opulence welling up around them and wished to draw a boundary between themselves and the arrivistes. In contrast to the newcomers' extravaganzas, the Bachelor's germans would be tasteful affairs held three or four times each winter, serving simple food in simply decorated halls, for refined guests who enjoyed dancing and conversation with their peers.

The Bachelor's exclusivity was controlled by a small nucleus of members. While invitations to the upcoming season's germans went out to as many as four hundred potential subscribers, subscription did not mean membership. Membership was limited to only about fifty men, and the membership list included the names of some of the oldest, most distinguished residents of the capital—Chew, Blair, Rodgers, Meigs. A board of governors and the chairmen of a host of committees—hall, engraving, flowers, music, supper, floor, and so on—were chosen from among the members and charged with the minutiae of maintaining the dignity of the germans. The chairman of the dressing room committee, for example, was admonished to be sure that "the W. C. is ventilated before hand and proper paper placed there." The chairman of the supper committee was to quiz the caterer about the costs of a modest buffet to include bouillon, tea, coffee, lemonade, ices, cakes, chicken croquettes, peas, oysters, chicken salad, potato salad, and beer and sandwiches for the musicians. "A *good* floor," read the instructions to the floor committee, "is of the first importance and the floor committee must watch closely to insure it—see that it is properly waxed, avoid too much wax, and is *slippery,* at least eight or ten hours before the Cotillion."

In the 1880s, as rich newcomers were pouring into Washington, the leaders of the Bachelor's became increasingly concerned with preserving the selectness of their group. In 1886–87, they issued an admonition to all members reminding them that the club

> should be kept for older Washingtonians rather than for the modern. The Club is a purely social one and should be kept free of the slightest suspicion of influence—Army, Navy, Political, Diplomatic, or Personal—The qualifications for either an invitation or membership should be the same—high social prestige, high cultivated and distinguished qualities, above all congenial to the body as a whole—It has been customary to choose the ladies to receive from the older residents . . . to avoid those who will without doubt ruin the Bachelor's German.

The members took pains to insure that their dances would stand in marked contrast to the showy affairs of the newcomers, where long buffets groaned under a plethora of expensive dishes and young ladies vied to see who would receive the greatest number of costly bouquets. Among the club's guidelines in 1888–89 were many that reflected these concerns:

> The german shall be a simple affair: dancing to be the feature rather than an elaborate supper or expensive decoration.

> The members shall let it be known that no lady will be allowed to carry bouquets into the ballroom.

> Every name for membership or invitation shall be submitted to the committee to be rigidly inspected and considered from a purely social standpoint.

> Two black balls exclude any name.

Gentlemen whose names have been proposed for membership—if not known personally—should be visited by one or more committee men and a report made if possible.

Again in 1888–89, on the Bachelor's twentieth anniversary, the governors reminded the membership:

The cooperation of members is necessary in keeping up the high standard which the Club has maintained for so many years. It is well understood that one uncongenial member can cause breaking up of the organization. It is therefore necessary to be particular in proposing for membership—not only the man himself but his associations should be known as far as possible.

The leaders of the Bachelor's had cause to worry. As family lines died out and native sons drifted away from the capital, it became harder and harder to find representatives of the city's oldest families to replace the club's aging founders. Members were forced to reconsider their proscription against newcomers in their search for recruits. While finally forced to compromise their old rule that the club "should be kept for older Washingtonians," however, members did not relax their standards for "high social prestige, high cultivated and distinguished qualities." It might be expedient to look for new members among the "modern element," but they could not be oafs or bores. The new blood flowing into the Bachelor's in the 1880s included Truxton Beall, the son of General Edward Beall, William Corcoran Eustis, grandson of William Corcoran, and Nicholas Longworth Anderson and Senator Thomas Francis Bayard, Sr, who represented the oldest and most refined families of Ohio and Delaware.

Still Flawlessly Correct

While increasingly identified with their veneration for long-dead ancestors, their disdain for officials and newcomers, and their pride in their relatively deep roots in Washington, the evolving Antiques never lost their strong, early identification with flawless etiquette. Their dominion over this arcane subject was conceded by the members of the capital's other social circles.

No one staked the Antiques' claim to impeccable correctness more assertively than Madeleine Vinton Dahlgren. The daughter of Samuel Vinton, a prominent Whig congressman from Ohio, Mrs. Dahlgren had grown up in Washington. In 1846 she married Daniel Goddard, assistant secretary of the newly formed Interior Department. After Goddard's death just five years later, she and their two children moved into her father's home, where she acted as his official hostess for more than a decade until his death in 1862. In 1865 she married Rear Admiral John Adolphus Dahlgren, a wealthy widower known for his contributions to the United States Coastal Survey and his work in naval ordinance. Together Admiral and Mrs. Dahlgren became one of the most prominent couples among the postwar capital's social, scientific, military, and intellectual elites.

After the Admiral's death in 1871, Mrs. Dahlgren retained her high status in Washington society and achieved prominence on her own as a leader of charitable activities, the author of many short stories and essays, and a founder of the Washington Literary Society in 1873. After his visit to Washington in 1882, Henry James drew a fictionalized portrait of the formidable Mrs. Dahlgren, then at the height of her powers, in his short story "Pandora." She appears thinly disguised as Mrs. Steuben, the grand dame of Washington society whose home was a famous literary meeting place. Mrs. Steuben "was the widow of a commodore," and, like Mrs. Dahlgren, who had the same scent about her, "had about her a positive strong odour of Washington." Mrs. Dahlgren was also one of several women in Washington who bore a striking resemblance to Madeleine Lee, the heroine of Henry Adams's *Democracy*. Both women were strong-willed; both had lost distinguished husbands; both restlessly sought outlets for their reformist drives; and, ultimately, after shedding their widow's weeds, both tried to refine Washington society. The fictional Mrs. Lee sought to improve one small corner of society by turning her elegant parlor into an exclusive salon. Mrs. Dahlgren was not content with so limited and passive a response. Hers was far more grand and direct. Mrs. Dahlgren was an activist for erudition and refinement.

Mrs. Dahlgren's hand in cultivating high moral purpose was most clearly visible in the Washington Literary Society. She wished "the Literary" to cast "a radiance over the conventional inanity of social life in Washington." It was to this end that she attempted to dominate the club's executive committee, leading one irritated cofounder to refer to it privately as the "Dahlgren Society." Mrs. Dahlgren abhorred controversy and spirited polemics and sought always to maintain decorous harmony. "Our aim and purpose is to *assimilate contraries,"* she proclaimed. "The Society claims to be neutral ground rather than a battlefield." Those instances when meetings of "the Literary" rose above readings of conventional poetry and lectures on world travels to challenge entrenched orthodoxies occurred despite Mrs Dahlgren's best efforts.

Lillie de Hegermann-Lindencrone, the charming American-born wife of the popular Danish minister, wrote a vivid description of one of the Literary's evenings that was probably typical of many more. Gently chiding the pompousness of both Mrs. Dahlgren, whom she easily mistook for its president, and the Literary, which she dubbed "The Brain Club," she described for her mother her initiation into the society in the spring of 1877:

> The first meeting was a ghastly affair. The subject to be discussed was the "Metamorphosis of Negative Matter." You may imagine that I was staggered. I had no more idea what negative matter was than the inhabitants of Mars. They took us alphabetically. When they got to "H," Mrs. Dahlgren (who, as president, sat in a comfortable chair with arms to it, while the others sat on hard dining-room, cane-bottomed chairs) turned to me and said, "Has Mrs. *Hegermann* anything to say concerning the Metamorphosis of Negative Matter?" I had on my blue velvet gown, and thought of it fast becoming chair-stamped, and I wondered if negative matter would comprise that. However, I wisely refrained from speech, and shook a sad smile from my closed lips. "H" to "K" had a great deal to say. Every one looked wise and wore an appearance of interest. They slid down to "L." Then Mrs. Dahlgren said, "Has Mrs. *Lindencrone* anything to say on the Metamorphosis of Negative Matter?" I answered that I had not discovered anything since the last time they asked me. They were not accustomed to one lady having two names, each beginning with a capital letter.

Madame Hegermann-Lindencrone felt the evening only partially redeemed by the introduction of positive matter in the form of scalloped oysters and chicken salad.

While well known as a founder and spokeswoman for the Literary, Mrs. Dahlgren left her most lasting imprint on Washington society as chief proselytizer for the Antiques. From the late 1860s until her death in 1898, Mrs. Dahlgren parlayed her own and her late husband's illustrious family pedigrees and her years of experience as a Washington hostess into a career as the capital's self-appointed arbiter of good taste and correctness. Her chief forum for disseminating the Antiques' philosophy was her extremely successful manners manual, *Etiquette of Social Life in Washington,* which first appeared in 1873. The reader received from it, in addition to detailed information on protocol, proper attire, and card-leaving, a large dose of Mrs. Dahlgren's aristocratic philosophy and her thinly disguised disdain for what she regarded as the rabble dominating official society. It was no accident that her volume appeared in the same year that the ostentation of the Grant administration was reaching its zenith. "Because we are a Republic," Mrs. Dahlgren informed her readers on the very first page, "we are not necessarily to be deprived of those amenities which render life agreeable, and assist to cultivate good feeling." To support her case for good manners and deference to age, lineage, and rank, she invoked the sainted, unassailable first president: "We all know that the venerated Washington and his stately wife, compelled a rigid observance of social etiquette towards the administration in its various branches."

Mrs. Dahlgren mixed concrete information on calling days and seating arrangements with increasingly strong doses of personal philosophy in each new edition. (The slim twenty-nine-page first edition of 1873 quickly grew to seventy-six pages by the fifth edition in 1881). First and foremost, she sought to "educate" the "newcomers to our city." Her targets were not the urbane patricians like the Hamilton Fishes, but the crude nouveaux riches with which Washington society suddenly seemed to be littered. Her advice regarding dinner-giving typifies the condescension that infuses her pages:

> As to the menu . . . , we would suggest not to yield implicitly to the caterer, who will be sure to prolong your dinner beyond the bounds of good taste. Especially should this be the case, where a sudden acquisition of fortune gives hospitable people the means of entertaining. Such persons, quite unaccustomed to judge for themselves of what is really proper, are readily imposed upon by those whose interest it is to provide lavish feasts. A banquet must be sumptuous rather in the careful choice and quality, than in the profuse quantity of the selected dishes. If you desire to spend money without stint when giving dinners, do so rather by the artistic elaboration of that which you present, than by an endless repetition of courses which pall upon the taste.

"No dinner," Mrs. Dahlgren warned, "however superb in prandial show, can be agreeable if the *convives* are dullards. . . . No sordid computation of dollars can buy or measure the Promethean light of conversational effect."

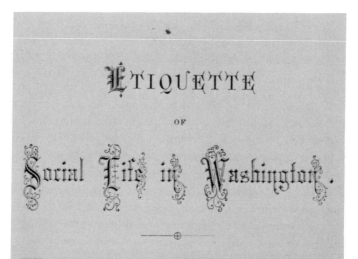

ℰTIQUETTE

OF

Social Life in Washington.

IF order is Heaven's first law, we should not regard as beneath careful attention, the proper recognition of rules which may tend to avoid confusion in social life.

Because we are a Republic, we are not necessarily to be deprived of those amenities which render life agreeable, and assist to cultivate good feeling.

Courtesy may be considered but as the mirror of charity, and, although it may often become an unmeaning semblance of benevolence, yet, if we assiduously cultivate, if only but the shadow, we may finally hope to gain the reality. Thus, by placing ourselves in excellent relations towards others, we may eventually acquire that sentiment of good will which may at first have been but a mere appearance.

That which is called good breeding is actually the golden rule carried into practice, and is therefore a very Christian accomplishment. Since egotism is the most dreaded bane of society, if we can learn so far to forget ourselves as to consider the just claims of others, we

Each successive edition of Mrs. Madeleine Vinton Dahlgren's popular *Etiquette of Social Life in Washington* contained stronger and stronger doses of "Antique" philosophy. (Madeleine Vinton Dahlgren, *Etiquette of Social Life in Washington,* 4th ed. [Lancaster, Penn., 1876])

Mrs. Dahlgren also sought to teach her socially unschooled readers that the old families of Washington deserved their deep respect and deference. She patiently explained that "in real solidity of social importance, the resident society must . . . be classed as of the very elite," and added, "The old families of Washington have an interest for us which none other in the land may claim, for their social life has gone hand in hand with that of the nation." She peppered each new edition with additional references to the Antiques' superior social position, in hopes that the eager parvenus who bought her books in great quantities would honor the "very elite" as they sought to emulate their good manners.

Washington's Antiques were not alone in claiming the realms of etiquette and good taste as their own. As Jaher points out in *The Urban Establishment,* Brahmins, Knickerbockers, and the other old urban social and cultural elites also sought to corner their local markets on gentility. Shaping standards of decorum was a gratifying exercise because it permitted the illusion of retaining some semblance of former hegemony. Defining good taste was an attempt to define the tangible evidence of success in one's favor. In matters of taste, most Antiques and other beleaguered old elites championed "the old over the new, the gentleman in business over the aggressive competitor"; they preferred "the patriarchal kinship group rather than the conjugal unit, ancestral homes to modern apartments, Henry Adams's 'Virgin' to the 'Dynamo.'"

By defending traditional style and taste, the old elite families repudiated two other measures of success—wealth and power—that were far more compelling to the rich and aggressive newcomers than polished tea-table manners. The rich newcomers were eager to do the right thing socially and happy for guidance from any quarter, but they were not willing to gauge their own personal success by the correctness of a table setting. The Antiques were bypassed by the new elites who followed other roads to hegemony, but their popular etiquette books publicized their continued existence and enabled them at least to retain their position as arbiters of taste and gentility.

While superior mastery of good manners would never regain for them their old dominion over Washington high society, some financially frayed Antiques discovered fiscal salvation in their command of proper etiquette and long familiarity with Washington. (Mrs. Dahlgren made a great deal of money from her *Etiquette* books even if much of her advice went unheeded.) While the sons of the Antiques left the capital in search of greener pastures, several of their daughters translated their good breeding into much-needed employment and joined the ranks of the social secretaries.

Although relatively new, the social secretary had rapidly taken hold in Washington, where a "social pilot" was especially helpful. "The calling," observed a reporter, "is one which in Washington, as the Capital of the nation, attains highest importance and realizes widest scope. Unlike all other cities of the union, in Washington it is an absolute necessity that the newcomer have advice and guidance." "Snares and pitfalls into which it is possible for persons in high authority to be thrown through ignorance of the niceties of official and diplomatic etiquette" lay in wait in the capital for newcomers ignorant of the city's ways. In Washington, "to err in seating diplomatic and official guests at table is fraught with consequences too far-reaching to be a matter lightly dealt with." One society reporter ticked off the Washington "social pilot's" most important qualities:

> She must be a sort of social Napoleon in petticoats. . . . She must have a rich and sure knowledge of Washington's customs, of its pitfalls and snares. She must be well-groomed, well-gowned. She must be possessed of some of the qualities of a Sherlock Holmes, for she must be mistress of all sorts of tricks for discovering the past, present, future, and, if need be, the hereafter of every person who comes within range of her patroness's eye.

Few young women were more expertly equipped to guide newcomers through the minefield of Washington etiquette than the young "well-groomed, well-gowned," and well-mannered Antiques, many of whom also were in need of paying jobs.

The Washington social secretary's duties could be by turns exalted and menial: in some houses, she presided over the tea table, while in others, said one secretary, she was expected to "air the dog and wash the baby." They might also require ruthlessness and bring vicarious satisfaction: "If there is any score to be paid off, or any snubbing to be done, she does it, not only in behalf of her patroness, but often in her own behalf, for it is in this way that she evens up things with the world." The job was hardly a sinecure. It required great social resources, "especially if her employer has that ghastly habit of not only putting her own foot in it on all occasions, but of dragging in other people's feet as well."

"For all this that she has to do and so effectively does, and for all that she does not do and yet is blamed for doing, what honorarium does this social secretary receive?" asked a reporter. "Generally, it is in proportion to what she can accomplish, or to the amount of raw material she must handle. In the case of one very famous social coach who carried a senatorial family brilliantly through one or two administrations, the entire senatorial salary was deemed barely sufficient." The pay of a social secretary was neither opulent nor paltry. For two hours a day on her first job as social secretary to the wife of British Ambassador James Bryce, Edith Benham received fifty dollars a month at the turn of the century. When Mrs. Theodore Roosevelt made Isabelle "Belle" Hagner, who had been her social secretary when her husband was vice president, the first White House social secretary in 1901, her salary was a respectable sixteen hundred dollars a year.

Edith Benham found her first position at the British Embassy thanks to kindly Mrs. Admiral William Sheffield Cowles, Theodore Roosevelt's sister Anna, who, along with her husband, was a leader of official Washington society in the 1890s. With her own niece Eleanor in mind, Mrs. Cowles felt a special sympathy for the daughters of the great old families who, despite their heritage, were financially disadvantaged. Mrs. Cowles was only one of several society matrons in Washington doing such rescue work. Another was Mrs. John Henderson, wife of the former Missouri senator and wealthy Washington lawyer, who made the daughters of the Antiques, like vegetarianism, one of her "causes."

When Miss Benham, the daughter of naval officer Andrew Ellicott Kennedy Benham and the granddaughter of New York Congressman John Henry Seaman, accepted her first position as a social secretary, she knew that the career held out a respectability few others offered young women of her class. That respectability had been secured by the pioneer of Washington social secretaries, Cornelia "Nellie" Hunt, daughter of William Henry Hunt, Secretary of the Navy under President Garfield and later minister to Russia. Miss Hunt's career as a social secretary began in 1889, after her father's death, when she was hired by Mrs. Levi Morton, the wife of the vice president. Upon her arrival in Washington, Mrs. Morton "at once perceived that her way would be beset with thorns unless it were possible to bring to her aid an adjutant as clever as herself." When she chose Miss Hunt, Mrs. Morton chose wisely. A reporter enumerated the qualities that made Miss Hunt the perfect "adjutant": "A woman of fine presence, suave, pleasant manners, accustomed from birth to the society of distinguished men and women in this country and

Europe, she was at the outset well equipped for the important duties that have from time to time fallen to her share."

Mrs. Morton's generous recognition of Miss Hunt's expertise and high standing in Washington society lent a respectability to the job of social secretary that eased the minds of other Antique young ladies considering the profession. "Miss Hunt," noted a *Saturday Evening Post* article in 1904, "was not only entrusted with the multitudinous duties attendant upon the secretary to the mistress of an immense establishment, but from the start, she was accorded by Mrs. Morton the very enjoyable dignities of a social equal."

Nellie Hunt's most famous protégée was Belle Hagner, the daughter of one of Washington's oldest Southern families. Before being hired by Mrs. Theodore Roosevelt, she had already served an impressive apprenticeship as social secretary to Mrs. Elihu Root, wife of President McKinley's secretary of war, and to Mrs. Chauncey Depew, wife of the extremely rich New York senator. Besides knowing Washington society thoroughly, Belle Hagner was fun-loving and companionable, and she fit into the rowdy Roosevelt ménage perfectly. She became Mrs. Roosevelt's accomplice in incognito forays to antique shops, and a popular, rollicking friend of the Roosevelt children. When Mrs. Roosevelt left the White House, she wrote Belle fondly, "You have been my eldest child for so many years."

There was considerable irony in the fact that while the rich officials and parvenus broke the old residential elite's grip on Washington high society, in a small way these same socially unschooled newcomers proved the financial salvation of a few Antique offspring. As one reporter noted, for the daughters of the old families the rise of the new profession of social secretary seemed providential:

> It would almost seem as though a beneficent Providence had specially decreed that most American statesman and officials who come to Washington should be of the self-made type, for no other reason than to insure a genteel occupation to well-bred, well-born, impecunious young women of blue-blooded families. . . . This occupation of the social piloting of families across the bar into society's harbor seems Heaven sent.

The Antiques' situation was actually doubly ironic, since in turning their special skills to a profit they gave aid and comfort to the enemy, the Parvenus.

From Antiques to Cave Dwellers

Sometime in the early 1890s, Washington's old families acquired the name they would carry with them into the twentieth (and the twenty-first) century. Ellen Maury Slayden, a very proud Maury of Virginia and a proud Antique as well, casually used the term in her diary in 1897, shortly after her return to Washington as the wife of Texas congressman James Slayden: "My many sweet 'cave dweller' Maury relatives have been most kind." By the turn of the century, if the capital's old aristocrats attracted the press's attention at all, "Cave Dweller" was the term most often used to describe them. The gossip-pedaling national society tabloid *The Club Fellow* routinely used the term when referring to the capital's old families, knowing full well its readers would understand the reference.

Just what did the term "Cave Dweller" imply? As this and the label "Antique" suggested, these Washingtonians were "old" in a variety of ways. They were old in the literal sense of age or longevity. The term implied, at the very least, several decades spent in Washington and, at best, a family whose claim to the Potomac region went back further than the capital's. Cave Dwellers were also old in another sense: they were passé. They were the "dying snails" retreating into their shells, the "has-beens," as one reporter ungraciously called them, whom a richer, more glamorous society had passed by.

The term also implied "relics" with perfect manners and impeccable taste. These Cave Dwellers had seen the crass handwriting on the wall of those whom they regarded as the true savages, Twain's Parvenus. They had retreated up into their comfortable Federal-period caves, pulled their ladders after them, and, from their lofty vantage point, declared genteel society in the capital dead. One Cave Dweller, a lady with soft white curls "worn after a long-gone-by fashion," explained her understanding of the label she proudly bore:

> Like David we have gone to our caves. You know David, my dear, who took refuge from Saul in the cave of Adullam? Well, many of us have fled from Saul, Saul being in this case in Washington, new-rich people with more money than manners, with more pride than pedigree, with more dinners than digestion.

By 1900, the press was using "Cave Dweller" broadly to include not only those who possessed the group's own narrowly construed attributes of ancient pedigree and long tenure in the capital, but all those who shared the old families' concern for the city, for personal integrity, and for subdued gentility. Thus, the title of Cave Dweller was bestowed upon the family of Nicholas Longworth Anderson, who hadn't come to Washington until 1879, but whose antecedents, handsome H. H. Richardson-designed home, gracious lifestyle, and donations to the city's charities and cultural life qualified them for inclusion.

Charles Glover's name was another that began to appear on lists of Cave Dwellers around 1900. Though the grandson of one of Washington's earliest settlers, Glover himself was born in North Carolina and had come to the capital as an orphan to be raised in reduced circumstances by his aged grandmother. Beginning as a clerk in the Riggs Bank, Glover rose steadily through the ranks to become chairman of the board. While on his way to becoming a very rich man, Glover allied himself with the city's old citizens rather than its wealthy newcomers. He married into the old families and, in 1880, he decided to live in their midst on passé Lafayette Square rather than build in the fashionable West End. It was, however, Glover's devotion to the city as chairman of the Corcoran Gallery of Art and a host of charities and park projects that most endeared him to the old families and won him admittance to their circle.

Few of the Cave Dwellers objected to the broader use of their old nickname. They were quite proud of the title. They "hugged it to their breasts," claimed one society reporter, "as a hallmark of distinction and exclusiveness." Most looked with favor on anyone under eighty years of age willing to keep alive their genteel traditions and share their love of Washington. Infusions of new blood were welcome, especially so as two of their cherished institutions, established to preserve their identity and integrity as a group—the Bachelor's and the Oldest Inhabitants—were foundering.

Shortly after the turn of the century, the *Club Fellow,* which regarded the Bachelor's as snooty and stuffy, began to hint at the club's demise with glee. In October 1906, it reported, "Several young men who had been kept cooling their heels outside the door of the membership committee of the Bachelor's for several seasons, decided to bolt the whole affair, and organize the Benedicts." The Benedicts had apparently given two cotillions the previous winter, which, in the *Club Fellow*'s opinion, were more "fun" than the Bachelor's stodgy dances. In 1907, the *Club Fellow* reported that still another group, the Sixty Couples, was on the verge of eclipsing the Bachelor's.

By the turn of the century, the Oldest Inhabitants had been reduced to a purely ceremonial organization. The three most important dates on its members' calendars were times for stirring up the embers of the glory days of the past: New Year's Day, George Washington's Birthday, and the Fourth of July. On January 1, the elderly members marched in a line to the White House where they were received by the president, just as President John Adams had received the city's leading inhabitants a century before. In 1800, the residential elite had been just about the president's only callers. By 1900, they were aged anachronisms, lost in a throng of thousands. On Washington's Birthday, the members would gather to listen to a reading of George Washington's farewell address, and, on the Fourth of July, they would read aloud the Declaration of Independence.

The membership of the Oldest Inhabitants was getting older, and new recruits were getting harder to find. Even when the required number of years of residence for eligibility was lowered from forty-five to forty and then to thirty-five, few sought the club out. Many of the Oldest Inhabitants' potential recruits were siphoned off by the new, more stimulating Columbia Historical Society, established in 1894. Though its mission was similar to that of the Oldest Inhabitants—"the collection, preservation and diffusion of knowledge respecting the history and topography of the District of Columbia and national history and biography"—the Columbia Historical Society drew together an exhilarating mixture of scholars, scientists, government officials, and longtime residents, and had no sex, age, or length of residency bars to membership.

The Oldest Inhabitants became the butt of jokes, and the group was identified with the relics its members collected. Ellen Maury Slayden, invited by one of the "most toploftical of the F.F.V's" to address the group in 1906 on the subject of her recent visit to Spain, described an evening where the whispers from the audience were mostly of "symptoms and ancestors":

If . . . asked to walk a tightrope for their delectation, the urge of my Virginian blood would have made me try it, but if I had known how old "old Washingtonians" were, or how volubly they slept, I wouldn't have accepted so lightheartedly. . . . The room was warm and the sound of my voice evidently the last touch of comfort they needed. One by one they fell asleep while I became almost hysterical wondering what I should do if not one of them was awake when I finished.

Though the title of Cave Dweller was applied more broadly than the label of Antique had been, the expanded group's reputation for impeccable manners and unflagging propriety remained undiminished. Even the *Club Fellow* acknowledged the Cave Dwellers' continuing superiority in this quarter. "The old fortunes," it noted in 1907,

> can not compare with the fabulous fortunes of the new generation of millionaires now residing in Washington. Still an affair of any sort given by the Eustises [Mr. and Mrs. William Corcoran Eustis], the Bealls [Mr. and Mrs. Truxton Beall], the Janins [Mr. and Mrs. Albert Covington Janin] or any other of the wealthy Cave Dwellers, would bear the hall-mark of aristocracy and refinement which is so sadly missing in those with which the Western wealthy set are wont to dazzle the National Capital nowadays.

After Mrs. Dahlgren's death in 1898, Violet Blair Janin succeeded her as the old families' arbiter of taste. Cave Dweller Marietta Minnigerode Andrews described the rows of homes around Lafayette Square where Mrs. Janin lived as the "veritable last stronghold of the Cave Dwellers" and Mrs. Janin as their "Queen":

> Queen of the Cave Dwellers, a lady lives in one of these old houses which bears on a brass plate the word "Blair." Her colonial traditions, her orthodox churchmanship, her conservative standards, her infallible decisiveness, her beautiful profile, have never changed; she lives in the same atmosphere as in her youth, under the same lofty ceilings, among the same priceless calf-bound books, even with the same venerable and unresponsive, faithful old servants! Unchanged, unchanging.

While still the undisputed leaders of the realm of dignity and refinement, the days when Mrs. Janin and her fellow Cave Dwellers had led high society in the capital were only a dim memory. The futility of their efforts to maintain the selectness of Washington society was strikingly cast up to them by Washington's first *Social Register,* published in 1900.

The old families had easily dismissed earlier attempts to catalogue the social elite of Washington, the most notable of which, the *Elite List,* first appeared in 1888. While the *Elite List* proclaimed itself a guide to the socially elect of the nation's capital, every senator, representative, cabinet member, Supreme Court justice, and official down to the first, second, third, fourth, and fifth auditors of the Treasury Department was listed on its pages in between advertisements for face creams and horsehair sofas. The *Elite List* indiscriminately included the old families—the Janins, the Hagners, and Mrs. Dahlgren—and the new—Mr. and Mrs. Washington McLean, Mr. and Mrs. John R. McLean, and the Leiters.

Every city had its equivalent of the *Elite List,* and the old families everywhere ignored them. But the *Social Register* was another matter. The first *Social Register* appeared in 1888 for New York City. Within its tasteful covers, on pages devoid of advertisements, it listed fewer than two thousand families (along with their winter and summer residences, yachts, clubs, and colleges) out of New York's more than a million inhabitants (two families for every thousand people). Not only was the *Social Register* an immediate success, but its discriminating pages were grudgingly acknowledged in many quarters truly to represent New York's social elite. Volumes of the *Social Register* quickly followed for Philadelphia, Boston, Chicago, and, in 1900, Washington. Each contained, as the preface noted, "those families who by descent or by social standing, or from other qualifications are naturally included in the best society of any particular city or cities."

The first Washington *Social Register* contained the names of about two thousand families at a time when the city's population totaled only three hundred thousand (six families for every thousand people). Washington's ratio of the "elect" to the total population was the highest of any of the *Social Register* cities. While this high ratio might have indicated that the capital had more families of quality than any other city in America, the Cave Dwellers did not see it that way. By their lights, nearly a third of those included had slipped in under the "other qualifications" clause, thereby greatly diluting the quality of the whole. Of the two thousand families listed, some eight hundred belonged to members of Congress, army and navy officers, cabinet members, justices, and foreign diplomats. These government officials had not been scrutinized for the same exacting qualifications for inclusion supposedly demanded of those outside of official life, but were included en masse irrespective of their forebears, their ill-gotten fortunes, or their divorces. As far as the Cave Dwellers were concerned, the *Social Register* was little better than the telephone directory or the *Congressional Directory.*

By the end of the century, the Cave Dwellers knew that the hope of exploiting the unique porousness of Washington's society would continue to draw to the capital parvenus who knew they could not successfully storm the gates of high society elsewhere. They knew, too, that of-

The listings in the first *Social Register* for Washington, published in 1900, show that the densest concentration of Cave Dwellers was centered around Lafayette Square. Violet Blair Janin, "queen of the Cave Dwellers," and her friends of "older blood" holed up in townhouses like those visible in this turn-of-the-century photograph of the west side of Jackson Place. (Historical Society of Washington, D.C.)

ficial society, with its increasing numbers of high-ranking members who were guaranteed prominent places at table by the protocol that ruled it, was not going to go away or yield back to them their old dominion over Washington. And they knew that the New Washington would continue to be a strong magnet, pulling more and more members of the growing national social elite—men and women whose *Social Register* entries were likely to include houses in New York and Newport as well as Washington—to the Potomac's shores each season.

Yet while they were greatly outnumbered, the Cave Dwellers' position at the end of the century was not totally bleak. They had unquestionably lost status and authority since the 1850s, when the old residential families had constituted the closest thing to an upper class that Washington would ever know. But they had not been obliterated, as it had once appeared they might be, in the years immediately after the war. Demonstrating great resiliency, the Cave Dwellers lived on as one of the several elite groups making up high society in the nation's capital. While one of the smallest of the social elites at the century's end, they took comfort in knowing they were also the most socially correct.

9 Conclusion

During the nineteenth century, Washington grew into a full-fledged city. When it was a dirty village at the century's beginning, few had come to the new capital who did not have to, and no one came solely to enjoy its nearly nonexistent social ambiance. The young federal government in Washington could barely control a handful of rowdy states, much less flex any muscle beyond its shores. By the century's end, the city, its society, and the government that had spawned both had all greatly matured. The city was handsome and spacious; its high society sparkled as brightly as any in the nation; the federal government exercised dominion over forty-five states that spanned the continent and even possessed foreign territories, the result of victory in the recent Spanish-American War. On the eve of the twentieth century, the historian of the Washington Literary Society neatly, and perhaps wistfully, summed up the city's transformation: "The old-time, dreamy Southern, do-nothing dynasty had passed forever; the bustling, energetic city-builders of the North and West poured in, and at once proceeded to make a wide-awake modern city out of a sleepy town."

In certain ways, high society in the new "wide-awake" capital bore little resemblance to what had passed for society in the old "do-nothing" town. The single wretched theater of the early 1800s offering only feeble diversion and the tiny handful of private homes offering decent food and conversation had given way to dozens of theaters, clubs, parks, and drives, and a dense mass of enormous mansions, each of which could accommodate almost as many people in its reception rooms as had lived in the whole District of Columbia a century earlier.

By 1900, Washington's social elite claimed membership in the national, rather than parochial, high society of rich, rootless men and women that had emerged in the 1890s, interlacing the East Coast cities and criss-crossing the country. The capital had become a prominent stop in this nomadic elite's seasonal trek. The rich put down their packs, unfurled their tents, and enjoyed Washington's unique attractions for a season before restlessly moving on to the next fashionable watering hole. The turn-of-the-century capital proved a delightful social pond in which to paddle. Julia Foraker reminisced about its fin de siècle charms:

> Washington society in the 'nineties was as brilliant as any that ever America has produced. The administrations had a certain ceremonious glory; there was an arresting group of men in the Senate, with a few remarkable leaders; the diplomatic set was distinguished and delightful and romantically mysterious in the old-time, old World manner. . . . In the 'nineties, too, our country's cornucopious bounty seemed to overflow. Never again shall any of us see such abundance and cheapness, such luxurious well-being as prosperous Americans then enjoyed. . . . What is so rare as a Washington morning in the season? The sunshine, the soft, sweet air, the brilliant come-and-go. Smart equipage! Horses! And the whole distinguished, cosmopolitan world abroad! Everybody knew everybody else. There was a great smiling and waving of greetings, a great many informal levees held at brougham doors. I know little about the life of European queens (there were more then), but I doubt if any of them ever held gayer matinee courts than we Washington women of the 'nineties.

In its fiftieth anniversary issue in 1902, the Washington *Evening Star* looked back over the changes that had taken place in the capital during the preceding half century. Among the aspects of Washington that had undergone the most dramatic changes, the *Star* concluded, were the physical city itself—its streets, buildings, and density—and its high society. The West End of Washington embodied both of these changes. Who would have guessed that the isolated banks of Slash Run, dotted with

"They Talk . . . About The Clothes Worn By The Grand Dames Of The Republic"

slaughterhouses and farmers' patches at the end of the Civil War, would emerge as the city's most fashionable neighborhood, with mansions costing nearly a million dollars crowding around a busy traffic circle that had until very recently been just a hypothetical dot on L'Enfant's original design for the city?

Boss Shepherd's improvements, the Honest Miners' development, William Stewart's Castle and the relocation of the British legation to the area all combined to make the West End the most attractive place in town for the rich newcomers looking for a place to alight. The turrets, spires, towers, and parapets of the colossal homes these new millionaires built cheek to jowl on the streets radiating from Pacific Circle (soon to be renamed Dupont Circle) transformed the city's skyline just as the influx of rich newcomers transformed its high society. By the turn of the century, noted the *Star,* the "storm center of high society"—the densest concentration of "the best" families—hovered over the elegant blocks of mansions in the West End. The Cave Dwellers and their old, sedate Federal and Georgian-style townhouses around Lafayette Square, for seven decades the "eye of the social storm," had become relics of the past.

"Her First Appearance At A
White House Reception"

Numerous magazine articles, enhanced with handsome drawings, painted vivid pictures of the elegance, excitement and cosmopolitan air of fin-de-siècle Washington. A long article in *The Century Magazine* in 1902 emphasized Washington's high standing with the national "smart set." The drawings by Charlotte Harding illustrating the article featured dashing diplomats and beautiful women enjoying the social whirl. (Henry Loomis Nelson, "The Capital of Our Democracy," *The Century Magazine,* 1902)

By 1900, the "storm center of high society" swirled above the enormous mansions packed together around Dupont Circle. A sparsely populated wilderness at the end of the Civil War, the West End proved fertile ground for the parvenus who arrived in the 1880s and 1890s. This aerial photograph from the early 1920s shows just how densely these mansions grew. The 55-room Leiter mansion is on the right; the Stanford White-designed home of the Pattersons of Chicago is on the left; the vacant lot where "Stewart's Castle" once stood is at upper right. (Library of Congress, Prints and Photographs Division)

The most important change in Washington's high society over the past fifty years, however, was not that its geographic center had shifted, but that its leadership had changed. In 1852, when the *Star* first appeared, the leaders of high society in Washington had been members of the residential elite, families with names like Corcoran, Riggs, Blair, Mercer, and Carroll, plus a few rich Southern Democrats in official life like the Clays of Alabama. These were the old Southern and Democratic families that called the tune to which the rest of Washington society had danced since 1800.

During the 1870s, the *Star's* society reporters found themselves covering the exploits of a completely new set of social leaders. The old

In contrast to the huge, flamboyant mansions of the arrivistes around Dupont Circle, the restrained, sedate homes of the city's Cave Dwellers clustered around Lafayette Square. The "eye of the social storm" had hovered over these homes of the city's residential elite for six decades before moving west. This impressive row of Greek Revival houses, built in the 1850s, lined H Street, one block north of the White House, at the turn of the century. Bancroft House, home of the eminent historian George Bancroft, is on the left; William Corcoran's house is in the distance on the right. (James Goode Collection, Library of Congress, Prints and Photographs Division)

Washington residents and Southern officials had been eclipsed by the cabal of Northern and Republican officials who took the capital by storm in the years just after the war and thoroughly dominated high society for a decade. Individuals—mostly women—like Julia Grant, Julia Fish, Kate Chase Sprague, Kate Williams, and Amanda Belknap replaced the old families who had provided social leadership in the young capital for half a century.

By 1902, still another group had come to the fore as leaders of high society in Washington, displacing the officials, just as the officials had displaced the old families. The days when the arrival and departure of congressmen for the convening and recess of Congress marked the beginning and end of the social season were gone. "Congress," claimed the *Star,*

> has less and less to do each year with mapping out a social program. The presence of the legislators has, of course, a bearing on matters polite, on hospitalities significant and on arrangements affecting a sudden increase in the population, but what is known as the "smart set" scarcely finds that this factor causes any special preparation on its part.

In the officials' place, said the *Star,* "a charming new group" of ladies shared the turn-of-the-century social honors. Among those the *Star* singled out were Mrs. Leiter, Mrs. DeKoven, Mrs. John R. McLean, and Mrs. Richard Townsend. These women represented the unofficial rich newcomers who first began to arrive in the New Washington in the 1870s and 80s. Made up of nouveaux riches, members of the social lobby, and scions of old fortunes from old cities looking for adventure, the rich newcomers had taken advantage of the "open door" policy leading to social prominence in the capital and moved right up to the top.

The *Star's* anniversary issue plainly spelled out what Washington's beleaguered old families and overshadowed, outspent officials already knew: at the turn of the century, the leaders of high society in the nation's capital were more likely to be Northern-born than Southern-born, nouveaux riches rather than old rich, members of unofficial society rather than official society, and seasonal visitors rather than permanent residents.

Much about Washington and its high society had changed during the nineteenth century, but not everything. In some ways it was still the same high society that Mark Twain encountered during his disastrous stint as a Senate staffer in the years just after the Civil War. Even President John Adams would have recognized aspects of this high society as close kin to the one whose members he had greeted in the half-finished White House in 1801.

In 1900, Washington was still the one and only capital of the United States. No one seriously talked of moving the capital anywhere else any longer. And the city remained a one-crop town, dominated by the business of government more thoroughly than ever before: one by one, the mills along the Potomac in Georgetown were closing, and river traffic consisted largely of excursion boats ferrying tourists to Mount Vernon and back. All of the special features of the city's high society that flowed from its special status as the nation's capital still applied, and in fact still apply. Official society endured, growing at what many regarded as an alarming rate, and continued to march to the beat of its own special protocol. Though tempests over precedence erupted periodically, George Washington and Dolley Madison would have quickly grasped that the same rules of seating they had once observed at official dinners were still scrupulously followed.

Transience was still the hallmark of this itinerate, all-male official elite. The revolving door of democratic electoral politics continued to turn out unlucky officials every other November. Fewer defeated or retiring congressmen chose to return to the bosom of their constituents (it was hard for many to go back to towns like Omaha or Des Moines after ten, or even two, years in the cosmopolitan capital), but if they remained in Washington, it was as members of the unofficial social elite.

Washington and its high society still resonated to national themes such as war, depression, and industrialization, each of which drew to the capital its own cast of characters to add to the mélange. And the capital and its social elite continued to hold the nation's imagination. Featuring photographs and flattering drawings, articles about Washington's high society regularly appeared in popular magazines, bringing news of the "social doings" in the capital into parlors across America. The energetic family of President Theodore Roosevelt provided endless copy for society reporters, whose readers found the first family endlessly fascinating.

Although high society had grown larger and the number of subcircles within it had multiplied by 1900, Mark Twain still could easily have picked out members of the "three distinct aristocracies" he had identified in the early 1870s. Antiques muttered and grumbled about the unvarnished manners of the arrivistes; officials multiplied like rabbits; and parvenus still flocked to this social mecca along the Potomac. The tide of rich newcomers, of which parvenus were the most visible subset, continued to rise each year. They sought out the capital in 1900 for the same reasons they had come in 1870: Washington's winters were warm; the embassies lent an air of international sophistication; and the federal government offered a myriad of powerful and interesting dinner guests. This city was different from all the others the rich vagabonds of the national social elite could choose from. As *Century Magazine* noted in 1902, "Washington is busy with nothing that absorbs the minds and occupies the energies of the typical American city."

Another extremely potent lure also continued to attract rich new-comers to the capital. In 1873, Twain's Henry Brierly had assured Laura Hawkins that she wouldn't need a crowbar to break into society there as she would in Philadelphia; in 1882, the reporter "Carp" had assured ar-rivistes that in Washington there was "more opportunity for a nobody to become a somebody than in the whirlpool of New York." As the century turned, there was still no Cerberus guarding the portals to Washington's high society. In 1902, *Harper's Weekly* confirmed that the situation was unchanged: "More and more every year people of means make Washington their winter residence . . . partly because, it is frequently said, it is easier to break into society in Washington than elsewhere."

For all of these reasons, Washington's high society was fascinating in 1800 as the federal government settled in, in 1865 as it emerged from a devastating civil war, and at the turn of the century when it took its place alongside other fashionable watering holes—and it still is today. As Henry Brierly said, it's not Philadelphia. And it's not New York, Boston, Chicago, or Los Angeles either. High society in Washington was, and still is, unique in America.

Notes

Chapter 1. Introduction

1   "unlike any other American city": "The New Washington," *Century Magazine,* March 1884.

2   "Money or beauty will open any door": Mark Twain and Charles Dudley Warner, *The Gilded Age: A Tale of Today,* 2 vols. (1873; reprint New York, 1915), 1:194.

3   "The 'seat of the Government'": "How Shall We Govern the National Capital," *The Nation,* June 11, 1874, p. 375.

4   "superciliousness or unnecessary reserve": George Washington, "Queries on a Line of Conduct to be Pursued by the President," in *The Writings of George Washington,* ed. John Fitzpatrick, 39 vols. (Washington, D.C., 1939), 30:319–21; William Seale, *The President's House: A History,* 2 vols. (Washington, D.C., 1986), 1:5–6.

4   Hamilton's rules for levees: Alexander Hamilton to George Washington, May 5, 1789, in *The Works of Alexander Hamilton,* ed. Henry Cabot Lodge, 12 vols. (New York, 1904), 8:83–84; Seale, *President's House,* 1:6.

4   Congressional community turnover: James Sterling Young, *The Washington Community: 1800–1828* (New York, 1966), p. 89.

5   "I live in a land of strangers": Margaret Bayard Smith, *The First Forty Years of Washington Society,* ed. Gaillard Hunt (New York, 1906), p. 165.

6   Meanings of *society*: *Oxford English Dictionary*, s.v. "society" (3c); T. B. Bottomore, *Elites and Society* (New York, 1964), p. 1.

6   "The Sociomaniac": quoted in Cleveland Amory, *Who Killed Society?* (New York, 1960), p. 1.

6   Features of the upper class: Frederic Jaher, ed., *The Rich, the Well Born, and the Powerful* (Urbana, Ill., 1973), pp. 2–3; Frederic Jaher, *The Urban Establishment* (Urbana, Ill., 1982), pp. 7–9; E. Digby Baltzell, *Philadelphia Gentlemen: The Making of a National Upper Class* (Glencoe, Ill., 1958), pp. 6, 59.

6   Intraclass elite: Jaher, *The Rich*, pp. 2–3; Bottomore, *Elites*, p. 1.

7   Pareto on elites: Vilfredo Pareto, *The Mind and Society: A Treatise on General Sociology*, trans. Andrew Bongiorno and Arthur Livingston, 4 vols. (New York: 1935), 3:1422–23.

7   Aggregates of specialized invididuals: Baltzell, *Philadelphia Gentlemen*, p. 59.

7   Works on elites: E. Digby Baltzell, *Puritan Boston and Quaker Philadelphia: Two Protestant Ethics and the Spirit of Class Authority and Leadership* (New York, 1979); Edward Pessen, *Riches, Class and Power before the Civil War* (Lexington, Mass., 1973). More general, but no less important, classic works on elites in America include Bottomore, *Elites*, and Philip Burch, *Elites in American History*, 2 vols. (New York, 1981). Thomas Bender's *Community and Social Change in America* (New Brunswick, N.J., 1978) offers important insights into the meaning of community, whether of class or of special interests. Dixon Wecter's *The Saga of American Society* (New York, 1937) is one of the first works to take a serious look at high society in America. Four decades later, Stephen Birmingham updated the saga in *The Right People: A Portrait of the American Social Establishment* (Boston, 1968). Birmingham's *Our Crowd: The Great Jewish Families of New York* (New York, 1967), Cleveland Amory's *The Proper Bostonians* (New York, 1947), and Helen Horowitz's *Culture and the City* (Louisville, Ky., 1976) on Chicago are three good older studies that examine elites in these respective cities. Recent studies of elites in American cities, several of which use criteria developed by Jaher, Baltzell, Pessen, and others, include Jan Cigliano, *Showplace of America: Cleveland's Euclid Avenue, 1850–1910* (Kent, Ohio, 1991); Walter Fraser, Jr., *Charleston! Charleston! The History of a Southern City* (Columbia, S.C., 1989); Richard Hogan, *Class and Community in Frontier Colorado* (Lawrence, Kans., 1990); Timothy Mahoney, *River Towns in the Great West: The Structure of Provincial Urbanization in the American Midwest, 1820–1870* (Cambridge, Eng., 1990); Richard Peterson, *Bonanza Rich: Lifestyles of the Western Mining Entrepreneurs* (Moscow, Idaho, 1991); Joseph Rishel, *Founding Families of Pittsburgh: The Evolution of a*

Regional Elite, 1760–1910 (Pittsburgh, 1990); James M. Russell, *Atlanta 1847–1890, City Building in the Old South and the New* (Baton Rouge, La., 1988); and Robert Vitz, *The Queen and the Arts: Cultural Life in Nineteenth-Century Cincinnati* (Kent, Ohio, 1989).

8   Model articulated by Jaher: In his essay "Style and Status: High Society in Late Nineteenth-Century New York," in *The Rich, the Well Born, and the Powerful,* Jaher notes that New York deviated more and more from this norm as the century wore on. See also Jaher, *Urban Establishment,* p. 9; Pessen, *Riches,* pp. 242–43.

9   A thoroughly Southern town: Seale, *President's House,* 1:327

9   Sudden loss of social leaders: Jaher, *Urban Establishment,* pp. 20–21, 171, 399.

9   Scientists and scholars: For good discussions of the intellectual elite that expanded so quickly in Washington after the Civil War see: James Kirkpatrick Flack, *Desideratum in Washington: The Intellectual Community in the Capital City, 1870–1900* (Cambridge, Mass., 1975), and Michael Lacey, "The Mysteries of Earth-Making Dissolve: A Study of Washington's Intellectual Community and the Origins of American Environmentalism in the Late Nineteenth Century," Ph.D. diss., George Washington University, 1980.

10   African-American elite: Constance McLaughlin Green, *The Secret City* (Princeton, 1967); Willard B. Gatewood, *Aristocrats of Color: The Black Elite, 1880–1920* (Bloomington, Ind., 1990).

11   "it will be most awkward": Marian Hooper Adams, *The Letters of Mrs. Henry Adams: 1865–1883,* ed. Ward Thoron (Boston, 1936), p. 252.

11   "a day of bubbling joy": *The Letters of Henry Adams,* ed. J. C. Levenson et. al. (Cambridge, Mass., 1982), 2:447.

12   "Mr. Blaine is blown up": ibid., 2:448.

12   Dillworthy and Pomeroy: Justin Kaplan, introduction to *The Gilded Age,* by Mark Twain and Charles Dudley Warner (Indianapolis, 1972), p. xv.

13   "Society is the handmaiden": Florence Howe Hall, *Social Usages at Washington* (New York, 1906), p. v.

Chapter 2. High Society Gets Underway in the New Capital: 1800–1860

14   "This Embryo Capital": The British poet Thomas Moore visited Washington in 1804 and lampooned the city's pretensions in verse:

> . . . This embryo capital, where Fancy sees
> Squares in morasses, obelisks in trees;

Where second-sighted seers e'en now adorn
With shrines unbuilt and heroes yet unborn
Though not but woods—and Jefferson—they see
Where streets should run and sages ought to be.

Beckles Willson, *Friendly Relations: A Narrative of Britain's Ministers* (Boston, 1934), p. 97.

14   a modest start: Gerald Carson, *The Polite Americans* (New York, 1966), p. 95; M. B. Smith, *First Forty Years*, p. 25; Seale, *President's House*, 1:87.

15   building a capital ex nihilo: Young, *Washington Community*, pp. 17–19.

15   a pastoral idyll: George Jones, *Washington: Yesterday and Today* (New York, 1943), p. 30.

15   auction of lots: Young, *Washington Community*, pp. 19–20; Wilhelmus B. Bryan, *A History of the National Capital*, 2 vols. (New York, 1914), 1:159–60, 204–5, 213–14.

15   Federal District population and housing: *United States Census: Second through Ninth, 1800–1870* (Washington, D.C., 1872); *Statistical View of the United States* (Washington, D.C., 1854), p. 192; Young, *Washington Community*, p. 22.

15   Rep. Griswold grumbled: letter to Fanny Griswold, December 6, 1800, quoted in Constance McLaughlin Green, *Washington: A History of the Capital, 1800–1951*, 2 vols. (Princeton, 1962), 1:23.

15   Secretary Wolcott was furious: Oliver Wolcott to his wife, July 4, 1800, quoted in Bob Arnebeck, *Through a Fiery Trial: Building Washington 1790–1800* (Lanham, Md., 1991), p. 574.

16   Sen. Morris: quoted in Young, *Washington Community*, pp. 46–50.

16   Washington was dull indeed: ibid, pp. 42, 47; Kenneth Bowling, *The Creation of Washington, D.C.: The Idea and Location of the American Capital* (Fairfax, Va., 1991), pp. 211–12.

17   crowded living conditions: Green, *Washington*, 1:6, 45; Young, *Washington Community*, p. 46; Christian Hines, *Early Recollections of Washington City* (Washington, D.C., 1866), p. 75; Roy Swanstrom, "The United States Senate: 1787–1801," Ph.D. diss., University of California, Berkeley, 1959, p. 183.

17   Jefferson's entertaining: Seale, *President's House*, 1:91–106; M. B. Smith, *First Forty Years*, p. 32.

18   social life under the Madisons: Barbara Carson, *Ambitious Appetites: Dining, Behavior, and Patterns of Consumption in Federal Washington* (Washington, D.C., 1990), pp. 104–5.

18   Washington Irving: quoted in Marie Smith, *Entertaining in the White House* (Washington, D.C., 1967), p. 43.

18   a Philadelphia merchant: Thomas P. Cope, *Philadelphia Merchant: Diary of Thomas P. Cope, 1800–1851,* ed. Eliza Cope Harrison (South Bend, Ind., 1978), pp. 261–62.

18   Dolley Madison brought warmth: Seale, *President's House,* 1:127.

18   the Monroes' protocol changes: Mary Smith Lockwood, *Yesterdays in Washington* (Rosslyn, Va., 1915), pp. 136–36; Green, *Washington,* 1:81; Bryan, *National Capital,* 1:47–53; M. B. Smith, *First Forty Years,* p. 141; Seale, *President's House,* 1:157.

19   The "social revolution": Josephine Seaton, *William Winston Seaton of the National Intelligencer* (Boston, 1871), pp. 136–39; Smith, *First Forty Years,* pp. 53–54.

21   Sen. Eaton's wedding day: M. B. Smith, *First Forty Years,* p. 252.

21   Sen. Barry defends Mrs. Eaton: quoted in B. Carson, *Ambitious Appetites,* p. 14.

22   Cabinet members resigned: Seale, *President's House,* 1:188–91.

22   "God help the women!": Peggy Eaton, *The Autobiography of Peggy Eaton* (New York, 1932), p. 209.

22   Van Buren's White House sparkled: Seale, *President's House,* 1:190–91, 213–14; Mary Cable, *The Avenue of the Presidents* (Boston, 1969), p. 101.

23   "ruffled shirt-wirt-wirt": Cable, *Avenue,* p. 101.

23   "Old Tippecanoe": Seale, *President's House,* 1:228.

23   Dolley Madison's stream of advice: ibid., 1:241–46, 255.

24   Dolley Madison's last years and funeral: ibid., 1:283–85; *Daily National Intelligencer,* July 14, 1849.

24   Rep. Hubbard: Thomas Hubbard, "Political and Social Life in Washington during the Administration of President Monroe," ed. Robert Hubbard, *Transactions of the Oneida Historical Society at Utica, New York* 9 (1903): 56–73.

24   Alfred Shelby: Alfred Shelby, "Mr. Shelby Goes to Washington," ed. John McDonough, *The Filson Club History Quarterly* 59 (April 1905): 214.

24   Stratford Canning: quoted in Cable, *Avenue,* p. 34.

25   disappointment of ministers: Willson, *Friendly Relations,* pp. 40–48; Green, *Washington,* 1:46–47; Augustus Foster, *Jeffersonian America* (San Marino, Calif., 1954), pp. 55–57.

25   nasty nationalistic response: Young, *Washington Community,* p. 220; Foster, *Jeffersonian America,* pp. 55–56.

25   revolving electoral door: Green, *Washington,* 1:119–23.

25   "quaking and trembling": M. B. Smith, *First Forty Years,* pp. 297–98.

25   massive housecleaning: Green, *Washington,* 1:122.

26   "empty, silent, dark": M. B. Smith, *First Forty Years,* p. 298.

26   Rep. Mitchill: "Dr. Mitchill's Letters from Washington: 1801–1813," *Harper's New Monthly Magazine* 58 (April 1879): 745.

26   Sen. Dallas: John M. Belohlevek, *George Mifflin Dallas: Jacksonian Patrician* (University Park, Penn., 1977), pp. 52–55.

26   Rep. Fairfield: John Fairfield to Anna Fairfield, December 4, 1835, and December 14, 1835, John Fairfield Collection, Manuscript Division, Library of Congress, Washington, D.C..

26   Frances Trollope: Frances Trollope, *Domestic Manners of the Americans* (1832; reprint, New York, 1904), p. 192.

27   congressmen lived the bachelor's life: Young, *Washington Community,* pp. 88–109; Busey, *Pictures,* p. 311.

27   looking for a "mess": Hubbard, "Political and Social Life," pp. 56–73.

27   Fairfield's fourth floor room: John Fairfield to Anna Fairfield, December 8, 1835, Fairfield Collection.

27   Rep. Randolph: Henry Adams, *John Randolph* (Boston, 1898), p. 275.

27   Rep. Quincy: quoted in Cable, *Avenue,* pp. 56–57.

27   Harriet Martineau: Harriet Martineau, *Retrospect of Western Travel,* 2 vols. (1838; reprint, New York, 1969), 1:238, 301.

27   Sen. Graham: quoted in Green, *Washington,* 1:151.

28   Grumbling was easier: Young, *Washington Community,* p. 50.

28   "The population of our city": M. B. Smith, *First Forty Years,* pp. 336–37.

28   officials blind to local problems: Bryan, *National Capital,* 1:64.

29   fledgling residential elite: Green, *Washington,* 1:5, 20; B. Carson, *Ambitious Appetites,* pp. 1–4, 92–102.

29   notable first residents: Green, *Washington,* 1:19–20; Arnebeck, *Fiery Trial,* pp. 215–20.

29   early residential society: B. Carson, *Ambitious Appetites,* pp. 1–4.

30   first residents and officials mixed: Green, *Washington,* 1:5, 20; M. B. Smith, *First Forty Years,* pp. 3–32, 390.

30   Tayloes of Octagon House: B. Carson, *Ambitious Appetites,* p. 128.

31   Mrs. Thornton recorded: Diary of Mrs. William Thornton, vol. 1, Manuscript Division, Library of Congress, Washington, D.C..

32   "we entered by the kitchen window": ibid.

32   "Reflections After Seeing": Undated poem among "Verses and Poems," Law Collection, Manuscript Division, Library of Congress, Washington, D.C.

32   "these Sunday assemblies": M. B. Smith, *First Forty Years,* pp. 13–14.

33   "lounging place of both sexes": ibid., pp. 94–95; cf. Young, *Washington Community,* p. 72.

33   growth of official society: U.S. Congress, *Biographical Directory of the American Congress* (Washington, D.C., 1972).

33   "Mr. and Mrs. Clay request": Young, *Washington Community,* pp. 224–25.

33   another arena: ibid., p. 47.

34   "other people's parties": M. B. Smith, *First Forty Years,* p. 213.

35   The Adamses' ball: Gretchen Schneider, preliminary draft of paper, "Mrs. Adams' Ball: A Political and Social Arena in Early Nineteenth-Century America," 1987, pp. 1–4.

35   "a snarling dinner": Louisa Catherine Adams, "Diary," December 19, 1823, Adams Papers, Massachusetts Historical Society, Microfilm Reel No. 265 (Boston, 1956).

35   "John's arguments": Louisa Catherine Adams, "Diary," December 20, 1823.

35   guest list: John Quincy Adams, "Diary," January 6, 1824, Adams Papers, Massachusetts Historical Society, Microfilm Reel No. 38, (Boston, 1954).

35   "number . . . exceeds belief": Louisa Catherine Adams, "Diary," December 27, 1823.

35   "society is divided into separate battalions": M. B. Smith, *First Forty Years,* p. 170.

35   "Party spirit is now fiery hot": Seaton, *William Winston Seaton,* p. 195.

36   Juliana Seaton belittled: ibid., p. 132.

37   "city is thronged with strangers": M. B. Smith, *First Forty Years,* pp. 312–13.

37   "increasing luxury of dress": ibid., pp. 377–78.

38   Southerners and Southern ways: Green, *Washington,* 1:53–54, 95–96; Walter C. Claphane, "The Local Aspects of Slavery in the District of Columbia," *Records of the Columbia Historical Society, 1898–1899,* (Washington, D.C., 1900), p. 225; Sandra Fitzpatrick and Maria Goodwin, *The Guide to Black Washington* (New York, 1990), p. 44.

38   mounting anxiety: Green, *Washington,* 1:178.

39   Southerners still dominate society: Margaret Leech, *Reveille in Washington: 1860–1865* (New York, 1941), p. 17.

39   "Feeling ran high": Virginia Clay-Clopton, *A Belle of the Fifties* (New York, 1905), p. 42.

39   "dancing over a powder magazine": ibid., p. 58.

40   "Not even to save the Nation": ibid., pp. 126–37.

40   Miss Lane's impossible task: Seale, *President's House,* 1:340–46.

41   "Mr. Tombs and General Scott": *Wartime Washington: The Civil War Letters of Elizabeth Blair Lee,* ed. Virginia Laas (Urbana, Ill., 1991), p. 23.

41   escalating crisis: Leech, *Reveille,* pp. 20–21; Cable, *Avenue,* p. 117.

41   a few days before Christmas: Seale, *President's House,* 1:355; Sara A. R. Pryor, *Reminiscences of Peace and War* (New York, 1905), pp. 111–12; Leech, *Reveille,* pp. 21–22.

42   a beleagured battleground: Green, *Washington,* 1: 232.

42   Rumors began to fly: ibid., pp. 231–33; Benjamin Cooling, *Symbol, Sword and Shield* (Hamden, Conn., 1975), pp. 12–18; Benjamin Brown French, *Witness to the Young Republic: A Yankee's Journal, 1828–1870,* ed. Donald B. Cole and John J. McDonough (Hanover, N.H., 1989), p. 339.

42   1860 census: *United States Census: 1860.*
42   "men bold and brave enough": *Richmond Examiner,* December 25, 1860.
42   "all Washington seemed to change": Clay-Clopton, *Belle of the Fifties,* p. 151.

Chapter 3. Washington Society Transformed: The Civil War and Its Aftermath in the Capital

43   Lincoln's inauguration: *Washington Evening Star* (hereinafter *Star*), March 1–6, 1861; Cooling, *Symbol,* pp. 12–27.
43   civil war had begun: *Star,* March 5–30, April 12–20, 1861; Green, *Washington* 1:240.
44   exodus of Southerners: Green, *Washington,* 1:241–48; *Star,* April 15–20, 1861; Albert Gallatin Riddle, *Recollections of War Times* (New York, 1895), pp. 7–10; Mary Mitchell, *Divided Town* (Barre, Mass., 1968), p. 36.
44   resignation of officers: *Star,* April 18–24, 1861; Leech, *Reveille,* pp. 61–62. By April 22, 1861, four days after Lee's resignation, Quartermaster General Joseph Johnston, Captain John B. Magruder, and Commodore Franklin Buchanan, all prominent members of society, had resigned and departed to serve the Confederacy; Cooling, *Symbol,* p. 34.
44   residential elite suffered losses: Mitchell, *Divided Town,* pp. 33, 118–19; Green, *Washington,* 1:236–72; Lee, *Wartime Washington,* pp. 25–48; Seale, *President's House,* 1:362.
45   "disgraced with Lincoln's low soldiery": Clay-Clopton, *Belle of the Fifties,* p. 151.
45   handsome homes for rent: Elden Billings, "Social and Economic Conditions in Washington During the Civil War," *Records of the Columbia Historical Society, 1963–1965* (Washington, D.C., 1966), pp. 192–93.
45   "Property . . . 'for a song'": George W. Smith, "A Critical Moment for Washington," *Records of the Columbia Historical Society, 1918* (Washington, D.C., 1919), p. 105.
45   Southerners who stayed behind: Leech, *Reveille,* pp. 94–96, 134–41, 148–51; Mitchell, *Divided Town,* p. 33; Alan H. Lessoff, "The Federal Government and the National Capital—Washington, 1861–1902," PhD diss., The Johns Hopkins University, 1990, p. 72.
45   "in the midst of traitors": quoted in Cooling, *Symbol,* p. 32.
45   rumors of collaboration: Leech, *Reveille,* pp. 94–96, 134–41, 148–54; Mitchell, *Divided Town,* p. 33; Lee, *Wartime Washington,* 170–72.
46   Fanny Kemble marvelled: letter of March 8, 1862, vol. 4, Fanny Kemble Collection, Folger Shakespeare Library, Washington, D.C.
47   freedmen and clerks: Green, *Washington,* 1:276–78.

47   tourists flooded in: Leech, *Reveille,* pp. 163–64.

47   "in quest of friends": Noah Brooks, *Washington During Lincoln's Time,*
ed. Herbert Mitgang (Chicago, 1971), p. 17. [Original edition first published in 1895.]

47   Confidence men, etc.: Leech, *Reveille,* pp. 121, 259–67; Green,
Washington, 1:251; Cooling, *Symbol,* p. 141. Throughout the war, articles
in the *Star* described and decried the charlatans and prostitutes preying
on the soldiers and citizenry, all the while running the advertisements of
some of the worst of the lot.

47   "Politicians of every grade": Julia Ward Howe, *Reminiscences: 1819–1899*
(1899; reprint, New York, 1969), p. 269. While in Washington, Howe tired
of listening to the Massachusetts regiments' endless choruses of "John
Brown's Body," and was inspired to write "The Battle Hymn of the
Republic," to be sung to the same tune, at dawn one morning in her
room at the Willard Hotel.

47   Louisa May Alcott: quoted in Cable, *Avenue,* p. 125.

48   hotels were crowded: Billings, "Economic Condition," p. 193.

48   "city now is a huge crowd": Mrs. John A. Kasson, "An Iowa Woman in
Washington, 1861–1865," *Iowa Journal of History* 52 (January 1954), p. 62.

48   Mary Todd Lincoln: Leech, *Reveille,* pp. 285–310; Jean Baker, *Mary Todd
Lincoln: A Biography* (New York, 1987), pp. 163–243.

48   "cold shoulder": Lee, *Wartime Washington,* p. 61.

48   Mrs. Lincoln's extravagance: Leech, *Reveille,* pp. 285–310; Baker, *Mary
Todd Lincoln,* pp. 205–207; Green, *Washington,* 1:269; *Star,* February
1–18, 1862. Several members of official society found the much-publicized
preparations for the reception obscene. Ohio Senator Ben Wade sent
harshly worded regrets: "Are the President and Mrs. Lincoln aware that
there is a civil war? If they are not, Mr. and Mrs. Wade are, and for that
reason decline to participate in feasting and dancing"; quoted in Leech,
Reveille, p. 295.

49   elegant drawingrooms: Thomas Belden and Marva Belden, *So Fell the
Angels* (Boston, 1956), pp. 24–26; Billings, "Economic Conditions," pp.
201–2.

49   the two women detested one another: Kate Chase, who believed her father
the rightful occupant of the White House, made her disdain for the Lincolns
clear at their first State dinner in March 1861. In an exchange repeated all
across the capital, Mrs. Lincoln greeted her, "I shall be glad to see you any
time, Miss Chase," to which Kate Chase insolently replied, "Mrs. Lincoln, I
shall be glad to have *you* call on *me* at any time"; Belden and Belden,
Angels, pp. 3–4, 33. The rivalry of Mrs. Lincoln and Miss Chase, in which
Miss Chase consistently held the upper hand, was noted with glee in the
press. One Ohio newspaper commented: "The Lincoln-Chase contest has

extended into the women's department. Mrs. Lincoln has got a new French rig with all the posies, costing $4,000. Miss Chase sees her and goes one better, by ordering a nice little $6,000 arrangement, including a $3,000 love of a shawl." *The Dayton Empire,* quoted in Carl Sandburg, *Abraham Lincoln: The War Years,* 3 vols. (New York, 1939), 2:256.

50   Kate Chase's wedding: The *New York Herald* had impudently suggested that Mrs. Lincoln, "with her usual good nature," would permit Miss Chase to hold her wedding reception in the East Room, "in order that in view of a certain possible event she may have an opportunity of judging how its associations suit her." *New York Herald* quoted in Leech, *Reveille,* p. 256. For weeks after the wedding, Washington society talked of little else. One reporter noted "who was there and who was not there; how the bride looked in her white velvet dress . . . how Mrs. Lincoln did not go because she is yet in black wear and an opportune chill betimes; . . . how the bride wore a 'tiara' of pearls and diamonds, the like of which was never seen in America . . . all of these things are good for Washington gossip, and the National Village is yet agitated"; Noah Brooks, quoted in Sandburg, *War Years,* 2:456.

50   bloated corpses: Green, *Washington,* 1:261. In the weeks after the battle of Ball's Bluff upriver in Virginia in October 1861, the *Star* carried stories of bloated bodies of dead soldiers being carried downriver to lodge against the bridges and piers.

50   "Washington seems crazy": Green, *Washington,* 1:268–69.

50   "One would hardly think": Harriet Balch to mother, February 10 and 15, 1863, quoted in Green, *Washington,* 1:269.

50   "something saddening, indeed revolting": the *London Times,* November 3, 1863, quoted in Emerson Fite, *Social and Industrial Conditions in the North during The Civil War* (New York, 1910), p. 259.

50   "mad with gaiety": *Springfield Republican,* February 20, 1864.

50   Violet Blair: Violet Blair Janin Diary, winter 1863–64, Albert and Violet (Blair) Janin Collection, the Huntington Library, San Marino, Calif.

50   "Gaiety has become an epidemic": Frederick Seward, quoted in Leech, *Reveille,* p. 284.

51   Noisy celebrations: *Star,* December 26–29, 1864, and April 4–12, 1865; B. French, *Witness,* p. 468.

52   the capital in mourning: *Star,* April 18–22, 1865.

52   Marian Hooper: M. Adams, *Letters,* pp. 4–10.

52   Major General Hayes: Emily Geer, *First Lady: The Life of Lucy Webb Hayes* (Kent, Ohio, 1984), p. 78.

52   "Pennsylvania Avenue was lined": entry for May 23, 1865, Isaac Bassett Diary, Office of the Curator of Arts and Antiquities, U.S. Capitol, Washington, D.C.; parade reported in the *Star,* May 24, 1865.

52   "this glorious old army": M. Adams, *Letters,* p. 7.

53   second day of Grand Review: *Star,* May 25, 1865.

54   "The pageant faded": Brooks, *Lincoln's Time,* p. 283. Altogether nearly 200,000 men marched down Pennsylvania Avenue in two days. The decimated regiments, the youthful appearance of the general officers, and the scarcity of field officers were sad reminders of the thousands who lay in hospital beds or graves far from home. Marian Hooper's sister Ellen wrote home, "It was a sad day too—you felt as if there were another army— larger and finer—marching above them"; M. Adams, *Letters,* p. 469. On May 26, Lucy Hayes wrote her mother, "While my heart filled with joy at the thought of our mighty country—its victorious noble army—the sad thoughts of the thousands who would never gladden home with their presence made the joyful scene mingled with so much sadness—that I could not shake it off"; Geer, *First Lady,* p. 78.

54   "old jog trot": B. French, *Witness,* p. 490.

54   clearly a changed city: Leech, *Reveille,* p. 418.

54   "returning parole bearer": Thomas C. DeLeon, *Belles, Beaux, and Brains of the 60's* (1907; reprint, New York, 1974), p. 33.

54   postwar crowds: *United States Eighth and Ninth Censuses,* (Washington, D.C., 1860, 1870); Green, *Washington,* 1:264, 306. Washington was not the only city experiencing phenomenal growth in the last half of the nineteenth century. Its population increase mirrored the urbanization taking place nationwide. While other cities could point to the discovery of gold or the opening of a rail line as the cause of their sudden growth, Washington was unique in two respects: its growth spurt was directly attributable to a national calamity (the war) and it was not in the West or Midwest where other mushrooming cities lay, but nestled among the older cities along the East Coast. Among other cities that grew rapidly in the last half of the century: Chicago, a muddy trading post of 350 people in 1833, a city of 30,000 in 1850, 100,000 in 1860, and 300,000 in 1870; Denver, which grew from 5,000 in 1870 to 100,000 in 1890; Birmingham, Alabama, nonexistent in 1870 but with 3,800 citizens by 1880; and New York City, which grew from 1,000,000 in 1870 to 1,500,000 in 1890. See Jaher, *Urban Establishment,* p. 453; Stanley Buder, *Pullman: An Experiment in Industrial Order and Community Planning* (New York, 1967), p. 4; John Garraty, *The New Commonwealth: 1877–1890* (New York, 1968), p. 180.

54   a capital physically shabby: Henry Glassie, "Victorian Homes in Washington," *Records of the Columbia Historical Society, 1963–1965* (Washington, D.C., 1966), p. 334; James Whyte, *The Uncivil War: Washington during the Reconstruction* (New York, 1958), pp. 13, 164; Green, *Washington,* 1:312, 328–29; Bowling, *Creation of Washington,* pp. 244–45.

55 agitation to move the capital: Lessoff, "The Federal Government," pp. 17–18.

55 petition for a territorial government: ibid., pp. 335–38; Francis C. Adams, *Our Little Monarchy: Who Runs It and What It Costs* (Washington, D.C., 1873), pp. 7, 9; *Star*, January 4, 1870.

55 The short life of the Territory: Green, *Washington*, 1:336; William Maury, "The Territorial Period in Washington, 1871–1874, with Special Emphasis on Alexander Shepherd and the Board of Public Works," Ph.D. diss., George Washington University, 1975, p. 41; Lessoff, "The Federal Government," p. 54.

55 Grant's crony Shepherd: Green, *Washington*, 1:339–62; Maury, "Territorial Period," pp. 1–37. Shepherd's control of Cooke and the entire territorial government was widely acknowledged. "Why," went a contemporary joke, "is the new governor like a lamb?" "Because he is led by A. Shepherd," was the riposte; *Washington Daily Patriot*, May 9, 1871.

56 congressional investigation: U.S. Congress, "Investigation into the Affairs of the District of Columbia," 42d Cong., 2d sess., H. Rpt. 72, Serial 1542, pp. 1–755; *Star*, March 3, 1873; Lessoff, "The Federal Government," pp. 62, 129–50. Shepherd had obligingly provided inside information on areas of the city to be developed to friendly officials, enabling several, like Nevada Senator William Stewart, Ohio Senator John Sherman, and General William T. Sherman, to reap fortunes in real estate. See Glassie, "Victorian Homes," pp. 342–47; Ruth Hermann, *Gold and Silver Colossus: William Morris Stewart and His Southern Bride* (Sparks, Nev., 1975), p. 239; Lessoff, "The Federal Government," pp. 62, 301–2; Walter Albano, "History of the Dupont Circle Neighborhood, Washington, D.C., 1880–1900," M.A. thesis, University of Maryland, 1982, p. 10; Russell Elliott, *Servant of Power: A Political Biography of William Morris Stewart* (Reno, Nev., 1983), p. 74. Shepherd's papers contain many letters from friendly officials, including Congressmen James Garfield and Thomas Platt of New York, who stood to profit by the cordial relationship; Alexander Shepherd Collection, Manuscript Division, Library of Congress, Washington, D.C.

56 District of Columbia was bankrupt: Maury, "Territorial Period," p. 115; Green, *Washington*, 1:357–58; *Star*, September 1–30, 1873.

56 a costly failure: U.S. Congress, "Investigation into the Affairs of the District of Columbia," 43d Cong., 1st sess., S. Rpt. 453, Serial 1590, 1591, 1592; Green, *Washington*, 1:359–60. In his doctoral dissertation, Alan Lessoff finds a strong correlation between citizen opposition to Shepherd's "Ring" and length of residence in the District. The longer the residence in Washington, the more likely an individual was to oppose Shepherd's plans. Lessoff, "The Federal Government," pp. 106–16.

57   Shepherd fled Washington: Maury, "Territorial Period," p. 210. Shepherd lived to see his tarnished image refurbished. In Mexico, he reopened an abandoned silver mine and recouped his fortune. When he visited Washington in 1887, the city staged an elaborate welcome. No mention was made of kickbacks or corruption, only of his vision and foresight. Marching bands met Shepherd at the station. In the parade that followed were banners reading "Population 1871, 80,000; 1887, 250,000," and "Washington suggested; Congress sanctioned; Shepherd made it." It was very gratifying for Shepherd, who eventually returned to Mexico where he died of a ruptured appendix in 1902; Green, *Washington,* 2:83.

57   "provincial Southern city is no more": Mary Clemmer Ames, *Ten Years in Washington: Life and Scenes in the National Capital As a Woman Sees Them* (Hartford, Conn., 1873), pp. 72–74.

57   Shepherd's New Washington: Morton Keller, *Affairs of State: Public Life in Late Nineteenth Century America* (Cambridge, Mass., 1977), pp. 39, 98–100; Young, *Washington Community,* pp. 28–31; Lessoff, "The Federal Government," pp. 1–5.

58   a Japanese visitor: Arinori Mori, *Life and Resources in America* (Washington, D.C., 1871), p. 39.

58   Joel Parker and E. L. Godkin: quoted in Keller, *Affairs of State,* p. 45–46.

59   "Adams was optimistic": *The Education of Henry Adams* (Boston, 1961), p. 237. [*Education* was first published in 1918.]

59   "young men like ourselves": Henry Adams, *A Cycle of Adams Letters,* ed. Worthington Chauncey Ford, 2 vols. (Boston, 1920), 1:196.

59   the new state's influence: Margaret Susan Thompson, "The 'Spider Web': Congress and Lobbying in the Age of Grant," Ph.D. diss., University of Wisconsin, 1979, p. 131; Thomas Bender, *Toward an Urban Vision* (Lexington, Ky.,1975), p. 189.

59   Congress was newly powerful: Thompson, "'Spider Web,'" pp. 27–28; Keller, *Affairs of State,* pp. 21–22, 108–10. The creation of a host of new congressional committees was testament to the new responsibilities Congress was shouldering: Coinage, Weights and Measures (1864), Mines and Mining (1865), Pacific Railroads (1865), Education and Labor (1867), Revision of the Laws (1868), War Claims (1873), Expenditures in the Department of Justice (1874), Levees and Improvements of the Mississippi River (1875), and Alcoholic Liquor Traffic (1879).

59   government was expanding: Young, *Washington Community,* p. 28; Thompson, "'Spider Web,'" pp. 43–44; U.S. Government, *Historical Statistics of the United States: Colonial Times to 1957* (Washington, D.C., 1961), p. 710.

59   special interest groups: Keller, *Affairs of State,* pp. 122–61, 170; Thompson, "'Spider Web,'" pp. 25–26.

60   Sen. Sherman: quoted in Claude Bowers, *The Tragic Era: The Revolution After Lincoln* (Cambridge, Mass., 1929), p. 115.

60   "The harpies": George Alfred Townsend, *Washington Outside and Inside* (Hartford, Conn., 1873), p. 22.

60   ruthless era: Thompson, "'Spider Web,'" p. 186. Vernon Parrington labeled these years "The Great Barbeque"; Richard Hofstadter, "The Age of the Spoilsmen"; Ray Ginger, "The Age of Excess"; and Matthew Josephson, "the saturnalia of plunder."

60   dishes at the Great Barbeque: Garraty, *New Commonwealth,* pp. 4–10; Whyte, *Uncivil War,* p. 194; Matthew Josephson, *The Politicos* (New York, 1938), p. 105; David Loth, *Public Plunder: A History of Graft in America* (New York, 1938), p. 180; Bowers, *Tragic Era,* p. 195. When their fledgling telephone company became embroiled in interminable lawsuits and potentially devastating patent disputes, both Alexander Graham Bell and his father-in-law, rich and influential Gardiner Greene Hubbard, moved to Washington to look out for their interests. Both built beautiful mansions in the city and they and their wives became leaders of the city's intellectual, scientific, and social elites. Lacey, "Mysteries of Earth-Making," pp. 82–91; Robert Bruce, *Bell: Alexander Graham Bell and the Conquest of Solitude* (Boston, 1973).

61   John Hay to John Nicolay: quoted in Belden and Belden, *Angels,* p. 169.

61   "waltzing the profession": H. Adams, *Education,* p. 256.

61   "literally central city": DeLeon, *Belles, Beaux,* p. 33

61   fate of Southern sympathizers: Green, *Washington,* 1:289, 294–95; Seale, *President's House,* 1:340.

61   Charleston: Fraser, *Charleston! Charleston!* pp. 265–75, 283–84.

62   social vacuum: Jaher, *Urban Establishment,* pp. 20–21, 171, 399.

62   "the rim of outer darkness": [Nelle Margaret Scanlan], *Boudoir Mirrors of Washington* (Philadelphia, 1923), p. 221.

63   Beatrice Webb: quoted in Leonore Davidoff, *The Best Circles: Society, Etiquette and the Season in London.* (London,1973), p. 63.

63   composition of Congress: U.S. Senate, *Senate Campaign Information* (Washington, D.C., 1978), pp. 396–97.

63   War heroes popped up: Thompson, "'Spider Web,'" p. 21; U.S.Senate, *Senate Campaign Information,* pp. 396–97.

64   Andrew Johnson's White House: Emily Edson Briggs, *The Olivia Letters* (New York, 1906), pp. 48–50, 69, 100; Ames, *Ten Years,* p. 244.

64   Charles Sumner: David Donald, *Charles Sumner and the Rights of Man* (New York, 1970), pp. 268–302. Sumner's social star shone briefly. Within a year of their marriage, the Sumners were providing grist for the society

gossip mill. There were rumors of great unhappiness on both sides, of loud quarrels, and of a handsome attaché at the Prussian Embassy. The Sumners separated, and in 1873 Sumner divorced his wife, the former Alice Hooper, on grounds of desertion. Donald, *Charles Sumner,* pp. 289–95, 312–20.

64   social gatherings to enhance political position: William McFeely, *Grant: A Biography* (New York, 1981), pp. 260–80. Throughout 1866 and 1867, the Radicals tried to "appropriate" Grant for their cause by securing his attendance at their parties. But Ulysses and Julia Grant were scrupulously hospitable to all of official society and accepted every invitation to the White House as well as invitations to the Radicals' receptions. However, after Grant broke with President Johnson in January 1868, the two men maintained separate "courts," and the social and political rivalry was only thinly veiled. For example, in late June, the Grants had a "private" reception, with the general and his aides in full uniform, to honor the members of the recently arrived Chinese legation. By labeling their evening as "private," the Grants did not have to invite the president. Later that year, the Grants pointedly kept their children home from the White House Christmas party. McFeely, *Grant,* pp. 245, 258, 284.

64   presidential fever struck Chase: Belden and Belden, *Angels,* pp. 167–83.

64   "The old monarchy's dying": Briggs, *Olivia Letters,* p. 37.

64   "passion for notoriety": Wilhelmus Bryan, *National Capital,* 2:585.

65   "Paris has Eugenie": Briggs, *Olivia Letters,* p. 70. Twain mocked the gushing prose of the new genre in his "account of a [Washington] reception" for the *Chicago Republican:* "The most fashionably dressed lady was Mrs. G. C. She wore a pink satin dress, plain in front, but with a good deal of rake to it—to the train, I mean; it was said to be two or three yards long. One could see it creeping along the floor some little time after the woman was gone. She had a beautiful complexion when she first came, but it faded out by degrees in the most unaccountable way. However, it was not lost for good. I found most of it on my shoulder afterward"; Mark Twain, *Chicago Republican,* February 8, 1868, article pasted in scrapbook in the David Mearns Collection, Manuscript Division, Library of Congress, Washington, D.C. Society columns began to appear in nearly all big-city newspapers in the years after the war, suggesting that high society was getting too large for its members to pass around gossip by word of mouth.

65   inaugural ball a fiasco: *Star,* March 4–6, 1869.

65   "tearing up of the icebergs": Briggs, *Olivia Letters,* pp. 97–99.

65   "Delicate women": Ames, *Ten Years,* p. 278–79.

Chapter 4. The Blossoming of Official Society: 1868–1872

66   a tidal wave of optimism: Allan Nevins, *Hamilton Fish: The Inner History of the Grant Administration* (New York, 1936), pp. 107–08.

67   "make it really democratic": *The Nation,* March 4, 1869.

68   official society's congressional component: U.S. Congress, *Biographical Directory,* pp. 47, 171–74, 193–97. The other two of the five new states were Kansas and West Virginia.

68   numbers of leading officers: U.S. Congress, *Congressional Directory,* 36th Cong., 1st sess. (Washington, D.C., 1860), pp. 33–35; U.S. Congress, *Congressional Directory,* 41st Cong., 1st sess. (Washington, D.C., 1869), pp. 75–78.

68   General Sherman was always happy to recount the particulars of his "march to the sea," and did so with great gusto. Nearly two decades after those battles, the general was still delighting dinner companions with the thrilling tale, as Marian Adams related to her father in a letter in December 1882: "Yesterday a dinner of fourteen at [Commissioner of Agriculture] G[eorge]. B[ailey]. Loring's; sat between a mild and dull New Yorker named Jay and the Secretary of State [Frederick T. Frelinghuysen]. At last in desperation I spoke across the table to General Sherman and he became very lively over his 'march to the sea' and repeated it with knives and forks on the tablecloth. Finally he swept the rebel army off the table with a pudding knife, much to the amusement of his audience." M. Adams, *Letters,* pp. 406–7.

68   growing diplomatic community: U.S. Congress, *Congressional Directory,* 36th Cong., 1st sess., pp. 36–38; *Congressional Directory,* 41st Cong., 1st sess., pp. 80–82.

68   the diplomatic community: The *New York Herald* headlined its account of President Grant's New Year's reception in January 1870 "A Gorgeous Nigger" and told of the arrival of the Haitian minister, General Alexander Tate, in a swallowtail coat with elaborate gold braid on the collar and lapels. The president cordially shook Tate's hand, but other diplomats and American officials snubbed him. Noticing this, Postmaster General John Creswell went over and had an amiable conversation with him. *New York Herald,* January 2, 1870; William McFeely, *Grant,* New York: 1981, p. 337.

Assignments to the American capital were still not greatly prized. One reason was the living conditions, which, while greatly improved since the war, still fell far below those of cities like Paris or London. The suffocating heat of a Washington summer was especially horrifying to Europeans. When Prevost-Paradol, Napoleon III's minister to Washington, committed suicide in July 1870, at the outbreak of the Franco-Prussian War, local wags claimed that the excessive heat, not international turmoil, had unhinged him. Green, *Washington,* 1:316; Nevins, *Hamilton Fish,* pp. 402–3.

69 "an asterisk is affixed": U.S. Congress, *Congressional Directory,* 29th Cong., 1st sess. (Washington, D.C., 1845), pp. 5–10.

70 an asterisk no longer sufficed: U.S. Congress, *Congressional Directory,* 36th Cong., 2d sess. (Washington, D.C., 1861), pp. 63–68.

70 symbols multiply again: U.S. Congress, *Congressional Directory,* 42d Cong., 2d sess. (Washington, D.C., 1872), pp. 120–25.

70 congressmen in hotels: James M. Goode, *Capital Losses: A Cultural History of Washington's Destroyed Buildings* (Washington, D.C., 1979), pp. 176–78; *Star,* December 16, 1902, and June 12, 1912; Washington *Post,* January 21, 1912, and May 19, 1912; Whyte, *Uncivil War,* pp. 179–80; Townsend, *Washington,* p. 180.

72 large private homes: Goode, *Capital Losses,* pp. 24–25.

72 official society's constant turnover: *Congressional Directory,* 36th Cong., 2d sess., and 41st Cong., 1st sess.; *Biographical Directory,* pp. 171–74, 193–97; Congressional Quarterly, *Congressional Quarterly's Guide to the U.S. Supreme Court* (Washington, D.C., 1979), pp. 808–23.

73 boom in etiquette books: Susan Williams, *Savory Suppers and Fashionable Feasts: Dining in Victorian America* (New York, 1985), p. 6.

73 the Washington etiquette book: Arthur M. Schlesinger, *Learning How to Behave: A Historical Study Of American Etiquette Books* (New York, 1946), pp. 33–34; Madeleine Vinton Dahlgren, *Etiquette of Social Life in Washington* (Lancaster, Penn., 1873); John Kasson, *Rudeness and Civility: Manners in Nineteenth-Century Urban America* (New York, 1990), pp. 48–51.

73 women as arbiters of taste: Jaher, *Urban Establishment,* p. 416; Jaher, *The Rich,* pp. 274–77.

73 "The courtesies": Hall, *Social Usages,* pp. v, 127.

73 "Politeness is power": Maurice Egan, *A Gentleman,* 2d ed. (New York, 1893), p. 15.

74 the importance of courtesy: Kasson, *Rudeness,* pp. 68–69.

74 congressional salaries: Congressional Quarterly, *Guide to Congress,* pp. 460–62.

75 Cries of poverty: *Congressional Globe,* 42d Cong., 3d sess. (Washington, D.C., 1873), pp. 2048–49.

75 Sen. Cameron: ibid., pp. 2046–47. Since 1853, the salary of a member of the cabinet had been $8,000. The 1873 compensation act raised it to $10,000.

75 Sen. Morton: ibid., p. 2047.

75 Sen. Scott, Sen. Morrill: ibid., pp. 2180, 2049.

76 Sen. Carpenter: ibid., p. 2181.

76   when the odious bill passed: ibid., p. 2184; *Guide to Congress,* pp. 461–62. The Senate vote for the salary increase was 36 to 27 with 10 members absent.

76   repeal the salary increase: Nevins, *Hamilton Fish,* p. 612; *Guide to Congress,* pp. 461–62. After the increase was repealed, congressional salaries remained at $5,000 for more than three decades, until 1907, when Congress ventured to raise them to $7,500 again.

78   to seal one's political doom: In 1883, Senator William Windom of Minnesota was largely defeated by the house he built on Vermont Avenue in the District. His opponent circulated photographs of the house and convinced enough voters that it showed too great a love for the good life and too little regard for Minnesota. David Barry, "Men and Affairs at Washington," *New England Magazine* 37(January 1908): 590.

78   Respected for his eloquence: *New York Times,* December 28, 1898; *Star,* December 28, 1898; William Parker, *The Life and Public Services of Justin Smith Morrill* (Boston, 1924), pp. 200–378.

80   Morrill's home on Thomas Circle: Parker, *Justin Smith Morrill,* p. 221; Goode, *Capital Losses,* pp. 44–45; *New York Times,* December 28, 1898.

80   Sen. Stewart of Nevada: R. Elliott, *Servant of Power,* pp. 1–47, 291; Hermann, *Gold and Silver Colossus,* pp. 1–223; *Star,* April 23, 1909.

81   Mark Twain and Sen. Stewart: Justin Kaplan, *Mr. Clemens and Mark Twain* (New York, 1966), pp. 50–58. Twain's hilarious piece on his Washington career was entitled "My Late Senatorial Secretaryship." Twain had Stewart in mind when he described a congressman as "the smallest mind and the selfishest soul and the cowardliest heart that God makes"; quoted in Wallace Stegner, *Beyond the Hundredth Meridian: John Wesley Powell and the Second Opening of the West* (Boston, 1954), p. 117.

82   Stewart's Castle: R. Elliott, *Servant of Power,* pp. 74–80; Hermann, *Gold and Silver Colossus,* p. 239–42; Albano, "Dupont Circle," p. 10; Effie Mona Mack, "William Morris Stewart, 1827–1909," *Nevada Historical Society Quarterly* 7 (1964): 62, 93–94; Goode, *Capital Losses,* pp. 77–79; Green, *Washington,* 1:344–45; *Star,* December 31, 1879 and January 12, 1930.

84   the Stewarts are eclipsed: Hermann, *Gold and Silver Colossus,* pp. 242–48, 285–305; Goode, *Capital Losses,* p. 79; *New York Times,* April 24, 1909; *Star,* December 31, 1879 and April 24, 1909.

84   huge Butler mansion: Goode, *Capital Losses,* p. 81. Butler's Capitol Hill house cost him $125,000. He had the architect incorporate into it an office for himself, and an apartment for his daughter Blanche and her husband, Mississippi Senator Adelbert Ames, a carpetbagger from New England. Butler's heirs sold the house to the government for $275,000 and the site is now the home of the Longworth House Office Building. Robert

Werlich, *"Beast" Butler* (Washington, D.C., 1962), p. 159; Richard S. West, Jr., *Lincoln's Scapegoat General: A Life of Benjamin Butler* (Boston, 1965), p. 352.

85   old New England stock: Hans Trefousse, *Ben Butler: The South Called Him Beast* (New York, 1957), pp. 1–80.

85   Butler's military career: Trefousse, *Ben Butler,* pp. 80–174; L. T. Merrill, "General Benjamin F. Butler in Washington," *Records of the Columbia Historical Society, 1936–1937* (Washington, D.C., 1938), pp. 78–80.

86   Butler easily recognized: Trefousse, *Ben Butler,* pp. 175–241; Merrill, "General Benjamin F. Butler," pp. 72–73, 80–83.

86   The early Grant years benefited Butler: Merrill, "General Benjamin F. Butler," pp. 71–97; Trefousse, *Ben Butler,* pp. 208, 241; Gamaliel Bradford, *Damaged Souls* (Boston, 1923), p. 229. Reporters twitted Butler on his opportunities for enhanced prosperity when admission of new states was considered, entailing new flags with additional stars.

86   parties and sailing: Merrill, "General Benjamin F. Butler," pp. 78, 96–97; Trefousse, *Ben Butler,* p. 212; *Star,* January 11, 1893; Bradford, *Damaged Souls,* p. 238. Sailing was Butler's chief recreation, and the *America,* after which the "America's Cup" was named, was a marvelous racing craft. In India-rubber coat and sou'wester, his face as red as a lobster, Butler would ply the Atlantic in *America* and relax.

86   Butler in political decline: Trefousse, *Ben Butler,* pp. 230–31; Merrill, "General Benjamin F. Butler," p. 75; Bradford, *Damaged Souls,* pp. 224–25; *Star,* January 11, 1893.

87   "fair, fat and forty": In fact, Julia Grant was forty-three when her husband took office. Mrs. Grant was indeed a solidly built woman—when, as tourists at the Paris Exposition in 1878, the Grants tested an elaborate scale on display, Ulysses weighed in at 165 pounds, Julia at 175. McFeely, *Grant,* pp. 24–25; Henry Adams quoted in Whyte, *Uncivil War,* p. 95; Briggs, *Olivia Letters,* p. 169; Seale, *President's House,* 1:474.

88   The nation delighted: *The Personal Memoirs of Julia Dent Grant,* ed. John Simon (New York, 1975), pp. 173–74; Whyte, *Uncivil War,* p. 95; McFeely, *Grant,* pp. 303–4; Briggs, *Olivia Letters,* p. 168.

88   "I felt a little shy": Grant, *Memoirs,* pp. 174–75, 177.

88   Mrs. Grant's innovation: Briggs, *Olivia Letters,* p. 257; Nevins, *Hamilton Fish,* p. 575; Ames, *Ten Years,* pp. 256–57.

88   "easy and pleasant for me": Grant, *Memoirs,* pp. 175–76

88   the Grants set their stamp on the White House: Seale, *President's House,* 1:456; Edna Colman, *White House Gossip: From Andrew Johnson to Calvin Coolidge* (Garden City, N.Y., 1927), p. 57; Briggs, *Olivia Letters,* pp. 200–205; Ames, *Ten Years,* pp. 171–72; Mary Abigail Dodge, *Gail Hamilton's Life in Letters* (Boston, 1901), p. 647.

90   Reporters like Briggs scrutinized: Briggs, *Olivia Letters,* pp. 168, 199–201; Seale, *President's House,* 1:474.

90   "a bright and beautiful dream": Grant, *Memoirs,* p. 182; McFeely, *Grant,* pp. 319–29.

90   collapse of the gold market ensnares the Grants: McFeely, *Grant,* pp. 319–29; Grant, *Memoirs,* p. 182.

93   Kate Sprague's precarious prominence: Mary Merwin Phelps, *Kate Chase, Dominant Daughter* (New York, 1935), p. 179; Belden and Belden, *Angels,* p. 164; Ishbel Ross, *Proud Kate: Portrait of an Ambitious Woman* (New York, 1953), pp. 212–13.

93   Sprague's sulphurous harangues: Senator Sprague's speeches on the Senate floor began on March 15, 1869, and continued through April 8. *Congressional Globe,* 41st Cong., 1st sess. (Washington, D.C., 1869); Briggs, *Olivia Letters,* pp. 112–16; *New York World,* April 23, 1869; Belden and Belden, *Angels,* pp. 216–40; Phelps, *Dominant Daughter,* pp. 219–20.

94   Mrs. Sprague was much subdued: Belden and Belden, *Angels,* pp. 242–43, 269–70

94   "I do not see Mrs. Sprague's name": Mrs. Lincoln to Mrs. J. H. Orne of Philadelphia, February 18, 1870, quoted in Ross, *Proud Kate,* p. 219.

94   "Mrs. Grundy": *New York World,* February 20, 1870.

94   "smooth waters of domestic life": Briggs, *Olivia Letters,* p. 291.

94   handsome Sen. Conkling: Briggs, *Olivia Letters,* pp. 212–13; Ross, *Proud Kate,* p. 219; David Jordan, *Roscoe Conkling of New York* (Ithaca, 1971), p. 205.

94   last and most elaborate reception: *New York World,* April 28, 1872.

95   "Gossip had it": Carl Schurz, *Reminiscences of Carl Schurz* (New York, 1907), p. 187.

95   widower George Williams: Sidney Teiser, "Life of George Williams: Almost Chief-Justice," Part 1, *Oregon Historical Quarterly* 47 (September 1946): 271–74; *Portland Daily Oregonian,* September 7, 1867.

95   "trying her repartee": *Oregon State Journal,* May 9, 1868.

95   "Mrs. Williams has no superior": ibid., January 22, 1870.

96   "the fair diplomatist": ibid., April 10, 1869; Teiser, "Almost Chief-Justice," Part 1, pp. 278–80.

96   Attorney Generalship: Teiser, "Almost Chief-Justice," Part 1, pp. 278–80.

96   the most expensive landau: Teiser, "Almost Chief-Justice," Part 2, *Oregon Historical Quarterly* 47 (December 1946): 418–25; *Oregon State Journal,* March 9, 1872; *Portland Daily Oregonian,* December 25, 1873, and January 5, 1874.

96   peremptory antics: Mrs. John A. Logan, *Reminiscences of a Soldier's Wife* (New York, 1913), pp. 271–72.

97   nasty gossip: Teiser, "Almost Chief-Justice," Part 2, pp. 424–25, 427;
      McFeely, *Grant,* p. 370.
97   "daughter of a steamboat man": Dodge, *Gail Hamilton,* pp. 682–83.
97   more salacious suggestions: Teiser, "Almost Chief-Justice," Part 2, pp.
      277–78.
98   Mrs. Grant admired Mrs. Fish: Grant, *Memoirs,* p. 188; Nevins, *Hamilton
      Fish,* p. 578. Louisa Dumeresg Hunt, daughter of a prominent, wealthy
      Boston family, was the wife of artist William Morris Hunt. Ellen Ruggles
      Strong, daughter of prominent New Yorker Samuel Ruggles, was married
      to New York lawyer George Templeton Strong.
98   easily intimidated: McFeely, *Grant,* pp. 235, 296–97.
98   husband had been a senator: Hamilton Fish had also been a member of
      the House for one term, from 1843 to 1845, but Mrs. Fish spent the time
      in New York.; Nevins, *Hamilton Fish,* pp. 44–45.
98   "lady *par excellence*": Dodge, *Gail Hamilton,* pp. 678, 685.
98   "Mrs. Fish—ah!": Briggs, *Olivia Letters,* p. 192.
98   Mrs. Fish took the first step: Nevins, *Hamilton Fish,* p. 94; Logan, *Soldier's
      Wife,* pp. 269–70.
99   admirably suited to entertain: Nevins, *Hamilton Fish,* pp. 122, 578–79;
      Goode, *Capital Losses,* p. 129; Benjamin Perley Poore, *Perley's
      Reminiscences of Sixty Years in the National Metropolis,* 2 vols.
      (Philadelphia, 1886), 2:298.
99   Grant's second inauguration: Ames, *Ten Years,* pp. 269–83; Logan,
      Soldier's Wife, pp. 320–24; *Star,* March 4 and 5, 1873.

**Chapter 5. Official Society Sullied by Scandal, Cleansed by Time:
1873–1900**

102   Crédit Mobilier: Nevins, *Hamilton Fish,* pp. 124–25, 610–13.
103   assessment of the damages: *The Nation,* January 30, 1873.
103   "Congress is practically demoralized": Hamilton Fish to Robert C. Schneck,
      February 20, 1873, quoted in Nevins, *Hamilton Fish,* pp. 611–12.
103   Cooke and Shepherd fall next: Ellis P. Oberholtzer, *Jay Cooke, Financier
      of the Civil War,* 2 vols. (Philadelphia, 1907), 1:121–11, 2:65–71, 181, 269,
      421, 453–75; Henrietta Larson, *Jay Cooke: Private Banker* (Cambridge,
      Mass., 1936), pp. 102–62, 200; Briggs, *Olivia Letters,* p. 340; Green,
      Washington, 1:339–62; Maury, "Territorial Period," pp. 153–212.
104   next trees to topple: Nevins, *Hamilton Fish,* pp. 660–62; *The Nation,*
      December 11, 1873; Teiser, "Almost Chief-Justice," Part 2, 420–23.
105   "the fair sex are to a man": C. H. Hill to Benjamin Bristow, December 19,

1873, Benjamin Bristow Papers, Box 2, Manuscript Division, Library of Congress, Washington, D.C.

105   "that unfortunate carriage": C. H. Hill to Benjamin Bristow, December 19, 1873, Benjamin Bristow Papers, Box 2.

105   "This constituent of mine": *Congressional Record,* 43d Cong., 1st sess., pp. 3375–78.

105   "numberless peccadilloes": Logan, *Soldier's Wife,* pp. 271–73.

106   spiteful gossip: Hamilton Fish diary, January 5, 1874, quoted in Nevins, *Hamilton Fish,* pp. 663.

106   "Mrs. W. is not a favorite": C. H. Hill to Benjamin Bristow, December 19, 1873, Benjamin Bristow Papers, Box 2.

106   "By Jupiter it is horrible": Jerome Stillson to Charles A. Dana, December 3, 1873, enclosed in Dana letter to Manton Marble, editor of the *New York World,* December 4, 1873, Manton Marble Papers, vol. 35, General Correspondence, Manuscript Division, Library of Congress, Washington, D.C.; Dana's note to Marble read, "The enclosed information may be as instructive to you as it has been to me."

106   Williams's position was hopeless: Teiser, "Almost Chief-Justice," Part 2, pp. 427–34. In deciding to press for Williams's resignation, Grant mentioned to Hamilton Fish anonymous, scurrilous letters sent to him, his family, and other cabinet members, which had been traced, by peculiarities of phrasing and handwriting, to Mrs. Williams; Nevins, *Hamilton Fish,* pp. 770–72, 818.

106   "Mrs. Williams's arrogance": Logan, *Soldier's Wife,* pp. 272–73.

106   news of Williams's withdrawal: Teiser, "Almost Chief-Justice," Part 2, pp. 430–32.

107   irregularities in the whiskey business: McFeely, *Grant,* p. 397; Nevins, *Hamilton Fish,* pp. 708–10.

107   Babcock had moved into the White House: Nevins, *Hamilton Fish,* pp. 762–804; Briggs, *Olivia Letters,* p. 394; McFeely, *Grant,* pp. 413–15.

107   Babcock counted on his friendship: Hamilton Fish diary, February 8, 1876, quoted in Nevins, *Hamilton Fish,* pp. 797–98, 802–3; McFeely, *Grant,* pp. 414–16. Orville Babcock was made an inspector of lighthouses, and, in 1884, while on an inspection trip, drowned at Mosquito Inlet in Florida.

108   Rebecca Felton: Rebecca Latimer Felton, *Country Life in Georgia in the Days of My Youth* (1919; reprint, New York, 1980), p. 133; *New York Tribune,* March 3, 1876. Appointed to the post by the governor of Georgia to fill a vacancy, eighty-seven-year-old Rebecca Latimer Felton became the first woman United States Senator on November 21, 1922. Her term was brief—one day.

108   Belknap confessed: McFeely, *Grant,* pp. 433–34.

108   "a dime novel": *New York Herald,* March 10, 1876.
108   bargain that paid for Amanda Belknap's clothes: McFeely, *Grant,* pp. 428–29.
109   "I do feel *so* sorry": Grant, *Personal Memoirs,* pp. 190–92; Hamilton Fish diary, March 26, 1876, quoted in Nevins, *Hamilton Fish,* pp. 808–9.
109   "The disclosure": "The Late Secretary of War," *Harper's,* March 18, 1876.
109   "The peril of official life": ibid. In fact, a cabinet member's salary was only $8,000; a member of Congress earned $6,000.
110   Belknap's trial: William Belknap remained in Washington and practiced law, but was never able to shake off the mortification he felt over his ethical lapses. Amanda Belknap, however, regained her stride. In 1889, she received national attention when she was seen at Coney Island in a bathing dress that revealed more of her than was thought respectable. She was traveling in October 1890 when her husband died in Washington. Various causes of death were suggested but Belknap's death was widely believed to have been a suicide. McFeely, *Grant,* p. 427; *New York Times,* October 15, 1890.
110   After her father's death: Belden and Belden, *Angels,* pp. 262–87; Ross, *Proud Kate,* pp. 229–31; Jordan, *Roscoe Conkling,* pp. 144–45, 202–4; Briggs, *Olivia Letters,* p. 107.
110   Sen. Conkling and Mrs. Sprague: Jordan, *Roscoe Conkling,* pp. 13, 144–45; Ross, *Proud Kate,* pp. 236–37; Belden and Belden, *Angels,* pp. 298–302.
111   "she was his mistress": Violet Blair Janin diary, February 2, 1880, Albert and Violet (Blair) Janin Collection, Huntington Library, San Marino, Calif. Mary Adams French, wife and cousin of sculptor Daniel Chester French, recalled that when she was a girl in Washington in the 1870s, "everyone talked about it [the Conkling-Sprague affair] on street cars and on corners." Her aunt was among the many enamored women who sent flowers (pink roses in her case) to Conkling on the Senate floor. The women of the city's leading unofficial families, who, not bound by the rigid rules of official protocol, could choose their guests with more freedom than official hostesses, would have nothing to do with Mrs. Sprague. Betty Blair Lee, a leader of residential society, referred to Kate contemptuously as "that person." Mrs. Daniel Chester French, *Memories of a Sculptor's Wife* (Boston, 1928), pp. 147–48; Belden and Belden, *Angels,* p. 299.
111   Kate Sprague's position and reputation were gone: Belden and Belden, *Angels,* pp. 297–99; *Washington Post,* August 19, 1879.
111   the diplomatic circle: Briggs, *Olivia Letters,* pp. 294–301.
111   "General Logan and I": Logan, *Soldier's Wife,* pp. 309–10.
112   "no end of card-leaving": Lillie De Hegermann-Lindencrone, *The Sunny Side of Diplomatic Life* (New York, 1914), p. 3.
112   "assemblage was promiscuous": ibid., pp. 8–9.

112   Nellie and "Algy": Grant, *Memoirs,* pp. 180–81; Marie Smith and Louise
       Durbin, *White House Brides* (Washington, D.C., 1966), pp. 81–89; *Star,*
       May 20, 21, and 22, 1874; *New York Herald,* May 22, 1874. Nellie Grant's
       wedding gifts were worth an estimated $75,000. A. J. Drexel gave a din-
       ner service valued at $4,500. The President and Mrs. Grant gave her
       diamonds and a check for $10,000. Walt Whitman sent a poem: "O
       Sweet Missouri Rose, O bonny bride! Yield thy red cheeks unto a na-
       tion's loving kiss"; Dee Brown, *The Year of the Century: 1876* (New
       York, 1966), p. 15. For a few years, the Sartorises appeared happy. By
       1880, however, there was open talk of Nellie's loveless marriage. In
       1889, the Sartorises separated, then divorced, and Sartoris soon died.
       Eventually Nellie and her widowed mother returned to Washington and
       Nellie entertained again. Years later she remarried; McFeely, *Grant,*
       pp. 400–5.

113   Centennial Exposition: Logan, *Soldier's Wife,* p. 351; *Star,* May 9, 10, and
       11, 1876. The diplomatic corps had been invited to Philadelphia at the
       nation's expense, and the de Hegermann-Lindencrones were among the
       many who accepted the offer. "Johan," Madame de Hegermann-
       Lindencrone wrote her aunt, "looked like an enormous poppy in his red
       uniform; the sun blazing through the glass roof almost set him on fire";
       de Hegermann-Lindencrone, *Sunny Side,* p. 13.

113   the *Star* retreated: *Star,* January 2, 6, 16, 19, 24, and 28, 1874.

114   "seldom wealthy men": [Hamilton, Gail], "The Display of Washington
       Society," *The Galaxy,* June, 1876.

115   thirst for social news slaked: Maurine Beasley, *The First Women
       Washington Correspondents* (Washington, D.C., 1976), pp. 10–14.

115   no wine or spirits: Mrs. Hayes's announcement caused a furor, espe-
       cially among the diplomatic corps, but she was unmoved. A month after
       the ban on alcohol went into effect, Madame de Hegermann-
       Lindencrone noted: "I think that the teetotality of the White House dis-
       pleases as much our country-people as it does the foreigners. At one of
       our musical parties Mr. Blaine came rather late, and, clapping his hands
       on Johan's shoulder, said, 'My kingdom for a glass of whiskey; I have
       just dined at the White House.' Others call the White House dinners 'the
       life-saving station'"; de Hegermann-Lindencrone, *Sunny Side,* p. 15.

115   Sunday evening hymn-singing: In describing the Hayes inaugural, reporter
       Mary Clemmer Ames referred to Mrs. Hayes as "the first lady of the land."
       It was apparently the first time the term was used and it was quickly
       picked up by the rest of the press. Geer, *First Lady,* p. 138.

116   Hayeses' social style: Bess Furman, *White House Profile: A Social History
       of the White House* (New York, 1951), p. 219; Margaret Leech, *In the Days
       of McKinley* (New York, 1959), p. 20; Colman, *White House Gossip,* pp.

116–25. Geer, *Lucy Webb Hayes,* pp. 144–56; Seale, *President's House,* 1:489–90.

117 Garfield White House: Margaret Leech and Harry Brown, *The Garfield Orbit* (New York, 1978), pp. 187–98, 224–25; Margaret Klapthor, *The First Ladies* (Washington, 1983), p. 49.

117 "All the world is paying court": *Letters of Mrs. James G. Blaine,* ed. Harriet Blaine Beale, 2 vols. (New York, 1908), 1:191.

117 "a mighty wrench": ibid., 1:197.

117 "The new house": ibid., 1:197, 208.

117 no reason to stay in Washington: ibid., 1:264, 274–78. The Blaines charged $1,000 a year to rent their Dupont Circle mansion. It was the highest rent ever asked for a residence in Washington, but it was not too expensive for a Chicago millionaire named Levi Leiter, who was looking for an elegant house to act as the springboard for his family's splash into Washington society; Albano, "Dupont Circle," p. 34.

118 "hailed as the rising sun": Thomas Donaldson quoted in Seale, *President's House,* 1:544–45.

118 Sir Lionel Sackville-West: Susan Mary Alsop, *Lady Sackville: A Biography* (New York, 1978), pp. 1–17.

118 A delicate question: ibid., pp. 18, 43; Arline Tehan, *Henry Adams in Love* (New York, 1983), p. 55; Blaine, *Mrs. James G. Blaine,* 1:261.

119 Adamses were charmed: M. Adams, *Letters,* pp. 317–18.

119 "a sweet girl": Henry Adams quoted in Tehan, *Henry Adams in Love,* p. 56.

120 "Sunday papers opened fire": M. Adams, *Letters,* p. 343.

120 the verdict was in her favor: For the next seven years, Victoria was the darling of official society. There was a slight chilling in enthusiasm in 1883, when Sackville-West brought his two younger daughters, Flora and Amalia, to Washington. Mrs. Cameron noted, "Washington thought the arrival of the two younger girls rather too much." But by 1885, when she organized a magnificent coming-out ball for Flora, there was only renewed praise for Victoria. Alsop, *Lady Sackville,* p. 66.

120 Horace Tabor sowed wild oats: Lewis Cass Gandy, *The Tabors: A Footnote of Western History* (New York, 1934), pp. 1–235; John Burke, *The Legend of Baby Doe* (New York, 1974), pp. 50–77.

120 Tabor's Senate appointment: Duane Smith, *Horace Tabor: His Life and Legend* (Boulder, Colo., 1973), pp. 212–35; Burke, *Baby Doe,* pp. 120–24.

122 thousand-dollar nightshirt: Burke, *Baby Doe,* p. 125.

122 "vulgar, ruffianly boor": John Ingalls, quoted in Burke, *Baby Doe,* p. 125; David Karsner, *Silver Dollar: The Story of the Tabors* (New York, 1932), pp. 210–13.

122 the Tabor wedding: Smith, *Horace Tabor,* pp. 225–26; Gandy, *The Tabors,*

pp. 235–40; *Washington Post,* February 26, March 1, 2, 1883; Burke, *Baby Doe,* pp. 125–131; Karsner, *Silver Dollar,* pp. 212–14; Mrs. E. N. Chapin, *American Court Gossip; or, Life at the National Capital* (Marshalltown, Iowa, 1887), p. 148.

124 made the "Senate blush": M. Adams, *Letters,* p. 445.

124 "Tabor has gone home": Henry Moore Teller, quoted in Smith, *Horace Tabor,* p. 229.

124 "uninteresting social figure": Frank Carpenter, *Carp's Washington,* ed. Frances Carpenter (New York, 1960), p. 32.

124 Cleveland's marriage: Smith and Durbin, *Brides,* p. 105; *Star,* June 3, 1882; Carpenter, *Carp's Washington,* pp. 46–47; Seale, *President's House,* 1:568.

125 "ran the gauntlet": Carpenter, *Carp's Washington,* p. 47

125 two richest men in Congress: Carpenter, *Carp's Washington,* pp. 92, 181; Goode, *Capital Losses,* pp. 93–95.

125 Hearst bought his way: W. A. Swanberg, *Citizen Hearst: A Biography of William Randolph Hearst* (New York, 1961), p. 9; Hearst was rumored to have spent $500,000 on his election. Richard Peterson, *Bonanza Rich: Lifestyles of the Western Mining Entrepreneurs* (Moscow, Idaho, 1991), pp. 122–23.

125 Hearst's West End mansion: Goode, *Capital Losses,* pp. 93–95; *Star,* March 12, 1890, February 27, 1890; Carpenter, *Carp's Washington,* pp. 88–89. George Hearst died in office in February, 1891, but his widow remained in the capital for another decade. Unlike most members of fashionable society, Mrs. Hearst supported many local charities. She was a founder of the Parent-Teacher Association, she established kindergartens in Washington and San Francisco, provided funds for the building of the National Cathedral School for Girls in Washington, helped preserve Mt. Vernon, and supported the education of the first female medical students in San Francisco. At the time of her death in 1919 in California, Mrs. Hearst had given away $21 million to charities, leaving the remainer of the Hearst fortune, some $11 million to her son, William Randolph Hearst. The huge Hearst home on New Hampshire Avenue was razed in 1964 to make way for an office building.

126 Benjamin Harrison's administration: When Mrs. Harrison died at the White House of tuberculosis in October 1892, society went into mourning, and when official mourning ended, Mary Harrison McKee acted as her father's hostess during the last few months of his term. Klapthor, *First Ladies,* p. 54; Colman, *White House Gossip,* pp. 207–13; Mary Abigail Dodge, *Biography of James G. Blaine* (Norwich, Conn., 1895), pp. 695–707.

126 Cleveland's second term: Seale, *President's House,* 2:604–5.

127 a petulant invalid: Leech, *Days of McKinley,* pp. 16–22, 432–37; Seale, *President's House,* 2:619.

127   dinner with Mrs. McKinley: Marguerite Cassini, *Never a Dull Moment* (New York, 1956), p. 121.

128   Mrs. Senator Keyes recalls her visit: Frances Parkinson Keyes, *Capital Kaleidoscope: The Story of a Washington Hostess* (New York, 1937), pp. 8–9. Mrs. McKinley knitted with a vengeance. Mrs. Senator John A. Logan, who was often called upon to help the First Lady receive, recalled: "Her busy fingers were constantly at work for charity. Before she left the White House she had finished more than three thousand five hundred pairs of knitted slippers for ladies and children, all of which had been given to friends for charity and invalids." Mrs. John A. Logan, *Thirty Years In Washington; or, Life and Scenes in Our National Capital* (Hartford, Conn., 1901), p. 732.

129   executive branch was lusterless: Mrs. Garret Hobart, *Memories* (New York, 1930), p. 32; Leech, *Days of McKinley,* pp. 99–101, 191, 329, 372–77.

129   "Millionaires Club": Rene Bache, "How Our Congressmen Live in Washington," *The Saturday Evening Post,* January 26, 1901, p. 3.

129   "It is hardly possible": ibid.

129   "It is expected": William E. Curtis, "Life in Washington, D.C.," *The Chautauquan,* August, 1897, pp. 471–73.

130   "The millionaire Senator": Bache, "How Our Congressmen Live," p. 2.

130   "a place of highest dignity": ibid., pp. 2–3.

130   Ten Bonanza Kings: Peterson, *Bonanza Rich,* pp. 107, 121–23.

131   senators fond of the title, not the work: ibid., pp. 2–7, 53, 83–87, 107, 122–23, 131. In the Sharon-Fair contest in 1880, votes, which usually sold for five to ten dollars, rose to as much as eighty.

131   "Senator Copper": Wallace Irwin, "Senator Copper's House" [written ca. 1911], *New York Times Book Review,* January 1, 1939, p. 15. The monstrous mansion that Clark built on Fifth Avenue in New York in 1906 inspired Irwin's poem. Reportedly costing more than $3 million, the house contained 131 rooms, including twenty-one bathrooms, thirty-one servant's rooms, four art galleries and an enormous swimming pool. Clark bought an entire stone quarry in New England to build his home. Robert Littell, "The House that Clark Built," *New Republic,* March 30, 1927, pp. 171–72; *New York Times,* March 3, 1925.

131   "The hospitable crowd": Julia Foraker, *I Would Live It Again* (New York, 1932), p. 191.

132   Elkins's rise to prominence: Goode, *Capital Losses,* pp. 116–18.

132   The Elkinses in Washington: All his life, Elkins was devoted to making money. His favorite greeting was, "Well, how are you doing? Are you making money?" *Washington Times Herald,* January 14, 1940; *Star,* November 22, 1936; Goode, *Capital Losses,* pp. 116–18.

132   "'Extra Post'": Ellen Maury Slayden, *Washington Wife: Journal of Ellen Maury Slayden,* ed. Walter Prescott Webb (New York, 1963), pp. 18–19.

133   Dewey mania: Leech, *Days of McKinley,* pp. 208–9; Adelbert M. and Louis M. Dewey, *The Life of George Dewey, Rear Admiral, U.S.N.* (Westfield, Mass., 1898), pp. 124–28.

133   Dewey's welcome: Leech, *Days of McKinley,* pp. 410–12; *Star,* October 3, 4, and 5, 1899.

133   Dewey euphoria died: Leech, *Days of McKinley,* pp. 413–31; *New York Tribune,* November 10 and 15, 1899; *Star,* November 1–31, 1899; Evelyn Walsh McLean, *Father Struck It Rich* (1936; reprint, Ouray, Colo., 1981), pp. 218–21.

133   The diplomatic corps: The wives of several prominent members of the diplomatic corps were American-born and many had grown up in official society, making them not only exceptionally competent hostesses but also women with access to many of Washington's interconnected social circles. Baroness Speck von Sternberg, wife of the chargé d'affaires at the German Embassy, was the former Lily Langhorn of Louisville; Baroness Moncheur, wife of the Belgian minister, was the daughter of Senator Powell Clayton of Arkansas; and Mrs. Dayrell Crackanthorpe, wife of the third secretary of the British Embassy, was the daughter of General Daniel Sickles of Washington. Foraker, *Live It Again,* p. 199.

134   "lest the storm might break": Hobart, *Memories,* pp. 36–43.

134   congratulated by "everyone": ibid.

134   John Hay, Theodore Roosevelt: quoted ibid., p. 43.

134   Marguerite Cassini's arrival: Cassini, *Never a Dull Moment,* pp.4–10, 94–105, 123.

135   "carefully worded acceptances": ibid., p. 124.

135   "Woodward and Lothrup's": ibid., p. 126.

135   "I sallied forth": ibid., p. 127. To "corner" a calling card meant to turn down one of the four corners just a bit. Each corner was significant. To turn down the upper right corner meant the caller was only paying respects and did not seek to be received. The upper left hand corner turned down signified "congratulations," and the lower left corner meant "condolences." A bend of the lower right corner meant "P.P.C.," or *Pour Prendre Congé,* the caller is leaving town for an extended period.

136   1899–1900 social calendar: ibid., pp. 135–37.

136   trouble over unorthodox seating: Theodore Bingham Papers, Box 15, Manuscript Division, Library of Congress, Washington, D.C.

138   unmarried offical hostesses: Leech, *Days of McKinley,* p. 472.

138   diplomatic dinner of 1899: Bingham Papers, Box 16. Baroness von Hengelmüller inadvertently suffered yet another cruel blow from Hay's hand that night. In his attempt to smooth all ruffled feathers, Hay had apparently forgotten the fate of the ill-starred Hapsburg, Maximilian, assassinated in Mexico, and partnered the Baroness, wife of the Austrian

minister, with the Mexican ambassador. The Baroness flatly refused to go in to dinner with him; Leech, *Days of McKinley*, pp. 472–73.

138   diplomatic dinner of 1900: *Star*, January 27, 1900; Bingham Papers, Box 15.

138   diplomatic dinner of 1901: Leech, *Days of McKinley*, p. 473; Bingham Papers, Box 5.

Chapter 6. The First Rich Newcomers Trickle into Washington:
1865–1880

141   "When the visitors swept": Twain and Warner, *Gilded Age*, 2:15.

141   "By and by the newspapers": ibid., 2:19.

141   "English with a foreign accent": ibid., 2:20.

141   nationwide rise of nouveaux riches: Pessen, *Riches*, pp. 16–23; Ray Ginger, *Age of Excess: The United States from 1877 to 1914* (New York, 1965), p. 93; John Tripple, "The Robber Baron in the Gilded Age," in *The Gilded Age: A Reappraisal*, ed. H. Wayne Morgan (Syracuse, N.Y., 1963), pp. 16–17.

142   cities awash with parvenus: The clash between the old urban aristocrats and the parvenus became a pervasive theme running through some of the best turn-of-the-century fiction. The contest in Boston, where the newly-rich from the New England hinterlands were flocking, was mirrored in William Dean Howells's *The Rise of Silas Lapham* (1885). The struggle between old and new wealth in Philadelphia, where fortunes earned from coal, iron, and steel vied with mercantile fortunes several generations old, was reflected in the pages of Theodore Dreiser's *The Financier* (1912). The manning of New York's social barricades was a central theme in novels of Edith Wharton (herself a member of an old Knickerbocker family) such as *The House of Mirth* (1905), *The Custom of the Country* (1913), and *The Age of Innocence* (1920). The contest in Washington found its way into fiction, too. In addition to Twain and Warner's hilarious and vicious *Gilded Age* (1873), there is Henry James's short story "Pandora," which appeared in the *New York Sun* in 1884, and Washington reporter John Wheelwright's novel *A Child of the Century* (1887).

142   lobbyists began to descend upon Washington: Thompson, "'Spider Web,'" pp. 44–131; James Deakin, *The Lobbyists* (Washington, D.C., 1966), pp. 57–58; Karl Schriftgiesser, *The Lobbyists* (Boston, 1951), pp. 1–23. Robert Walker lobbied Congress for the Russian government during the Alaska Purchase negotiations in 1868; see William Dunning, "Paying for Alaska," *Political Science Quarterly* 27 (September 1912): 385–88; Paul Holbo, *Tarnished Expansion: The Alaska Scandal, the Press, and Congress, 1867–1871* (Knoxville, 1983), pp. 4–29.

143 "Floating in Congressional waters": Briggs, *Olivia Letters,* pp. 92–93.

143 Joining Huntington: Deakin, *Lobbyists,* p. 58; Briggs, *Olivia Letters,* p. 94.

143 the "social lobby": "Law Making by Means of Dinners," *The Literary Digest,* July 16, 1927, p. 46; "The Lobbyist," *Harper's Monthly,* August 4, 1888.

144 the "lobbyess": George Townsend, *Washington,* pp. 455–56; Dr. John Ellis, *The Sights and Secrets of the National Capital* (New York, 1869), p. 183; Ames, *Ten Years,* pp. 120–26. The beautiful high-society lobbyess first began to appear in novels in the 1870s. While Twain's Laura Hawkins is best known, another is the beautiful Mrs. Buffington in reporter Charles Murray's *Sub Rosa: A Novel* (1880.) The official society woman who tried to turn her and her husband's influence to profit also began to appear in fiction at this time. An example is Sylvia Granger, wife of Secretary of State Ralph Granger (possibly based on Harriet and James G. Blaine), who compromised her husband and caused his resignation from the cabinet, in newspaper correspondent Theron Clark Crawford's 1894 novel, *A Man and His Soul: An Occult Romance of Washington Life.* (Donald A. Ritchie, "A Novel With A Key," manuscript. This article examines Crawford's novel in detail.)

144 "a luscious, mellow banana": Briggs, *Olivia Letters,* p. 91.

145 "conspicuous consumption": Thorstein Veblen, *The Theory of the Leisure Class* (1899; reprint, New York, 1934), pp. 68–101.

147 city's lack of "bustle": "How Shall We Govern," pp. 375–76.

147 "The pleasant thing": Leon Edel, *Henry James: The Conquest of London, 1870–1883* (London, 1962), p. 30.

147 "compared to New York": The Very Reverend S. Reynolds Hale, quoted in Green, *Washington,* 2:77.

147 "air of comfort": G. W. Stevens quoted in Green, *Washington,* 2:77.

147 "the rich men": Hall, *Social Usages,* p. 116.

147 "gossip and great men": Carpenter, *Carp's Washington,* pp. 8–9.

148 "money or beauty": Twain and Warner, *Gilded Age,* 1:194.

148 other East Coast cities: Frederic Jaher, "Style and Status: High Society in Late Nineteenth-Century New York," in Jaher, *The Rich,* pp. 263–65; Frederic Jaher, "Nineteenth Century Elites in Boston and New York," *Journal of Social History* 6 (Fall 1972): 6; Jaher, *Urban Establishment,* p. 535.

148 "The 'one-price emporium'": John Wheelwright, *A Child of the Century* (New York, 1887), p. 50.

149 "impression of a great hotel": Maurice Low, "Sundays at the Capital," *Harper's Weekly,* April 13, 1912, p.9.

149 "Washington society is so constituted": Carpenter, *Carp's Washington,* pp. 110–11.

150 premier marriage mart: Barry, "Men and Affairs at Washington," p. 574;

Barry Bulkley, *Washington Old and New* (Washington, 1914), p. 97; Hall, *Social Usages,* p. 59; Amory, *Who Killed Society?* pp. 229–35.

151   "millionaire ex-tradesmen": Marie Columbia, "The Capital City and the Smart Set," *Delineator* 65 (January 1905): 79–83.

151   Sam Ward's rise to prominence: Maud Elliott, *Uncle Sam Ward and His Circle* (1938; reprint, New York, 1975), pp. 1–143; [Lately Thomas], *Sam Ward: King of the Lobby* (Boston, 1965), pp. 1–48.

152   "the old Puritan morals": M. Elliott, *Uncle Sam Ward,* p. 446.

152   "I have my own crockery": ibid., p. 456.

152   Ward accepted annual fees: Thomas, *Sam Ward,* pp. 228–31, 300–13, 336–37; *New York Times,* July 11, 1889; *New York Sun,* July 11, 1889. Barlow recognized in Sam a fellow epicure and wit. Their business correspondence was full of puns and discussions of brandies. In one note, Sam's recipe for Paraguayan maté preceded his vital news that "it has taken me a week to corral my Congressional elephants and I am at length able to write you favorably touching both your projects." This, like other letters between the two men, was sent in confidence, and bore the hieroglyph "On the □," a Masonic symbol that put a communication under a seal of strictest secrecy. Thomas, *Sam Ward,* pp. 248–49.

152   a sort of Figaro: M. Elliott, *Uncle Sam Ward,* pp. 496, 554.

152   What "everybody wanted": Thomas, *Sam Ward,* pp. 248, 351, 409–30; Carpenter, *Carp's Washington,* pp. 279–80; M. Elliott, *Uncle Sam Ward,* pp. 554–55; John W. Forney, *Anecdotes of Public Men* (1873; reprint, New York, 1970), p. 394. Sam Ward filed and annotated seating charts and menus and wrote down his own rules of cookery, sometimes in verse: "To roast spring chickens is to spoil 'em / Just split 'em up the back and broil 'em."

153   "the one man who knows everybody": "The Men of the Day," *Vanity Fair,* January 10, 1880, p. 25.

154   Ward "knew more of life": H. Adams, *Education,* p. 253.

154   "diner-out par excellence": de Hegermann-Lindencrone, *Sunny Side,* pp. 78–79.

154   "He treated his friends so well": Carpenter, *Carp's Washington,* p. 280.

154   "my little lamb": Thomas, *Sam Ward,* pp. 336, 340, 355. Only once, Ward claimed, did he resort to stronger tactics. He wrote to his friend Henry Wadsworth Longfellow of an exploit too delicious to hold back. It concerned "a client, eager to prevent the arrival at the committee of a certain member before it should adjourn at noon, who offered me $5,000 to accomplish his purpose, which I did by having his [the Congressman's] boots mislaid, while I smoked a cigar and condoled with him until they could be found at 11:45! I had the satisfaction of a good laugh, a good fee in my pocket, and of having prevented a conspiracy!"

154   Ward's Pacific Mail testimony: U.S. Congress, "On the Pacific Mail Subsidy Bill," 43r Cong., 2d sess., H. Rpt. 268, pp. 408–10.

155   still scratching for a living: Thomas, *Sam Ward,* pp. 398–400.

155   saw little more of Sam Ward: New York became Sam Ward's headquarters, and there his last fortune disappeared as quickly as its predecessors. As they had in the past, Sam's loyal friends came to his aid, and he traveled happily in Europe, growing older and weaker but no less witty and bright. In May 1880, Sam Ward died in Italy with his dog-eared copy of Horace beneath his pillow and Omar Khayyam's *Rubaiyat* open beside him.

156   Ned Beale had arrived: Stephen Bonsal, *Edward Fitzgerald Beale: A Pioneer in the Path of Empire, 1822–1903* (New York, 1912), pp. 1–86; Marie Beale, *Decatur House and Its Inhabitants* (Washington, D.C., 1954), pp. 70–83.

157   Beale's early career: In the early 1850s, while on a trip back East, Beale convinced Secretary of War Jefferson Davis to try camels in the West to solve the problem of supplying far-flung Army stations. Davis dispatched a ship to Tunis to get the "ships of the desert," and gave Beale command of the first and last camel corps. When Davis left the War Department, the camels lost their most influential supporter, and they were ordered sold at auction. Loyal to his humped friends, Beale bought most of them and let them roam free at Tejon Rancho. Beale, *Decatur House,* pp. 87–90; Bonsal, *Edward Beale,* pp. 198–255; Mrs. Terry B. Morton, "General Edward Fitzgerald Beale," *Historic Preservation* 19 (July–December 1967): 69–82.

159   the Beales and Decatur House: Morton, "General Beale," pp. 69–71; Beale, *Decatur House,* p. 106; Bonsal, *Edward Beale,* pp. 293–298. One of the first private residences on Lafayette Square, Decatur House was designed by Benjamin Latrobe and built for Commodore Stephen Decatur, a young naval hero of the War of 1812. Decatur and his wife Susan moved in in 1819 and for the next year the house was the social center of the young capital city. In March 1820, Decatur was killed in a duel by Commodore James Barron, his one-time mentor. Decatur's beautiful house went through several owners and tenants before Beale bought it. In 1944, Mrs. Truxtun Beale, the General's daughter-in-law, ordered the Grant-era sandstone trim torn off and the house restored in accordance with the original Latrobe drawings. In 1956, she bequeathed the house to the National Trust.

161   the Beales' three children: Mrs. Hazel Detwiler, "The Truxtun Beale Years," *Historic Preservation* 19 (July–December 1967):83–86; McLean, *Father,* pp. 171–74. In the early 1900s, all three of General Beale's children lived in Washington again. After several years in California following

his divorce in 1896, Truxtun and his second wife, Marie Oge Beale, moved into Decatur House. George Bakhmeteff was named Imperial Russian Ambassador to the United States in 1911, and the Bakhmeteffs' famed barouche, emblazoned with the Romanoff crest and attended by footmen in wine-colored livery, became a familiar sight on Washington's streets. Beale, *Decatur House,* pp. 115–32; George Abell and Evalyn Gordon, *Let Them Eat Caviar* (New York, 1936), p. 102.

161   Shepherd's large bluestone mansion: Goode, *Capital Losses,* pp. 152–54; Glassie, "Victorian Homes," p. 344.

162   rich thanks to Shepherd's New Washington: Maury, "Territorial Period," pp. 173, 210. German-born architect Adolph Cluss, who designed Shepherd's home (and one for himself next door) and Stewart's Castle, was among those who profited handsomely from the New Washington. Cluss made a fortune as a society architect and became a member of the postwar capital's social elite. See Tanya Edwards Beauchamp, "Adolph Cluss: An Architect In Washington during Civil War and Reconstruction," *Records of the Columbia Historical Society, 1971–1972* (Washington, D.C., 1973), pp. 338–58.

162   tale of Amzi Barber: Goode, *Capital Losses,* pp. 97–99; James Severance, "Amzi Lorenzo Barber," *Oberlin Alumni Magazine* 5 (June 1909): 341–46; *Chicago Daily Tribune,* April 19, 1906; photocopies of miscellaneous Barber biographical material provided by Oberlin College Alumni Office, Oberlin, Ohio.

163   Barber's ventures immensely profitable: Goode, *Capital Losses,* pp. 97–99; Ronald Johnson, "LeDroit Park," in *Washington in Home,* ed. Kathryn Smith (Northridge, Calif., 1988), pp. 139–41.

164   "asphalt king": Goode, *Capital Losses,* pp. 97–99; miscellaneous biographical material from Oberlin College.

164   any luxury he chose: Severance, "Amzi Lorenzo Barber," pp. 341–46. Just after the turn of the century, Barber moved his headquarters to New York. He paid half a million dollars for a Manhattan residence on Fifth Avenue. Barber, the "asphalt king," who had begun his Washington career as an idealistic teacher of freed Negroes in 1868, died in 1909.

165   "attract a respectable class": "How Shall We Govern," p. 376.

165   "more and more of a resort": Godkin to Norton quoted in Green, *Washington,* 1:355–56.

165   "a place of winter residence": Helen Nicolay, *Our Capital on the Potomac,* New York: 1924, p. 437.

165   "blaze in the social sky": Briggs, *Olivia Letters,* p. 357.

165   "a new woman": Ames, *Ten Years,* p. 261.

166   "veneer furniture": Poore, *Perley's Reminiscences,* 2:527.

166   "demoralizing haste": Townsend, *Washington,* p. 684.

166   "Ill-gotten and well-gotten": [Gail Hamilton], "The Display of Washington Society: Considered the Origin of Evil in the Universe," *Galaxy* 21(June 1878): 762.

166   "least possible pleasure": Green, *Washington,* 1:395.

Chapter 7. A Rising Tide of Rich Newcomers Floods the Capital: 1881–1900

167   "wedge was driven": Columbia, "Capital City," pp. 79–83.

168   "Since the retirement": Briggs, *Olivia Letters,* p. 413.

168   "Its mild climate": "The New Washington," *Century Magazine* 27 (March 1884): 652–53.

169   "beautiful white and brown mushrooms": Columbia, "Capital City." pp. 79–83.

169   "gayest of the gay": *Cleveland Leader,* September 30, 1883.

169   More reporters than ever: Beasley, *Washington Correspondents,* pp. 1–24; Carpenter, *Carp's Washington,* pp. ix–xv.

169   "Washington is like no other": Carpenter, *Carp's Washington,* pp. 4–5.

170   "There is enough silk": ibid., p. 91.

170   "Washington nabobs": ibid., p. 92.

171   "genial and amusing": Edel, *Henry James,* pp. 26–32.

171   Anderson family: Anderson Family Clipping Files, Cincinnati Historical Society, Cincinnati, Ohio; "Larz Anderson," *Cathedral Age* 12 (Spring 1937); *Star,* April 26, 1931; *Letters and Journals of General Nicholas Longworth Anderson,* ed. Isabel Anderson (New York, 1942), pp. 7–8; *Larz Anderson: Letters and Journals of a Diplomat,* ed. Isabel Anderson (New York, 1940), pp. 13–37; Clara Longworth De Chambrun, *The Making of Nicholas Longworth* (1933; reprint, New York, 1971), pp. 7–54.

172   "Nick Anderson turned up": M. Adams, *Letters,* p. 277.

173   "We have had Mr. Richardson here": Mrs. Anderson quoted in James M. Goode, *Capital Losses,* pp. 90–91. Two years later, when Henry Adams and John Hay commissioned Richardson to design their adjoining houses, the General wrote to Larz in November 1885: "I am afraid I am bitterly revenged on the Adamses for the fun they had with my architect troubles, for their house is not nearly finished and Mrs. A. is suffering from nervous prostration. The two houses exteriorly do not meet public expectations, and are ranked after ours, but their interiors will be of unusual magnificence and beauty and corresponding costs"; N. Anderson, *Letters and Journals,* p. 250.

173   "Mr. Richardson is with us": N. Anderson, *Letters and Journals,* pp. 207–8.

Architect Richardson was an enormous man. He had ballooned from the slim undergraduate that General Anderson and Henry Adams remembered into a rotund figure weighing nearly three hundred pounds. In February 1883, while on another inspection tour of the new house, Richardson again stayed with the Andersons. This time, Mrs. Anderson wrote Larz, the bed broke under his weight, sending Richardson crashing to the floor in the dark with a loud thud. (Mrs. Anderson to Larz Anderson, February 11, 1883, unpublished typescript, Society of the Cincinnati, Washington, D.C.)

173   massive Romanesque house: Goode, *Capital Losses*, pp. 89–91; "A Glimpse of Some Washington Homes," *Harper's Magazine*, March, 1885, pp. 520–33; N. Anderson, *Letters and Journals*, p. 226.

174   "Washington is growing": N. Anderson, *Letters and Journals*, pp. 210–11. The Casino proved too ambitious a project and failed. A year later, General Anderson reported: "I am sorry to tell you that our Casino will shortly go into bankruptcy. I am very sorry for the Casino and all the pleasures it promised, but I am far sorrier for my $3,000.00 which is buried in the ground on Connecticut Avenue"; ibid., p. 223.

175   Sources of quotations on pp. 175–79 from N. Anderson, *Letters and Journals:* "I hate to come back," p. 238; "swarms of strangers," p. 256; "wealth and snobbery," "vanity fair," p. 265; "Eight years ago," p. 296; "Picnics are all the rage," "Thirty of us," p. 211; "invited to dine with the Secretary," p. 214; "If a Democrat should be," p. 229; "I am not one of those," p. 234; "I rather imagine," p. 239; "We in Washington," p. 242; "Your Mother begins to-day," p. 250; "A big *mi-carême* ball," "Our mid-Lent ball," p. 267; "We are still dining," p. 269; "The new Secretary of War," pp. 304–5.

179   General's obituaries: Anderson Family Clipping Files, Cincinnati Historical Society. Mrs. Anderson continued to take an active part in Washington society until her death in 1917.

179   Washington McLean: Charles Greve, *Centennial History of Cincinnati*, 2 vols. (Chicago, 1904), 2:840; McLean Family Clipping File, Cincinnati Historical Society, Cincinnati, Ohio.

180   John R. McLean: McLean Family Clipping File, Cincinnati Historical Society; McLean Family Clipping File, Historical Society of Washington, Washington, D.C.; McLean Family Clipping File, Washingtoniana Division, Martin Luther King Public Library, Washington, D.C.

180   Washingtonians baffled by the match: Jonathan Daniels, *The End of Innocence* (1954; reprint, New York, 1972), pp. 276–77.

180   power he was beginning to wield: McLean became a major stockholder and director of both the local American Security and Trust Company and the Riggs National Bank, president of the Washington Gas Light

Company, co-founder of the Old Dominion Railway, developer of the prominent suburb of McLean, Virginia, and owner of the *Washington Post.* (McLean Family Clipping Files, Cincinnati Historical Society, Martin Luther King Library, Historical Society of Washington; *New York Times,* June 10, 1916.) Under McLean, the *Post* deteriorated rapidly. Good reporting was replaced by sensational, syndicated stories; crime and scandal were pushed to the fore; egregious errors abounded. When the Mona Lisa was stolen from the Louvre in Paris in 1911, for example, the *Post* reproduced the wrong painting.

181   Renaissance-style villa: Goode, *Capital Losses,* pp. 129–33; "The Washington House of Mr. John R. McLean," *Town and Country,* April 26, 1913, pp. 31–34, 62.

182   Levi Leiter: Leiter Family Clipping File and Scrapbook Files, Historical Society of Washington, Washington, D.C.; Leiter Family Clipping File and Scrapbook Files, Washingtoniana Division, Martin Luther King Public Library, Washington, D.C.; Nigel Nicholson, *Mary Curzon* (New York, 1977), pp. 3–7.

182   decided they should enter society: Nicholson, *Curzon,* pp. 7–17.

182   Rebuffed by Chicago's high society: Clipping files, Historical Society of Washington and Washingtoniana Division; Goode, *Capital Losses,* pp. 112–14; Nicholson, *Curzon,* pp. 12–26.

183   a glamorous social stage: Sylvia Jukes Morris, *Edith Kermit Roosevelt: Portrait of a First Lady* (New York, 1980), p. 149; Henry Adams, *Henry Adams and His Friends,* ed. Harold Dean Cater (1947; reprint, New York, 1970), p. 302; Journal of Mary Theresa Leiter, May 1886–December 1887, Leiter Collection, Chicago Historical Society, Chicago, IL.

183   a home of their own: Goode, *Capital Losses,* pp. 112–14; Nicholson, *Curzon,* pp. 46–47.

183   "naively pleased": Cassini, *Never a Dull Moment,* p. 116.

183   Duchess/Malaprop: *The Club-Fellow,* June 27, 1906; Cassini, *Never a Dull Moment,* p. 113; Margaret Terry Chandler, *Roman Spring: Memoirs* (Boston, 1934), p. 208; Nicholson, *Curzon,* p. 7.

183   Mrs. Leiter's daughters: Cassini, *Never a Dull Moment,* p. 116; Nicholson, *Curzon,* pp. 20–26; Mary Theresa Leiter Journal, May to December 1887.

184   Many thought Mary Leiter arrogant: S. Morris, *Roosevelt,* p. 149; H. Adams, *Friends,* p. 302; Virginia Peacock, *Famous American Belles of the Nineteenth Century* (1900; reprint, Freeport, NY, 1970), pp. 267–272; Leiter Family Clipping Files and Scrapbooks, Historical Society of Washington and Washingtoniana Division; Nicholson, *Curzon,* pp. 41, 72.

184   "She never swerved": Chandler, *Roman Spring,* p. 208

185   Curzon-Leiter marriage: *Star,* April 20, 22, and 23, 1895; *Washington Herald,* April 10, 1938; Peacock, p. 272; Leiter Family Clipping Files and

Scrapbooks, Historical Society of Washington and Washingtoniana Division; Nicholson, *Curzon,* pp. 76–79.

185 Her joy was unbounded: Mrs. Leiter had the satisfaction of seeing all three of her daughters marry prominent Englishmen—Daisy married the Earl of Suffolk and Nancy married Colonel Colin Campbell of the British Army. Their only son, Joseph, gave the Leiters a more difficult time. Joseph Leiter tried to corner the wheat market in 1897, but lost nearly $10 million overnight when he was outmaneuvered by Chicago meat packer Philip Armour. Levi Leiter covered his son's debts, recouped his fortune, and was worth $30 million at his death in 1904. After her wedding, Mary Leiter Curzon never saw the United States again. Lady Curzon died shortly after her father in 1906. Nicholson, *Curzon,* pp. 103–4; Goode, *Capital Losses,* pp. 112–14; *Washington Herald,* April 12, 1932, April 10, 1938; *Star,* October 30, 1942.

186 Edmund Patten struck it rich: Henry Corbin Papers, Box no. 17 and Scrapbook no. 15, Manuscript Division, Library of Congress, Washington, D.C.

186 militantly Irish: ibid., Scrapbook no. 15; *Washington Post,* August 31, 1946.

186 soon entertaining everybody: Henry Corbin Papers, Box no. 17 and Scrapbook no. 15.

186 Katherine Patten's wedding: ibid., Box no. 17.

187 After Anastasia Patten's death: ibid.; Jonathan Daniels, *Washington Quadrille: The Dance Beside the Documents* (New York, 1968), p. 94.

187 young Winthrop Chandlers: Chandler, *Roman Spring,* pp. 180–213.

187 Mrs. Chandler soon grew unhappy: ibid., pp. 214–32.

187 the Tuckerman family: Goode, *Capital Losses,* p. 105; *Washington Post,* May 16, 1965, February 10, 1967; *Evening Star,* January 8, 1939.

188 Brainerd Warner: Green, *Washington,* 2:14, 31–33, 88–89; Newspaper Clipping Files and Scrapbooks, Historical Society of Washington, Washington, D.C.; Warner Clipping File, Washingtoniana Division, Martin Luther King Public Library, Washington, D.C.

188 Thomas Franklin Schneider: Goode, *Capital Losses,* pp. 109–10; Newspaper Clipping Files, Historical Society of Washington; Schneider Clipping File, Washingtoniana Division, Martin Luther King Public Library, Washington, D.C.

188 "Attracted by the social advantages": Curtis, "Life in Washington, D.C.," p. 467.

189 a real estate boom: ibid., p. 467; Green, *Washington,* 2:12–13.

189 ill financial winds: Green, *Washington,* 2:18–19, 77; Cable, *Avenue,* p. 171.

189 "a thorough chaos": H. Adams, *Friends,* p. 289.

191   "busted": ibid., pp. 301–2.

191   flow of rich newcomers resumed: Jaher, *Urban Establishment,* pp. 501,
       535; Anna Farwell DeKoven, *A Musician and His Wife* (New York, 1926),
       pp. 186–206; Ralph Martin, *Cissy* (New York, 1979), pp. 16–40, 61–65.

192   George Pullman: Buder, *Pullman,* pp. 28–31; Liston Leyendecker, *Palace
       Car Prince: A Biography of George Mortimer Pullman* (Niwot, Colo.,
       1992), pp. 120–22. Pullman died in 1896, but his widow had become very
       fond of Washington's milder winters, and decided to continue to spend
       part of each social season there. She built a beautiful mansion on presti-
       gious 16th Street as a background for her social triumphs. Mrs. Pullman's
       neighbors eventually included two other prominent Chicago widows: Mrs.
       Norman Williams, widow of one of the co-founders of the Pullman Car
       Company, and Mrs. Marshall Field. Clipping Files, Historical Society of
       Washington; Goode, *Capital Losses,* pp. 133–34.

192   The rest of the Midwest: Goode, *Capital Losses,* pp. 68–70; Walter M. W.
       Ecker, *Dumbarton Oaks, The History of a Georgetown House and Garden,
       1880–1966* (Cambridge, Mass., 1967); Clipping Scrapbooks,
       Washingtoniana Division, Martin Luther King Public Library, Washington,
       D.C.; *Star,* March 14, 1943; Amory, *Who Killed Society?* p. 520; Julia
       Foraker, *I Would Live It Again* (New York, 1932), p. 215; Elden Billings,
       "Social and Economic Life in Washington in the 1890s," *Records of the
       Historical Society of Washington, 1966–1968* (Washington, D.C., 1968), p.
       169.

192   Hendersons of Missouri: Goode, *Capital Losses,* pp. 106–8; *Washington
       Post,* May 31, 1981; Seale, *President's House,* 2:637–38; Mrs. Garret Hobart,
       Memories, New York: 1930, pp. 51–52. Mrs. Henderson became an even
       more formidable figure in Washington after the turn of the century and
       after her husband's death in 1913. Her main passion was 16th Street,
       which she personally developed into the handsomest drive in the city by
       purchasing nearly all the lots adjacent to her "Castle" and building on
       them more than a dozen beautiful mansions, which she rented to individ-
       uals or foreign governments for embassies.

193   newcomers from older East Coast cities: Goode, *Capital Losses,* pp. 82,
       118; Alsop, *Lady Sackville,* p. 44; Nathaniel Burt, *The Perennial
       Philadelphians: The Anatomy of an American Aristocracy* (Boston, 1963),
       pp. 252–53; *Star,* March 2, 1936.

193   "New York-crowd-with-the-names": Foraker, *Live It Again,* p. 6.

193   Tom Walsh of Colorado: McLean, *Father,* pp. 27–32.

194   "Colorado Croesus": Peterson, *Bonanza Rich,* pp. 85, 119.

194   "we were in": McLean, *Father,* p. 72.

194   "a reception at the White House": ibid, p. 111.

194   a Washington mansion: ibid., pp. 114–20; *Star,* December 1–30, 1903;

McLean Family Clipping Files, Historical Society of Washington and Washingtoniana Division; Evalyn Walsh McLean Collection, Box 1, Manuscript Division, Library of Congress, Washington, D.C.; Peterson, *Bonanza Rich,* p. 85. Tom Walsh died in 1910, but the seven years he reveled in the glory of "2020" were happy ones for him. Famed for her diamond "dog collar" necklace and gold table service made from nuggets from the Camp Bird Mine, Mrs. Walsh continued entertaining at "2020" until her death in 1932. Mrs. Walsh left an estate worth an estimated $100 million. McLean, *Father,* pp. 186–92, 259, 329–30; McLean Clipping Files, Historical Society of Washington and Washingtoniana Division. 2020 Massachusetts Avenue is currently the Indonesian Embassy.

195   Patten weddings: Cassini, *Never a Dull Moment,* p. 336; Henry Corbin Papers, Clipping Scrapbooks and Box 17. As the years passed and their husbands died, Augusta and Edythe moved back in with their sisters. The quintet continued to entertain on Sundays until death picked them off one by one. Edythe outlived them all. She remained active, distributing the fortune her father had dug from the earth nearly a century earlier among her favorite Catholic charities, until 1959, when she died in her nineties. *Washington Post,* August 31, 1946; *Star,* March 31, 1945, May 3, 1959.

196   Elsie Anderson: *Star,* June 7, 1899; Anderson Family Collection, Society of the Cincinnati, Washington, D.C.

196   Larz Anderson: L. Anderson, *Larz Anderson,* pp. 99–149.

196   Reporters disputed: *Chicago Tribune,* June 10, 1897; Anderson Family Clipping Files, Cincinnati Historical Society, Historical Society of Washington and Washingtoniana Division.

196   Anderson-Perkins wedding: Anderson Family Clipping Files, Cincinnati Historical Society, Historical Society of Washington and Washingtoniana Division.

197   Anderson House: L. Anderson, *Larz Anderson,* pp. 149, 160, 293, 354; Isabel Anderson, *Presidents and Pies: Life in Washington, 1897–1919* (New York, 1920), p. 13; *Washington Post,* February 18, 1962. The Andersons continued to lead one aging segment of Washington society into the 1930s. Instantly recognized as they were chauffeured about the city in a purple Rolls Royce, they persisted in a formal, opulent style of entertaining few others could afford to emulate had they wanted to; *Washington Daily News,* November 4, 1948. In 1929, on the eve of the Great Depression, Mrs. Anderson wrote, "We remained, I believe, the only house in Washington, except the Embassies, which turned out the servants in full-dress livery, shorts and stockings, buckled shoes, braided coats. These dinners were swan songs to the old order"; L. Anderson, *Larz Anderson,* p. 558.

Chapter 8. "Dying Snails": The Old Elite Withdraws into Its Shell

199   "dying snails": Briggs, *Olivia Letters*, pp. 340–41.

199   "'old resident' element": "The New Washington," pp. 652–53.

199   Puritan fathers: Amory, *Who Killed Society?* pp. 30–33.

199   Every fading elite: Jaher, *Urban Establishment*, p. 280.

200   "beruffled barbarians": E. L. Godkin quoted in Peterson, *Bonanza Rich*, p. x.

200   elite recruitment vs. exclusivity: Jaher, *Urban Establishment*, p. 114.

202   trickling out of human resources: Green, *Washington*, 1:194–95.

202   founding of the Oldest Inhabitants: Ames, *Ten Years*, p. 244; James Gannon, "Washington at the Turn of the Century," *Records of the Columbia Historical Society, 1963–1965* (Washington, D.C., 1966), p. 315; William C. Corcoran, *A Grandfather's Legacy* (Washington, D.C., 1879), p. 219; *Star*, December 6, 1931, and December 3, 1939; Association of Oldest Inhabitants Collection, Historical Society of Washington, Washington, D.C.

203   Oldest Inhabitants' constitution: *The Washington Times*, April 29, 1900; Scrapbook no. 9, Historical Society of Washington, Washington, D.C.

204   requirements for admission: *Washington Times*, April 9, 1900; *Star*, December 6, 1931, December 3, 1939.

204   without clout: Green, *Washington*, 1:333.

204   other old urban elites: Jaher, *Urban Establishment*, pp. 276–77, 417, 646.

204   the same impetus: ibid., pp. 276–77. Often in the audience at the Oldest Inhabitants' lectures, always as a guest since her sex barred her from membership (born in the city in 1850, she could have easily met the length of residence requirement), was Violet Blair Janin, one of the most formidable of the Antiques. Mrs. Janin was among the many Antiques who took refuge in filiopietistic societies like the Oldest Inhabitants. Her long list of memberships was typical of many of Washington's grandes dames. Mrs. Janin was founder of the Colonial Dames of the District of Columbia, registrar of the Maryland chapter of the Daughters of the American Revolution, treasurer general of the Children of the American Revolution, and a member of the Daughters of the Cincinnati, the Association for Preservation of Virginia Antiquities, and "about twenty other societies," including the National Society Opposed to Women's Suffrage; "Violet Blair Janin," *American Biographical Directories: District of Columbia* (Washington, D.C., 1909), p. 205. Another Antique active in patriotic and historical organizations aimed at preserving family traditions and national values was Britannia Peter Kennon, great-granddaughter of Martha Washington, who lived her long life (1815–1911) at Tudor Place in Georgetown, the home her father had built early in the century. In 1893,

Britannia Kennon became a founder and first national vice president of the National Society of the Colonial Dames of America and president of the District of Columbia chapter; Tudor Place Foundation Collections, Tudor Place, Washington, D.C.

205   cordial to well-bred newcomers: Green, *Washington,* 1:375–76.

205   "They drove up": Twain and Warner, *Gilded Age,* 2:12.

206   cordiality began to chill: Green, *Washington,* 1:376–77; Marian Gouveneur, *As I Remember: Recollections of American Society* (New York, 1911), pp. 359–64.

206   "the old citizens are more likely": [Gail Hamilton], "The Display of Washington Society," *Galaxy,* June 1876, p. 768.

207   "two dead presidents": Violet Blair Janin Diary, January 10, 1883, Albert and Violet (Blair) Janin Collection, Huntington Library, San Marino, Calif.

207   "a race apart": Edith Benham Helm, *The Captains and the Kings* (New York, 1954), p. 38.

207   "I am an Apley": John P. Marquand, *The Late George Apley* (Boston, 1937), pp. 26–27.

208   corrupting American life: Jaher, *Urban Establishment,* p. 119.

208   "more easily meet the needs": ibid., p. 120.

208   "statesmen series": Marie Columbia, "Washington: Its Cave Dwellers and Its Social Secretaries," *Delineator* 55 (February 1905): 248–49.

209   Bishop Satterlee: quoted in Green, *Washington,* 2:193–94.

209   Orphan Asylum: Lee, *Wartime Washington,* pp. 101–2.

210   old families generously supported: Green, *Washington,* 1:310, 2:61–76.

210   establishment of Louise Home: William Corcoran Papers, Boxes 10, 11, 12, 13, and 14, Manuscript Division, Library of Congress, Washington, D.C.; "Letter From William W. Corcoran to the Trustees [of the Louise Home]," December 4, 1870, in Corcoran, *A Grandfather's Legacy,* pp. 35–40; James M. Goode, *Capital Losses,* pp. 226–29; *Star,* January 25, February 1, 8, and 15, 1920, and March 3, 1946.

210   Corcoran was mindful of the pride: Goode, *Capital Losses,* pp. 226–29.

211   "tender and touching tribute": Miss Letty Lewis of Sweet Springs, West Virginia, to William W. Corcoran, September 8, 1875, in Corcoran, *A Grandfather's Legacy,* pp. 476–78.

212   "Tuesday, a birthday party": M. Adams, *Letters,* p. 316. Henry and Marian Adams spent their first winters in Washington in handsome houses near Lafayette Square rented from William Corcoran, first at 1501 H Street and later at 1607 H Street.

212   "ladies cultured and refined": William Corcoran quoted in Goode, *Capital Losses,* p. 228.

213   "last port of comfort": Isabel McKenna Duffield, *Washington in the 90s: California Eyes Dazzled by the Brilliant Society of the Capital* (San

Francisco, 1929), pp. 105–6. In 1947, the trustees sold the Louise Home
building to real estate developers and moved to the Codman House at
Decatur Place and 22nd Street, NW. With the advent of social security and
other benefits for the aged, fewer and fewer women requested to become
"guests" at the Louise Home. The Home closed in 1976. The remaining
"guests" and Corcoran's bequest were combined with the Lisner Home.
Goode, *Capital Losses,* p. 229.

213   establishment of "the Bachelor's": Bachelor's German Club Collection,
Club Ledgers, Manuscript Division, Library of Congress, Washington, D.C.

213   the dignity of the germans: ibid., Instructions to Committee Chairmen for
the 1888–1889 social season, Club Ledgers.

214   "for older Washingtonians": ibid., Club Ledger for the 1886–1887 season.

214   club's guidelines: ibid., Rules and Guidelines for the 1888–1889 season.

215   "The cooperation of members": ibid., Admonitions to Board Members for
the 1888–1889 season, Club Ledger.

215   new blood in the 1880s: ibid., Subscription Lists, 1881–1889.

216   Mrs. Dahlgren: Flack, *Desideratum,* pp. 14–15; Household Accounts and
Social Register (1877–1885) of Madeleine Vinton Dahlgren, John A. B.
Dahlgren Collection, Manuscript Division, New York Public Library, New
York, New York. Mrs. Dahlgren wrote under the pen names "Corinne"
and "Cornelia." Her works include *Thoughts on Female Suffrage* (she was
adamantly against it); *Memoir of Ulric Dahlgren; South Sea Sketches; South
Mountain Magic; Memoir of John A. Dahlgren; A Washington Winter;
Lights and Shadows of a Life; Divorced;* and *The Secret Directory.* She
translated *Idealities: An Essay on Catholicism, Authority and Order,* and
The Executive Power in the United States (from Spanish and French, re-
spectively). *South Mountain Magic* is the least pedestrian of her many
stories.

216   James drew a fictionalized portrait: Henry James, "Pandora," in *Stories
Revised* (1885; reprint, New York, 1975). James also cast his friends Henry
and Marian Adams in "Pandora" as the stuffy but witty Mr. and Mrs.
Bonnycastle.

216   Mrs. Dahlgren also resembles Madelaine Lee: [Henry Adams], *Democracy*
(New York, 1880); Flack, *Desideratum,* pp. 14–15, 43–48.

216   Washington Literary Society: Flack, *Desideratum,* pp. 42–48; Christopher
C. Cox, "To the Members of the Dahlgren Literary Society," Box 5, Literary
Society Papers, Manuscript Division, Library of Congress, Washington,
D.C.; Madeleine V. Dahlgren, "Statement of the Purposes of the Literary
Society of Washington," Box 5, Literary Society Papers. "The Literary"
drew its members from an unusually broad cross section of Washington's
many elites. There were Dorseys and Footes from the old families, and
Representative James A. Garfield, Senator John Ingalls, Supreme Court

justices, and many other members from official society. Geologist John
Wesley Powell and Alexander Graham Bell represented the scientific elite,
while Librarian of Congress Ainsworth Spofford and writers like Francis
Hodgson Burnett represented the literary elite. Box 1, Vol. 1, Literary
Society Papers.

217   "a ghastly affair": de Hegermann-Lindencrone, *Sunny Side,* pp. 16–17.

217   chief proselytizer of the Antiques: Household Accounts and Social
       Register (1877–1885) of Madeleine Vinton Dahlgren, John A. B. Dahlgren
       Papers.

218   "Because we are a Republic": Dahlgren, *Etiquette,* pp. 3–4. George
       Washington was repeatedly invoked by the spate of etiquette book writ-
       ers that emerged after the Civil War in their campaign to improve taste
       and conduct. Appearing within a span of four years were *George
       Washington's Fifty-Seven Rules of Behavior* (1886); *Washington's Rules of
       Civility and Decent Behavior* (1888); and *George Washington's Rules of
       Civility Traced to Their Source* (1890). See Flack, *Desideratum,* p. 29.

218   "As to the menu": Dahlgren, *Etiquette,* 1873 edition, p. 20.

218   "No dinner": Dahlgren, *Etiquette,* 1881 edition, p. 50.

220   "in real solidity of social importance": Dahlgren, *Etiquette,* 1873 edition,
       p. 22.

220   "the old over the new": Jaher, *Urban Establishment,* p. 112.

220   defending traditional style and taste: ibid., pp. 112–14.

221   "The calling": Katherine Elwes Thomas, "How Washington Entertains,"
       The Saturday Evening Post, October 22, 1904, pp. 10, 14.

221   "to err in seating": Columbia, "Cave Dwellers," p. 252.

221   "social Napoleon in petticoats": Columbia, "Cave Dwellers," p. 253.

221   "If there is any score": letter to Jonathan Daniels from Edith Benham
       Helm, quoted in Daniels, *Washington Quadrille,* p. 71.

221   "dragging in other people's feet": Columbia, "Cave Dwellers," p. 253.

221   "what honorarium?": Columbia, "Cave Dwellers," p. 253.

222   pay of a social secretary: Daniels, *Washington Quadrille,* p. 71; Isabelle
       Hagner James, "A Cave Dweller as Social Secretary," first chapter of an
       unpublished memoir, Curator's Office, The White House, Washington,
       D.C. For comparison, while Miss Hagner received a salary of $1,600 a
       year, senators and representatives still received only $5,000 a year. The
       "famous social coach" alluded to was probably Mr. T. Sanford Beatty, an
       ambitious young man who "made" the family of Senator Calvin S. Brice of
       Ohio in 1891. A 1904 article on Washington social secretaries described
       this exceptional case:

       The late Senator Calvin S. Brice realized on going to Washington
       that he had neither time nor inclination to society. . . . At that time

Mr. T. Sanford Beatty was desirous of securing a foreign consulate, and was at the Capital to urge his claims through the family of President Harrison, who had known him from earliest boyhood. The Senator's attention was called to the young man and, looking him well over, he thereupon made an offer to install him in his own household as social secretary, at a salary considerably larger than that of a Cabinet officer, with *carte blanche* for expenses of the social campaign. . . .
That first winter at the Arlington Hotel, when Mr. Beatty was at the helm to guide the family successfully through the maelstrom, amply proved to the Senator from Ohio the wisdom of his selection.
Quotation is from Thomas, "Washington Entertains," p. 11.

222   Edith Benham: Daniels, *Washington Quadrille,* pp. 43, 63; S. Morris, *Roosevelt,* pp. 160–61; Helm, *Captains,* pp. 5–35, 38; Columbia, "Cave Dwellers," p. 252. Miss Benham later became social secretary to first ladies Edith Bolling Galt Wilson and Eleanor Roosevelt, niece of her old patroness Mrs. Cowles. Helm, *Captains,* pp. 5–35.

222   "beset with thorns": Helm, *Captains,* p. 35.

222   "A woman of fine presence": Thomas, "Washington Entertains," p. 10.

223   "dignities of a social equal": ibid., p. 11.

223   Belle Hagner: Miss Hagner's father, Alexander Hagner, Associate Justice of the District of Columbia Superior Court, had been born in Washington in 1826. "Alexander Hagner," *American Biographical Directories,* p. 194; Columbia, "Cave Dwellers," p. 253; Thomas, "Washington Entertains," p. 11; Helm, *Captains,* p. 35; S. Morris, *Roosevelt,* p. 226; Daniels, *Dance,* p. 71. Belle Hagner remained at the White House as social secretary to first ladies Helen Taft and Ellen Axson Wilson. The respectability of the social secretary was further attested to by their subsequent lives. After their years as social secretaries to first ladies, both Miss Hagner and Miss Benham made good marriages: Miss Hagner to wealthy Baltimore businessman Norman James, and Miss Benham to naval officer James Helm. When she was widowed, Mrs. Helm returned to her old career as social secretary to first lady Eleanor Roosevelt. Daniels, *Dance,* pp. 73, 249, 253; S. Morris, *Roosevelt,* p. 418.

223   "a beneficent Providence": Columbia, "Cave Dwellers," p. 252.

224   " 'cave dweller' Maury relatives": Slayden, *Washington Wife,* p. 6.

224   term most often used: Columbia, "Cave Dwellers," pp. 248–53. The term "Cave Dweller" is still routinely used by the *Washington Post* to refer to "old" (circa World War II), wealthy Washingtonians.

224   "has-beens": Columbia, "Capital City," 80.

224   "Like David": Columbia, "Cave Dwellers," p. 249.

225   Charles Glover: Goode, *Capital Losses,* pp. 119–120; Allen Clark, "Charles Carroll Glover," *Records of the Columbia Historical Society, 1938* (Washington, D.C., 1939), pp. 141–48. Archbold-Glover Park in northwest Washington commemorates the memory of Charles Glover.

225   demise of the Bachelor's: *Club Fellow,* October 17, 1906 and January 9, 1907. In her memoirs, socialite Isabel McKenna Duffield referred to "Bachelors turned Benedicts" at the turn of the century. Duffield, *California Eyes Dazzled,* p. 77.

226   three most important dates: *Star,* April 29, June 18, July 13, 1928; *The Washington Times,* April 29, 1900.

226   recruiting increasingly difficult: *Star,* December 3, 1939, and January 30, 1944. The Association of Oldest Inhabitants endures. In the mid-1950s, when their clubhouse, the old Union Engine Company at H and 19th Streets, NW, was demolished, the members elected to donate their extensive collection of Washingtoniana to the Smithsonian Institution and the Columbia Historical Society, but a few aged members still gathered infrequently to reminisce; *Star,* March 21, 1956. Included among the founders of the Columbia Historical Society in 1894 were Henry Adams and John Hay; W. J. McGee and G. Brown Goode, noted scientists and administrators at the Smithsonian Institution; Marcus Baker and John Wesley Powell with the Geological Survey; Librarian of Congress Ainsworth Spofford; James Welling, president of the Columbian University; and, representing longtime Washingtonians with a great love for their city, Lawrence Gardner, secretary of the Washington Beneficial Endowment Association, Judge Alexander Hagner, Theodore Noyes, editor of the *Star,* physician J. M. Turner, and real estate agent Michael Weller. *Star,* January 30, 1944; "The Columbia Historical Society," publication of the Society, 1985. The Columbia Historical Society changed its name to the Historical Society of Washington, D.C. in 1989.

226   "If asked to walk a tightrope": Slayden, *Washington Wife,* p. 84.

227   "The old fortunes": *Club Fellow,* January 9, 1907.

227   "Queen of the Cave Dwellers": Marietta Minnigerode Andrews, *My Studio Window* (New York, 1928), p. 34.

227   catalogue the social elite: *The Elite List* (Washington, D.C., 1888).

228   first *Social Register:* Wecter, *Saga,* pp. 232–36.

228   Washington *Social Register:* Wecter, *Saga,* pp. 234–35; Green, *Washington,* 2:88–89; Social Register Association, *Social Register— Washington* (New York, 1900).

229   Cave Dwellers lived on: Green, *Washington,* 2:90; Andrews, *Window,* pp. 101–2; Wecter, *Saga,* pp. 233–36.

Chapter 9. Conclusion

230 "do-nothing dynasty": "History," Box no. 12, Literary Society Papers, Manuscript Division, Library of Congress, Washington, D.C.

231 "Washington society in the 'nineties": Foraker, *Live It Again,* pp. 6–7, 190–91.

236 "Congress has less and less to do": *Star,* 50th Anniversary Supplement, December 16, 1902.

236 Mrs. Richard Townsend: Mrs. Townsend was the heir of Pennsylvania Senator William Scott, who had made his fortune in coal and the Pennsylvania Railroad. The Townsends arrived in Washington in 1885 and became leaders of the "young set." In the 1890s, they bought the Curtis Hillyer mansion on Massachusetts Avenue, but found it too small for their large-scale entertainments. Mrs. Townsend, however, was superstitious and refused to tear the house down. Instead, she hired a French architect to design a huge marble mansion *around* the Hillyer house. Richard Townsend was killed in a fall from a horse in Rock Creek Park before the house was finished, but Mrs. Townsend and their daughter Matilde moved in and entertained with what Marguerite Cassini called "seldom matched elegance." *Washington Post,* March 24, 1931; Cassini, *Never a Dull Moment,* p. 190.

238 "Washington is busy": Henry Loomis Nelson, "The Capital of Our Democracy," *Century Magazine,* 1902.

238 "More and more every year": Low, "Sundays at the Capital," p. 9.

Bibliography

1. Unpublished Sources

Manuscript Collections

Adams Papers, Diary of John Quincy Adams. Massachusetts Historical Society, Boston, Mass. (Microfilm Reel #38, Massachusetts Historical Society, 1954.)

Adams Papers, Diary of Louisa Catherine Adams. Massachusetts Historical Society, Boston, Mass. (Microfilm Reel #265, Massachusetts Historical Society, 1956.)

Anderson Family Clipping and Manuscript Collection. Cincinnati Historical Society, Cincinnati, Ohio.

Anderson Family Collection. Society of the Cincinnati, Washington, D.C.

Association of Oldest Inhabitants Collection. Historical Society of Washington, D.C., Washington, D.C.

Bachelor's German Club Collection. Manuscript Division, Library of Congress, Washington, D.C.

Isaac Bassett Diary. Office of the Curator of Arts and Antiquities, U.S. Capitol, Washington, D.C.

Theodore Bingham Papers. Manuscript Division, Library of Congress, Washington, D.C.

Benjamin Bristow Papers. Manuscript Division, Library of Congress, Washington, D.C.

Frances Carpenter Collection. Manuscript Division, Library of Congress, Washington, D.C.

Records of the Commission of Fine Arts. Record Group 66. National Archives and Records Administration, Washington, D.C.

Henry Corbin Papers. Manuscript Division, Library of Congress, Washington, D.C.

William W. Corcoran Papers. Manuscript Division, Library of Congress, Washington, D.C.

John A. B. Dahlgren Collection. New York Public Library, New York, N.Y.

Records of the District Courts of the United States. Record Group 21. National Archives and Records Administration, Washington, D.C.

John Fairfield Collection. Manuscript Division, Library of Congress, Washington, D.C.

Benjamin Brown French Collection. Manuscript Division, Library of Congress, Washington, D.C.

Samuel Peter Heintzelman Papers. Manuscript Division, Library of Congress, Washington, D.C.

Edith (Benham) Helm Collection. Manuscript Division, Library of Congress, Washington, D.C.

Albert and Violet (Blair) Janin Collection. The Huntington Library, San Marino, Calif.

Kemble Papers Collection. Folger Library, Washington, D.C.

Thomas Law Collection. Manuscript Division, Library of Congress, Washington, D.C.

Mary Theresa (Carver) Leiter Collection. Chicago Historical Society, Chicago, Ill.

Literary Society Papers. Manuscript Division, Library of Congress, Washington, D.C.

Manton Marble Papers. Manuscript Division, Library of Congress, Washington, D.C.

Evalyn Walsh McLean Collection. Manuscript Division, Library of Congress, Washington, D.C.

David Mearns Collection. Manuscript Division, Library of Congress, Washington, D.C.

Records of the Office of Public Buildings and Public Parks of the National Capital. Record Group 42. National Archives and Records Administration, Washington, D.C.

Pike Family Scrapbooks and Clipping Files. Cincinnati Historical Society, Cincinnati, Ohio.

Alexander Shepherd Collection. Manuscript Division, Library of Congress, Washington, D.C.

Diary of Michel Shiner. Manuscript Division, Library of Congress, Washington, D.C.

Margaret (Bayard) Smith Collection. Manuscript Division, Library of Congress, Washington, D.C.

Mary Amelia Curtin Taylor Collection. Manuscript Division, Library of Congress, Washington, D.C.

Diaries of Anna Marie (Brodeau) Thornton. Manuscript Division, Library of Congress, Washington, D.C.

Tudor Place Foundation Collections. Tudor Place, Washington, D.C.

Monographs and Theses

Albano, Walter. "History of the Dupont Circle Neighborhood, Washington, D.C., 1880–1900." Master's thesis, University of Maryland, 1982.

Anderson, Elizabeth Kilgore. "Letters of Mrs. Nicholas Longworth Anderson to Her Son Larz Anderson, 1882–1916." Edited by Isabelle Anderson. Carbon transcript, Society of the Cincinnati, Washington, D.C.

James, Isabelle Hagner. "A Cave Dweller as Social Secretary." Unpublished memoir, Curator's Office, The White House, Washington, D.C.

Lacey, Michael James. "The Mysteries of Earth-Making Dissolve: A Study of Washington's Intellectual Community and the Origins of American Environmentalism in the Late Nineteenth Century." Ph.D. diss., George Washington University, 1980.

Lessoff, Alan H. "The Federal Government and the National Capital—Washington, 1861–1902." Ph.D. diss., Johns Hopkins University, 1990.

Maury, William M. "The Territorial Period in Washington, 1871–1874, with Special Emphasis on Alexander Shepherd and the Board of Public Works." Ph.D. diss., George Washington University, 1975.

McLoud, Melissa. "Craftsmen and Entrepreneurs: Builders in Late Nineteenth-Century Washington." Ph.D. diss., George Washington University, 1988.

Ritchie, Donald A. "A Novel With a Key." Draft of an article examining Theron Crawford's 1894 novel, *A Man and His Soul,* in relation to what it reveals about a possible scandal involving James and Harriet Blaine in 1880–81, lent to the author.

Schneider, Gretchen. "Mrs. Adams' Ball: A Political and Social Arena in Early Nineteenth Century America." Draft of a paper for a conference jointly sponsored by the Committee on Research in Dance and the American Dance Guild, 1987, lent to the author.

Swanstrom, Roy. "The United States Senate: 1787–1801." Ph.D. diss., University of California, Berkeley, 1959.

Thompson, Margaret Susan. "The 'Spider Web': Congress and Lobbying in the Age of Grant." Ph.D. diss., University of Wisconsin, Madison, 1979.

2. Published Sources

Published Autobiographies, Letters, Diaries, and Memoirs

Adams, Francis C. *Our Little Monarchy: Who Runs It, and What It Costs.* Washington, D.C.: F. A. Fills, 1873.

Adams, Henry. *A Cycle of Adams Letters.* Edited by Worthington Chauncey Ford. 2 vols. Boston: Houghton Mifflin, 1920.

———. *The Education of Henry Adams: An Autobiography.* Boston: Houghton Mifflin, 1961. [First published in 1918.]

———. *Henry Adams and His Friends.* Edited by Harold Dean Cater. 1947. Reprint. New York: Octagon Books, 1970.

———. *The Letters of Henry Adams.* Edited by J. C. Levenson and Ernest Samuels. 3 vols. Cambridge, Mass.: Harvard University Press, 1982.

Adams, Marian Hooper. *The Letters of Mrs. Henry Adams: 1865–1883.* Edited by Ward Thoron. Boston: Little, Brown, 1936.

Ames, Mary Clemmer. *Ten Years in Washington: Life and Scenes in the National Capital As a Woman Sees Them.* Hartford, Conn.: Worthington, 1873.

Anderson, Isabel. *Presidents and Pies: Life in Washington, 1897–1919.* New York: Houghton Mifflin, 1920.

Anderson, Larz. *Letters and Journals of a Diplomat.* Edited by Isabel Anderson. New York: Fleming H. Revell, 1940.

Anderson, Nicholas Longworth. *Letters and Journals of General Nicholas Longworth Anderson.* Edited by Isabel Anderson. New York: Fleming H. Revell, 1942.

Andrews, Marietta Minnigerode. *My Studio Window.* New York: E. P. Dutton, 1928.

Blaine, Mrs. James G. *Letters of Mrs. James G. Blaine.* Edited by Harriet S. Blaine Beale. 2 vols. New York: Duffield, 1908.

Briggs, Emily Edson. *The Olivia Letters.* New York: Neale Publishing, 1906.

Brooks, Noah. *Washington in Lincoln's Time.* Edited by Herbert Mitgang. Chicago: Quadrangle Books, 1971. [First published in 1895.]

Busey, Samuel. *Pictures of the City of Washington in the Past.* Washington, D.C.: William Ballantyne and Sons, 1898.

Butler, Benjamin Franklin. *Autobiography and Personal Reminiscences of Major-General Benjamin F. Butler: Butler's Book.* Boston: A. M. Thayer, 1892.

Carpenter, Frank. *Carp's Washington.* Edited by Frances Carpenter. New York: McGraw-Hill, 1960.

Cassini, Countess Marguerite. *Never a Dull Moment.* New York: Harper and Brothers, 1956.

Chandler, Margaret Terry. *Roman Spring: Memoirs*. Boston: Little, Brown, 1934.

Clay-Clopton, Virginia. *A Belle of the Fifties*. New York: Doubleday, Page, 1905.

Cope, Thomas P. *Philadelphia Merchant: Diary of Thomas P. Cope, 1800–1851*. Edited by Eliza Cope Harrison. South Bend, Ind.: Gateway Editions, 1978.

Corcoran, William. *A Grandfather's Legacy*. Washington, D.C.: Henry Polkinhorn, 1879.

De Hegermann-Lindencrone, Lillie. *The Sunny Side of Diplomatic Life*. New York: Harper and Brothers, 1914.

DeKoven, Anna Farwell. *A Musician and His Wife*. New York: Harper and Brothers, 1926.

Dodge, Mary Abigail. [Gail Hamilton, pseud.]. *Gail Hamilton's Life in Letters*. 2 vols. Boston: Leed Shepard, 1901.

Duffield, Isabel McKenna. *Washington in the '90's: California Eyes Dazzled by the Brilliant Society of the Capital*. San Francisco: Overland Monthly, 1929.

Eaton, Peggy. *The Autobiography of Peggy Eaton*. New York: Charles Scribner's Sons, 1932.

Felton, Rebecca Latimer. *Country Life in Georgia in the Days of My Youth*. 1919. Reprint. New York: Arno Press, 1980.

Foraker, Julia. *I Would Live It Again*. New York: Harper and Brothers, 1932.

Forney, John W. *Anecdotes of Public Men*. 1873. Reprint. New York: DaCapo Press, 1970.

French, Benjamin Brown. *Witness to the Young Republic: A Yankee's Journal, 1828–1870*. Edited by Donald B. Cole and John J. McDonough. Hanover, N.H.: University Press of New England, 1989.

French, Mrs. Daniel Chester [Mary French]. *Memories of a Sculptor's Wife*. Boston: Houghton Mifflin, 1928.

Garfield, James A. *The Diary of James A. Garfield*. Edited by Harry J. Brown and Frederick D. Williams. 4 vols. East Lansing, Mich.: Michigan State University Press, 1967–81.

Gouveneur, Marian. *As I Remember: Recollections of American Society during the Nineteenth Century*. New York: D. Appleton, 1911.

Grant, Julia Dent. *Personal Memoirs of Julia Dent Grant*. Edited by John Simon. New York: Putnam, 1975.

Hamilton, Alexander. *The Works of Alexander Hamilton*. Edited by Henry Cabot Lodge. 12 vols. New York: Putnam, 1904.

Helm, Edith Benham. *The Captains and the Kings*. New York: G. P. Putnam's Sons, 1954.

Hines, Christian. *Early Recollections of Washington City*. Washington, D.C.: Chronicler Book and Job Print, 1866.

Hoar, George Frisbee. *Autobiography of Seventy Years*. 2 vols. New York: Charles Scribner's Sons, 1903.

Hobart, Mrs. Garret [Jennie Hobart]. *Memories.* New York: Carroll Hall, 1930.

Howe, Julia Ward. *Reminiscences: 1819–1899.* 1899. Reprint. New York: Negro Universities Press, 1969.

Hubbard, Thomas. "Political and Social Life in Washington during the Administration of President Monroe." Edited by Robert Hubbard. *Transactions of the Oneida Historical Society at Utica, N.Y.* 9 (1903).

Kasson, Mrs. John A. "An Iowa Woman in Washington, 1861–1865." *Iowa Journal of History* 52 (January 1954).

Keyes, Frances Parkinson. *Capital Kaleidoscope: The Story of a Washington Hostess.* New York: Harper and Brothers, 1937.

King, Horatio. *Turning on the Light.* Philadelphia: J. B. Lippincott, 1895.

Lee, Elizabeth Blair. *Wartime Washington: The Civil War Letters of Elizabeth Blair Lee.* Edited by Virginia Jeans Laas. Urbana: University of Illinois Press, 1991.

Logan, Mrs. John A. [Mary S. Logan]. *Reminiscences of a Soldier's Wife.* New York: Charles Scribner's Sons, 1913.

———. *Thirty Years in Washington; or, Life and Scenes in Our National Capital.* Hartford, Conn.: A. D. Worthington, 1901.

Longworth, Alice Roosevelt. *Crowded Hours.* New York: Charles Scribner's Sons, 1933.

McLean, Evalyn Walsh. *Father Struck It Rich.* 1936. Reprint. Ouray, Colo.: Bear Creek Publishing, 1981.

"Dr. Mitchill's Letters from Washington: 1801–1813." *Harper's New Monthly Magazine* 58 (April 1879).

Nicolay, Helen. *Our Capital on the Potomac.* New York: Century, 1924.

Pepper, Charles M. *Everyday Life in Washington with Pen and Camera.* New York: Christian Herald, 1900.

Poore, Benjamin Perley. *Perley's Reminiscences of Sixty Years in the National Metropolis.* 2 vols. Philadelphia: Hubbard Brothers, 1886.

Pryor, Sarah A. R. *Reminiscences of Peace and War.* New York: MacMillan, 1905.

Riddle, Albert Gallatin. *Recollections of War Times.* New York: G. P. Putnam's Sons, 1895.

Schurz, Carl. *Reminiscences of Carl Schurz.* New York: McClure, 1907.

Seaton, Josephine. *William Winston Seaton of the National Intelligencer.* Boston: James R. Osgood, 1871.

Shelby, Alfred. "Mr. Shelby Goes to Washington." Edited by John McDonough. *The Filson Club History Quarterly* 59 (April 1985).

Slayden, Ellen Maury. *Washington Wife: The Journal of Ellen Maury Slayden from 1897–1919.* Edited by Walter Prescott Webb. New York: Harper and Row, 1963.

Smith, Mrs. Samuel Harrison [Margaret Bayard Smith]. *The First Forty Years of Washington Society.* Edited by Gaillard Hunt. New York: Charles Scribner's Sons, 1906.

Stewart, William Morris. *Reminiscences of Senator William M. Stewart of Nevada.* New York: Neale Publishing, 1908.
Washington, George. *The Writings of George Washington.* Edited by John C. Fitzpatrick. 39 vols. Washington, D.C.: Government Printing Office, 1939.
Willets, Gilson. *Inside History of the White House.* New York: The Christian Herald, 1908.

Secondary Sources

Abell, George, and Evelyn Gordon. *Let Them Eat Caviar.* New York: Dodge Publishing, 1936.
Adams, Henry. *Democracy.* New York: Henry Holt, 1880.
———. *John Randolph.* Boston: Houghton Mifflin, 1898.
"All About Sam Ward." *New York Daily Graphic,* February 1, 1875.
Alsop, Susan Mary. *Lady Sackville: A Biography.* New York: Doubleday, 1978.
Amory, Cleveland. *The Proper Bostonians.* New York: E. P. Dutton, 1947.
———. *Who Killed Society?* New York: Harper and Brothers, 1960.
Arnebeck, Bob. *Through a Fiery Trial: Building Washington 1790–1800.* Lanham, Md.: Madison Books, 1991.
Bache, Rene. "How Our Congressmen Live in Washington." *Saturday Evening Post,* January 26, 1901.
Baker, Jean H. *Mary Todd Lincoln: A Biography.* New York: W. W. Norton, 1987.
Baltzell, E. Digby. *Philadelphia Gentlemen: The Making of a National Upper Class.* Glencoe, Ill: The Free Press, 1958.
———. *Puritan Boston and Quaker Philadelphia: Two Protestant Ethics and the Spirit of Class, Authority and Leadership.* New York: The Free Press, 1979.
Barry, David. "Men and Affairs at Washington." Occasional column in *New England Magazine,* 1907–1908.
Bartley, Numan V. *The Creation of Modern Georgia.* Athens: University of Georgia Press, 1983.
Batchelder, Frank Roe. "Washington Homes of New England Statesmen." *New England Magazine,* December, 1900.
Beale, Marie. *Decatur House and Its Inhabitants.* Washington, D.C.: National Trust for Historic Preservation, 1954.
Beasley, Maurine Hoffman. *The First Women Washington Correspondents.* George Washington University Studies no. 4. Washington, D.C.: The George Washington University, 1976.
Beauchamp, Tanya. "Adolph Cluss: An Architect in Washington during Civil War and Reconstruction." *Records of the Columbia Historical Society, 1971–1972.* Washington, D.C.: The Columbia Historical Society, 1973.
Belden, Thomas, and Marva Belden. *So Fell the Angels.* Boston: Little, Brown, 1956.

Belohlavek, John M. *George Mifflin Dallas: Jacksonian Patrician.* University Park: Pennsylvania State University Press, 1977.

Bender, Thomas. *Community and Social Change in America.* New Brunswick, N.J.: Rutgers University Press, 1978.

————. *New York Intellect.* New York: Alfred A. Knopf, 1987.

————. *Toward an Urban Vision.* Lexington: University Press of Kentucky, 1975.

Billings, Elden. "Social and Economic Conditions in Washington during the Civil War." *Records of the Columbia Historical Society, 1963–1965.* Washington, D.C.: Columbia Historical Society, 1966.

————. "Social and Economic Life in Washington in the 1890's." *Records of the Columbia Historical Society, 1966–1968.* Washington, D.C.: Columbia Historical Society, 1969.

Birmingham, Stephen. *Our Crowd: The Great Jewish Families of New York.* New York: Harper and Row, 1967.

————. *The Right People: A Portrait of the American Social Establishment.* Boston: Little, Brown, 1968.

Bonsal, Stephen. *Edward Fitzgerald Beale: A Pioneer in the Path of Empire.* New York: G. P. Putnam's Sons, 1912.

Bottomore, T. B. *Elites and Society.* New York: Basic Books, 1964.

Bowers, Claude. *The Tragic Era: The Revolution after Lincoln.* Cambridge, Mass: Houghton Mifflin, 1929.

Bowling, Kenneth. *The Creation of Washington, D.C.: The Idea and Location of the American Capital.* Fairfax, Va.: George Mason University Press, 1991.

Boynton, Henry. "The Press and Public Men." *Century Magazine,* October, 1891.

Bradford, Gamaliel. *Damaged Souls.* Boston: Houghton Mifflin, 1923.

————. "Mrs. Benjamin F. Butler." *Atlantic Monthly,* April, 1925.

Brinkley, David. *Washington Goes to War.* New York: Alfred A. Knopf, 1988.

Brown, Dee. *The Year of the Century: 1876.* New York: Charles Scribner's Sons, 1966.

Browne, Charles. *A Short History of the British Embassy at Washington.* Washington, D.C.: By the Author, 1930.

Bruce, Robert. *Bell: Alexander Graham Bell and the Conquest of Solitude.* Boston: Little, Brown, 1973.

Bryan, Wilhelmus. *A History of the National Capital.* 2 vols. New York: Macmillan, 1916.

Buder, Stanley. *Pullman: An Experiment in Industrial Order and Community Planning, 1880–1930.* New York: Oxford University Press, 1967.

Bulkley, Barry. *Washington Old and New.* Washington, D.C.: Washington Printing, 1914.

Burch, Philip, Jr. *Elites in American History.* 2 vols. New York: Holmes and Meier Publishers, 1981.

Burke, John. *The Legend of Baby Doe*. New York: G. P. Putnam's Sons, 1974.
Burnley, James. *Millionaires and Kings of Enterprise*. Philadelphia: J. B. Lippincott, 1901.
Burt, Nathaniel. *The Perennial Philadelphians: The Anatomy of an American Aristocracy*. Boston: Little, Brown, 1963.
Cable, Mary. *American Manners and Morals*. New York: American Heritage Publishing, 1969.
————. *The Avenue of the Presidents*. Boston: Houghton Mifflin, 1969.
Carr, Roland. *Thirty-Two President's Square*. Washington, D.C.: Acropolis Books, 1980.
Carson, Barbara. *Ambitious Appetites: Dining, Behavior, and Patterns of Consumption in Federal Washington*. Washington, D.C.: The American Institute of Architects Press, 1990.
Carson, Gerald. *The Polite Americans: A Wide-Angle View of the More or Less Good Manners over Three Hundred Years*. New York: William Morrow, 1966.
Chapin, Mrs. E. N. *American Court Gossip; or, Life at the National Capital*. Marshalltown, Iowa: Chapin and Hartwell, Bros., 1887.
Cigliano, Jan. *Showplace of America: Cleveland's Euclid Avenue, 1850–1910*. Kent, Ohio: Kent State University Press, 1991.
Claphane, Walter. "The Local Aspects of Slavery in the District of Columbia." *Records of the Columbia Historical Society, 1898–1899*. Washington, D.C.: Columbia Historical Society, 1900.
Clark, Allen. "Charles Carroll Glover." *Records of the Columbia Historical Society, 1938*. Washington, D.C.: Columbia Historical Society, 1939.
Colman, Edna. *White House Gossip: From Andrew Johnson to Calvin Coolidge*. Garden City, N.Y.: Doubleday, Page, 1927.
Columbia, Marie. "The Capital City and the Smart Set." *The Delineator,* January, 1905.
————. "Washington: Its Cave-Dwellers and Its Social Secretaries." *The Delineator,* February, 1905.
Congressional Directory. 1823–1825. Washington, D.C.: Daniel Rapine, 1825.
Congressional Directory. 1829–1831. Washington, D.C.: S. A. Elliott, 1831.
Congressional Directory. 1833–1835. Washington, D.C.: Jonathan Elliott, 1835.
Congressional Quarterly's Guide to the United States Congress. Washington, D.C.: Congressional Quarterly, Inc., 1976.
Congressional Quarterly's Guide to the United States Supreme Court. Washington, D.C.: Congressional Quarterly, Inc., 1979.
Cooling, Benjamin. *Symbol, Sword and Shield*. Hamden, Conn.: Archon Books, 1975.
Crawford, Theron Clark. *A Man and His Soul: An Occult Romance of Washington Life*. New York: By the Author, 1894.

Cross, Wilbur, and Ann Novotny. *White House Weddings.* New York: David McKay, 1967.

Curtis, William Elroy. "Life in Washington, D.C." *The Chautauquan,* August, 1897.

Dahlgren, Madeleine Vinton. *Etiquette of Social Life in Washington.* Lancaster, Penn.: Inquirer Publishing, 1873. [Through 8th ed., 1883.]

Daniel, Pete, and Raymond Smock. *A Talent for Detail: The Photographs Of Frances Benjamin Johnston, 1889–1910.* New York: Harmony Books, 1974.

Daniels, Jonathan. *The End of Innocence.* 1954. Reprint. New York: DaCapo Press, 1972.

———. *Washington Quadrille: The Dance beside the Documents.* Garden City, N.Y.: Doubleday, 1968.

Davidoff, Leonore. *The Best Circles: Society, Etiquette and the Season in London.* London: Croom Helm, 1973.

Deakin, James. *The Lobbyists.* Washington, D.C.: Public Affairs Press, 1966.

De Chambrun, Clara Longworth. *The Making of Nicholas Longworth.* 1933. Reprint. New York: Books for Libraries, 1971.

DeLeon, Thomas C. *Belles, Beaux and Brains of the '60's.* 1907. Reprint. New York: Arno Press, 1974.

Detwiler, Mrs. Hazel. "The Truxtun Beale Years." *Historic Preservation* 19 (July–December 1967).

Dewey, Adelbert, and Louis Dewey. *The Life of George Dewey, Rear Admiral, U.S.N.* Westfield, Mass: Dewey Publishing, 1898.

Dodge, Mary Abigail. *Biography of James G. Blaine.* Norwich, Conn.: Henry Bill Publishing, 1895.

———. "The Display of Washington Society." *The Galaxy,* June, 1876.

Donald, David. *Charles Sumner and the Rights of Man.* New York: Alfred Knopf, 1970.

Dunning, William A. "Paying for Alaska." *Political Science Quarterly* 27 (September 1912).

Ebner, Michael H. *Creating Chicago's North Shore: A Suburban History.* Chicago: University of Chicago Press, 1988.

Ecker, Walter. *Dumbarton Oaks: The History of a Georgetown House and Garden, 1880–1966.* Cambridge, Mass: Harvard University Press, 1967.

Edel, Leon. *Henry James: The Conquest of London, 1870–1883.* London: Rupert Hart-Davis, 1962.

Egan, Maurice. *A Gentleman.* 2d ed. New York: Benzinger Brothers, 1893.

The Elite List. Washington, D.C.: Elite Publishing, 1888.

Ellet, Mrs. Elizabeth. *The Court Circles of the Republic; or, The Beauties and Celebrities of the Nation.* Hartford, Conn.: Hartford Publishing, 1870.

———. *The Queens of American Society.* New York: Charles Scribner, 1867.

Elliott, Maud Howe. *Uncle Sam Ward and His Circle*. 1938. Reprint. New York: Arno Press, 1975.

Elliott, Russell R. *Servant of Power: A Political Biography of Senator William M. Stewart*. Reno: University of Nevada Press, 1983.

Ellis, Dr. John. *The Sights and Secrets of the National Capital*. New York: U.S. Publishing, 1869.

Eskew, Garett L. *Willard's of Washington: The Epic of a Capital Caravan*. New York: Coward-McCann, 1954.

Fite, Emerson. *Social and Industrial Conditions in the North during the Civil War*. New York: Macmillan, 1910.

Fitzpatrick, Sandra, and Maria Goodwin. *The Guide to Black Washington*. New York: Hippocrone Bookes, 1990.

Flack, James Kirkpatrick. *Desideratum in Washington: The Intellectual Community in the Capital City, 1870–1900*. Cambridge, Mass: Schenkman Publishing, 1975.

Foster, Augustus. *Jeffersonian America*. San Marino, Calif.: Huntington Library, 1954.

Fraser, Walter J., Jr. *Charleston! Charleston! The History of a Southern City*. Columbia: University of South Carolina Press, 1989.

Friedrich, Otto. *Clover*. New York: Simon and Schuster, 1979.

Furman, Bess. *White House Profile: A Social History of the White House, Its Occupants, and Its Festivities*. New York: Bobbs-Merrill, 1951.

Gallman, J. Matthew. *Mastering Wartime: A Social History of Philadelphia during the Civil War*. Cambridge, Eng.: Cambridge University Press, 1990.

Gandy, Lewis Cass. *The Tabors: A Footnote of Western History*. New York: Press of the Pioneers, 1934.

Gannon, James. "Washington at the Turn of the Century." *Records of the Columbia Historical Society, 1963–1965*. Washington, D.C.: Columbia Historical Society, 1966.

Garraty, John. *The New Commonwealth: 1877–1890*. New York: Harper and Row, 1968.

Gatewood, Willard B. *Aristocrats of Color: The Black Elite, 1880–1920*. Bloomington: Indiana University Press, 1990.

Geer, Emily. *First Lady: The Life of Lucy Webb Hayes*. Kent, Ohio: Kent State University Press, 1984.

Ginger, Ray. *Age of Excess: The United States from 1877–1914*. New York: Macmillan, 1965.

Glassie, Henry. "Victorian Homes In Washington." *Records of the Columbia Historical Society, 1963–1965*. Washington, D.C.: Columbia Historical Society, 1966.

"A Glimpse of Some Washington Homes." *Harper's New Monthly Magazine*, March, 1885.

Goode, James M. *Best Addresses.* Washington, D.C.: Smithsonian Institution Press, 1988.

————. *Capital Losses: A Cultural History of Washington's Destroyed Buildings.* Washington, D.C.: Smithsonian Institution Press, 1979.

Green, Constance McLaughlin. *The Secret City.* Princeton: Princeton University Press, 1967.

————. *Washington: A History of the Capital, 1800–1950.* 2 vols. Princeton: Princeton University Press, 1962.

Greve, Charles. *Centennial History of Cincinnati.* 2 vols. Chicago: Biographical Publishing, 1904.

Grover, Kathryn, ed. *Dining in America 1850–1900.* Amherst: University of Massachusetts Press, 1987.

Hall, Florence Howe. *Social Usages at Washington.* New York: Harper and Brothers, 1906.

Hermann, Ruth. *Gold and Silver Colossus: William Morris Stewart and His Southern Bride.* Sparks, Nev.: Dave's Printing and Publishing, 1975.

Hinman, Ida. *The Washington Sketch Book: A Society Souvenir.* Washington, D.C.: Hartman and Cadwick, 1895.

Hogan, Richard. *Class and Community in Frontier Colorado.* Lawrence: University Press of Kansas, 1990.

Holbo, Paul. *Tarnished Expansion: The Alaska Scandal, the Press, and Congress, 1867–1871.* Knoxville: University of Tennessee Press, 1983.

Hooker, Richard J. *Food and Drink in America: A History.* Indianapolis: Bobbs-Merrill, 1981.

Horowitz, Helen. *Culture and the City.* Louisville: University of Kentucky Press, 1976.

"How Shall We Govern the National Capital." *The Nation,* June 11, 1874.

Hurd, Charles. *Washington Cavalcade.* New York: E. P. Dutton, 1948.

Jaher, Frederic. "Nineteenth Century Elites in Boston and New York." *Journal of Social History* 6 (Fall 1972).

————. *The Urban Establishment.* Urbana: University of Illinois Press, 1982.

————, ed. *The Rich, the Well Born, and the Powerful: Elites and Upper Classes in History.* Urbana: University of Illinois Press, 1973.

James, Henry. "Pandora." In *Stories Revised.* 1885. Reprint. New York: Books for Libraries Press, 1975.

Jones, George. *Washington: Yesterday and Today.* New York: Ginn, 1943.

Jordan, David. *Roscoe Conkling of New York.* Ithaca, N.Y.: Cornell University Press, 1971.

Josephson, Matthew. *The Politicos.* New York: Harcourt, Brace, 1938.

Junior League of Washington. *The City of Washington.* New York: Wings Books, 1977.

Kaplan, Justin. "Introduction" to *The Gilded Age: A Tale of Today,* by Mark
Twain and Charles Dudley Warner. Indianapolis: Bobbs-Merrill, 1972.

———. *Mr. Clemens and Mark Twain.* New York: Simon and Schuster, 1966.

Karsner, David. *Silver Dollar: The Story of the Tabors.* New York: Covici-Friede
Publishers, 1932.

Kasson, John. *Rudeness and Civility: Manners in Nineteenth-Century Urban
America.* New York: Hill and Wang, 1990.

Keller, Morton. *Affairs of State: Public Life in Late Nineteenth Century America.*
Cambridge, Mass: Harvard University Press, 1977.

Klapthor, Margaret Brown. *The First Ladies.* Washington, D.C.: The White House
Historical Association, 1983.

Larson, Henrietta. *Jay Cooke: Private Banker.* Cambridge, Mass: Harvard
University Press, 1936.

"Larz Anderson." *Cathedral Age* 12 (Spring 1937).

"The Late Secretary of War." *Harper's Weekly,* March 18, 1876.

"Law Making by Means of Dinners." *The Literary Digest,* July 16, 1927.

Leech, Margaret. *In the Days of McKinley.* New York: Harper and Brothers, 1959.

———. *Reveille in Washington: 1860–1865.* Garden City, N.Y.: Garden City
Publishing, 1941.

———, and Harry Brown. *The Garfield Orbit.* New York: Harper and Row,
1978.

Lessoff, Alan. The Nation and Its City: Politics, Corruption and Progress in Washington, D.C., 1861–1902. Baltimore: Johns Hopkins University Press, 1994.

Leyendecker, Liston. *Palace Car Prince: A Biography of George Pullman.* Niwot:
University Press of Colorado, 1992.

Littell, Robert. "The House that Clark Built." *New Republic,* March 30, 1927.

"The Lobbyist." *Harper's Weekly,* August 4, 1888.

Lockwood, Mary Smith. *Yesterdays in Washington.* Rosslyn, Va.: The
Commonwealth, 1915.

Loth, David. *Public Plunder: A History of Graft in America.* New York: Carrick
and Evans, 1938.

Low, Maurice. "Sundays at the Capital." *Harper's Weekly,* April 13, 1912.

Mack, Effie Mona. "William Morris Stewart, 1827–1909." *Nevada Historical
Society Quarterly* 7 (Winter 1964).

Mahoney, Timothy. *River Towns in the Great West: The Structure of Provincial
Urbanization in the American Midwest 1820–1870.* Cambridge, Eng.:
Cambridge University Press: 1990.

Marquand, John P. *The Late George Apley.* Boston: Little, Brown, 1937.

Martin, Ralph. *Cissy.* New York: Simon and Schuster, 1979.

Martineau, Harriet. *Retrospect of Western Travel.* 1838. Reprint. New York:
Greenwood Press, 1969.

McClelland, Donald. *Where Shadows Live: Alice Pike Barney and Her Friends.* Washington, D.C.: National Collection of Fine Arts, 1978.

McFeely, William. *Grant: A Biography.* New York: W. W. Norton, 1981.

Mearns, David. "A View of Washington in 1863." *Records of the Columbia Historical Society, 1965.* Washington, D.C.: Columbia Historical Society, 1966.

"Men of the Day: Mr. Samuel Ward." *Vanity Fair,* January 10, 1880.

Merrill, L. T. "General Benjamin F. Butler in Washington." *Records of the Columbia Historical Society, 1937.* Washington, D.C.: Columbia Historical Society, 1938.

Miller, Hope Ridings. *Embassy Row: The Life and Times of Diplomatic Washington.* New York: Holt, Rinehart and Winston, 1969.

Mitchell, Mary. *Divided Town.* Barre, Mass.: Barre Publishers, 1968.

Morgan, H. Wayne, ed. *The Gilded Age: A Reappraisal.* Syracuse, N.Y.: Syracuse University Press, 1963.

Mori, Arinori. *Life and Resources in America.* Washington, D.C.: By the Author, 1871.

Morris, Edmund. *The Rise of Theodore Roosevelt.* New York: Coward, McCown and Geaghegan, 1979.

Morris, Sylvia Jukes. *Edith Kermit Roosevelt: Portrait of a First Lady.* New York: Coward, McCann and Geaghegan, 1980.

Morton, Mrs. Terry B. "General Edward Fitzgerald Beale." *Historic Preservation* 19 (July–December 1967).

Murray, Charles T. *Sub Rosa: A Novel.* New York: G. W. Carleton, 1880.

"Nellie Grant Sartoris and Her Children." *The Midland Monthly* 7 (February 1897).

Nelson, Henry Loomis. "The Capital of Our Democracy." *Century Magazine,* 1902.

Nevins, Allan. *Hamilton Fish: The Inner History of the Grant Administration.* New York: Dodd, Mead, 1936.

"The New Washington." *Century Magazine,* March, 1884.

Nicholson, Nigel. *Mary Curzon.* New York: Harper and Row, 1977.

Nolan, Dick. *Benjamin Franklin Butler: The Democrat Yankee.* Novato, Calif.: Presidio Press, 1991.

Nye, Russell. *George Bancroft: Brahmin Rebel.* New York: Octagon Books, 1972.

Oberholtzer, Ellis. *Jay Cooke: Financier of the Civil War.* Philadelphia: George W. Jacobs, 1907.

O'Toole, Patricia. *The Five of Hearts: An Intimate Portrait of Henry Adams and His Friends.* New York: Clarkson Potter, 1990.

Pareto, Vilfredo. *The Mind and Society: A Treatise on General Sociology.* Translated by Andrew Bongiorno and Arthur Livingston. 4 vols. New York: Dover Publications, 1935. [Translation of 1916 edition.]

Parker, William. *Life and Public Services of Justin Smith Morrill*. Boston: Houghton Mifflin, 1924.

Pavllin, Charles. "Early British Diplomats in Washington." *Records of the Columbia Historical Society, 1943*. Washington, D.C.: Columbia Historical Society, 1943.

Peacock, Virginia Tatnall. *Famous American Belles of the Nineteenth Century*. 1900. Reprint. Freeport, N.Y.: Books for Libraries Press, 1970.

Pessen, Edward. *Riches, Class and Power before the Civil War*. Lexington, Mass: D. C. Heath, 1973.

———, ed. *Three Centuries of Social Mobility in America*. Lexington, Mass: D. C. Heath, 1974.

Peterson, Richard. *Bonanza Rich: Lifestyles of the Western Mining Entrepreneurs*. Moscow: University of Idaho Press, 1991.

Phelps, Mary. *Kate Chase, Dominant Daughter*. New York: Thomas Y. Crowell, 1935.

Proctor, John Clagett, ed. *Washington: Past and Present*. 4 vols. New York: Lewis Historical Publishing, 1930.

Ratner, Sidney, ed. *New Light on the History of Great American Fortunes: American Millionaires of 1892 and 1902*. New York: Augustus M. Kelley, 1953.

Rishel, Joseph. *Founding Families of Pittsburgh: The Evolution of a Regional Elite, 1760–1910*. Pittsburgh: University of Pittsburgh Press, 1990.

Rose, William Ganson. *Cleveland: The Making of a City*. Kent, Ohio: Kent State University Press, 1990.

Ross, Ishbel. *Proud Kate: Portrait of an Ambitious Woman*. New York: Harper and Brothers, 1953.

Rozwenk, Edwin, and Thomas Bender. *The Making of American Society*. 2 vols. New York: Alfred A. Knopf, 1978.

Russell, James M. *Atlanta 1847–1890: City Building in the Old South and the New*. Baton Rouge: Louisiana State University Press, 1988.

Sandburg, Carl. *Abraham Lincoln: The War Years*. 3 vols. New York: Harcourt, Brace, 1939.

Scanlan, Nelle M. B*oudoir Mirrors of Washington*. Philadelphia: John C. Winston, 1923.

Schlesinger, Arthur M. *Learning How to Behave: A Historical Study of American Etiquette Books*. New York: Dodd, Mead, 1946.

Schriftgiesser, Karl. *The Lobbyists: The Art and Business of Influencing Law Makers*. Boston: Little, Brown, 1951.

Seale, William. *The President's House: A History*. 2 vols. Washington, D.C.: White House Historical Association, 1986.

Secretary of the Senate. *Senate Campaign Information*. Washington, D.C.: Government Printing Office, 1978.

"Seeing Washington through a Megaphone." *Ladies' Home Journal,* August, 1907.

Severance, James. "Amzi Lorenzo Barber." *Oberlin Alumni Magazine* 5 (June 1909).

Smith, Duane. *Horace Tabor: His Life and Legend.* Boulder: Colorado Associated University Press, 1973.

Smith, Elbert B. *Francis Preston Blair.* New York: The Free Press, 1980.

Smith, George. "A Critical Moment in Washington." *Records of the Columbia Historical Society, 1918.* Washington, D.C.: Columbia Historical Society, 1919.

Smith, Kathryn, ed. *Washington at Home.* Northridge, Calif.: Windsor Publications, 1988.

Smith, Marie. *Entertaining in the White House.* Washington, D.C.: Acropolis Books, 1967.

————, and Louise Durbin. *White House Brides.* Washington, D.C.: Acropolis Books, 1966.

Social Register Association. *Social Register: Washington.* New York: The Social Register Association, 1900.

Stegner, Wallace. *Beyond the Hundredth Meridian: John Wesley Powell and the Second Opening of the West.* Boston: Houghton, Mifflin, 1954.

Stevens, William Oliver. *Washington: The Cinderella City.* New York: Dodd, Mead, 1943.

Swanberg, W. A. *Citizen Hearst: A Biography of William Randolph Hearst.* New York: Scribner, 1961.

Tehan, Arline. *Henry Adams in Love: The Pursuit of Elizabeth Sherman Cameron.* New York: Universal Books, 1983.

Teiser, Sidney. "Life of George H. Williams: Almost Chief-Justice." *Oregon Historical Quarterly* 47 (September, December 1946).

Thernstrom, Stephen, and Richard Sennett, eds. *Nineteenth Century Cities: Essays in the New Urban History.* New Haven: Yale University Press, 1969.

Thomas, Katherine Elwes. "How Washington Entertains: The Social Secretary and Her Share in Some Recent Washington Successes." *Saturday Evening Post,* October 22, 1904.

Thomas, Lately. *Sam Ward: King of the Lobby.* Boston: Houghton Mifflin, 1965.

Thompson, Margaret. "Corruption or Confusion? Lobbying and Congressional Government in the Early Gilded Age." *Congress and the Presidency* 10 (Autumn 1983).

Tompkins, Lizzie. "Some Washington Homes." *Cosmopolitan,* March, 1889.

Townsend, George Alfred. *Washington Outside and Inside.* Hartford, Conn.: James Betts, 1873.

Trefousse, Hans. *Ben Butler: The South Called Him Beast.* New York: Twayne Publishers, 1957.

A Tribute to W. W. Corcoran of Washington City. Philadelphia: Porter and Coates, 1874.

Trollope, Frances. *Domestic Manners of the Americans.* 1832. Reprint. New York: Howard Wilford Bell, 1904.

Twain, Mark [Samuel Clemens], and Charles Dudley Warner. *The Gilded Age: A Tale of Today.* 2 vols. New York: Harper and Brothers, 1915. [Originally published in 1873.]

U.S. Congress. *Biographical Directory of the American Congress.* 100th Cong., 2d sess. Washington, D.C.: Government Printing Office, 1989.

U.S. Congress. *Congressional Directories.* 29th Cong., 36th Cong., 41st Cong., 42d Cong. Washington, D.C.: Government Printing Office, 1847, 1859, 1869, 1871.

U.S. Congress. House. "Investigation into the Affairs of the District of Columbia." 42d Cong., 2d sess., 1872. H. Rept. 72.

U.S. Congress. Senate. "Investigation into the Affairs of the District of Columbia." 43d Cong., 1st sess., 1874. S. Rept. 453.

U.S. Congress. House. "Pacific Mail Steamship Subsidy." 43d Cong., 2d sess., 1873. H. Rpt. 268.

U.S. Government. *Historical Statistics of the United States: Colonial Times to 1957.* Washington, D.C.: Government Printing Office, 1961.

Veblen, Thorstein. *The Theory of the Leisure Class: An Economic Study of Institutions.* 1899. Reprint. New York: Modern Library, 1934.

Vitz, Robert C. *The Queen and the Arts: Cultural Life in Nineteenth-Century Cincinnati.* Kent, Ohio: Kent State University Press, 1989.

Washburn, Wilcomb. "Influence of the Smithsonian Institution on Intellectual Life in Mid–Nineteenth Century Washington." *Records of the Columbia Historical Society, 1963–1965.* Washington, D.C.: Columbia Historical Society, 1966.

"The Washington House of Mr. John R. McLean." *Town and Country,* April 26, 1913.

Wecter, Dixon. *The Saga of American Society.* New York: Charles Scribner's Sons, 1937.

Werlick, Robert. *"Beast" Butler.* Washington, D.C.: Quaker Press, 1962.

West, Richard S., Jr. *Lincoln's Scapegoat General: The Life of Benjamin Butler.* Boston: Houghton Mifflin, 1965.

Wheelwright, John T. *A Child of the Century.* New York: Charles Scribner's Sons, 1887.

Whyte, James. *The Uncivil War: Washington during the Reconstruction.* New York: Twayne Publishers, 1958.

Williams, Susan. *Savory Suppers and Fashionable Feasts: Dining in Victorian America.* New York: Pantheon Books, 1985.

Willson, Beckles. *American's Ambassadors to England: 1785–1928.* 1928. Reprint. Freeport, N.Y.: Books for Libraries Press, 1969.

Young, James Sterling. *The Washington Community: 1800–1828.* New York: Columbia University Press, 1966.

Newspapers and Periodicals

While dozens of newspaper clippings and journal and magazine articles, often unattributable to any source, fill the clipping files at the Washingtoniana Division of the Martin Luther King Public Library and the Historical Society of Washington, D.C., and proved most valuable, the following newspapers and periodicals were systematically examined for information relevant to the topic:

The Club Fellow: The National Journal of Society.
Harper's Weekly Magazine.
Harper's Monthly Magazine.
The Nation.
New York Daily Graphic New York City, New York).
New York Herald (New York City, New York).
New York Times (New York City, New York).
Washington Daily News (Washington, D.C.).
Washington Daily Patriot (Washington, D.C.).
Washington Evening Star (Washington, D.C.).
Washington Herald (Washington, D.C.).
Washington Post (Washington, D.C.).
Washington Times (Washington, D.C.).

Index